The Big Jump

OUR HERO
Capt. Charles Lindbergh

New York

Paris

"We Did It"

The Big Jump

Lindbergh and the Great Atlantic Air Race

Richard Bak

WILEY

John Wiley & Sons, Inc.

Copyright © 2011 by Richard Bak. All rights reserved

Photo Credits: Page 13: First Across Association; pages 16 left, 25, 33, 55, 59, 86, 104, 117, 124, 135, 137, 173, 180, 182, 212: Library of Congress; page 21: Vickers; page 26: New York Public Library; pages 42, 52, 114, 120, 150, 155, 159: Musée de l'Air et de l'Espace; page 65: Sikorsky Archives; pages 94, 167, 188: Smithsonian Institution; pages 95, 235: *Record Flights*; pages 108, 217, 221, 256: National Archives; page 241: *Skyward*; pages 243, 247: *L'Illustration*.

Published by John Wiley & Sons, Inc., Hoboken, New Jersey
Published simultaneously in Canada

For general information about our other products and services, please contact our Customer Care Department within the United States at (800) 762-2974, outside the United States at (317) 572-3993 or fax (317) 572-4002.

Wiley also publishes its books in a variety of electronic formats and by print-on-demand. Some content that appears in standard print versions of this book may not be available in other formats. For more information about Wiley products, visit us at www.wiley.com.

Library of Congress Cataloging-in-Publication Data:
Bak, Richard, date.
    The big jump : Lindbergh and the great Atlantic air race / Richard Bak.
        p. cm.
    Includes bibliographical references and index.
    ISBN 978-0-471-47752-5 (hardback); ISBN 978-1-118-04376-9 (ebk);
ISBN 978-1-118-04377-6 (ebk); ISBN 978-1-118-04378-3
    1. Aeronautics–Competitions–History–20th century. 2. Transatlantic flights–History–20th century. 3. Aeronautics–United States–History–20th century. 4. Aeronautics–History–20th century. 5. Lindbergh, Charles A. (Charles Augustus), 1902-1974. 6. Air pilots–United States–Biography. 7. Air pilots–Biography. I. Title.
    TL537.B35 2011
    629.13092–dc22
                                    2011010967

Printed in the United States of America

10 9 8 7 6 5 4 3 2 1

To the memory of my father,
Edward Joseph Bak

Contents

Acknowledgments

While the pursuit of the Orteig Prize by Charles Lindbergh, Clarence Chamberlin, Richard Byrd, Charles Nungesser, René Fonck, Paul Tarascon, and others is the focal point of this narrative, the race to be the first to connect New York and Paris by air plays out against the broader backdrop of North Atlantic flight, from the initial crossings in 1919 through the flurry of attempts in 1927 and concluding with the first Paris-to-New York flight in 1930. To more fully present the French side of the story, a viewpoint typically given short shrift in the many accounts of Lindbergh's epochal flight, my research necessarily involved locating and deciphering materials that challenged my meager foreign-language skills. I consider myself fortunate to have found Carolyn Miller, an archival researcher fluent in French, who expertly and expediently translated many documents for me. My daughter Rosemary also translated several items, often on short notice, proving that her year of study in Marseilles still held value. Additionally, librarians, archivists, curators, booksellers, historians, and aviation aficionados on both sides of the Atlantic contributed in various ways to the completion of this work, and to each of them I offer my deepest thanks. My editor, Hana Umlauf Lane, and my literary agent, Jim Donovan, both deserve some sort of prize of their own for their patience. Finally, thanks to Wiley Senior Production Editor John Simko for his forbearance and attention to detail.

Prologue

Instant Fame—or Flaming Gasoline

The barrier was both physical and psychological, and cost more than a few lives. Flying over water was far more dangerous than flying over land, where any flat space was a suitable landing field for a 1920s craft. The Atlantic had its stepping-stones like the Canadian coast, Bermuda, the Azores, England, and Ireland, but for the big jump the pilots poised at the edge of the water, like small children waiting for somebody else to stick a toe in first.

—George Vescey and George C. Dade, *Getting Off the Ground*

In the early-morning gloom, all eyes were on the little monoplane with its distinctively burnished cowling. As the nine cylinders of the Wright Whirlwind engine issued a powerful, monotonous roar, the young pilot inside the cramped cabin weighed the risks of trying to leave Long Island, New York, under less than ideal conditions against those of waiting an additional day. By then his rivals in what reporters, odds-makers, and the rest of the enthralled public were calling "the world's greatest air derby" likely would be ready for departure as well. Like all airplanes attempting to make the "big jump" across the cold, treacherous expanses of the North Atlantic, his machine, with nearly a ton and a half of fuel on board, was essentially a flying gas tank. In this situation, with a single engine straining to lift the overloaded aircraft off a sticky, unpaved

1

runway, nobody would have faulted him for postponing his departure until the sun dried out the field and the air.

"It's less a decision of logic than of feeling," was the pilot's explanation. "The kind of feeling that comes when you gauge the distance to be jumped between two stones across a brook." And if he had gauged wrong—well, that was the advantage of going it alone. He had no one to answer to except himself.

He buckled his safety belt and pulled down his goggles.

"What do you say," he said. "Let's try it."

The wheel blocks were kicked out. A handful of men pushed against the wing struts to free the plane from the ooze, then ran alongside to help send it on its way. After a hundred yards the last of the helpers dropped off and the fishtailing craft was moving on its own, churning through the muck in the general direction of the ambulance parked ominously at the end of the runway.

John Miller, a youthful aviation buff, had spent a sleepless night on the floor of the lobby of the Garden City Hotel, waiting for history to be made. "I think most of the non-aviation people out there expected a crash," he said of the curiosity-seekers who had flocked to Roosevelt Field in the wee hours of a dreary, rainy morning. "They were out there to see a disaster."

"Disaster" had become the operative word in the transatlantic sweepstakes the *New York Times* had labeled "the greatest sporting event of the age." During the previous eight months a series of catastrophes had claimed some of the world's finest airmen as they chased aviation's most prestigious prize. Four men had been killed outright, while two others had disappeared somewhere over the ocean and were presumed dead. Several other fliers, including such familiar names as Richard Byrd and Floyd Bennett, the conquerors of the North Pole; Tony Fokker, the builder of Germany's famous fighters; and René Fonck, the Allies' leading ace during the Great War, had either been seriously injured or narrowly escaped death in mishaps. One *Times* reporter who watched the string of aspirants roll down the runway and into the headlines sardonically handicapped each pilot's chances for the elusive Orteig Prize. It was either going to be instant fame, thought John Frogge—or flaming gasoline.

Within just a few years of Orville Wright's brief but historic 1903 flight off a North Carolina sand dune, daring aeronauts were knitting together odd corners of the map. One July morning in 1909, the Frenchman Louis Blériot created a sensation by being the first to fly across the English Channel, a twenty-two-mile hop that in its day was as celebrated a long-distance feat as *Apollo 11*'s round trip to the moon sixty years later. One hundred thousand Parisians cheered Blériot upon his return. "This transformation of geography is a victory for the air over sea," flight pioneer Alberto Santos-Dumont declared in a congratulatory note. "One day, thanks to you, aviation will cross the Atlantic."

The French, with their traditionally romantic self-image, were especially smitten with *les chevaliers de l'air*, making the cult of the poet-pilot an integral part of their national culture even as more than a hundred young French fliers died in the period between Blériot's channel crossing and the outbreak of the Great War five summers later. Enthusiasts insisted that powered flight was above all a spiritual undertaking, a deeply aesthetic experience that offered the potential for self-transcendence and a rejuvenation of the soul. It seems almost quaint today, but in the early years of aviation there was a widespread mysticism attached to communing with the clouds, a belief that something so rapturous would somehow develop into a benevolent instrument of social change. That nations would co-opt flying machines for purposes of war was perhaps inevitable, but military applications did hasten vast improvements in aeronautics and demonstrated aviation's practical side.

As the industry came of age in the postwar years, airplanes and airships continued to transport man ever higher, faster, and farther through the sky, creating excitement and adventure and opening up unlimited possibilities for their use. Progress was steady, with each new achievement building on the spectacular triumphs—and often-fatal failures—of a swelling fraternity of tinkerers, mechanics, engineers, daredevils, and scientists. By the early 1920s airplanes were being catapulted off the decks of ships, used to "sky-write" advertising messages ten thousand feet above the earth, and journeying to some of the most isolated parts of the planet. Hardly a day went by when one didn't pick up a newspaper and read of some airman flying faster, farther, and at greater peril than the one before him. Frontiers and records—along with a corresponding number of pilots and planes—fell with the regularity of autumn leaves.

One major challenge loomed largest in the news: the $25,000 Orteig Prize, the purse to be awarded for the first direct nonstop flight between the two great cities of New York and Paris. The inspiration behind the

Orteig Prize was Raymond Orteig, a onetime shepherd boy who had made his fortune after coming to America. An admiring friend once toasted the Manhattan millionaire as "a worthy son of mother France, a conscientious citizen of the United States, and a brother to your fellow man." The dapper hotelier had created the prize in 1919 to encourage scientific progress while also rebuilding strained relations between his native and adopted countries. During the immediate postwar years, as airlines established regular passenger service between the major cities of Europe, and as distance and speed records steadily increased, the Orteig Prize remained tantalizingly out of reach of the world's best pilots and planes. But due to rapid improvements in aircraft design and technology, especially in the form of lighter and more reliable engines, by the mid-1920s a New York–Paris flight was not only feasible, it was inevitable. By then scores of people had already crossed the Atlantic in a variety of lighter- and heavier-than-air crafts, often in stages. The initial flights over the North Atlantic, as chancy and conspicuous as they were in their day, usually followed abridged routes that carried no immediate commercial implications. Shorter flights over the South Atlantic, while important in their own right, inspired little passion among ordinary Americans and Europeans.

However, connecting New York and Paris in a single bound meant an epic journey of more than thirty-six hundred miles, roughly twice the distance of previous transatlantic crossings. It also meant having the spotlights of the media and cultural capitals of the world shining directly on the men and planes involved, ensuring maximum coverage and impact. To certain dauntless and adventuresome types, the Orteig Prize was an almost intoxicating challenge. Whether one landed in Paris or New York or fell into the ocean somewhere in between, a splash of some type was guaranteed—glory, riches, the kind of fame that accompanies even spectacular failure. By the time the major contenders were lined up on both sides of the Atlantic in the spring of 1927, the question was no longer *can* the Orteig Prize be won, but by whom?

Years earlier, pioneer balloonist Augustus Post had provided a clue to the winner's identity and alluded to the acclaim that awaited him. "A man is now living who will be the first human being to cross the Atlantic Ocean by air," he wrote in a remarkably prescient article published in 1914.

"He will cross while he is still a young man. All at once Europe will move two days nearer; instead of five days away, it will be distant only thirty hours. . . . Imagine, then, the welcome that awaits the Columbus of the air. The cable warns of his departure before he flies; the wire announcing his progress; ship after ship, awaiting the great moment, gets a glimpse of the black spot in the sky. Ocean steamers bearing each a city full of human beings, turn thousands of glasses on the tiny winged thing, advance herald of the aerial age. The ocean comes to life with gazing humanity. Above all, he rides, solitary, intent. There will have been no time to decorate for his coming. Flags will run up hurriedly; roofs in an instant turn black with people; wharves and streets white with upturned faces, while over the heads of the multitude he rides in to such a shout as the ear of man has never heard.

"No explorer ever knew such a welcome," concluded Post, "and no conqueror ever knew such a welcome as awaits the Columbus of the air."

The little silver plane surged down the runway, splashing through puddles and picking up momentum. As it ate up more and more of the nearly mile-long strip, the young man at the controls resisted the temptation to abort. He had earlier marked the spot on the runway where, if he felt that he had not gathered enough speed to lift off, he would throttle back and attempt to coast the brakeless craft to a stop, but now pilot and plane roared past the point of no return. The wheels bounced once . . . twice . . . a third time . . . and then the *Spirit of St. Louis* finally lifted free of the sticky earth, slowly rising above and then past the web of telephone wires at the end of the field.

The barograph required by the National Aeronautic Association, installed and sealed a few hours earlier, began its official recording of time and altitude. It was 7:54 a.m., Friday, May 20, 1927.

A local youngster, Anne Condelli, had joined her parents and brother in seeing Charles Lindbergh off. "There was a great relief," she recalled many years later. "But there was no clapping, no joyful noises at all. Just relief that his plane had cleared those wires."

John Miller watched the plane disappear into the mist. He shook his head and said to no one in particular, "We'll probably never see the poor guy again."

1

"We've Come to Fly the Atlantic"

An aura of unreality seemed to surround us as we flew onward towards the dawn and Ireland . . . the distorted ball of a moon, the weird half-light, the monstrous cloud shapes, the fog below and around us, the misty indefiniteness of space, the changeless drone, drone, drone of the motors.

—Lieutenant Arthur "Teddy" Whitten Brown

At the turn of the last century, most outsiders viewed the Dominion of Newfoundland as little more than a high-walled wedge of ancient rock and timeless timber rising out of storm-tossed, cod-filled waters. Cool, bleak, and sparsely inhabited save for a couple of small towns inland and the fishing villages dotting its fringe, the giant island off the eastern coast of Canada was considered one of the British Empire's more isolated and uninviting outposts. An airplane had never touched its stony soil. But in the early spring of 1919, just months after the Armistice stilled guns and grounded aero squadrons across Europe, several teams of aviators and mechanics, along with a flock of reporters, began converging on the capital of St. John's. "We've come," one late arrival explained to an uncommonly busy innkeeper, "to fly the Atlantic."

It was about time. It had been six years since Lord Northcliffe, owner of London's populist newspaper the *Daily Mail*, had announced a prize of £10,000 ($50,000) to the first person to cross the ocean by a heavier-than-air flying machine. (Lighter-than-air apparatus—a category that included balloons and all airships held aloft by bags of helium or hydrogen gas—were barred from the competition.) Northcliffe's challenge, issued on April 1, 1913, stipulated that the flight be made in fewer than seventy-two hours and that the takeoff and landing points be somewhere in the United States, Canada, or Newfoundland on one side, and the British Isles on the other. The rules further stated that the start could be made from land or water, but in the latter case the plane had to cross the coastline in flight. Stoppages were allowed on water, and a competitor's craft could be repaired en route.

The competition was administered by the Royal Aero Club and was open to any pilot of any nationality who held a license issued by the Paris-based Federation Aéronautique Internationale, aviation's international governing body. All that was required were a £100 ($500) entry fee, registration with the club fourteen days prior to the first anticipated flight, and a suitable plane. At the time Northcliffe issued his challenge there was no airplane capable of making the crossing, which was just shy of nineteen hundred statute miles at its shortest distance, between Newfoundland and Ireland. Then the Great War caused the competition to be suspended.

When it was renewed in 1918, the situation had materially improved for interested parties. The prize money, augmented by offers from a tobacco firm and a private citizen, now totaled £13,000 ($65,000). The combination of more efficient engines, better instruments, smarter design, and a deeper understanding of aerodynamics promised to significantly increase the odds of any postwar attempt, though the obstacles remained formidable and a successful crossing was by no means a sure thing. A few plucky pilots were persuaded that the right plane just might remain airborne long enough for the twenty to thirty hours needed to cross the ocean. Manufacturers, their eye on the huge commercial potential of hauling passengers, mail, and freight, were understandably anxious to outfit them in such an aircraft.

All told, there were eleven competitors in various stages of preparation for the prize by early 1919. All but one were British. In renewing his challenge after the war, Lord Northcliffe had tweaked the rules. Now "aeroplanes of enemy origin or manufacture" were prohibited from entering, which kept Germany's large and nimble Gotha bombers out of the race. Although there had been reports that France and Italy were preparing to field teams, neither country posted an entry. An accident in New Jersey cost two Swedes their plane, removing the only non-British contender.

Because the prevailing winds in the Northern Hemisphere blow eastward, helping to push aircraft toward Europe, all but one of the competitors planned to follow a west-to-east course. The one who didn't was Major J. C. P. Woods, pilot of a single-engine biplane called the *Shamrock*. On April 18, 1919, Woods set off from England for his planned departure point of Limerick, Ireland. The converted torpedo bomber promptly dropped into the Irish Sea with a dead engine. Woods and his navigator were rescued by nearby picnickers, but the plane was ruined. "The Atlantic race," declared its soggy pilot, "is pipped."

The *Shamrock* was the exception that proved the rule. Any aircraft hoping to cross the Atlantic from east to west would have to battle ornery headwinds that, depending on their velocity, could trim ten, twenty, or more miles off a plane's hourly pace while draining its fuel supply in the process. It obviously was more advantageous to sail along on the westerlies. Hence the aviation world's new center: St. John's, Newfoundland, one of the oldest and easternmost settlements in North America. Its proximity to European shores had prompted radio pioneer Guglielmo Marconi to receive the first transatlantic wireless message there in 1901. Now, nearly two decades later, several airplanes were being crated and making the long trek to St. John's by steamer, along with their crews and mechanics. Eventually four teams would be in St. John's.

Wagering was fierce in England. It was hard to bet against test pilot Harry Hawker, a clear-eyed Australian who had set a variety of speed, distance, and altitude records around the British Isles. The slightly built thirty-year-old, who also had made a name as an auto racer, neither drank nor smoked, believing either vice would affect his greatest asset: his steady nerves. He hadn't fought in the war, but in his line of work he'd taken more risks and suffered more injuries than many who had. The press, always on the lookout for a properly hyperbolic tagline, took to calling this survivor of multiple crashes "the man who won't be killed."

Hawker's navigator was Lieutenant Commander Kenneth Mackenzie Grieve, a career naval officer with just four hours of flying experience behind him. Their single-engine biplane, the *Atlantic*, had been specially designed at the Sopwith factory at Brooklands, outside London, where all the major British airplane manufacturers built and tested their machines. The *Atlantic* boasted a unique streamlining feature. Hawker planned to pull a lever shortly after takeoff, releasing the wheeled undercarriage. The sudden loss of several hundred pounds of weight, coupled with the improved wind resistance, figured to increase the *Atlantic*'s speed to a brisk 100 miles per hour over the ocean. This goodly clip meant Hawker could plan on a controlled crash some seventeen to twenty hours later in Ireland, assuming no mechanical breakdowns or navigational errors en route. There would be, at a minimum, some significant bruising of the crew and plane in attempting a belly-flop landing. But the gain in speed was considered well worth it. The men would share a single cockpit and, in the event of a forced water landing, the detachable lifeboat built into the upper part of the fuselage.

Not to be outdone was the Martinsyde Company, which fielded a smaller two-seater. It was lighter and more streamlined and could hum along at 110 miles per hour, despite having a less powerful engine than the *Atlantic*. It was called the *Raymor* after its pilot, Freddie Raynham, and his navigator, Captain Fairfax Morgan, whose cork leg was an unfortunate souvenir of his naval air service in the war. Another manufacturer, Handley Page Ltd., entered the largest plane available, the new V/1500 bomber. It measured 126 feet wingtip to wingtip, and had four Rolls-Royce Eagle engines driving two tractor and two pusher propellers. It carried a crew of four, including its fifty-five-year-old commander, Admiral Mark Kerr, who in 1914 had become the first British flag officer to learn how to fly.

Each team sought the best spot to build an aerodrome—a rather grand term for the primitive takeoff strips that would have to be carved out of the raw and rocky countryside. "Everybody thought Newfoundland in spring would be teeming with flat green fields like England, ideal for flying," Morgan recalled. "It turned out to have very little but low hills and a lot of uneven ground that I could see was going to be swampy when the winter snow melted." To make room for the requisite length of runway each plane needed to get airborne, fences, trees, and stumps were removed, ditches filled, and boulders carted away. In Kerr's case, houses and outbuildings also had to be knocked down.

Meanwhile, waiting for the arrival of their converted Vickers Vimy bomber were Captain John Alcock and his navigator, Lieutenant Arthur Whitten Brown, just two of the many demobilized airmen determined to continue their aviation careers any way they could after the war.

Both hailed from Manchester, though "Teddy" Brown's parents were American. Brown, a slender and quiet man, had spent the prewar years working in electrical engineering at Westinghouse prior to enlisting. He survived the trenches at Ypres and the Somme before entering the Royal Flying Corps in 1916. He walked with a permanent limp, the result of a leg injury suffered when he was shot down over German lines during a reconnaissance mission. He wound up spending fourteen months in a prisoner-of-war camp. Alcock was sturdy, gregarious, and a natural leader. He had some forty-five hundred hours in the air, many of them piloting long-range bombing missions, and was awarded the Distinguished Service Cross. At twenty-seven he was five years younger than Brown. Alcock also was a former POW, having been brought down over Turkey in the closing months of the war. While in captivity each man had whiled away the time exploring various aspects of transatlantic flight. Afterward they became acquainted while applying for jobs at the Vickers factory. They got along so well that Brown, a self-taught student of celestial navigation, put off his wedding to an American girl named Kathleen Kennedy to go to Newfoundland.

Vickers' biplane bomber had been developed at the close of the war with the intention of bombing Berlin, but that particular mission never materialized. The Vimy was nearly 44 feet long, had a 68-foot wingspan, and was outfitted with a pair of reliable Rolls-Royce 360-horsepower engines that made it capable of sustained cruising at a speed of 100 miles per hour. Among the modifications for the Atlantic flight was ripping out all of the now unnecessary military hardware to create space for additional fuel tanks and installing a wireless set.

Wireless radio had already proved to be an indispensable survival tool. Two-way radio—that is, separate sets capable of transmitting and receiving messages—was rapidly becoming standard equipment on ships at sea. For airplanes, a transmitter was more valuable than a receiver, allowing an airman to broadcast positions and distress messages, albeit over a limited range. However, wireless sets also were heavy, cumbersome, expensive, and susceptible to mechanical breakdowns during flight, considerations that made it an easier decision for most experienced pilots to simply fly without one. Alcock intended to use radio as a directional guide to complement Brown's sextant. In their words, they planned to "hang their hats" on the masts of the Marconi wireless station at Clifden, on the Errislannan peninsula.

That is, if their plane ever got to Newfoundland first. It wasn't until nearly the middle of May that the plane was finally torn down, packed into crates, and placed on a steamer. By then the other planes—Hawker's *Atlantic*, Raynham's *Raymor*, and Kerr's V/1500—had already been assembled and started test flights. Only a long stretch of frustratingly bad weather kept any of them from setting off. Reporters, pilots, and the public grew impatient. "Sir, do buck up and start," implored a pair of self-described "cablettes" from the cable office of the British War Mission in New York. "We cannot stand the suspense much longer."

Putting the spur to the Brits was the arrival of the U.S. Navy, in the form of a fleet of flying boats officially designated "NC," for Navy-Curtiss. Each "Nancy" had a seaworthy wooden hull and four lightweight 400-horsepower Liberty engines that could carry the 14-ton craft through the air at 80 miles per hour or propel it through the water when surface operations were called for. Its wingspan, like that of the more massive V/1500, was an amazing 126 feet. The prototype had originally been built by famed New York aviator and inventor Glenn Curtiss to pursue the *Daily Mail* prize in 1914. Curtiss, a former bicycling champion who'd become one of the world's top competitive fliers, had already paid his entry fee when war broke out just days before his scheduled attempt. He subsequently worked with the navy to develop his seaplane into a long-range hybrid that could theoretically reach European shores.

Peace came before the Nancy could be battle-tested against Germany. However, the navy remained anxious to test its capabilities. By the spring of 1919, plans had been drawn up to send a squadron of four Nancys from Newfoundland to Portugal, sandwiched around a refueling stop in the Azores Islands. The logistical support was unprecedented: a daisy chain of sixty-five U.S. warships, stationed fifty miles apart, stretching across the Atlantic. The vessels, belching dark smoke into the sky during the day and using flares and searchlights at night, would act as navigational aids for the low-flying planes. Connected with each other and the Nancys by wireless, the guard ships also would flash weather reports and be close at hand for any emergency.

The navy chose to describe the costly large-scale air-sea operation as the "development of a wartime project" and did not post an entry for the *Daily Mail* prize. According to one of the participating pilots, Lieutenant William Hinton, the navy "could not well have hesitated between the two possible methods of crossing the Atlantic. One way, the world knows, was to make the flight a great sporting event. The other possibility was to keep it, as closely as possible, to a well-organized scientific expedition. Obviously the American Navy could not, even if it would, choose sport in preference to science. Dignity and efficiency forbade that." Technically, the naval aviators did not even qualify for Northcliffe's prize. Ocean stoppages along the way were no longer permitted, effectively eliminating the American aeroboats from capturing the prize. But the revised rules would not prevent the Nancys from claiming the title of "first across the Atlantic," which would be a boast of considerable national pride to make.

On May 8, the four Nancys, each carrying a six-man crew, left the naval station at Rockaway Beach, New York, on their shakedown flight to Newfoundland. Almost immediately the *NC-2* experienced mechanical problems and had to turn back. Then the *NC-4*, which had previously lost a crew member when his hand was sliced off by a propeller, blew two engines and was forced down at sea. After spending the next few days seeing to repairs and battling a gale, the hard-luck craft the press dubbed the "Lame Duck" finally rejoined the *NC-1* and the *NC-3* at Trepassey Bay. Newsmen, tired of waiting out the wet weather with the British teams, hurried to the American camp sixty miles south of St. John's. They turned a railroad car into living quarters, labeled it the "Nancy-5," and filed dispatches flavored with Hawker's and Grieve's disdainful remarks. Among them was Hawker's offer to eat any American flying boat that made it across the Atlantic.

In the early evening of May 16, the trio of Nancys lifted off from Trepassey Bay, flying into the "deflected glow of a sunset," remembered Lieutenant Hinton. For the first several hours the Liberty engines roared in a reassuring monotone while the naval vessels, a few hundred feet below, "were passed as regularly as train stations." The weather soon grew angry. Fog and clouds enveloped the formation, causing a near-collision and finally forcing two of the Nancys into the water. Heavily damaged and low on fuel, they came dangerously close to sinking in the rough seas. The wireless sets didn't work, making communication with

The U.S. Navy flying boat *NC-4* arrives in the Azores.

nearby navy vessels impossible. As the *NC-1* and the *NC-3* struggled in the darkness, the *NC-4* made it to safe harbor in Horta in the western Azores, cutting its engines some fifteen hours after first firing them up in Newfoundland. News of its arrival created a sense of urgency back in St. John's. British pilots decided to cast aside caution in an attempt to head off the Americans.

By the following day, May 18, the seasick crew of the wrecked *NC-1* had been picked up by a passing Greek merchant ship and then transferred to a U.S. destroyer. Shortly after six-thirty that Sunday evening, as the whereabouts of the other missing seaplane, the *NC-3*, remained unknown, Hawker and Grieve took off from Glendenning's Farm in their overloaded Sopwith. Tests had not been completed, the runway was spongy, the wind was fickle, and the weather over the Atlantic was dicey, but it was now "win or die" for the impatient aviators. "Tell Raynham I'll greet him at Brooklands," Hawker shouted before advancing the throttle. The surging *Atlantic* barely negotiated the trees at the end of the field before staggering off into the clear sky. Two hours later, the *Raymor* trundled over the ground at the nearby village of Quidi Vidi. This time the crosswinds held the craft tantalizingly aloft for about a hundred yards before violently pushing it back to earth. The crack-up cost one-legged Fairfax Morgan an eye and dashed Freddie Raynham's hopes of overhauling his cocksure rival.

By the next day, May 19, Hawker's *Atlantic* was lost. There had been no reports of a landing and no sightings by ships at sea. By evening it was obvious that Hawker and Grieve—who'd had enough fuel for roughly twenty-two hours of flight—had dropped into the ocean. Their fate remained as uncertain as that of the crew of the *NC-3*. It was hard not to assume the worst. Over the next several days, flags were flown at half-mast, a memorial service for the two fliers was held, and Lord Northcliffe gallantly offered to provide for their widows for the rest of their lives. As England first learned of the loss of Hawker and Grieve, the missing Nancy turned up in the Azorian port of Ponta Delgada, joining the *NC-4* already docked there. The *NC-3* had barely survived the storm through a herculean effort by its hungry, exhausted, and waterlogged crew. With its left lower wing destroyed, the flying boat was forced to taxi through heavy seas for sixty-two hours. It actually traveled the last couple hundred miles backward, using its oversized tail fin as a sail, to reach port. The *NC-3* was in no condition to continue to Portugal. It would be up to the sole remaining Nancy, the *NC-4*, to finish the mission that the four flying boats had originally set out on.

On May 25, as the Americans in Ponta Delgada waited for the weather to clear, startling news arrived. Hawker and Grieve had been found and were safe! After a week of anxiety and mourning, disbelief over the news quickly turned into jubilation. Extras on both sides of the ocean told of the airmen's ordeal. Eleven hundred miles into their flight, an over-heated radiator had caused them to ditch their craft into the sea, just as a gale was whipping it into a gray, foamy frenzy. Hawker had buzzed a passing Danish tramp steamer, the *Mary*, before expertly dropping the *Atlantic* into a trough between the twelve-foot waves and then releasing the lifeboat built into the fuselage. It took an hour and a half for the mariners to finally hoist the pair of drenched aviators out of the frigid, heaving waters. With no radio, however, the captain of the *Mary* couldn't transmit the news of their rescue. It took six agonizing days before the vessel reached Scotland and delivered the wayward airmen into the embrace of a disbelieving public. Hawker and Grieve made their way back to England via destroyer and train, hailed as heroes at every stop. Impromptu speeches were made and celebratory rounds drunk. At King's Cross, more than a hundred thousand people turned out to raise a cheer. On May 27, two days after their miraculous reappearance, they were received at Buckingham Palace by King George V. Lord Northcliffe awarded Hawker and Grieve £5,000, half of the original purse, as a consolation prize in recognition of "the determined nature of their effort, which has filled their countrymen and women with admiration."

The same day Hawker and Grieve were received at court for their "magnificent failure," the *NC-4* set down in Lisbon Harbor, completing an eight-hundred-mile flight from Ponta Delgada in a little less than ten hours. Their twilight arrival was greeted with a twenty-one-gun salute and congratulatory wires from around the world. "We are heartily proud of you," President Woodrow Wilson cabled from Paris, where the postwar peace conference was being held. "You have won the distinction of adding further laurels to our country." It had taken nearly three weeks—of which forty-one hours and fifty-eight minutes had actually been spent in the air—but the Atlantic Ocean had successfully been traversed by a flying machine for the first time in history.

Lieutenant Commander Albert "Putty" Read, the sawed-off, taciturn New Englander who navigated the *NC-4* throughout, had transmitted the following message upon the craft's arrival in Lisbon: "We are safely on the other side of the pond. The job is finished." Not quite. As a public relations gesture, the six Americans were ordered on to Plymouth, England, symbolically splashing down four days later near the spot where the first Pilgrims had left three centuries before on the *Mayflower*. They were escorted by a bevy of British planes, which "danced many lazy figures of sheer joy-riding and of the aviators' brotherly interest in the great victory achieved," reported a correspondent on the scene. Cheering crowds filled the streets, and the front page of the *Daily Mirror* declared RAH! RAH! FOR READ. In addition to Read, the crew members of the *NC-4* who could forever claim to be "first across" were First Lieutenant Elmer F. Stone (pilot), Lieutenant Walter Hinton (copilot), Ensign Herbert C. Rodd (radio operator), Lieutenant James Breese (pilot and engineer), and Chief Machinist Mate Eugene S. Rhoads. All were navy personnel except Stone, who served in the coast guard.

Most aviation historians agree that the landmark flight of the *NC-4* doesn't get the level of recognition it deserves. The plane with the porpoise-gray hull and yellow wings may not have flown point-to-point, but it was the first flying device of any kind—balloon, airship, seaplane, land plane—to link the continents, to prove that the Atlantic was indeed traversable by air. The public was suitably impressed by the accomplishment, though the drawn-out drama of the *NC-4*'s twenty-three-day journey from Rockaway Beach to Plymouth lacked the emotional wallop of Hawker and Grieve's shocking back-from-a-watery-grave tale.

Hawker's comments at a luncheon following his rescue were characteristically flippant. He dismissed the U.S. effort as not a serious one, with a ship stationed "every twenty yards." This did not go over well, even inside a room full of British airmen. Hawker, destined to die two years later in a fiery crash during a test flight at Brooklands, later explained that he had been misunderstood, that his barb was directed at critics unhappy with the British government for failing to provide similar support for his flight. "Nothing was further from my mind," he insisted, "than to criticize the Americans." Hawker was there to greet the Yankees of the *NC-4* when they arrived in England. It had been "a jolly good effort," he admitted.

While all this was taking place, John Alcock and Teddy Brown chafed. The ocean had been crossed, airmen had been lost and then miraculously found, and several thousand pounds sterling silver of Lord Northcliffe's

Captain John Alcock (left) and Lieutenant "Teddy" Brown.

fortune had been dispersed. It was easy to temporarily lose sight of the fact that nobody had actually yet *won* the *Daily Mail* prize.

Alcock and Brown's plane finally arrived in Newfoundland on May 26. The Vimy had been packed into thirteen wooden crates, and it took two weeks for the imported Vickers crew of mechanics and riggers to reassemble the craft. The large plane had to be constructed outdoors, forcing the mechanics to work long hours in consistently miserable weather. Sympathetic newsmen occasionally left the shelter of a cow-shed to pitch in, helping to lift heavy parts into place. But "rubbernecks" were a problem, these curious bystanders often testing the plane's fabric, as well as the crew's patience, with the point of an umbrella. Other than that, St. John's "showed us every kindness," Brown said.

Alcock and Brown took the Vimy up for the first time on June 9 and put it through its paces. The bomber performed smoothly, but all fliers were stymied by the gale that delivered several more days of nasty weather. Alcock and Brown decided to risk an attempt when the winds finally slackened. They moved to a recently cleared site called Lester's Field, named after the friendly drayman who offered its use as a depar-ture point. Vickers support crew filled the Vimy with 865 gallons of gasoline and 40 gallons of oil and picked stray rocks off the improvised airstrip. At takeoff, the plane would be expected to carry a thousand pounds over its designed maximum load. Its overburdened wheels sank into the spring mud.

The Vimy remained grounded until the crosswinds died down on the afternoon of Saturday, June 14. "The conditions seemed propitious," Alcock said, "so Brown and I decided to 'chance our arms.' Under the wings of our aeroplane we had our last meal, a fairly hearty one, as one never knows." A crowd of picnickers showed up in a festive mood, some fully expecting the two Brits to kill themselves. Shortly after four o'clock, the heavily laden ship wobbled down the 1,500-foot-long runway, Alcock practically *willing* it to rise in the unpredictable winds. As anxious spectators winced, the plane barely skipped over a stone dike and a line of trees before sagging briefly out of sight on the other side of a hill beyond. There were cries of alarm, but the Vimy quickly regained altitude and set off across the Atlantic, its nose aimed at Ireland.

All went relatively smoothly during the first hour or so. Zipped into their Burberry flying suits, protected by a windscreen, and heated by the plane's radiator, Alcock and Brown stayed warm if not comfortable, squeezed into the cramped open cockpit. They sat side by side on a cushioned wooden board, with Alcock's right hand never leaving the joystick nor his feet the rudder throughout the entire flight. However, the wind-powered generator to the wireless set quickly broke, ending the men's ability to transmit to ship or shore. Then a potentially lethal problem developed when a section of the exhaust pipe on the starboard engine split, melted, and blew away. The flames from half of the damaged engine's twelve cylinders, instead of being safely deflected, now roared menacingly close to a bracing wire and the canvas skin of the wings and the fuselage. There was a chance the entire plane could become a flying torch. The men's concern subsided as they flew on and nothing happened, though the deafening noise from the damaged exhaust forced them to communicate exclusively by notepad and hand signals throughout the rest of the flight.

Soon a huge fogbank left the men incapable of seeing either sky or ocean. Unable to climb above it, they flew through the disorienting thick haze for several hours. A break in the clouds finally allowed Brown to line up the stars and use his sextant. To both men's relief, he determined they were on course. Eight hours after leaving Lester's Field, they had traveled about 850 miles and were almost halfway to Ireland. Alcock, looking to reduce stress on the engines and preserve fuel, throttled back and dropped the Vimy from 6,000 to 4,000 feet. There they sailed briskly along at about two miles a minute, assisted by strong tailwinds. During the night they ate sandwiches and chocolate and drank hot liquids from a vacuum flask.

As a new day broke, the plane plowed into towering thunderheads. The strong winds caused the Vimy to buck and swing wildly. Zero visibility disoriented the men. The airspeed indicator jammed, preventing Alcock from realizing the plane was slowing dangerously. An accurate airspeed reading is critical to maintaining heavier-than-air flight. If a plane is going too slowly, it is in danger of stalling; if it is traveling too fast, the stress can cause it to break apart. The Vimy shuddered, stalled, and plunged into a blind spin. The men were pressed back in their seats. Soon they were at 500 feet. With the dead engines eerily silent, Alcock and Brown could hear the roar of the sea rushing up to meet them.

Suddenly the plane burst out of the fog into light. The Atlantic came into view, but it was above, not below them. They were almost upside down and would crash into the sea in seconds. With a quick glimpse at the horizon, Alcock regained his equilibrium, pulled the Vimy out of its spin, and full-throttled the engines to level the plane 50 feet above the water. They had averted disaster and certain death by mere moments. They sailed on, rattled and relieved. A short while later, Brown glanced at the compass and realized they were heading west, back to Newfoundland. Alcock laughed and swung the plane around.

More crises loomed. The Vimy soon headed into another monstrous gathering of cumulonimbus, one of the storied Atlantic fronts that stretch for miles in every direction, as vast and imposing as a mountain range. As Alcock attempted to climb over the storm, a thick, driving rain enveloped the plane. In minutes, the rain turned to snow, then sleet. Every pilot recognized ice as a potential killer. Its accumulation could affect the forward flying surfaces, freeze ailerons and rudders in place, and pile weight onto a plane. There also was the buildup of ice on the faces of the various instruments and gauges to worry about. In the early years of aviation, not all the devices were arranged on the instrument panel; some were on the struts, engine casings, and fuselage. As snow and sleet continued to pelt the Vimy, Brown twisted around in the cockpit and saw that the gasoline overflow gauge attached to the center strut was blocked with snow, rendering it unreadable. This vital gauge showed whether the fuel supply to the engines was correct; otherwise there was a risk of fouling the carburetors, causing engine failure.

Without consulting Alcock, Brown clambered out and gingerly worked his way along the top of the fuselage, wiping the instrument's glass face free of snow. Then he used his pocketknife to chip away at the ice clogging each engine's air intake. While doing so he knelt on the glazed wing, just inches from the violently whirling propeller, stung by sleet and clinging to a single strut wire to keep from pitching into the howling black void. He repeated the maneuver several more times. In a classic display of British understatement, Brown later recalled his experiences out on the wing as "startlingly unpleasant."

As the morning wore on, Alcock climbed incrementally higher, seeking a gap in the sleet that was pummeling the Vimy. It was very possible the storms had thrown them significantly off course, but Brown needed to get a reading to figure out where they were. Alcock was at about eleven thousand feet when the sun momentarily broke through the thick, drifting clouds. Brown pulled off his thick gloves. With hands numbed by cold, he quickly took his sun shot and made his calculations.

They were about eighty miles from the Irish coast. It was 7:20 a.m. After some fifteen hours of chancy flying and excruciating concentration, a safe arrival seemed in sight. At eight o'clock the men shared a bit of breakfast, "partly to take our minds from the rising excitement induced by the hope that we might sight land at any instant," Brown said. At eight-fifteen, Alcock grabbed Brown's shoulder and pointed. Ahead in the mist were the two small islands of Eeshal and Turbot. Eleven minutes later they crossed the coast of Ireland.

There was enough gasoline left to reach London if they wanted, but Alcock was anxious to put the Vimy down before a hilltop popped out of the dangerously low-lying clouds. After circling the village of Clifden for a bit, he sighted a smooth green meadow, cut the engines, and touched down. However, what appeared from the air to be an ideal landing place was actually the Derrygimlagh bog. The machine rolled through the marsh for a hundred feet, then slowly pitched onto its nose in the muck. And there it stuck, its tail in the air—a rather undignified climax to a perilous, exhausting, and unprecedented adventure. The two men climbed out, Brown with a sore nose of his own and Alcock sporting a black eye, swollen lips, and a huge grin.

"What do you think of that for fancy navigation?" Brown asked.

"Very good," Alcock replied. They shook hands. Fatigue and stress were etched into their faces.

Sixteen hours and twenty-eight minutes after leaving Newfoundland, the intrepid Englishmen had made it. They had crossed 1,890 miles of the Atlantic and, unlike their Yankee counterparts in the NC-4, they had done so without a stop and in a land plane. "We have had a terrible journey," Alcock admitted in the Daily Mail. "The wonder is we are here at all."

Wonder, indeed. To the astonished folks on the Errislannan peninsula, having this beastly, flame-spitting contrivance swoop down from nowhere and into their midst on a Sunday morning truly was a marvel. When the first locals arrived on the scene, they thought the fliers were joking when they insisted they had come all the way across the sea from North America. A sack filled with envelopes stamped in St. John's—history's first transatlantic air mail—finally convinced the last of the skeptics.

Leaving their fractured aircraft behind for soldiers to guard and locals to gawk at, Alcock and Brown returned to England. Both were bone tired. Alcock was suffering major permanent hearing loss from listening to the Vimy's exhaust "rattling like a machine gun battery" for sixteen straight

The Alcock-Brown flight ended in an Irish bog.

hours. The flurry of celebratory affairs included a luncheon at London's Savoy Hotel. Winston Churchill, the secretary of state for war and air, presented Alcock and Brown with a check for the prize money, a sizable chunk of which they shared with their deserving mechanics. "I really do not know what we should admire the most in our guests," Churchill told a room full of beaming admirers, "their audacity or their good fortune." Luck had indeed rode with them, in the form of a couple of toy stuffed cats (Lucky Jim and Twinkletoes) brought along as charms and the horseshoe a rigger had nailed under Alcock's seat. The following day the two national heroes were knighted by King George V at Windsor Castle.

Good fortune, seasoned airmen knew, could be as vaporous as the spectral mist they regularly flew through. Six months later, on December 18, 1919, Sir John Alcock was delivering a new Vickers flying boat to an air show in Paris when he clipped a tree in the fog and crashed in the French countryside. A farmer tended to his broken body, but he died without ever regaining consciousness. The "lesson of his fate," opined the *New York Times*, "is that, however skillful and experienced an aviator may be, 'flying' in a heavier-than-air machine is always attended with risks." Sir Arthur Whitten Brown, who at the time of the crash was in

San Francisco on his honeymoon, concurred. He worked as an engineer for Vickers and lived another twenty-nine years, but he never flew again after his friend's death.

The craft that carried Alcock and Brown across the ocean was recovered and rebuilt by Vickers, then donated to the Science Museum in South Kensington just three days before Alcock's fatal crash. The historic plane has been on display ever since, a testament to a pair of dauntless airmen whose exploits were a prelude to even more harrowing Atlantic adventures to come.

2

"Where Does France Come In?"

[Raymond Orteig] was deeply stirred by the unfaltering courage of aviators during the World War. It caught his imagination as few things had ever done. . . . There was to him something very fine in the bravery of these men to whom defeat meant death, for whom there was no such thing as surrender and who could not even if they would give quarter or take it.

—George Buchanan Fife

One winter evening in early 1919, Captain Eddie Rickenbacker rose to address the members and guests of the Aero Club of America at its annual dinner in New York. Rickenbacker had been one of the country's most accomplished race car drivers before the war, its top air ace during it, and now in a whirl of speeches and appearances shortly after the Armistice was using the power of his fame to focus attention on the human detritus left by the conflict—war orphans, disabled veterans, the hastily buried and easily forgotten dead. One in three U.S. airmen sent to the front had died. Two hundred thirty-seven had been killed, most battling "Hun machines" in the skies over the Western Front, while roughly four times that number had died of accidents and disease.

"I recall a little graveyard just outside of Toul," began Rickenbacker, who went on to describe the final resting place in French soil of such flying comrades as Raoul Lufbury, Hoby Baker, and Blair Thaw. He talked of visiting his hometown of Columbus, Ohio, and seeing a make-shift memorial on Main Street dedicated to "the boys of Columbus." The names of the fallen were inscribed on it. Locals explained it would have to suffice until a permanent monument could be subscribed for and built.

"And I thought this evening would be a good time to bring up and suggest such a memorial for this little graveyard just outside of Toul, which we all know so well," Rickenbacker continued, "and something to perpetuate the memory of the boys left behind. . . . If I had my way about it, the parents of the boys left in France, the mothers, would have the decorations which I have today. In years to come we can say with a clear conscience that those who gave their all for the cause which brought us fame are the men whose memories shall stand out, and the future generations of America's air fleet, America's eagles, will look back with that realization." Rickenbacker wrapped up his heart-tugging talk by suggesting that "each and every one of you present will do your share" in contributing to what soon became, under the Aero Club's aegis, the Airmen's Memorial Fund.

Among the guests moved by Rickenbacker's remarks was a middle-aged Manhattan hotelier and restaurateur named Raymond Orteig, a Frenchman in love with American democracy and fascinated by the skills and courage of the aviators he came in regular contact with. Orteig was not a pilot, and not even a member of the Aero Club until that evening. But one of his business establishments, the Hotel Lafayette, had become a favorite gathering spot for airmen during and after the war. Many of them were French officers on temporary duty in the States. Others were Americans, including some who had served in the Lafayette Escadrille. The squadron of volunteers was named after the Marquis de Lafayette, the idealistic nobleman who had come to America's assistance during the Revolution. Talking with these pilots about their exploits and their aspirations reassured Orteig of man's nobler impulses in a world gone to pieces and spurred his own interest in the seemingly limitless possibilities of manned flight.

Orteig knew all about possibilities, for his life was an almost embar-rassingly bathetic version of the American dream. He was born on January 30, 1870, in the village of Louvie-Juzon in southern France, near Pau, on the Spanish border. As a barefoot boy tending his father's sheep on the scraggy slopes of the Pyrenees he had heard stories of his

Manhattan hotelier Raymond Orteig, donor of the $25,000 prize bearing his name.

uncle Joseph, who had left for the United States several years earlier and entered the restaurant business as a butcher. Raymond's grandmother encouraged the boy to do the same, to go to this golden land on the other side of the ocean and "see what you can do."

Orteig, the oldest of six children, was twelve years old when he crossed the Atlantic for the first time, arriving in New York one October day in 1882 with thirteen francs stuffed into his clothes. The trip via steamship took nearly two weeks, a voyage that helped feed his adult imagination. *"De l'eau, l'homme doit passer à l'air,"* he would later say, quoting Victor Hugo, the great Romantic writer of the period. "From the water, man must go through the air."

Orteig moved in with his uncle, who taught him English, and worked as a two-dollar-a-week bar porter at Wengler's restaurant on Williams Street. On a foggy, drizzly autumn day four years later, a million celebrants gathered for the unveiling of the Statue of Liberty, a gift to the United States from its oldest ally. Although the giant copper lady was not fully appreciated in 1886 (it had taken years of fund-raising to pay for the statue's pedestal in New York Harbor), during his lifetime Orteig would watch it grow into America's favorite icon and the most enduring symbol of the historic, if not always harmonious, relationship between France and the United States.

As a young man Orteig went to work for Jean-Baptiste Martin, who operated a four-story hotel, complete with café, restaurant, and billiards room, on University Place at Ninth Street. The proprietor of the Hotel Martin proudly flew the French tricolor on his roof and offered his transatlantic visitors translation services; a selection of *journaux français*; and, most notably, a menu of authentically prepared French cuisine that drew lovers of fine dining from all over the city. Orteig first worked as a waiter, eventually becoming the maître d'. The restaurant was "the gourmet's paradise," recalled artist and illustrator Reginald Birch, a regular customer. "With such material and an ideal host, is it a wonder that it was constantly full of the best known people in New York?" When Martin moved uptown to Broadway in 1902, he sold the business to Orteig, who renamed the place the Lafayette and installed a bust of its namesake in the lobby.

At about this time Orteig and a partner ambitiously took out a lease on the Hotel Brevoort, just two blocks away. The five-story brick hotel at the northeast corner of Fifth Avenue and Eighth Street was a faded landmark, having once been the home for visiting European royalty. Orteig remodeled it and made dishes such as *coq sauté au vin* and *filet mignon sauce Bordelaise* the centerpieces of the Brevoort, just as they had

The Hotel Brevoort, circa 1912.

been for decades at the Martin-cum-Lafayette. Nearly everything at both establishments, from the marble-topped tables to the chefs and waitstaff, was imported. For years the hors d'oeuvres were brought in from the Brasserie Universelle in Paris.

Both of Orteig's establishments were in Washington Square, a once-elegant nineteenth-century neighborhood evolving into the bohemian enclave known as Greenwich Village. Apartment buildings started to replace many of the brownstone mansions that had given lower Fifth Avenue its signature "old New York" feel. As the machine age gathered speed, the Brevoort stood out as a "curiously European oasis" in a rapidly changing city. Its elegant, low-ceilinged dining rooms catered to intimate meals and formal banquets. Patrons in the main room could gaze out the French windows overlooking Fifth Avenue while a trio of ladies played soothing music in a small alcove by the door. Familiar faces such as Louis, headwaiter for nearly half a century, and Alphonse, the maître d', attended to the needs of such notables as O. Henry, Mark Twain, H. L. Mencken, Edith Wharton, Helen Keller, Theodore Dreiser, Richard Harding Davis, and Diamond Jim Brady. The downstairs crowd was more boisterous. Writers, poets, dancers, feminists, and proponents of free love, the Dada movement, and James Joyce's *Ulysses* could all be found at one time or another in the trendy Parisian-style café in the Brevoort's basement. The Lafayette's handsomely paneled dining rooms featured the same moneyed clientele and unhurried atmosphere as Orteig's other property, but it was the Lafayette's tile-floored corner café that was most fondly recalled in later years. Within, an interesting blend of journalists, artists, radicals, and faddists rubbed shoulders with the local habitués, who sipped their cognac while playing dominoes or reading the latest Paris paper. The Brevoort and the Lafayette both enjoyed remarkably loyal followings among staff, customers, and hotel guests. Some people who were residents when Orteig acquired the hotels were still living there when he died nearly forty years later.

Every summer when he could, Orteig returned to Louvie-Juzon to relax, renew acquaintances, and shop for the best wine to bring back to New York. Orteig was a popular and respected figure in the area, a successful and philanthropic American who never forgot his roots. In fact, he intended to retire there. After the war he bought the Henri IV in Pau, a four-story Old World hotel that catered to the growing number of Anglo-American tourists. Whenever he returned to New York, he left the establishment in the care of a local fabric salesman whom he jokingly referred to as "my cousin from Germany."

Pau was a popular center for wealthy sportsmen, the more daring of whom launched large, bulbous balloons and flew frail-looking aircraft. It also was home to the French Army's main pilot training facilities. Orteig was never a pilot but always an enthusiastic passenger. There is no record of when he first tasted the sensation of manned flight, but it wouldn't be surprising if the experience occurred one summer day in the sun-kissed skies over Pau. His biggest dream, he often said, would be to fly directly between New York and Paris, a trip that still took the better part of a week by ocean liner. He hoped to live long enough to see that day.

Orteig worked hard, married well, and networked tirelessly. He threw himself into a variety of charitable and fraternal activities. Over time the immaculately groomed entrepreneur with the impeccable manners, sophisticated wit, and suave Gallic charm became recognized as a leading figure in New York's French community and hailed as one of the city's great restaurateurs. One day he would be made a *chevalier* of the Légion d'Honneur, the highest decoration that France can confer on one of its citizens. He and his French American wife, Marie Ruisquès, had three sons—Evariste, Raymond Jr., and Jean—all of whom followed their father into his line of work. The two oldest boys married the daughters of his longtime friend and partner, Elie Daution, further tightening the bonds between family and business. Both the Lafayette and the Brevoort, reported the *New York Times*, were highly regarded as "authentic, transplanted bits of France." Reflecting Orteig's dual devotion, American and French flags hung at each hotel.

On Thursday, May 22, 1919, the man known by well-traveled members of the international community as simply "Raymond at the Lafayette" sent a typed letter on that hotel's stationery to Alan Ramsay Hawley. Hawley was an accomplished airman (he had won the 1910 Gordon Bennett International Balloon Race) and president of the Aero Club of America, headquartered at 207 Madison Avenue. *Aviateurs courageux* were in Orteig's thoughts. On this day the British airmen Hawker and Grieve were missing at sea and presumed dead; at the same time, the formation of American flying boats had fallen into alarming disarray in the gray, choppy swells of the Atlantic. Orteig's letter read:

Gentlemen: As a stimulus to the courageous aviators, I desire to offer, through the auspices and regulations of the Aero Club of America, a prize of $25,000 to the first aviator of any Allied country crossing the Atlantic in one flight, from Paris to New York or New York to Paris, all other details in your care.

Yours very sincerely,
RAYMOND ORTEIG

Twenty-five thousand dollars was a lot of money in 1919, a time when fat Sunday newspapers cost a nickel and Broadway tickets topped out at $2.50. A Manhattan town house could be bought for those five figures. Although it's always a little tricky trying to compare the purchasing power of a dollar from different eras, Orteig's prize money was roughly equivalent to $350,000 today. Indications are that he could well afford it. He had recently purchased twenty-one acres in Westchester County, adding to his valuable real estate holdings between Briarcliff and Pleasantville, where he made his home. Later, when asked by reporters to explain the reasons behind his proposition, Orteig mentioned Captain Rickenbacker's inspirational speech one winter night at the Aero Club. He continued in his accented English: "I had read so much about flights from Canada to Ireland, and New York to the Azores, Lisbon, and England, and I said to myself, 'Where does France come in?' I wanted to offer some inducement for a flight which would include France."

It went deeper than that. Like the father of two fractious sons he loved equally, Orteig was anguished by the bickering then taking place between France and the United States at the Paris Peace Conference. Beginning in January 1919 and continuing for several contentious months, frock-coated diplomats from more than thirty countries hammered out the shape of the postwar world. It had been American arms and money that had finally tipped the outcome of the Great War in the Allies' favor. But America's contributions (4.7 million of its citizens served in uniform, including Orteig's two oldest sons) paled in comparison to the losses suffered by the other major Allied powers, France and England. A generation of young men had been slaughtered, including Orteig's brother-in-law, who was killed at the Marne while defending Paris in the first great battle of the war. Ten thousand square miles of northern France lay in ruins, its churned, spoiled earth still coughing up bodies and unexploded shells to this day. Someone had to account for this tragedy. Under the terms of the Treaty of Versailles, Germany was forced to accept blame for the war and pocket the bill—a staggering schedule of reparations and a humiliating list of conditions designed to cripple it as a power for the next hundred years. Georges Clemenceau, the aging, barrel-chested, and still vital premier of France, was particularly obstinate inside the salons. At one point he accused President Woodrow Wilson, initially heralded as the "Savior of Europe" for his principled idealism, of being "pro-German." This was a tough accusation for the average American to swallow when, at the time, some twenty thousand wounded doughboys were arriving home from France each month and almost seventy-six thousand others lay in hastily constructed cemeteries. Friction between the two countries would continue for years over a variety of issues—unpaid war debts, the failure of the League of Nations, the invasion of France by tourists and expatriates, the trial of anarchists Sacco and Vanzetti—adding spice to the developing rivalry between both nations' aviators.

In arriving at his decision to reward the first successful nonstop flight connecting America's largest city with the capital of France, Orteig was well aware of the scientific and public relations value of sponsoring such a high-profile race. However, in his admirable optimism he also believed his proposed prize could serve as an instrument of rapprochement between his native and adopted countries. Harmony would be worth every penny—or franc.

On May 26, the Aero Club's secretary responded with delight to Orteig's unexpected proposition:

> My Dear Mr. Orteig—I have the honor to acknowledge receipt of your letter of May 22d offering a prize of $25,000 to the first aviator crossing the Atlantic in one flight, from Paris to New York or New York to Paris, and of any allied nationality, leaving the details to the Aero Club of America.
>
> A meeting of the Board of Governors is convened for this coming Wednesday, when I shall be very glad to lay your splendid offer before them.
>
> In the meantime, and to substantiate your initial offer as contained in your letter of May 22, would you be so kind as to give us a bank guarantee or put up this amount of $25,000

in escrow and draw up a formal deed of gift to the Aero Club of America to be presented at the meeting of the board for its official action.

I wish to tender on behalf of the Aero Club of America, its officers and members, our very great appreciation of this offer you have made and for the co-operation and support you are affording to the development of ocean travel. Yours gratefully,

AUGUSTUS POST Secretary

Three days later, with the Memorial Day weekend at hand, Orteig followed up with a letter that proved his offer was serious. By now the American flying boat *NC-4* had safely arrived in Lisbon, and the British airmen were reported rescued, buoying spirits and provoking more enthusiasm over the possibilities of transatlantic flight.

Gentlemen—Your letter of May 26, through Mr. Augustus Post, Secretary, received, and in reply I beg to advise you that in pursuance of your suggestion of a bank guaranty as assurance of the fulfillment on my part of the offer proposed by me, I have made preliminary arrangements with my bankers, A. Iselin & Co., for the guaranty of $25,000 to the Aero Club, to be paid by the club to the first aviator of any of the allied nations crossing the Atlantic in one continuous air flight, from New York to Paris or vice versa, in accordance with terms and conditions to be laid down by the Aero Club and acquiesced in by me. The offer to remain good for a period of five years from date.

If you will please submit to me the proposed terms and conditions of the club governing the flight, and with which it will be necessary for the aviator to comply in order to be entitled to the prize, I will write you a formal letter embodying the proposition in its final shape, together with the bank guaranty in relation to same.

Very truly yours,

RAYMOND ORTEIG

Directors of the Aero Club quickly approved the creation of what became known as the Orteig Prize and set down a limited number of conditions for the competition. Applicants were required to register with the organization at least sixty days before their first planned attempt. The club's counterparts in Paris would cooperate in the judging of all flights, via cable, regardless of their point of origin. The rules stipulated that a sealed barograph be installed in any competing aircraft to prove it had not set down anywhere during the course of its flight. Otherwise, reported the press, "There will be no restriction whatever upon the size or type of plane, its power, motors, equipment, personnel or any other details, because the Aero Club officials believe that the greatest freedom should be given for the development of aviation."

Capturing the Orteig Prize was a far more daunting task than the phrase "from Paris to New York or New York to Paris" prosaically typed on a piece of hotel stationery suggested. The span between two of the world's great cities was 3,635 miles. This was double the distance Alcock and Brown would cover in their arduous flight from Newfoundland to Ireland just weeks after Orteig announced his challenge. It made quaint the achievement of aviation pioneer Henry Farman, who just eleven years earlier had been the first European to connect two towns by air—a sixteen-mile journey from Buoy to Reims, France. No airplane even remotely capable of attempting a New York-to-Paris run existed in the spring of 1919. However, Aero Club members in Manhattan, impressed by the rapid pace of aeronautical progress, were confident the flight would be made well within the time limit of five years. "If it is not won in that time," said Alan Hawley, "it will surprise me, and that failure will be new in aviation."

The public was still buzzing over the recent string of harrowing transoceanic adventures by American and British airmen when the dirigible *R-34* left its moorings at East Fortune, Scotland, in the wee morning hours of July 2, 1919. No lighter-than-air apparatus had ever crossed the Atlantic. By 1919, however, the *R-34* was just one of a trio considered capable of the journey. The U.S. Navy had a blimp poised to tackle the Atlantic, until gale-force winds blew the docked airship out to sea in May. Germany, whose Zeppelin raids over England and France had killed hundreds of civilians, had built a monstrous 750-foot-long dirigible in the closing months of the war for the sole purpose of bombing New York City. Only the Armistice prevented it from being used then, and only political sensibilities—nobody at the Paris peace talks cared to be reminded of what Germany's hydrogen-filled gas bags were capable of—kept it in its hangar now.

This left the field wide open for the *R-34*, whose mission was financed and coordinated by the British government. The great airship was held aloft by helium and powered by five engines. It had originally been designed to conduct retaliatory bombing raids against Berlin. It was commanded by Major G. H. Scott of the Royal Air Force and carried thirty-three crew members and observers, plus the first stowaway in aviation history. (William Ballantyne, a husky rigger scratched from the crew because of weight concerns, was discovered on a narrow catwalk eight hours into the flight.) The *R-34*, weighed down by nearly fifteen tons of fuel, flew low, its ponderous-looking shadow darkening the hills and fields of Scotland and Ireland before heading out over the Atlantic. A cylinder jacket on one of the engines cracked en route, but an enterprising mechanic with strong jaws solved the problem by seizing every last stick of chewing gum on board and jamming the unholy wad into the fissure.

The *R-34* battled high winds and an electrical storm as it approached the American coast. It finally docked safely at Mineola, New York, on

The pilothouse of the *R-34* as the British dirigible sets down at Mineola, New York, on July 6, 1919.

Sunday morning, July 6, having traveled 3,260 miles in 108 hours, 12 minutes. The trip took just over four and a half days to complete, a mediocre time that did nothing to diminish the size of the achievement. The *New York Times* devoted its first eight pages to stories and pictures of the unprecedented flight. Over the next three days, as the crew was feted and repairs were made, nearly seventy-five thousand people came out to marvel over the dirigible, which was as long as a sixty-six-story skyscraper placed on its side. On the evening of July 9, the *R-34* slipped its moorings on Long Island and retraced its path across the Atlantic, but not before first circling Manhattan and playfully lighting up Times Square with its searchlights. The airship arrived at Pulham, Norfolk, early on the morning of July 13, having covered the distance in an impressive three days, three hours, and three minutes, thanks to a healthy tailwind. A "delighted" Major Scott told reporters it was "a good thing that Britain had collared first blood in both aeroplane and airship single-hop flights."

The round-trip voyage of the *R-34* was the climax to what had proved to be a remarkable flying season. In all, four successful crossings of the Atlantic were made in 1919, with no lives lost. In this age of marvels, who could doubt that expeditious passenger service from shore to shore, be it by airplane or airship or flying boat, was just around the corner? Certainly not the League of Aerial Pioneers, a British group already planning to book seats on the first scheduled passenger flight to New York, nor the London firm of Marshall & Snelgrove, keen to sell rugged but fashionable "ladies' flying costumes" for such a journey. Popular magazines had fun imagining the possibilities. *Scientific American* optimistically headlined one of its features, "Lunch in America—Breakfast in Europe," while an article in *Century* coyly suggested, "Let's Drop in on England." In *Ladies' Home Journal*, science fiction writer Kaempffert Waldemar predicted passengers would in a few short years be zipping across the ocean at two hundred miles per hour and at a cost of five dollars per pound of body weight. Meanwhile, in Manhattan, a bartender caught up in the excitement blended a new cocktail for his customers. The concoction was called, perhaps inevitably, the Transatlantic.

3

"The Ace with the Wooden Leg"

There is a strong possibility right now of a Paris–New York flight, for which a prize was created last year. We have at last been told the names of those audacious men who will attempt this adventure: the pilot will be Tarascon, the flying ace with the amputated foot [and] the navigator will be François Coli. . . . All the good wishes of sportsmen go with them. If they succeed, they will know the glory of Louis Bleriot, for the Channel in 1909, of Roland Garros for the Mediterranean in 1913, of the Englishmen Alcock and Brown for the Atlantic (Nova Scotia–Clifden) in 1919.

—*Le Petit Journal*, April 30, 1925

After an initial outburst of enthusiasm aroused by the flurry of Atlantic crossings in the spring and summer of 1919, a long period of relative inactivity settled over the world's mightiest ocean. The British, enjoying the satisfaction of claiming the first nonstop transatlantic flights by an airplane and an airship, had scant interest in trying to tie together the principal cities of France and the United States. Instead they moved on to the more pressing matter of connecting the home country with various outposts of their unraveling postwar empire. Along with France, Holland, Germany, Belgium, and other countries where civil aviation enjoyed generous government subsidies, Great Britain concentrated resources on developing safe and reliable domestic airline service. International trips became common. By the middle 1920s most of the major cities in the Old World were linked by such firms as the Netherlands' KLM, England's Imperial Airways, and Germany's Lufthansa, which in 1925 became the first carrier to offer in-flight movies—silent one-reelers.

European progress contrasted sharply with apathy in the United States, where industrialists, financiers, politicians, and the general public all failed to grasp aviation's potential. To be sure, American pilots such as General Billy Mitchell and lieutenants Jimmy Doolittle and Russell A. Maughn were as brave and competent as those found anywhere. At the end of 1923, U.S. airmen held at least thirty-three various world records for speed, distance, and altitude, many of them at the expense of France. But one French flying official scoffed at what they all meant. "Records, yes, but they are a façade," he said. "Back of them there is nothing!" By then France was connected by air to a dozen countries—a dozen more than the United States. The world's most powerful country lacked a national aviation policy. Unlike Europe, there were no airlines offering regular passenger service, no colleges teaching aeronautical science, not even a governing body to issue licenses and inspect aircraft. The only "success" story was the airmail service, a lethal and unprofitable venture, subsidized by taxpayers and which Congress was regularly threatening to pull the plug on. Even getting Washington to recognize airpower as a vital element of national defense was a struggle, as became apparent when General Mitchell was famously court-martialed for accusing the Navy and War departments of "incompetency" and "criminal negligence" in continually stonewalling attempts to create a separate air branch of the military. To the average American of the early 1920s, flying was a fascinating but foolhardy activity best left to the barnstormers performing barrel rolls and loop-the-loops at the state fair.

During this period there was little public mention of the Orteig Prize and no official entrants. There was interest, but the requisite technology still was not in place for such a monumental flight. There was no shortage of adventurous airmen, however. In 1922, three years after the sagas of Harry Hawker, the *NC-4*, and Alcock and Brown focused the world's attention on the North Atlantic, the South Atlantic was crossed by air for the first time, though not in the fashion that might cause the average New Yorker or Londoner to buy two or three extra editions each day to keep abreast of the latest news. On March 30, 1922, two Portuguese naval officers left Lisbon in a two-wing seaplane for Rio de Janeiro. Using the Canary and Cape Verde islands as stepping-stones, and changing planes twice en route, Captains Gago Coutinho and Arturo de Cabral-Sacadura finally made it to Brazil on July 5, more than three months after they started. To the countries directly affected, as well as other European nations with colonial ties to Latin America, this and subsequent flights had significant social and economic implications. But for a variety of reasons the South Atlantic failed to stir the imagination of U.S. pilots and the American public. For one thing, it wasn't perceived as being especially challenging. The distance between this particular ocean hop's closest points—roughly fifteen hundred miles from Dakar, Senegal, to Natal, Brazil—was not even as formidable as what Alcock and Brown had traversed. The weather was more cooperative, with less fog and no ice to contend with. However, the winds in the Southern Hemisphere blew from east to west, the opposite of the North Atlantic, further dissuading U. S. pilots already put off by the logistics of launching an attempt from South America. Lastly, the incentives were disappointing. There were no cash prizes to win, no major cities to be feted in, and no real prestige involved. All of this is not to say that flying the South Atlantic was easy. Despite the equatorial region's balmy image, its treacherous winds and waters would claim its share of airmen over the years.

Two years after the first aerial crossing of the South Atlantic, eight handpicked members of the U.S. Army Air Service garnered international laurels when they became the first aviators to circumnavigate the globe. This time the Atlantic was a bit player rather than the star of the production, which saw the "world cruisers" start their journey in Seattle, Washington, on April 6, 1924, and end it there 175 days later. The Americans flew biplanes specially created for the trip by a talented young aircraft designer named Donald Douglas. Each two-seater, crewed by a pilot and a co-pilot/mechanic, was powered by a single 400-horsepower engine. The planes had 50-foot wingspans and landing wheels that could be replaced with pontoons as the situation warranted. The 'round-the-world fliers enjoyed maximum logistical support. Fuel dumps, supply depots, and rescue ships were strategically placed along the carefully plotted route, which avoided hostile weather systems such as the typhoon season in Southeast Asia and storms in the North Atlantic. The grueling adventure included seventy-two scheduled stops during nearly six months, including such exotic locales as Shanghai, Bangkok,

Karachi, Baghdad, Constantinople, and Reykjavik. At Kagoshima, Japan, the shore "was black with people" waving American flags, recalled one world cruiser. "It was an inspiring scene."

One of the planes crashed in the Aleutian Islands early in the cruise, but the rest of the squadron flew on. On the afternoon of July 14, Bastille Day, the "dog-tired" world cruisers—now more than halfway through their journey—were met by an enthusiastic crowd of several thousand at Le Bourget, the airfield built northeast of Paris during the war to protect the city from German raids. With Paris in the midst of hosting the Olympic Games, the French capital was filled with even more tourists than usual. French president Gaston Doumergue and John J. "Black Jack" Pershing, the overall commander of U.S. troops in the war, both formally received the "Magellans of the Air," who were roundly toasted by fellow aviators and given the freedom of the city. The public displays of fraternity were heartening. At one point the Americans looked in on the establishment of a fellow named Langer on the Champs-Élysées. "Lieutenant Leigh Wade was spotted by the proprietor instantly," observed a reporter tagging along with the group, "and was recognized as an old war acquaintance, and was kissed on both cheeks. The keys of both cellar and kitchen were given to him, and in honor of the occasion Langer grabbed a violin and led the orchestra. So far as the restaurateur was concerned, nobody else existed and he ignored all of his other patrons, who appeared glad to be ignored for the sake of the American heroes." After two days in Paris, the American fliers left for England, where their planes were fitted with pontoons for the east-to-west Atlantic crossing. It took three hours to fly from Paris to London, but a full month to make it over the ocean. The world cruisers stopped at the Orkney Islands, Iceland, and Greenland before officially touching down in North America at Icy Tickle, Labrador. During the crossing a second plane went down near the Orkneys, providing a reminder that the Atlantic could not be taken for granted. From there what remained of the formation flew on to Newfoundland, Nova Scotia, and nearly a score of cities on the U.S. mainland before finally calling it quits in Seattle on September 28, 1924. Fifty thousand people showed up to welcome the men home. Only two of the original four planes lasted the entire 27,533 miles (they were joined by a third, replacement plane in the last month of the flight), but despite the pair of crashes, nobody was seriously injured or killed during the unprecedented globe-girdling achievement.

The world fliers were still soaking in the public adulation when street-corner newsies began hawking the story of another transatlantic achievement. This time a German airship droned like a fat bumblebee across the ocean and into the headlines. The *ZR-3*, built specifically for the U.S. Navy as part of Germany's menu of war reparations, was piloted by Dr. Hugo Eckener, a pioneer in lighter-than-air craft. The 658-foot-long dirigible left the Zeppelin works at Friedrichshafen on October 12, 1924, carrying a crew of twenty-seven along with four American observers. Three days, two hours, and fifty-six minutes later, the "reparations ship" arrived at the Lakehurst Naval Air Station in New Jersey. Its docking concluded an uneventful delivery but still historic crossing: the first direct air connection between Germany and the United States.

The airship—rechristened the USS *Los Angeles* and its hydrogen replaced with less volatile helium by its new owners—proved to be a surprisingly popular instrument of rapprochement between the two former enemies. President Calvin Coolidge received Dr. Eckener and his crew at the White House. The Sunday after their arrival, fifty thousand people jammed the roads for miles around Lakehurst for the chance to see the airship and mingle with the celebrated airmen. New York threw a ticker-tape parade for *die triumphierenden Flieger*, many of whom had participated in deadly bombing raids over Paris and London just a few years earlier. Newspapers noted the millions of Americans of German heritage and insisted the country was "Zeppelin mad."

France, which had long wanted the Zeppelin works destroyed under the terms of the Treaty of Versailles, was cool to this almost giddy show of reconciliation between the United States and Germany. In 1923, after France's "eternal enemy" defaulted on its reparations payments, French troops had seized the Ruhr, the heart of Germany's steel and coal industries. Passive resistance by German citizens led to a severe economic slowdown and hyperinflation. The crisis wasn't resolved until representatives from the five major Allied countries met and agreed to a U.S. initiative known as the Dawes Plan. In effect, American loans to Germany would help that country restore its economy, stabilize its currency, and allow it to resume a now scaled-back schedule of payments to France and other debtor nations. France, suffering its own postwar economic woes and with its own obligations to meet, had no choice but to go along. Not only was a large part of its national budget dependent on German reparations, it also owed billions of dollars to the United

States for loans taken out during and after the war. The Dawes Plan was enacted in September 1924, concurrent with the growing hype over the *ZR-3*'s impending transatlantic voyage. At the very time the "peace ship" was being hailed throughout the United States and Germany as the latest demonstration of goodwill between the two countries, France was reluctantly preparing to withdraw from the Ruhr as a condition of the agreement.

Raymond Orteig's thoughts on the state of Franco-German relations and the blow to French national prestige are unrecorded, but they can be surmised. The five-year time limit on his $25,000 prize had recently expired. As he made steps to renew the challenge, eligibility remained limited to fliers and planes of "any allied nationality."

The gracefully aging head of Raymond Orteig, Inc., continued to enjoy the fruits of his hard-earned success as the 1920s roared on, though he was unhappy that Prohibition was costing him customers. The difficulty of cooking French cuisine without sherry, port, or maroschino, coupled with the loss of alcohol sales, was causing French-oriented restaurants everywhere to close their doors. Nonetheless, Orteig managed to keep his two establishments going. "These things must be borne with fortitude," he said.

Now in his middle fifties and reportedly worth somewhere close to $1 million, Orteig had eased into semiretirement, entrusting much of the daily operations of his hotels and restaurants to his three sons and his partner, Elie Daution. In early 1925, Orteig announced an ambitious $200,000 makeover of the Brevoort. The old-fashioned exterior of the landmark hotel—which actually was a collection of several nineteenth-century residences that had been haphazardly connected together over the years—would undergo a major face-lift. The interior also would undergo major structural changes. A good deal of the property's leafy and eccentric Old World charm would be sacrificed in the name of progress, but that could be said of the Washington Square neighborhood in general, where high-rise apartment buildings and sandwich shops continued to sprout.

The Orteig Prize also underwent renovation. On June 1, 1925, Orteig formally reissued his transatlantic challenge, which had expired the previous spring. During the yearlong period of abeyance Orteig had let it be known that he would continue to honor his commitment to reward the first to fly between New York and Paris nonstop. Under the new agreement his attorneys had put together, what was now officially called the Raymond Orteig $25,000 Prize was in the hands of a seven-man board of trustees. It was chaired by James G. Harbord, a retired army major general and the president of Radio Corporation of America. The vice chairman was George W. Burleigh, a colonel in the army reserves and a principal in Delafield, Thorne & Burleigh, the Wall Street law firm that had long represented Orteig's interests. Colonel Franklin W. Brown, president of the Army and Navy Club of America, was treasurer. Orteig's eldest son, Raymond Jr., was secretary. The other trustees were Maxime Mongendre, the consul general of France; Lucien Jouvaud, president of the French Benevolent Society; and Colonel Walter Scott, a kindly and much-honored philanthropist who had risen from a two-dollar-a-week messenger to vice president of Butler Brothers, a leading general wholesaling firm. Orteig deposited $25,000 in negotiable securities at Bryant Bank and had a trust agreement executed to transfer the funds should an aviator successfully make the flight.

Prize rules specified that the "start or landing may be made from land or water." If a land plane was used, the point of starting or landing had to be within fifty miles of Paris or New York. If a seaplane or flying boat was used, the starting or landing had to be made from a point within fifty miles of New York or on any point on the coast of France. To be properly entered on the register of contestants, an applicant was required to fill out a two-page form listing name, address, pilot license number and issuing authority, type of plane (monoplane, flying boat, etc.) being used, and any general particulars relating to the aircraft. Technical details also were required: the wing area in square feet; the load per square foot; the approximate capacity of the fuel tanks; and the make, type, and displacement of the engine or engines. The entry form was then to be signed, notarized, and mailed, along with a certified check for $250, to the board of trustees, in care of the Army and Navy Club of New York. The entry fee was intended as a gesture of good faith and was refundable.

The National Aeronautic Association agreed to administer the actual flights through a fourteen-man panel, with Orteig leaving the interpretation of the prize rules entirely in their hands. The Washington-based NAA had been formed in 1922 through its predecessor's merger with the

Raymond Orteig is flanked by Paul Tarascon (left) and François Coli in a photograph taken in Paris in August 1925.

debt-ridden Aero Club of America, which under Alan Hawley had never progressed much beyond its New York sport-flying roots. The flight committee consisted of the prize's board of trustees and seven notable members of the aviation community, including colonels Carl F. Schory, Lloyd Collis, and Harold E. Hartney. The NAA would work with the Aéro Club in Paris, operating under the auspices of the Fédération Aéronautique Internationale, in officiating all attempts. As was the case with the original challenge, a five-year time limit was attached to the Orteig Prize.

Work began on the Brevoort in the early summer of 1925. As Orteig and his wife boarded a liner for their annual vacation abroad, preparations for the first significant attempts to capture the prize were being made by a couple of French teams. The most advanced endeavor was that of Captain François Coli and Lieutenant Paul Tarascon, a pair of maimed war veterans in their early forties. The other effort involved the Farman Aviation Works, one of Europe's leading plane manufacturers. Orteig, delighted over the prospect of a New York-bound flight leaving

French soil that summer, expressed the hope that he would be able to personally witness at least one takeoff at Le Bourget.

Flying the Atlantic had been the dream of several accomplished French airmen long before Orteig's offer officially pricked their national pride. During the last year of the war, with the *Daily Mail* prize still unclaimed, two of the country's best-known pilots, Roland Garros and René Fonck, had been observed off by themselves, engaged in deep discussion. "You look like you're plotting something with Garros," an acquaintance teased Fonck one day. "Keep this to yourself," Fonck replied, "but we're getting ready to cross the Atlantic." Garros had gained fame by being the first to fly nonstop over the Mediterranean Sea in 1913. Any hopes of duplicating the feat over the Atlantic died with him when he was shot down on the eve of his thirtieth birthday, just a month before the Armistice. Fonck, however, would survive to have a pair of transatlantic aircraft built for him.

Henri Roget was another candidate for Atlantic honors who saw his potential snuffed out at an early age. Handsome, brave, and daring, the Lyons native had joined the 20th Dragoons upon his eighteenth birthday in 1911. He served on horseback and as dismounted infantry during the first three years of the war. Recovering from wounds received during a shelling, and attracted by "the glorious risks of aviation," he left the trenches for the Service d'Aéronautique, the French Air Service, in 1917, and ultimately flew bombers.

After the war Roget continued his long-distance flying with a series of *grand raids*—that is, "spectacular flights," as the French termed the cease-less and increasingly ambitious hops between Point A and Point B that characterized aviation between the two world wars. He piloted several notable flights linking France and the Mediterranean, including an effort in May 1919 to fly from Paris to Brazil in stages. That ambitious attempt to be the first to cross the South Atlantic ended prematurely with a crash outside Rabat, Morocco.

Roget also set altitude records while testing early turbocharged machines for the military. Once, in 1920, he zipped along at 156 miles per hour at 18,000 feet while covering the 285 miles between Paris and Lyons in well under two hours. The turbocharging apparatus used gas from the engine's exhaust to compress the air in the rarefied atmosphere,

allowing the propeller to maintain the same driving force as when operating in normal atmosphere. However, due to the greatly reduced resistance at high altitudes, a plane could travel much faster and farther using
the same amount of horsepower and fuel. In the immediate postwar era
French engineers believed turbocharging was the key to future ten-hour
flights between Paris and New York. When that day came, observed the
New York Times, "we will have a nightly service of airplanes following the
dawn across the Atlantic and dropping down in New York in time for
breakfast." The problem was that man and machine took a beating up in
the "evil heights." Engines fell apart and pilots risked succumbing to the
effects of "boiling blood," a condition where the lack of pressure causes
nitrogen bubbles to develop in the bloodstream and travel to the brain,
heart, and joints. Looking to assist the fledgling science of aeronautical
medicine, Roget unselfishly submitted to physiological testing inside a
large pneumatic chamber. On August 31, 1921, the twenty-eight-year-
old pilot died of "cardiac turbidity" at a military hospital. "French aviation loses in him one of its most brilliant glories and one of its more
luminous hopes," mourned a Paris daily.

Among the pallbearers at Roget's funeral was François Coli, the navigator on several of his flights, including the failed attempt to cross the
South Atlantic. Coli, who had discussed the possibility of a Paris-to-New
York flight with Roget, was now obliged to look elsewhere for a partner-
ing pilot. Paul Tarascon seemed an obvious choice.

Coli and Tarascon were an intriguing duo. Collectively the prospective ocean fliers had three good legs, three good eyes, and the kind of
indomitable spirit needed for such an undertaking. Coli had proved
himself equally capable at sea, on land, and in the air. He was born in
Marseilles on June 5, 1881, and grew up in a seafaring family. After studying navigation at the naval academy based there, he served a year in the
French Navy before following his father and uncles into the merchant
marine. He spent a decade aboard ship, rising to the rank of ship's officer
before leaving in 1912. Two years later he was in Argentina on family
business when war broke out. Although he wasn't mobilized, patriotism caused him to hurry back to France. When the best duty he was
offered was an assignment on a hospital ship, he resigned and joined
the infantry as a private in October 1914. Within fifteen months he had
been wounded twice in the trenches and earned several battlefield pro-
motions, ultimately commanding a company with the rank of captain. A

severe case of frostbitten feet, however, rendered him unfit for infantry duties. Looking to stay in the war, Coli asked to be transferred to the Air Service, where he received flight training and his pilot's brevet. In late 1916 he joined the Escadrille N. 62, a fighter squadron whose ranks included a hobbled pilot jocularly referred to as *l'as la jambe de bois*—"the ace with the wooden leg."

The Paris press knew Tarascon as a "gallant, opinionated, courageous man." Born on December 8, 1882, in the Provencal village of Le Thor, he had almost been killed in the crash of a Blériot monoplane while taking flying lessons in 1911. He spent eight months in the hospital and had his crushed right foot amputated above the ankle. Tarascon was in Casablanca when the war started. The examining physician at the local mobilization center somehow overlooked his handicap and assigned him to the infantry. Unfit for the trenches, he requested a transfer to the Air Service, which had no established eligibility requirements for pilot candidates and gladly accepted rejects from the infantry and the artillery. Tarascon earned his brevet and was made an instructor in two-seaters at Pau. Among his pupils were future aces Georges Guynemer and Alfred Heurtaux. Tarascon was itching to see action himself, and his request to join a combat unit was granted in early 1916, just in time to participate in the Battle of the Somme. According to one of his many citations, Tarascon proved himself a "remarkable pilot by his devotion, skill, coolness and initiative." These qualities helped him bring down a dozen German aircraft. On one mission his plane was hit more than a hundred times by enemy bullets, but he survived to fly again. Such escapades were in keeping with the cartoonish rooster he had painted on the side of his Nieuport 24. It was a rendition of Zigomar, a popular film character of the day that was always finding itself in some sort of trouble. Tarascon's fellow pilots liked his personal insignia so much that they adopted a slightly more ferocious version of it for the squadron insignia.

Tarascon was a true knight of the air, reminiscing in his old age of encounters such as the duel he once had with a red Albatros piloted by the great Oswald Boelcke, at the time the preeminent ace of the war. The two fought until both exhausted their ammunition and broke off the engagement. "I can still see the black leather helmet of Boelcke as I crossed him like a flash and he tossed me a sporting salute," Tarascon would say. "Our combat was without mercy, for Honor, but of such a dignity, such a knightliness, that, if our combat had been favorable to me, I would have solicited for him, for this knight of the air, privileged treatment." A few weeks later, when Boelcke was killed, the Royal Flying Corps dropped a wreath above the German aerodrome. It read: "To the memory of Captain Boelcke, a brave and chivalrous foe." These were the type of ennobling experiences romantics such as Raymond Orteig found irresistible.

Coli, as fearless in the air as he had been in the trenches, rapidly assumed command of the 62nd "Cocks." On March 10, 1918, the engine on his Spad VII failed, causing him to crash into a hangar. His right eye was ripped out in the accident. Displaying a quick and dark wit, Coli posted an order prohibiting pilots from entering a hangar by any means other than the doors designed for that purpose. By war's end Coli was commanding an entire air group. His eye patch gave him a somewhat raffish look, as if he were a character plucked from the pages of *Treasure Island*.

The bond that had formed between Coli and Tarascon continued after the war. By 1924 the pair was seriously considering a bid for the Orteig Prize, though financing was, as with all hopefuls, the major hurdle. Finally, an arrangement was reached with Henri Potez, an innovative engineer from Albert who had built propellers during the war and was now on the cusp of attaining notable success as an aircraft manufacturer. Potez had just received a government order for 150 of his new Potez 25 single-engine biplanes and was opening a plant in Meaulte to fulfill it. Within seven years his aircraft factory would be the largest in Europe and his durable two-seater would be exported by the thousands, becoming the workhorse for Aéropostale and other airmail companies. To demonstrate the multipurpose plane's reliability, range, and versatility to prospective clients, Potez entered it in many races, rallies, and promotional flights. There could be no better advertisement for the Potez 25 than somebody flying it from Paris to New York.

A special version of the plane was built for Tarascon and Coli inside a hangar at the Villacoublay aerodrome, south of Paris. The fuselage was modified to accommodate three large fuel tanks, while the lower wing was slightly altered to assist in lifting the greater load. To decrease drag and increase fuel efficiency, the wheel gear was designed to be dropped shortly after takeoff from Le Bourget. Press reports often mistakenly described the craft as a hydroplane. The Potez actually was built with grass, not water, in mind. Tarascon had it fitted with wooden skids, which would enable him to land toboggan-style on the thick rough of the Westchester Country Club at Rye, New York, the trip's planned terminus.

Its power plant was a single air-cooled radial Gnome-Rhone motor. The nine-cylinder "Jupiter" engine of British design was rated at 425 horsepower. The advantages of air-cooled engines over the more widely used liquid-cooled engines started with weight and simplicity. Air-cooled engines did not require the same cumbersome and complicated cooling system, which translated into easier maintenance and a weight savings of roughly three-quarters of a pound per unit of horsepower. A 400-horsepower air-cooled engine, for example, weighed about 300 pounds less than its liquid-cooled counterpart. Air cooling also made engines more reliable by eliminating the chief hazards of liquid-cooled engines: radiator leakage and stoppage. A third of all forced landings could be traced to this dangerous mechanical fault, including Harry Hawker's "magnificent failure" in 1919. The Jupiter was far from perfect, however. Like other early air-cooled engines, it had to gulp a rich air-fuel mixture to keep its cylinders from overheating. The Jupiter's poor exhaust valve cooling and comparatively short valve life continually frustrated technicians. Some joked that the Jupiter's consumption was more correctly measured in terms of exhaust valves than fuel.

On April 29, 1925, Tarascon and Coli publicly announced their intention to make the Paris-to-New York hop that summer. They hoped to leave by June or July, generally considered the most favorable months to fly the Atlantic. Their planned itinerary would take them across the English Channel to Ireland, from where they would head out across the ocean, following the Greenland-to-Newfoundland route before dropping down the eastern seaboard to New York. Tarascon, as pilot of the proposed flight, had filled out a notarized entry form on April 25, thus becoming the first person to formally compete for the Orteig Prize in the six years since it was created.

As would often be the case with challengers for the Orteig Prize, Tarascon was being overly optimistic about the planned departure date. By midsummer it was clear that the modified Potez needed more load, speed, instrumentation, and fuel consumption tests before it could be deemed fit for its mission. In late July Tarascon fixed a new date for takeoff. He and Coli would leave on August 25, he said, or as soon after that as weather allowed.

On July 30, the Potez was flown on what the press called a "secret" test flight—a round trip between Paris and Strasbourg, 300 miles to the east, on the German border. Sailing along on a tailwind, the outward flight took two hours, five minutes, roughly 145 miles per hour. On its return, this time flying into the wind, the Potez needed three hours, ten minutes, which translated into an airspeed of 95 miles per hour. Fuel economy was the major concern. Even allowing for a better pace as gas burned off and the plane's weight decreased en route, and assuming no straying off course due to high winds or navigational errors, Tarascon and Coli still figured to fall short of reaching New York. The Potez was already being asked to carry 792 gallons of gas on takeoff, increasing the plane's weight from one and a half tons to nearly four tons. The solution was not to try to load the craft with even more fuel, but to get the engine to burn a leaner, more economical mix without its cylinders frying up over the Atlantic.

Should the Potez wind up in the ocean, Tarascon and Coli were prepared. Ideally, they would have enough time to cut the fabric from the lower wing before hitting the water, which would enable the plane to float for a couple of hours. If help was not immediately forthcoming, they planned to pump dry the gas tanks, which would gain them another four hours. After that they would be forced to saw the bars holding the 735-pound engine in place, dropping the motor into the deep for the sake of improving the craft's buoyancy. Left with nothing but the frame, the men theoretically could ride the waves for as long as their supplies held out. These included fifteen days' worth of rations and a dozen rockets to fire as distress signals. The men remained supremely confident that they would not have to resort to using these precautionary measures. Tarascon was a proven pilot, if not yet over long distances, and Coli's experience and maritime background made him an unparalleled navigator over water. Concerned friends called it a fools' errand and tried to dissuade them.

As the summer of 1925 wore on and the testing and experimentation continued at Villacoublay, Tarascon felt increasing pressure from the Farman works, whose roster of experienced pilots included Maurice Drouhin and Lucien Bossoutrot. In a way, both men had been preparing for a transatlantic flight since joining Farman. Bossoutrot, born in 1890 and decorated several times during his four years with the French Air Service, would set twenty-seven different world records in civilian aviation during the 1920s and early 1930s. Drouhin was a wiry thirty-four-year-old Parisian with dark, penetrating eyes and a craving for adventure. As a member of the 24th Dragoons he had participated in cavalry charges in the fluid opening stages of the war, then become a motorbike messenger when the conflict devolved into a meat-grinding stalemate. He switched to the army's air arm and became a highly valued instructor of Farman aircraft.

One weekend in the fall of 1922, the pair had garnered headlines by flying nonstop for nearly a day and a half in a modified "Goliath" biplane over a controlled course outside Paris. With its 87-foot wingspan and pair of 300-horsepower Renault engines, the standard Goliath was everything its name suggested. It had originally been designed as a bomber, but its boxy fuselage was quickly retrofitted for commercial service after the war. In fact, it was the first long-range passenger plane, beginning regular Paris-to-London service in early 1919 with Bossoutrot piloting the inaugural two-and-a-half-hour flight. Its cabin normally could accommodate a dozen customers comfortably seated in wicker chairs. For the endurance flight of October 14–15, 1922, however, it was fitted with giant tanks brimming with three and a half tons of gasoline. During the two-day ordeal, Drouhin hung on despite suffering severe cramps from drinking cold coffee, while Bossoutrot had to wrap himself in furs to ward off the freezing temperatures. "Physical endurance proved superior to mechanical devices," reported a wire service correspondent, "as the engine gave out before the pilots. . . . Bossoutrot was a sorry looking sight as he alighted with bloodshot eyes and puffed face from the extreme cold, while Drouhin staggered from the fuselage, where he had been attempting to repair the left motor." The disheveled test pilots had established a world's record for uninterrupted time in the air: 34 hours, 19 minutes, and 7 seconds, breaking the mark set the previous year by U.S. fliers Eddie Stinson and Lloyd Bertaud. "I have been to America and halfway back again," Bossoutrot said.

Nearly two years later, on July 16–17, 1924, as Paris was busy hosting the Olympics and saying au revoir to the American world fliers, Drouhin created a new endurance record. This time he and copilot Lucien Coupet spent 37 hours, 50 minutes, and 10 seconds inside a circling F. 62 Goliath, this one with a wingspan expanded by four feet and powered by a single 520-horsepower engine placed in the redesigned nose. These endurance trials testing man and machine were crucial to any transatlantic

undertaking. Later, when speaking of the Orteig Prize, Drouhin liked
to say that in his mind he had already made the Paris-to-New York trip,
though, of course, the record attempts took place over a measured course
under strictly controlled conditions. Each time the plane was in regular
radio contact with observers, had no significant navigational challenges
to speak of, and was not flying over water or consistently bucking headwinds. The real thing promised to be far more difficult and hazardous.

In the predawn hours of Friday, August 7, 1925, Drouhin and copilot
Jules Landry took off from the airfield at Étampes, about thirty miles
south of Paris, intent on setting new standards for duration and distance.
This was promoted as a prelude to a transatlantic attempt. The Goliath
was fully laden with gasoline and oil and weighed a little over seven
tons when it began the grind: 44 circuits of a 100-kilometer (62-mile)
course between Étampes and Chartres. For the next couple of days the
roads and hillsides in the vicinity of the two towns were crowded with
spectators, many of them American tourists. By three o'clock Sunday
morning, when Drouhin and Landry finally landed with less than two
gallons of gas remaining, they had been aloft for a record-shattering
45 hours, 11 minutes, and 59 seconds. "If their flight had been a straight
line," observed a reporter on the scene, "they would easily have crossed
from Paris to New York with the plane." The record 4,400 nonstop
kilometers (2,733 miles) Drouhin and Landry had covered actually fell
several hundred miles short of what needed to be traversed to reach New
York. Nonetheless, Farman's latest triumph was viewed as one more step
toward achieving its goal of a proper transoceanic plane.

French newspapers, which typically were only four to eight pages long,
gave spare coverage to preparations for the Orteig Prize. The limited
space was largely given over to the financial and political upheaval of the
summer, particularly rebellions in the colonies of Morocco and Syria,
the deepening crisis with the franc, and security guarantees involving
Germany. Of the little commentary published about the Tarascon-Coli
effort, much of it revolved around its nationalistic aspects. Jacques
Mortane, writing in Le Petit Journal, was worried that Tarascon's plane
would use a German engine: "Up to this point, the Germans have never
had an idea of accomplishing such a feat with a French engine, even one
made in Germany, and we see things their way." The French government
did not favor the flight, offering scant assistance beyond issuing the fliers
the necessary permit and sharing meteorological information.

In the States, few knew a transatlantic bid was taking shape. Most of the administrative work for the competition was being handled by George Burleigh, Orteig's attorney and personal representative in Manhattan, and Carl Schory, secretary of the National Aeronautic Association in Washington. Both men were in the dark as to the details. While occasional reports from overseas correspondents were describing the ongoing preparations, there had been no direct communications between Tarascon and the Aéro Club in Paris or the NAA regarding the supervision of officials to properly monitor its start and finish. Also, after four months the entrant had yet to submit the required $250 good-faith fee, another discomfiting sign of the nature of the project. In early August, Orteig cabled his concerns over any possible delays to Burleigh: "Just met Tarascon. I hope you will accept his entry. . . . Flight will take place around September fifth."

On September 5, an editor at World Traveler Publishing Company forwarded Tarascon's entry fee to the NAA, along with the pilot's request to "make arrangements for an American landing field, etc." The editor added: "Will you kindly inform me of any formalities which must be met to give these chaps (Tarascon and Coli) a claim upon this prize in the event of a successful flight." The pilots' precise relationship with the Park Avenue publisher is unclear but presumably involved editorial rights for *World Traveler* magazine. With the flight apparently imminent and a check in hand, the contest committee finally moved on Tarascon's entry. On September 10, it approved the French pilot's paperwork and waived the sixty-day waiting period between approval and takeoff. This meant that Tarascon and Coli were free to leave any time they felt ready. Burleigh had a long conversation with Raymond Orteig Jr. in New York about procedural and ceremonial matters, but admitted, "we cannot do anything until we have more information."

Two weeks of waiting for favorable weather over the Atlantic followed. The men kept busy with all the sundry matters involved in an expedition of such magnitude. Presently, an announcement was made: Tarascon would attempt to break Drouhin's recently set endurance record while using the closed-circuit flight as a final rehearsal for an Atlantic attempt. At noon on September 25, 1925, Tarascon left Étampes in the Potez, its tanks fully loaded. Coli, occupied with his charts, did not accompany him this time. In his place was Lieutenant Louis Favreau, who, like Coli, had switched to aviation after being wounded in the trenches. Favreau had

The special modified Potez 25 biplane built for Paul Tarascon and François Coli for their transatlantic attempt is pictured at Villacoublay in early September 1925, shortly before it was destroyed in a crash.

become a test pilot for Potez in 1923 following several years of flying the mail between Paris and London. In eleven hundred mail runs he had not suffered a single accident.

Owing to high winds, the results were disappointing. After thirteen trips around the Étampes–Chartres–Orléans circuit, the Potez was averaging only 87 miles per hour while expending half of its fuel supply. The thirteenth lap ended at Étampes at two o'clock in the morning of September 26, just as the weather deteriorated. Violent gusts blew through the area. Spotters anxiously kept their binoculars and spotlights trained on the turbulent skies, but when there was no sign of the plane by four o'clock, a ground search was ordered. Airplanes joined the hunt at first light.

At ten o'clock the remains of the shattered and burned Potez were discovered near a small wooded area outside Dreux. Tarascon and Favreau were badly shaken up but still alive. As Favreau later explained it, he had taken over the controls from Tarascon to allow the fatigued pilot some rest when the plane soon was driven off course by the gale-force winds. Hindered by a malfunctioning compass and unable to read the altimeter after the lights on the instrument panel failed, he continued navigating *au pifomètre*, but the old airmail practice of "following one's nose" proved costly. Dropping low to get his bearings, he clipped a treetop in the darkness, with the Potez somersaulting over the uneven ground before exploding. Tarascon struggled to leave the burning plane. Favreau, thrown clear, managed to pull him out of the mangled cockpit. Favreau was slightly injured, while Tarascon suffered severe but not life-threatening burns. The craft was a total loss. However, Tarascon was not unnerved. He insisted to the French press that he would be back for another try.

Burleigh and Schory, initially unaware of the circumstances surrounding the abrupt cancellation of the Tarascon-Coli effort, griped two days after the crash that "no reasons exist in encouraging aviators who are not serious in their intention of making a flight." They were unfairly referring to Tarascon, but they could just as well have had others in mind. There was Harry G. Yerg of Nutley, New Jersey, who on the day of Tarascon's catastrophic flight wrote the contest committee to "kindly send me a list of prizes offered for various feats of flying, such as the flight from Paris to New York. . . . I am interested in money prizes only." Yerg, who claimed a hundred hours aboard British scout planes during the war, also inquired as to how he might acquire a private pilot's license before setting off across the Atlantic. Earlier, George Kirsch and Antoine Mourr, a pair of high-speed fiends who had flown together in the war, declared that they had sailed to New York specifically to compete for the Orteig Prize. "They did not bring planes with them," observed the reporter who greeted them, "nor had they any definite idea as to what type of machine would be the best for a transatlantic flight." They also had no backers. Untroubled by the lack of a plane, plan, and money, the Frenchmen confidently said they would be setting off for Paris in just a few weeks, in October, given favorable conditions. They made it to Paris—by liner.

As Tarascon healed and work continued inside the shops of Potez and Farman, winter weather settled in over the North Atlantic. All plans to have a go at the Orteig Prize would have to wait at least until the following spring. By then one of France's most decorated war heroes would already be in New York, preparing his own bid for glory.

4

The Fortune of the Air

Flirting with danger offers to the one who accepts the risk special satisfactions. We have moments of nostalgia, and it is then that one undertakes sublime follies, incomprehensible to other people.

—René Fonck

French pilots weren't the only ones warming to the Orteig Prize, as the winter of 1925–1926 saw stepped-up activity on the American side of the Atlantic. In the forefront were two separate efforts spearheaded by reserve officers. Lieutenant Commander Noel Davis, in charge of the Massachusetts Naval Reserve Station at Boston, publicly declared his intention to form an expedition, though he was finding it difficult to obtain a plane and financial support. Colonel Harold E. Hartney, who commanded the famous 1st U.S. Pursuit Group during the war, already had an organization in place. Backed by a pair of New Hampshire businessmen, he had teamed up with Homer M. Berry, a former air-mail pilot and a second lieutenant in the Army Air Reserve, to create Argonauts, Inc., the first American syndicate specifically set up to pursue the Orteig Prize.

Hartney was president of General Airways System, a struggling operation with a business office in the Fisk Building on 57th Street in Manhattan and a variable number of airworthy craft parked at Mitchel Field on Long Island. A lawyer in his native Canada before going overseas with the Royal Flying Corps, Hartney had been shot down four times—

54

Colonel Harold Hartney helped organize the Argonauts, the first American attempt to capture the Orteig Prize.

once, he claimed, by the great Baron von Richthofen himself. In 1918 he took charge of the 1st Pursuit Group, whose ranks included the likes of Eddie Rickenbacker and the "Arizona balloon-buster," Frank Luke, the only airmen of the war to receive the Medal of Honor. Hartney, a much-decorated ace himself, left the military in 1921, became a U.S. citizen two years later, and put his legal and flying backgrounds to good use as a civilian adviser to various aviation concerns. He was instrumental in organizing the National Aeronautic Association and was its general manager and secretary for many years. In 1923 he started General Airways with a view toward making his mark in airmail, freight, and passenger service on a national—and ultimately international—basis. To that end he was on the lookout for a dependable long-distance aircraft.

Working out of a tumbledown barn on a Long Island chicken farm was an immensely talented but chronically broke Russian engineer named Igor Ivan Sikorsky. In time Sikorsky's name would become synonymous with helicopters—so much so that he came to whimsically twirl a finger above his head when introduced at cocktail parties. In the 1920s, however, he was just another hardworking dreamer trying to establish a toehold in the uncertain marketplace of American commercial aviation.

Sikorsky was born in Kiev in 1889 and educated in Russia and Paris. Leonardo da Vinci's centuries-old drawings of flying machines intrigued him as a boy, leading to a lifelong fascination with flight. He was only twenty when he designed and built his first aircraft, a helicopter that failed to fly. However, he soon gained greater success with fixed-wing aircraft, building and piloting planes of remarkable range and size. In 1913 he unveiled the first successful four-engine plane, *Le Grand*, which featured the first enclosed cabin. He followed up with the *Ilia Mourometz*, an astounding aircraft for its time. It had a wingspan of 102 feet and weighed five tons. It offered its sixteen passengers a washroom, dining table, upholstered seats, and even an exterior promenade deck! During the war he delivered about seventy-five of his oversize planes as bombers. Sikorsky, the grandson of a poor village priest, probably would have gone on building ever-larger planes for Russia had the czar not been overthrown. Instead he fled the Bolshevik revolution—first to France, where he could not find a position in the downsized postwar aircraft industry, and then to the United States, where he arrived one early spring day in 1919 to equally dismal prospects. To support himself he taught mathematics to Russian immigrants, gave lectures on astronomy and aviation, and restricted himself to a strict meal allowance of 80 cents a day. Meanwhile he scraped together enough money to begin work on a twin-engine passenger plane numbered the S-29-A, with the "A" standing for America. He put his fellow Russian émigrés to work. Most of them were cabdrivers, cigarette makers, and cabaret dancers who pitched in during their free time. At a particularly critical moment, Sikorsky's favorite composer, the renowned pianist Sergei Rachmaninoff, subscribed $5,000 to his company. The money allowed Sikorsky to move his ragtag operation into a hangar at Roosevelt Field in Mineola, twenty miles east of Manhattan. There, the *New Yorker* later reported, a score of multilingual mechanics "calling each other Baron, Count, or General, like inmates of an asylum, and making tools of anything handy," worked under Sikorsky's direction.

Roosevelt Field was named after the youngest son of former president Theodore Roosevelt, Quentin, who was killed in a dogfight over the Western Front while serving in Harold Hartney's command. The airfield was adjacent to an airstrip once known as Hazelhurst, but renamed Curtiss Field in 1921 when Glenn Curtiss bought the property to develop airplanes for the government. Roosevelt and Curtiss fields were separated by a partially fenced twenty-foot bluff, with the Curtiss confines occupying the lower ground. The joint complex of shops, sheds, hangars, factories, offices, and unpaved runways was evolving into one of the hubs of American aviation. Rachmaninoff was named vice president of the Sikorsky Aero Engineering Corporation, an impressive-sounding name for what was still a shoestring operation. Employees received little or no pay, while their boss continued to give lectures at night and on weekends to help make ends meet. Somehow the S-29-A got built. After overloading caused it to crash on a golf course during its initial flight in the spring of 1924, the plane was repaired and successfully flown four months later. It could whisk fourteen people through the air at a cruising speed of a hundred miles per hour and fly, if needed, on just one engine. It was a wonderful machine, but there was no flood of orders, just irregular freight-transport jobs and chartered sightseeing gigs. The United States was still on the cusp of discovering commercial aviation.

Although the United States lagged far behind Europe in passenger air service, in one aspect of aviation it led the world: airmail delivery. The federal government began a cursory airmail service between Washington and New York in 1918; within two years a rudimentary transcontinental service was in place. Despite the loss of many pilots in the early going and millions of dollars throughout, America's subsidized airmail system steadily progressed to the point that the government was ready to turn it over to private operators. The Kelly Act, passed by Congress in February 1925, provided for the establishment of "feeder lines" between major cities, with these Contract Air Mail (CAM) routes open to bids. As an incentive, independent contractors would be allowed to keep the lion's share of all airmail revenue.

Hartney, Sikorsky, and Homer Berry joined forces. At the same time the overly ambitious Hartney was preparing a bid on four of the CAM routes, he was finalizing plans for an overnight airline connecting New York and five other major cities. He searched for a plane to make all this possible. One March day in 1925 Berry took Sikorsky's plane, bearing twenty-one passengers, to four thousand feet over Manhattan. The demonstration impressed, but did not convince, would-be investors. Starved for financing, the passenger airline didn't pan out as planned, and the airmail bid failed. Orteig's prize offer had recently been renewed. Berry, hungry for something more adventurous than hauling sacks of letters, squeamish businessmen, and the occasional piano between cities, convinced Hartney that they should shift their energies toward winning the prize. Accomplish that, and the world would come rushing to them.

Homer Berry was a tall, ruddy-faced Oklahoman. He had taken up barnstorming in 1912, when he was sixteen, and worked his way across the country to a flying school in New York. His adventures included briefly flying for Mexico during the Huerta revolution and several years of active duty in the Philippines, the Far East, and France. A postwar accident had netted him a lump-sum disability payment of $2,000, which he intended to invest as seed money in the inchoate transatlantic organization. Hartney tolerated a certain indulgence by the self-promoting Berry, who used his commission south of the Rio Grande as justification for presenting himself as "Captain" Berry. It may have been Berry's idea to call the group the Argonauts—after all, a pilot named Homer was bound to feel some kinship with Greek mythology. The name referred to the band of fifty heroes who accompanied Jason on the ship *Argo* in his fabled quest for the Golden Fleece. As it developed, there were to be no heroes in this modern version of the epic odyssey.

After buttonholing any number of potential investors, Berry and Hartney were finally able to line up two principal backers. One was Robert Jackson, a wealthy paper manufacturer from Concord, New Hampshire. The other was John B. Jamison, also of Concord, who invested $10,000. As the major contributor Jackson received the title of president of Argonauts, Inc., while Hartney was named vice president and general manager. Jackson, Hartney, and Jamison each held a 25 percent share of the stock. In recognition of his ongoing contributions (which included working for no salary and paying all his own expenses), Berry received a 10 percent stake in the syndicate. Most important to his ambitions, Berry also was promised that he would be a pilot on any Paris-bound flight.

Sikorsky continued to flirt with insolvency until, one weekend in 1925, he had a chance meeting with Arnold C. Dickinson of Fitchburg, Massachusetts, who was having his portrait painted by one of Sikorsky's Russian friends. Dickinson, a colonel in the war, was the eldest son of Charles Dickinson, who had made millions in real estate and utilities. Warmed by the struggling plane-maker's story and convinced of his potential, the Dickinsons decided to invest $100,000 in the company. Sikorsky was happy to step aside and have Arnold Dickinson assume the administrative chores as president of what was now called the Sikorsky

Manufacturing Company. The transfer of power allowed the freshly minted vice president of engineering to concentrate on what he did best: building cutting-edge planes with Old World craftsmanship.

The new company's first customer was the Argonauts. Hartney and Berry attested to the superior handling and performance of the S-29-A. Could Sikorsky build a craft similar to that, but with greater range and power, one that could carry a small band of modern-day Argonauts from New York to Paris? Sikorsky, a master of multiengined aircraft, confidently said that he could. The Argonauts placed an order and put down a deposit, and by early 1926 work had commenced inside the Sikorsky hangar.

In early May, Raymond Orteig gave a dinner for the French ace who had emerged as the most high-profile contender for his prize yet. René Fonck had just arrived in New York from a five-and-a-half-day crossing on the liner *Paris*. Now that he was on this side of the ocean, he planned to knock off four days from that time on his return trip by air. To get him where he wanted to go, he had signed on with the Argonauts.

René Fonck, the French "Ace of Aces," aboard an ocean liner in the early 1920s.

Fonck would naturally have preferred to launch his flight from native soil, but practical considerations had brought him to the States. The prevailing winds over the Atlantic were an immutable meteorological fact that continued to stack the odds against any east-to-west attempt. Much more important was the issue of financing. France was in the midst of a worsening monetary crisis, and the buying power of its currency continued to plummet. The exchange rate changed from 21 to 56 francs per dollar between 1925 and 1926 (meaning the Orteig Prize was now worth 1.4 million devalued francs). This was great news for Americans living or traveling abroad, but bad news for any Frenchman, no matter how famous, looking for domestic funding for a transatlantic attempt. In the Argonauts Fonck had found a willing underwriter to his personal ambition.

Given his druthers, Berry also would have preferred that Fonck launch his flight from France, and with a French syndicate. It was Berry's original intention to conduct an all-American flight: an American plane built with American capital and flown by an American crew. However, toward the end of 1925, while Berry was in South America on business, Fonck had come to the States. He met with Hartney and Sikorsky, reviewed their plans and the plane, and indicated that he would welcome an invitation to join their venture—as chief pilot, of course.

The organization's new backers were thrilled. Unlike Homer Berry, René Fonck was a marquee name, and the Argonauts intended to capitalize on that. The contract Fonck ultimately signed paid him $250 a week and called for him to use his connections with the French government— especially the air-minded minister of war, Paul Painlevé—to garner whatever support he could for the project. At Painlevé's direction, three 450-horsepower Gnome-Rhone Jupiter engines, collectively valued at $27,000, were shipped to New York, along with sophisticated radio gear from Radio des Industries. Technicians were assigned to deliver, set up, and monitor the donated equipment. Fonck was granted an indefinite leave of absence from the army to concentrate on the undertaking.

Many who read Fonck's postwar chronicle of his exploits, *Mes Combats*, were moved by the passages describing the brotherhood between French and American pilots. At one point in his book Fonck grieved over the sacrifice of Sergeant Phelps Collins, who lost consciousness while going after a German high-altitude bomber over Paris: "Death claimed him quite gently, without a shock. He will be among those whose sacrifices will probably be unknown—and Paris, our beautiful Paris, will never know that on the day of this first bombardment a brave American pilot, enlisted in our ranks, met his death while trying to defend it." This kind of "poignant melancholia," Fonck wrote, was characteristic of his people. "The French are built in such a way that the satisfaction of pride moves them more than material reward."

The short, dapper Fonck was driven by pride, to the point of being annoyingly arrogant at times. Now thirty-two years old, he was by his own reckoning the most prolific murderer of airmen in the Great War. His fame rested on that distinction, even if his total of "kills" was impossible to verify. He had 75 confirmed and 52 unsubstantiated victories, which in his personal ledger meant he had rid the skies of 127 *Boche* planes. Unwilling to have anyone finish ahead of him in the rankings of the war's greatest aces, especially a German, Fonck was careful to emphasize his combined total of confirmed and unconfirmed kills whenever discussing his record. Thus, over time his unofficial figure of 127 victories acquired a kind of legitimacy through its repetition in the press. It made Fonck the de facto "ace of aces," ahead of Germany's famous "Red Baron," Manfred von Richthofen, whose 80 official victories were the most of any airman on either side.

Fonck was born on March 27, 1894, in Saulcy-sur-Merthe, a village in the mountainous Vosges region. His Alsatian ancestors included a German general and a marshal in Napoleon's army. When conscripted in August 1914, his engineering studies landed him a position with the ground troops, where his work involved building trenches and fixing roads. Within six months he had obtained a transfer to the air service. It was a branch better suited to Fonck's ego, for no country more shamelessly promoted its air "aces" than France. Its best pilots were assigned to *Les Cigognes*, the famous Storks squadrons. Their ranks included the dashing but frail Georges Guynemer, whose gallantry and soulful dark eyes made him a national hero.

Fonck joined the Storks in 1917. Reportedly the youngest and smallest of France's pursuit pilots, he was by his own definition a virtuoso—a master tactician and a superb marksman. On two separate occasions he shot down six enemy aircraft in one day. Once he knocked down three German planes in three perfectly timed bursts of gunfire, an episode that took all of ten seconds. "I sent my bullets at the target as though directing them by hand," he said. As his neatly trimmed mustache and tightly tailored uniform suggested, Fonck was a fastidious man. He also was a loner. In the air he had preferred solo missions, where he was free to "perform those little coups of audacity which amuse me." On the ground, he rarely fraternized with fellow pilots, choosing to do calisthenics or press his uniforms while others were out drinking and carousing. Some claimed his best friend was the squadron's mascot, a pet stork named Helen.

In contrast to Guynemer, the very embodiment of French élan, Fonck's persona was that of a coldly calculating killer who took few risks. He never attacked observation balloons, for example, leaving the most hazardous form of air-to-air combat to others. One September day in 1917 the great Guynemer flew into a cloud and never came out. Searches turned up neither plane nor body. As France alternately mourned and held out hope that Guynemer—then the war's top ace—would miraculously materialize, the Germans claimed that one of their own aces, Kurt Wissemann, had shot him down. German soldiers were said to have buried Guynemer at some location in no-man's-land, a grave that quickly became lost in the muddy chaos of war. Three weeks later, Fonck came across a German two-seater. In his usual economical fashion, Fonck fired two short bursts, and the plane crashed inside Allied lines. When the dead pilot was identified as Wissemann, Fonck trumpeted himself as "the tool of retribution," meting out justice to "the murderer of my good friend." His boasting ignored the fact that Guynemer, like nearly all members of the Storks, had thought Fonck a pompous self-promoter and thus had little to do with him. "He is not a truthful man," said Lieutenant Claude Marcel Haegelen, a Storks ace who counted himself among Fonck's few friends. "He is a tiresome braggart, and even a bore, but in the air, a slashing rapier, a steel blade tempered with unblemished courage and priceless skill. . . . But afterwards he can't forget how he rescued you, nor let you forget it. He can almost make you wish he hadn't helped you in the first place."

Fonck remained in the army after the war. He was elected to the Chamber of Deputies, the lower house of France's bicameral legislature, representing his native Vosges. He remained widely respected inside and outside aviation circles for his wartime accomplishments. He was president of the Aeronautic League of France, the youngest commander in the Legion of Honor, and the author of books and articles, many describing the threat posed by German aviation. His fame was such that in 1925 he was approached by the leader of a group of rebellious Moroccan tribesmen to organize a small air force against the Spaniards.

After listening to various glowing tributes on this spring evening in Manhattan, Fonck reiterated that he was "not out for the money." Speaking through a translator (for all of his expressions of fraternity with the United States, Fonck never bothered to learn even a smattering of English), he told the gathering he was only interested in seeing "the bonds between France and America, forged by Lafayette, strengthened, and I want copartnership between American and Frenchman in this flight from the biggest city in your country to the capital of France." Should the enterprise succeed, Fonck, Sikorsky Aircraft, and the Argonauts would all be on the ground floor of a potentially lucrative transoceanic airline business. The honors and offers that would naturally come their way could make everybody's fortunes.

Fonck had previously announced that he would leave from New York's Central Park and land in the Bois de Boulogne, a sprawling green oasis on the western edge of Paris. Now the plan was for the giant Sikorsky plane currently being built to embark from Roosevelt Field. From there it would travel the "Great Circle" route that followed the curvature of the earth, from Long Island over Rhode Island and Cape Cod, then on a beeline to Nova Scotia and Newfoundland, bisecting both in turn. There the most dangerous part of the passage began, the course carrying the plane over the ocean, north of the shipping lanes, then back to a point ten miles south of Cape Clear, Ireland. From there it would pass over Falmouth, England, then Cherbourg, France, before setting down at Le Bourget.

Fonck added that the plane would not be outfitted with pontoons. He was interested in reaching Paris, not merely the shores of France, as the rules allowed. "It is either fly or sink," he said.

On April 19, 1926, Harold Hartney submitted Fonck's notarized Orteig Prize entry. He also filed an entry for himself, as agent for the Argonauts, just to be safe. Eleven days later he sent a second, amended form, this time including some minor technical omissions. The entries, along with the letters and telegrams he regularly sent to the contest committee apprising them of every little change in plans and asking clarification of certain rules and procedures, indicated he was taking no chances. As he put it, "this organization sincerely hopes to accomplish this flight . . . before some one else gets there ahead of us."

Money was a concern. Hartney and Berry had previously approached a New York publisher with the idea of helping to bankroll the Argonauts, but the newspaper magnate, while interested in the public relations value of the flight, ultimately decided the costs and risks of the enterprise were too great. Soon afterward Robert Jackson and John B. Jamison came aboard as financial angels, but their combined investment still left the Argonauts chronically scrambling for cash. The pinch became especially acute after the expensive decision was made to replace the two Liberty water-cooled motors on Sikorsky's work in progress with a trio of new air-cooled engines. The prize committee had no interest in how an entrant financed his effort, "providing it is done honestly," said George Burleigh. One potential source was the Daniel Guggenheim Fund for the Promotion of Aeronautics, which in January 1926 announced it would spend $2.5 million over the next ten years to foster aeronautical science. Citing lagging public support of flying because of a fear "stimulated by the sensational recital of airplane disasters," the fund's principal objectives were research, education, and the development of safety in aviation. Hartney, looking to tap into this wellspring of private money, wrote Orville Wright, hoping he would intercede on his behalf. Wright forwarded the letter to Harry F. Guggenheim, president of the fund. Guggenheim explained his position to Wright: "I have taken the view, in the numerous proposals that have been made to me for financial assistance in Transatlantic flights and other similar demonstrations, that these projects were very expensive means of propaganda and that we would be unwise to disburse our resources in this way."

In the words of Igor Sikorsky, throughout the spring and summer of 1926 the "huge, elegant, efficient and modern-looking airplane gradually took shape in the old, leaky hangar" at Roosevelt Field. The S-35, as the craft was numbered, was a sesquiplane. At 76 feet, the lower wing was much smaller than the upper wing, which was stretched from its normal 76 feet to a width of 101 feet by adding of a pair of 12½-foot panels. The additional wing area was needed to lift the extra weight of the fuel. The wings and the entire framework were made of duralumin, a rarity at the time. Fabric was used for the exterior covering. A streamlined

Designer Igor Sikorsky (right) poses in front of the Argonauts' three-engine aircraft with chief pilot René Fonck in the summer of 1926.

1,100-gallon fuel tank was positioned behind each outboard motor, and the third engine was fitted into the nose. The cockpit had dual controls and was fully enclosed, with sliding windows at its top and sides and a door that opened to the cabin.

On August 17 the plane was rolled out of its hangar for the first time, Sikorsky at the controls. He taxied it for thirty minutes, declaring afterward that every part of the craft—motors, controls, everything—"worked to perfection." Soon it was being put through its paces, the plane being flown with one engine out, then two, and with various loads. A demonstration flight to Washington a couple of weeks later impressed government officials. Carrying a load of 8,000 pounds, the plane climbed at the rate of over 800 feet a minute and maintained a cruising speed of more than 120 miles per hour. Thanks to self-compensating rudders, the plane could be flown on any two engines without affecting control. The machine's performance "remained unsurpassed by any plane of similar size and power" for years, Sikorsky later claimed. As equipment, tanks, and furnishings were added, the weight naturally increased. Sikorsky intended the S-35 to be a prototype airliner, so he lavished great care on its interior. Under the direction of a professional decorator the 15-foot

cabin was luxuriously appointed with carpeting, drapes, and mahogany
trim, with wicker chairs and a red leather couch that could be converted
into a bed. Sikorky wanted a methodical series of tests for every aspect
of the flight, especially in the critical areas of takeoff capability and fuel
consumption, and he was willing to postpone the takeoff for Paris until
the following spring to do so. But he was only the builder. While his
opinion was respected and considered, ultimately the Argonauts, who
had hired him, had the final say in the matter. The person who had the
most pull with the Argonauts was René Fonck.

During his time in the States Fonck stayed in a luxury suite at the Hotel
Roosevelt, with a male secretary to handle correspondence, translations,
and a demanding calendar. The pilot-hero's celebrity, his Frenchness,
and the novelty of his mission made him a much-sought-after guest.
The summer became an unending string of banquets, media interviews,
and personal audiences with luminaries of all stripes. Fonck didn't drink
(although he allowed himself a glass of wine with meals when possible,
Prohibition be damned) or visit nightclubs. His grooming was impeccable, and no matter how hot it got, he dependably wore his wool army
uniform with polished leather puttees or a crisply pressed suit with shiny
dress shoes. One muggy afternoon he was photographed in shirtsleeves
and suspenders, an image he said made him feel "ashamed" as he unsuccessfully tried to block its publication. The *New Yorker* described him as
"the quietest celebrity ever to visit these shores. . . . He seldom speaks, and
then quickly, and it is doubtful if he could talk at all were his hands tied."

As Fonck familiarized himself with the S-35 in test flights above
Long Island, the size and composition of the crew were likewise up in
the air. In addition to the pilot and copilot, there would be a navigator
and a radio operator, though some duties could be combined. Fonck's
contract allowed him to name his own crew, provided the copilot was
an American. It was always assumed by Homer Berry that he would
be that man; indeed, he was involved in the first tests. With hundreds
of applications pouring in, Fonck asked the Navy Department to help
him select the other crew members. Lieutenant Allan P. Snody, the aide
to the naval air chief, Rear Admiral William A. Moffett, was chosen to
be navigator. Captain John R. Irwin was picked to handle the radio.
Lieutenant George O. Noville, a thirty-six-year-old technical expert
who had supervised the base camp at Spitzbergen during Richard Byrd's
recent Arctic expedition, was named flight engineer. On a long and

difficult flight such as this, crew cohesiveness should have been a priority. Instead, it devolved into almost an afterthought. One by one, the original crewmen dropped out of the flight. Noville resigned following a disagreement over the type of lubricating oil to be used. Irwin also withdrew. And for reasons that were never fully explained, Berry was frozen out.

An early discordant sign was when Fonck and Snody skipped a formal Rotary Club function at which they and Berry were to receive platinum wristwatches. Soon Berry's name was pointedly absent in public discussions of the flight. On August 28, rumors of dissension became an ugly fact when Berry learned that Snody, the navigator, would now be Fonck's relief man at the controls. When he confronted Fonck about this at the airfield, Fonck responded evenly, "If a third pilot is to be taken, it will be you, Captain Berry."

Every airman knew that including a third pilot on a three- or four-man crew was so improbable as to be almost a joke—or an insult. "When I left for South America last December," Berry angrily told the press, "I had never heard Captain Fonck's name mentioned in connection with this flight. It was my understanding that as soon as the plane was ready I was to return to the United States to pilot it. Then when I came back I was told I was to be co-pilot with Captain Fonck. I was later informed that Lieutenant Snody was going as navigator. Then I was relegated to third pilot, and now today I find I am out in the cold altogether." Berry produced a letter written by Hartney, dated June 9, 1926, affirming the conditions of the original agreement between Berry and the syndicate. If a three-man crew undertook the flight, Berry would be the third man. On it were written "O.K." and Fonck's signature.

Fonck, unimpressed by the document he had evidently signed, responded by describing Berry to reporters as an "outsider," a term that boiled the blood of the original Argonaut. "So, he calls me an outsider, does he?" Berry fired back. "I will show him he is badly mistaken. No Frenchman, no matter how many medals he has, can come over here and push me out of this flight. I made this flight possible. I had planned it and had approached the backers before anyone ever dreamed of René Fonck taking part in it."

What was behind the feud? It was hard to question Berry's capabilities. He had logged twice as many air miles as Fonck and had far greater experience behind the controls of large multiengine planes. (A few years later, when Berry ferried a huge American bomber to England in treacherous weather, a journalist along for the ride marveled that Berry "handled the giant just as a nurse might juggle a fat baby.") Berry had a westerner's bluntness, was transparently ambitious, had a penchant for embroidering his accomplishments, and was not properly reverential toward the French ace. In other words, he was perhaps a bit *too* American for Fonck's taste. Even Fonck's admirers conceded his bloated ego, but there were indications that Berry's own flying helmet had expanded a couple of sizes. Among the signs was his hiring of a personal publicity agent.

"The best thing for Captain Berry to do is to keep quiet," Fonck advised. "I won't say any more. I won't talk to newspapermen. There is so much damned nonsense in the papers." Fonck managed to keep his vow of silence for only a day or so before letting it slip to reporters that "Captain" Berry had obtained his military title in Mexico, and that he had the unappealing habit of borrowing money and not paying it back.

Hartney at first tried to mediate the dispute, but when Fonck failed to come around, he closed ranks with Berry. He filled in the press on several details of Fonck's arrangement with the Argonauts, including the ace's failure to secure the engines as promised. It developed that the cash-strapped syndicate had to take out a $27,000 bond before the French government would release them on loan. Fonck's inability to deliver the engines cost him the 10 percent stake in the Argonauts he was to have received in return. This meant that Berry was the only crew candidate with a shareholder's interest in the flight, a legal distinction that was bound to help him if and when an injunction was filed against the plane taking off for Paris. Such a nasty legal maneuver seemed to be on the horizon when Hartney had the Argonauts' attorney draft a letter to Sikorsky Manufacturing on the evening of September 2. In it the plane's builder was informed that since the S-35 technically was the property of the Argonauts, the syndicate had the right to refuse Fonck and Snody access to it until some kind of resolution was reached. Meanwhile, though, Sikorsky personnel could continue performing tests. Not all of the flight's principals agreed with Hartney's presumptive action, however, and the controversy continued to be thrashed out behind closed doors.

Just as troubling as the disharmony was the sense of urgency that had crept into the flight as August turned into September. The snowballs of media scrutiny and public expectations were rolling downhill, so to speak, picking up size and momentum. Six months earlier, when Fonck was lining up support for his effort among French officials, he had told reporters in Paris, "It is a big job to undertake to fly a distance of 6,000 kilometers. It cannot be carried out without the most careful preparation of every small detail." It was that kind of attention to detail that had made him a great and virtually untouched fighter pilot. Now he was starting to resemble a subway commuter anxiously eyeing a timetable. The series of graduated load tests Sikorsky desired were time-consuming. Each test required water to be pumped into, and then out of, the auxiliary fuel tanks, followed by a thorough cleaning of the fuel system—a procedure that took days. Fonck decided that certain tests could be sacrificed. It was fast approaching now-or-never time. The flying season was almost at an end. If a flight didn't happen soon, the whole effort would have to be shelved until the following year, which would give rivals on both sides of the Atlantic several months to catch up.

Fonck may also have had his contract in mind. Depending on how one interpreted its language, his agreement with the Argonauts ended either August 28 (four months from the date of his arrival in the States) or, at the latest, on the last day of summer, which Hartney took to mean September 25. That made sense of Fonck's public comments that the flight would leave no later than that day. The deadline may have added pressure to Fonck's desire to launch the flight before Sikorsky was wholly comfortable in doing so. While rumors swirled that the flight's backers had held talks with Richard Byrd and Colonel Billy Mitchell, one editorial asked, "Why Not Make It an All-American Non-Stop Flight to Europe?"

> There has never been a convincing reason why this flight should not be made all-American in origin, personnel and spirit. This country is amply supplied with airmen competent to conduct the interesting experiment and reap for America whatever renown success would bring. With prompt action there should still be time to convert the flight to that more inspiring basis. That would end the present bickering and insure a keenness of interest which would not be felt if the American aviator chiefly responsible for the preliminary organization of the undertaking were at the last moment crowded out.

Adopting a less chauvinistic tone, the *New York Times* recognized the havoc that continued dissension could wreak—not only to the upcoming flight, but also to American aviation in general. "The New York to Paris flight, for which Captain René Fonck has been engaged as chief pilot, has excited great interest in this country," it opined.

> Without the support of public opinion the development of commercial aviation would be hopeless. If dissension among those engaged in promoting the flight results in its abandonment, or if failure should occur because it was not well organized, a long time may pass before Americans will concern themselves about transatlantic flying. . . . The flight is predictable from the engineering point of view. But with the prospect for success so fair a dispute about the number of those who should accompany Captain Fonck has overclouded it. In that controversy the public, which ultimately must pay the cost of transatlantic transportation if it can be made profitable, is not interested, except to entertain the view that efficient leadership and harmony on board the airplane are essential.

The ordinary folks who flocked in ever-growing numbers to Roosevelt Field didn't really understand all of the technical details, meteorological wrinkles, or personality conflicts that kept the S-35 grounded. All they knew was that the most expensive plane yet built was being piloted by the world's greatest living ace in pursuit of aviation's biggest plum. When was it going to finally take off for Paris? French aviation and government officials, busily working out the details of receiving the plane and its crew on their end, wondered themselves. Robert Jackson, president of the Argonauts, had already sailed for Europe, taking with him four trunks of Fonck's belongings. Jackson, who had a home in Paris, planned to greet the aviators when they arrived at Le Bourget. He buoyantly declared the odds of success fifty to one in their favor. Lloyd's of London was less confident but still placed the odds of a successful crossing at four to three. Lloyd's also quoted an insurance premium of $30,000 to cover the plane, which was valued at $105,000. Meanwhile, at New York's Hotel McAlpin, staff stood ready to prepare and hustle over to Roosevelt Field the hot celebratory dinner to be carried along on the flight: Manhattan clam chowder, roast Long Island duck, Baltimore terrapin, and Vermont

turkey. Chefs planned to take the gourmet feast off the range and immediately place it in vacuum containers, which would then be transferred
into a heavily insulated food cabinet installed inside the S-35. Upon
landing, the triumphant crew would share their repast with dignitaries
in a gala reception at the palatial Hotel de Crillon on the Place de la
Concorde. On a certain layman's level, this was basically what all the
money, technology, planning, and risk behind such a flight represented:
a meal cooked in New York one day could be served piping hot in Paris
the next. Wasn't progress wonderful?

Late in the afternoon of September 6, the turbulence surrounding
crew selection finally ended. After a day-long conference, Hartney and
John B. Jamison, the Argonauts' other principal backer, drove out to
Roosevelt Field to announce that all opposition to the flight had been
dropped. Berry had visited Fonck's hotel suite and asked if there was
any way of settling the differences between them. The flight had been a
"baby" of his for a long time; by his own calculations he had plunged at
least $5,000 worth of time and money into the venture. Fonck remained
unmoved. Berry, who previously had vowed "a fight to the last ditch,"
capitulated. "My innermost wish is to do nothing to interfere with the
transatlantic flight," he told Fonck. "I have my personal ambitions, of
course, and my disappointment therefore is sincere and deeply felt. But
the flight must go on. As you have expressed yourself against me, I am
here to wish you all the luck in the world. I will do everything in my
power to help you without embarrassing you with my company on the
flight. Here is my hand on it." The two embraced and Berry left.

Hartney said nothing was more important than not further jeopardiz-
ing the mission or Franco-American relations, a sentiment Berry echoed
in his public statements. Left unspoken was Hartney's own resignation
from the Argonauts. Two days after peace was declared, Jimmy Walker
traveled to Roosevelt Field to christen the Sikorsky ship. Prohibition
forced New York's mayor to crack a bottle of mineral water over the
spindle of the center motor instead of the traditional bottle of French
champagne. An Episcopalian priest blessed the aircraft, now optimistically known as the *New York–Paris*. A mechanic had already painted a
stork, the insignia of *Les Cigognes*, on the fuselage. Fonck was pleased
with this prominently placed reminder of his military pedigree.

Reporters caught up with Raymond Orteig in Paris, where he was
preparing to leave for New York after summering in Biarritz. He

was his usual composed self, his patrician face and bald pate toasted brown by weeks of sun. The restaurateur clearly wanted no part of the Fonck-Berry controversy. He had no opinion about the delays or the constant shuffling of crew members. "The details of the Fonck flight and those to be made by other contenders are in the hands of experts and there is nothing I can say about them," he said, handling each difficult question as adroitly as he would a ruffled dinner patron. "The experts, I take it, know what they are about."

On September 15, the *New York–Paris* was readied for takeoff. Reports had come in overnight indicating a break in the bad weather over the Atlantic. However, all of the preparations amounted to a dress rehearsal. Mechanics discovered a leak in a fuel tank, and the flight was scrubbed. The cancellation frustrated Fonck and the Argonauts team, who increasingly thought they could hear rivals' footsteps gaining on them. News items described the ongoing activities of three French teams, including one that was said to be ready to go by October 5. Richard Byrd, fresh off his triumphant aerial adventure over the North Pole, reportedly was contemplating a Paris flight, and Noel Davis (who had officially filed for the prize on April 27) and Clarence Chamberlin were making noises about getting planes for their own separate crossings. There were subtle signs of pressure everywhere Fonck turned. By now newsreel shorts covering preparations for the upcoming flight of the *New York–Paris* had been seen by millions of moviegoers (including Fonck, an inveterate film fan) inside theaters across the country. In the latest, Fonck could be seen in the cockpit of the giant plane mouthing the words, "Paris, here I come!" New York stores were stocking a close-fitting ladies' hat that resembled a pilot's cloth helmet and was known as "the Fonck chapeau." *Time* had already put Fonck on the cover of one of its August issues. The September number of the influential *Aero Digest* had a special ten-page advertising section featuring various firms involved with building the Sikorsky plane, from tie-rod and turnbuckle manufacturers to the maker of the French cane chairs in the cabin; all offered testimonials to a transatlantic plane that, two weeks after Labor Day, had yet to do what it had been built for. "Start," an old friend cabled Fonck from Paris, "even if it means that you will fall into the sea and have to swim."

Meanwhile, the crowds at Roosevelt Field grew larger, with hundreds of automobiles parked up and down Old Country Road between Mineola and Westbury. As many as ten thousand rubberneckers jammed the airfield on a single day, milling around hangars, taking photographs, asking inane questions, trying to climb into the plane, and generally making a nuisance of themselves. There were actors and actresses seeking publicity, and producers and agents trying to strike deals. Finally, a deputy sheriff and two sailors from the Brooklyn Navy Yard were assigned to guard the Sikorsky hangar. Ropes were strung to keep the crowds at a safe distance. Smoking by all parties—including Fonck, a chain smoker whose cigarette holder was like a sixth finger—was strictly prohibited. The reason why could be gleaned from a publicity photo taken at this time. Fifty barrels, each holding fifty gallons of gasoline, and forty large cans of oil were lined up in front of the aircraft. This represented the amount of fuel and oil to be carried on the *New York–Paris*, some seven and a half tons in all.

The cancellation on September 15 gave the public an opportunity to observe the final makeup of the crew. Lieutenant Snody, who throughout the controversy with Berry had literally stood by Fonck, inside and outside the cockpit, came down with acute bronchitis and was forced to leave the flight. Taking his place at the last moment was Lieutenant Lawrence W. Curtin, an experienced navigator and pilot who was about to embark on a navy flight from Philadelphia to Panama when he received notice to hurry to Long Island. Curtin joined the Fonck expedition on September 14, "bubbling over with enthusiasm all day," observed the *New York Times*.

In addition to Curtin, Fonck had decided on Jacob Islamov and Charles Clavier to round out his crew. Islamov, a twenty-eight-year-old graduate of the Russian Naval Academy, had served in the imperial navy and on a polar expedition. He had been in the States since early 1923 and just taken out citizenship papers. A dear friend of Sikorsky, the gaunt Islamov was an instrument expert who had assisted in every phase of the plane's construction. His chief responsibility on this flight was keeping close tabs on the tricky valve connections between the gas tanks and engines and monitoring fuel consumption. Charles Clavier had been in New York since spring, when he delivered the specially developed wireless equipment from France. He would be the radio operator on the flight. Short, moon-faced, and chronically happy, the thirty-three-year-old Parisian—who held several patents but not an actual radio operator's license—was anxious to return home to his wife and three children. "I will never leave France again," he promised. It was quite an international crew—two Frenchmen, an American, and a Russian immigrant—but the men had had very little time to work together as a team.

Several more days of delays and fidgeting followed before weather reports again turned favorable. On the evening of September 20, Fonck and Sikorsky were informed that fog along the eastern seaboard and off Newfoundland was shifting rapidly, opening up a window of opportunity. The decision was made to leave at daybreak. While the crew grabbed a few hours' sleep, Sikorsky spent the night supervising preparations, all the while worrying over the lack of even a slight breeze to assist liftoff.

In the predawn hours of Tuesday, September 21, mechanics finished fueling the *New York–Paris*. The plane, which Sikorsky taxied to the east end of the runway, "was groomed as a race horse before a race," commented one observer. An excited crowd of two or three thousand gathered, and hundreds of cars wrapped Roosevelt Field in a necklace of headlamps. Fonck and his cosmopolitan crew drove up and changed into their flying suits. Fonck's smartly tailored blue uniform (including his Croix de Guerre with twenty-six palms, each signifying a repeat of the award) was carefully stowed away inside the cabin, as was Curtin's. They would be donned once the plane landed for the benefit of the photographers and newsreel cameramen. Curtin was smiling, confident. "We'll be in Paris in thirty-seven hours," he said.

News of the impending flight had already reached France, quelling criticism of the continuous delays. Reporters visited Fonck's mother. Although her bachelor son purposely kept most of the details of his flying activities to himself, so as not to worry her, she expressed supreme confidence in his ability. "René has always had luck; why wouldn't he succeed?" she said. "I'm waiting for it, you see; before the end of this week, I'm sure he will be back to give me a kiss!"

As the three big engines warmed up and departure grew imminent, a woman stepped out of the crowd and grasped Fonck's hand.

"*Bon voyage*," she said.

Fonck saluted formally and replied, "*Merci, madame. Au revoir.*"

At the last moment a man with a long beard arrived with a box of pastries. It was a parting gift from Mr. Orteig, he said. Fonck contemplatively held the box in his hand, made a face, and tossed it into the cabin. The plane, already seriously overweight, would have to suffer the additional load of a dozen freshly baked croissants.

Fonck and Curtin climbed up into the open cockpit. Clavier couldn't stop smiling. He was coming home to his family, a hero no less. He exuberantly shouted, "Dinner in Paris Wednesday night!" before entering the plane. Gifts for his wife and children had already been packed on board. Now he and Islamov, who was quietly anticipating a postflight reunion with his parents in Constantinople, seated themselves in the rear cabin. The wheel chocks were pulled, Fonck opened the throttles, and the *New York–Paris* lumbered down the soft-sand-and-clay runway, accelerating slowly. Controlling the crowd was a chore for Nassau County deputies, with motorists merrily driving parallel to the big rolling plane as it gathered momentum.

The *New York–Paris* weighed more than 28,000 pounds, roughly half of which were gasoline and oil. Its wings, designed to carry 19 pounds per square foot, were being asked to lift 26 pounds—an unprecedented burden for a plane of any type. Sikorsky had calculated that his mammoth craft needed to hit 80 miles per hour within 48 seconds of takeoff to have enough speed to lift safely off the ground. This was double the time needed to get the plane airborne when it was tested at 20,000 pounds. To distribute the increased load, Sikorsky had fitted the *New York–Paris* with an auxiliary wheeled undercarriage. Once the flight was under way the undercarriage, having outlived its sole purpose, would be discarded with the pull of a lever. The system had been successfully tested on several practice flights, though not with the weight it was carrying now.

What nobody took into consideration was the slightly rutted service road that crossed the runway about a thousand feet down from the plane's starting point. As the *New York–Paris* rumbled heavily over these inadvertent speed bumps, one of the auxiliary wheels broke and flew off. The plane swerved. Islamov pulled the lever, releasing the entire undercarriage. Parts shot off and ricocheted into the tail section, tearing away a piece of the lower left rudder. The rushing plane veered before straightening out; then it slued again. Fonck and Curtin leaned their full weight against the rudder bars to correct the sluing, which was slowing them down, but their efforts were to no avail. The damaged elevator refused to rotate in its socket. Fonck had to quickly decide whether to continue or to reduce power and hope that disaster could be averted. Like all planes of the period, there were no brakes. If he decelerated too quickly the stationary wheels would collapse under the strain and the plane would nose over. He could try to steer it to either side, but that meant plowing into the crowd. If he gained enough speed, surely he could make a safe landing after scaling the bank at the end of the runway. But the tail failed to lift and the straining engines never got the plane past 65 miles an hour. By now it was like trying to coax a stampeding elephant into a high jump. The aircraft charged down the mile-long runway to the end, its tail dragging all the way, before pitching over the bank and disappearing from sight. Fonck's final desperate hope of making a controlled landing on the other side evaporated when the overburdened plane smacked down on the hard surface of Curtiss Field. The wheel on the right side snapped like a toothpick under the tremendous weight, the right lower wing dipped and struck the ground, and the *New York–Paris* violently cartwheeled to a stop.

There were several long seconds of suspenseful silence . . . then a monstrous explosion rent the air. Gasoline had spilled onto the red-hot exhausts, and seven tons of fuel exploded into a fireball. Sikorsky and Homer Berry had joined the mass of people running toward the crash. Berry yelled, "Oh, what a shame! What a shame! Those poor men!" as tears streamed down his face. A deputy sheriff briefly held off a rush of ghoulish souvenir hunters before the eruption drove everybody back. He, too, was crying.

It was an inferno. A tower of thick, greasy, black smoke climbed high into the early morning sky. At first it was thought the entire crew was incinerated, but two men were spotted stumbling away from the wreckage. A reporter recognized one of them, his face streaked with smoke and his forehead bloody from a cut. It was Fonck—"no longer the dapper, confident aviator, but a bewildered and staggering man unable to speak." The other survivor was Curtin. Both had managed to squeeze through a foot-wide opening in the crumpled cockpit and, in their mad dash to safety, had somehow avoided being sliced into ribbons by the still-spinning propellers. Islamov and Clavier, trapped inside the back of the cabin, were not as lucky. Within minutes an ambulance was on the scene and firemen were pouring water onto the wreckage, but by then it was too late for the two crew members. Sikorsky, panting after sprinting the length of the runway, stared at the funeral pyre in stunned disbelief, then somehow found his way back to his Mineola home. An hour later firemen were still soaking what was left of the *New York–Paris*, trying to cool down the charred bones of the plane and the victims.

Fonck regained his composure inside a hangar, his fighter pilot's fatalism evident in his comments. He said he had been in other dangerous situations. He fended off criticism for not switching off the motors as soon as trouble arose. "I tried to slacken speed because I knew if I stopped too quickly after the first accidents to the landing gear, the wheels would give way altogether. But I could not do so. I could not control the plane with that great weight. When the right wheel gave way after the drop I knew it was all over. It is the fortune of the air. It could not be helped." Fonck blamed Islamov for prematurely releasing the undercarriage.

Sikorsky was milder in his criticism of Islamov, suggesting it "would have been better" for his friend not to have pulled the lever. "We will go ahead," Sikorsky listlessly told a visitor to his home that evening. "Aviation must be prepared to meet these things as they occur. From the disaster itself may come great strides forward. No one who flies ever becomes disappointed by death and discouragement."

Charles Clavier (left) and Jacob Islamov were the first airmen to die in the quest for the Orteig Prize.

The coroner determined that Islamov and Clavier had both suffered a crushed skull and two broken legs. This suggested that the victims had been knocked unconscious—or possibly killed outright—while being flung about the cabin. One newspaper reported that the men were buried by an "avalanche" of baggage and oil cans. It helped explain why they were not able to escape through an easily accessible door in the rear of the fuselage in the moments prior to the explosion. Islamov, a Muslim, was buried two days after the crash, a drawn-out ceremony during which Fonck was notably ill at ease. A mullah from New Jersey recited prayers in Arabic inside the hangar and later at graveside at Cedar Grove Cemetery. Meanwhile, Clavier's remains were stored at the Brooklyn Navy Yard in anticipation of a French destroyer taking them home.

The day following Islamov's funeral, a full investigation by Nassau County officials began at the town hall in Westbury to see if any charges of criminal negligence were warranted against the plane's manufacturer, its crew, or the flight's backers. A sworn statement by Harold Hartney was entered, and it was damning to Fonck. Hartney said Fonck was too incompetent to handle such a large plane, that "there was no team work in the crew and that he seemed to be working toward one end only, namely that he would get all the prize money, all the publicity, and had this uppermost in his mind rather than the desire to make the flight a great success."

All of the principals involved in the flight testified, with Curtin refusing to pin any blame on Fonck. Although the two survivors disagreed on a number of points, Curtin insisted that Fonck was perfectly capable of handling the plane and had done everything humanly possible to prevent the catastrophe. At one point George Honneur, the motor expert who had accompanied the three engines from France, was called as a witness.

"Was everything done properly according to your ideas?" he was asked.

"Everything was done according to the ideas of Captain Fonck," Honneur replied.

"Do you believe Captain Fonck was a capable pilot?"

Honneur gave no direct answer, vaguely citing a directive he had received that morning from his bosses at Gnome-Rhone not to "interfere with the normal course of investigation."

Hartney was seen by some as trying to distance himself from the disaster to maintain his credibility in the industry. In Paris, experts blamed the accident on the plane's faulty construction, not pilot error. "The wheels were much too weak to support the weight of such a heavy plane," said a French aviation official. "It was a defect which I and other experts pointed out some time ago. All planes which have established records with 12,000 pounds freight or more on board have had to have specially built wheels for taking off." *L'Humanité* dispensed with the cold, technical analysis and saw the catastrophe as the cruel climax to a summer's buildup of national propaganda. "It's finished, this whole monstrous stunt that's been going on for months. So long to glory and the $25,000 prize from Orteig. It's done with, this big joke, this theft of heroism." In the end, investigators chose to holster an accusatory finger, declaring the crash "an unfortunate accident," and Hartney retracted some of his more forceful comments about Fonck.

Amid all the grieving and second-guessing, Fonck and Sikorsky agreed to work together on a new plane to make a second bid for the Orteig Prize. They would need fresh backers, though; the bankrupted Argonauts quietly disbanded after the tragedy. Although Fonck was officially cleared of any wrongdoing, Sikorsky was concerned over the blow to his own reputation. He returned to his drafting table and Fonck went back to France, leaving cynical habitués of Roosevelt Field to ponder whether the fighter ace's roster of kills should be expanded to include the two airmen incinerated in the crash of the *New York–Paris*.

5

Slim

The life of an aviator seemed to me ideal. It involved skill. It commanded adventure. It made use of the latest developments of science. I was glad I failed my college course. Mechanical engineers were fettered to factories and drafting boards, while pilots had the freedom of wind in the expanse of sky. I could spiral the desolation of a mountain peak, explore caverns of a cloud, or land on a city flying field and there convince others of aviation's future. There were times in an airplane when it seemed I had partially escaped mortality, to look down on earth like a god.

—Charles A. Lindbergh

The spectacular failure of René Fonck and the *New York–Paris* had airmen everywhere debating what had gone wrong. One was a quietly intense twenty-four-year-old pilot flying the mail between St. Louis and Chicago. "Had he demanded too much of wings on air?" Charles Lindbergh asked himself during one of his long spells of solitude in the sky. Was it a case of pilot error—Fonck not cutting the switches immediately—or was it a case of overloading? Lindbergh rolled over the problem in his mind, probing all the angles, computing what his own approach to such a flight would be. A plane hoping to make it to Paris "should be stripped of every excess ounce of weight," he decided. "It certainly doesn't take four men to fly a plane across the ocean." Or three. Not even two. Just one.

Unlike others contemplating the Orteig Prize in the fall of 1926, Lindbergh was a virtual unknown. He had earned no medals, served in no war, won no races, set no records, mapped no exotic virgin territory. He had no prominent or well-heeled backers. His sole claim to fame, if it could be called that, had the taint of failure: he had successfully parachuted out of more disabled aircraft than any other known pilot. Lindbergh's anonymity would remain intact for several months until that spring day when he dropped into New York, seemingly out of nowhere, and suddenly found himself dealing with a pack of largely irresponsible big-city reporters. "Depending on which paper I pick up," he would later complain, "I find that I was born in Minnesota, that I was born in Michigan, that I was born in Nebraska; that I learned to fly at Omaha, that I learned to fly at Lincoln, that I learned to fly at San Antonio." The inaccuracies and fabrications concerning his background galled Lindbergh, a notorious stickler for detail and a fiercely private person. Still, it was probably a good thing for the young pilot's universally whole-some image that, at the time, neither he nor the sensationalistic press corps knew the full particulars of his ancestry. For the Lindbergh story begins with a Swede on the lam.

One day in 1859, Lindbergh's paternal grandfather, Ola Mansson, crossed the Detroit River from Canada into the United States, looking for a fresh start. The fifty-one-year-old immigrant, accompanied by his much younger wife and their year-old child, desperately needed one, because the life he had left behind in Sweden was a mess. An unschooled dairy farmer who had risen to become a radical in the Swedish parliament, Mansson had been in the middle of a promising political career as a social reformer when he self-destructed. While his wife and eight children remained on their Baltic farm six hundred miles away, Mansson shared his free time in the capital city of Stockholm with a pretty waitress named Lovisa Callen. In 1858 Lovisa had a son by Mansson. He was named Karl August and duly registered in Stockholm's book of bastards. Mansson also stood accused of embezzlement, the result of accepting small commissions in return for helping to secure loans in his position as a bank officer. The Supreme Court of Sweden formally stripped Mansson of his civil rights. By then, however, the disgraced defendant had already acquired a passport, taken some rudimentary English-language courses, provided for his abandoned family, and fled Sweden with his mistress and their baby boy.

The family settled into a crude sod house in Melrose, Minnesota. Mansson changed his name. Exchanging Ola for Augustus, and then borrowing from the Swedish words for mountain and the linden tree, he constructed a new identity: August Lindbergh. His son's name was anglicized to Charles August Lindbergh.

August Lindbergh faced the rigors of the frontier with the pluck and resourcefulness that would characterize all generations of Lindberghs in America. These traits were never more evident than when he suffered a near-fatal sawmill accident not long after his arrival in Minnesota. While delivering some logs to be cut into planks for the new frame house he was building, he stumbled into a running saw. The blade carved off a chunk of his left arm and sliced deep enough into his back that horrified witnesses could see his heart beating through the gaping wound. "It was hot weather and there was no surgeon within fifty miles," recalled the local churchman who helped load him onto a cart. "I followed him to his home and we did not think that he could live. I picked out the sawdust and rags from his wound and kept the mangled arm wrapped in cold water." It was three days before a doctor finally arrived. August remained stoic and uncomplaining throughout the ordeal, calmly applying pressure to stop the bleeding and directing his wife and young Charles to bring cold, fresh spring water to bathe his injuries and to keep his fever down. August's arm was amputated at the shoulder and his back wound sewn up. Once recovered, the enterprising patient devised a harness that allowed him to swing a scythe. He also grew a long, shaggy beard, which he frequently employed as a makeshift towel for his remaining hand.

Over the next thirty years, August and his growing family (he fathered seven more children) scratched out a living on two hundred acres of land. By the time August died in 1892, Charles—commonly called "C. A."—was married and enjoying success as a lawyer in Little Falls, about fifty miles from the family farm. The young attorney was much admired for his principled and commonsensical approach to life and the law. Like his father, he believed in fostering self-reliance. A favorite expression when counseling someone with a problem was, "Now, you have a head, haven't you?"

In the spring of 1898, C. A.'s pregnant wife died. Distraught, he sent his two young daughters to live with relatives while he moved into a local hotel. Taking a room at the same time was the new science teacher at Little Falls High School, twenty-four-year-old Evangeline Lodge

Land. Evangeline descended from two prominent Detroit families. Her mother was one of eleven siblings, several of whom became physicians. Her father, Dr. Charles Land, was a kindly, mildly eccentric inventor best known for his pioneering but controversial use of porcelain in dentistry. Strong-willed and independent, Evangeline had graduated from C. A.'s alma mater, the University of Michigan. "He was an Apollo for physical beauty," Evangeline's uncle, John C. Lodge, observed of the tall, chiseled widower, "and my niece was soon swept off her feet." They married in 1901 and settled into a house C. A. built for them on a secluded bluff overlooking the Mississippi River. It was more of an estate than a farm, with C. A. giving the 120-acre property a name, Lindholm, to please his refined wife.

The new bride soon became pregnant. She returned to her parents' house in Detroit, where she was tended to by one of her physician-uncles. Early in the morning of February 4, 1902, Evangeline delivered a healthy nine-and-a-half-pound boy. The baby's blue eyes drew comment, as did his large feet. He was named Charles Augustus Lindbergh Jr., a slight variation of his father's name.

The marriage eventually dissolved due to the couple's conflicting temperaments. Whereas C. A. was stoic and undemonstrative, Evangeline was imperious and given to sudden mood swings. Contributing to the household tension was the presence of young Charles's half sisters, Lillian and Eva, who were fourteen and nine, respectively, when C. A. remarried. The girls never warmed to their stepmother. "She made life miserable for all of us," was Eva's recollection. Years later, when Lillian was dying of tuberculosis in California, Eva refused to allow Evangeline to see her. It was a snub that Charles, then a teenager, never forgave. Throughout the rest of his life he would have little to do with his surviving half sister.

C. A. served five terms in Congress as the representative from the Sixth District of Minnesota. The Lindberghs moved to Washington. While Charles mourned the lack of streams and meadows, Evangeline and C. A. quarreled over money issues and his philandering. In the summer of 1909, when Charles was six years old, Evangeline asked for a divorce. C. A. refused. He knew even a legal separation would be political suicide. There was their son's welfare to consider as well, he argued. Weighing these considerations, Evangeline compromised. For the rest of their lives Evangeline and C. A. lived apart. With this, the peripatetic pattern of Charles's adolescence was established. He would spend each school year in Washington (when he saw his father every day), and summers on the family farm in Minnesota (which C. A. visited regularly), interleaved with regular trips to Detroit with his mother to visit her relatives.

Because he was always late starting school in the fall and prematurely ending it in the spring, Charles was chronically behind in his studies. His academic deficiencies made the already shy boy retreat deeper into his shell. It was a rootless, friendless childhood. For the most part he amused himself with solitary pursuits. He built collections of all stripes—buttons, bottle caps, rocks—and played out fantasies of martial glory with armies of lead soldiers. He never had anything to do with girls or dances or team sports. He much preferred a tramp through the woods, a dog usually at his side, observing firsthand the wonders of the natural world. A favorite roost was in the large elm tree on their Minnesota farm. There he played the lone scout, on the lookout for renegades.

Charles eagerly anticipated his father's visits. The congressman was a physically fit outdoorsman who taught Charles how to shoot a rifle, pitch a tent, make a fire, and paddle a canoe. C. A. continually encouraged his son to test his own stamina, strength, and courage. Risks and challenges were all part of life. Recalled Charles, "He'd let me walk behind him with a loaded gun at seven, use an axe as soon as I had strength enough to swing it, drive his Ford car anywhere at twelve." The deal was utterly simple. The boy got freedom; all that his father expected in return was responsibility. "You and I can take hard knocks," C. A. told him. "We'll get along no matter what happens."

The Great War began in 1914. Charles was fifteen when the United States officially entered the conflict three years later. C. A. was heavily involved in the drawn-out debate over American involvement, ultimately seeing his political career unravel because of his unbending noninterventionist views. To Charles, however, the terrible conflict had an undeniable element of romance. "I dreamed often of having a plane of my own," he later wrote. "After war started, I searched newspapers for reports of aerial combats—articles about Fonck, Mannock, Bishop, Richthofen, and Rickenbacker. In one of the monthly magazines we subscribed to, I followed the fictional account of 'Tam o' the Scoots,' a British pilot who displayed new feats of heroism with each issue." The war ended long before Charles had a chance to enlist, but it didn't extinguish his fascination with aviation. As a boy he often stretched out in the tall grass and watched birds and clouds and the occasional biplane drift gracefully through the open expanses of the sky. How free, he'd think, how beautiful. "How wonderful it would be if I had an airplane—wings with which I could fly up to the clouds and explore their caves and canyons—wings like that hawk circling above me."

By the time he graduated from Little Falls High School, he was feeling vaguely dissatisfied. The urge to experience some great adventure, the desire to see more of the world, the pull of the transient lifestyle he had grown accustomed to as a boy—all conspired to move the restless teenager out of Little Falls. But to where? In the fall of 1920 he reluctantly entered the University of Wisconsin as a mechanical engineering student. He had a nimble mind—too nimble, for it tended to wander inside the classroom. During his sophomore year the struggling student was dropped from the university. The dismissal stung Lindbergh, though the direct result of his aborted formal education was to put him into the cockpit of an airplane—the exact spot where he was destined to succeed. For months he had been musing about taking flying lessons, sifting through brochures. He settled on an aircraft company in Lincoln, Nebraska, which had agreed to accept him as a student for $500. "It was a price my father and mother could afford," he remembered, "and to me the name 'Nebraska' was full of romance."

Lindbergh reported to Lincoln Standard Aircraft in April 1922 and immediately began learning aviation from the ground up. Inside the hangar he helped tear down engines and learned to "dope" the fabric skin with a waterproof varnish—routine chores to veteran pilots, but tasks that were endlessly fascinating to Lindbergh.

One Saturday, the newcomer and a sixteen-year-old Lincoln Standard employee named Harlan "Bud" Gurney went on their first airplane ride together. The pair squeezed into the front cockpit of one of the company's reconditioned army trainers. The chief engineer revved the engine, checked the instruments and wind direction, then taxied down the sod field before lifting off into space. After a fifteen-minute flight over the Nebraska countryside, the trio returned safely to earth. For the pilot it was just another up-and-down excursion, but Lindbergh was euphoric. Cows appeared as rabbits, he remembered, and houses and barns as toys, as the earth fell away beneath them. The experience changed his life forever. "My early flying seemed an experience beyond mortality," he would write half a century later. "There was the earth spreading out below me, a planet where I had lived but from which I had astonishingly

Fellow barnstormers Charles Lindbergh (left) and Bud Gurney in 1923.

risen. It had been the home of my body. I felt strangely apart from my body in the plane. I was never more aware of all existence, never less aware of myself. Mine was a god's-eye view." A crusty ex-army flight instructor, Ira Biffle, gave Lindbergh his first flying lessons. Demonstrating exceptional eyesight and reflexes, the student was a quick learner. "The actual flying of the ship is easy, also the take-off," he wrote a friend. "But the landing is Hell." When the company owner sold the training plane to a local barnstorming pilot, Lindbergh went along as his assistant.

The postwar glut of pilots and army surplus planes made barnstorming a popular and occasionally lucrative occupation. A gypsy pilot would fly in and out of a town at treetop level, stopping just long enough to give adventurous farmers a ten-minute ride for a few dollars apiece before moving on to the next village or county fair. Accomplished barnstormers had a complete repertoire of daredevil feats to draw paying customers, including barrel rolls, figure eights, and loop-the-loops. Stunts such as wing-walking and parachute jumping often were employed to attract larger crowds. It was a dangerous way to make a living, but the rubber-legged novice was not dissuaded by his fears. In the summer of 1922, Lindbergh joined a local pilot named "Shorty" Lynch on a barnstorming tour of Kansas, Nebraska, Wyoming, and Montana. He was promoted as "Aerial Daredevil Lindbergh," but his seemingly suicidal stunts actually were well thought out and thus of negligible risk. He was held in place by heel cups, wire cable, and a harness that were invisible to spectators. Although always a publicly modest person when it came to his accomplishments, Lindbergh quietly enjoyed the deference given him. "Ranchers, cowboys, storekeepers in town, followed with their eyes as I walked by. Had I been the ghost of 'Liver-Eating Johnson' I could hardly have been accorded more prestige. Shooting and gunplay those people understood, but a man who'd willingly jump off an airplane's wing had a disdain for death that was beyond them."

In April 1923, Lindbergh bought his first plane, a war-surplus Curtiss JN4-D "Jenny" that cost five hundred dollars. Jennies were slow and unstable, but their durability and affordability made them the popular choice of barnstormers. He traveled to Souther Field in Americus, Georgia, to take delivery. He had no license, but that was okay because a pilot didn't need one at the time. However, Charles had never soloed. In fact, at this point he had less than ten hours' flying time, all of it operating dual controls with an instructor on board. His inexperience became embarrassingly clear on his first takeoff, which he quickly aborted after the plane had climbed just a few feet into the air. The Jenny landed drunkenly on one wheel, the wingtip skidding across the clay. A young pilot named Henderson was idly watching and offered his help. He suggested that the two of them practice a few takeoffs and landings until Charles felt comfortable with the controls. By five that afternoon Lindbergh was ready to attempt it alone. The neophyte pilot spent the next week at Souther Field, perfecting his takeoffs and touchdowns, before lumbering off in the underpowered Jenny.

Charles gravitated toward Lambert Field in St. Louis, a converted cornfield that was the home base of the 110th Observation Squad of the Missouri National Guard. Acting on a local pilot's suggestion, he applied to the War Department for admission to the one-year aviation training program. In February 1924 he received a letter instructing him to report to Brooks Field near San Antonio, Texas. In terms of pure flying ability and overall aviation savvy, Lindbergh was far ahead of the average recruit. By now he had about 350 hours in the air, but his habitually poor study habits threatened to flunk him out. The once-indifferent student quickly changed his ways, frequently pulling all-nighters in the latrine to keep up with the books. "The Army schools taught me what

I had never learned before—how to study, even subjects in which I had no interest," he said. "For the first time in my experience, school and life became both rationally and emotionally connected." Even the grief that accompanied his father's death from a brain tumor was not enough to knock him off track.

As an aviation cadet Lindbergh excelled as a student inside and outside of the cockpit. The most important lesson he learned was that when it came to flying an airplane, imprecision could be fatal. It was a lesson that he came to apply to every other aspect of his life, in time becoming an almost maddening model of exactitude and careful preparation no matter what the endeavor. He was one of only 33 cadets (of an original class of 104) to move on to advanced training at Kelly Field, outside San Antonio. After six months of rigorous instruction in gunnery, observation, pursuit, and close-formation flying, he and eighteen other cadets were graduated on March 14, 1925, and commissioned second lieutenants in the air service reserve corps. Lindbergh finished first in his class.

He almost didn't make it to graduation. Eight days earlier, during a mock attack exercise involving three planes, he and his instructor collided. The planes locked together and both men jumped to safety. As far as anybody could tell, this was the first time two pilots had survived a midair collision. Lindbergh's succinct report of the incident revealed a matter-of-fact approach to the perils of flying. No mistake about it: aviation was a dangerous occupation, a reality driven home by the nearly daily news reports of crashes and pilot deaths in one part of the world or another. At the time the estimated life span of an aviator was roughly nine hundred flying hours. But Lindbergh had already made a pact, of sorts, with the devil. Back in Nebraska he had decided that if he could fly for ten years before dying in a crash, then "it would be a worthwhile trade for an ordinary lifetime."

The freshly minted reserve officer moved his base of operations to Lambert Field, where he made a living as a flight instructor and as an occasional barnstormer billed as the "Flying Fool." At times Lindbergh served as a test pilot, on one occasion narrowly surviving the crash of an experimental four-passenger plane called the "Plywood Special" into a potato patch. This crack-up on June 2, 1925, earned its pilot a dislocated shoulder and another distinction. According to an informal fraternity of lucky fliers known as the Caterpillar Club, Lindbergh was the only pilot in America known to have twice saved his life through an emergency parachute jump.

By now Charles was known to just about everyone as "Slim," a moniker coined by Bud Gurney and inspired by his bladelike figure. He stood a shade over six feet, two inches tall and weighed about 150 pounds. He had a twenty-nine-inch waist. With his blue eyes, dimpled chin, and tousled hair, he had grown into a handsome young man. He was the very image of the dashing aviator and could have collected all the women he wanted. Instead, he seemed a man without vices. He didn't smoke, drink, or gamble. He had no use for curse words, his strongest expression being "Jesus Christ on a bicycle!"

"He could make you feel mighty guilty after the third beer," said Gurney, "and didn't approve at all of girl-chasing, which was something every other youngster around indulged in. On the other hand, he was always a great one for risqué jokes, and some of them he told came quite close to the bone." He was perhaps overly fond of practical jokes: sprinkling hot pepper in someone's underwear, hiding grasshoppers in their bed, placing their belongings on the roof. One day at Lambert Field, he filled a water bucket with kerosene, as literal a "gag" as poor Gurney—who took two deep swallows of the stuff before realizing what he was drinking—ever experienced.

In the spring of 1925, the two friends signed with Dunlap's Flying Circus for a barnstorming tour of southern Illinois that ended when the show's promoter vanished owing everybody money. For the short time the tour lasted, "The Flying Fool" was billed as "Beans Lindbergh" and Gurney was touted as "Captain Gurni, the great French ace." An airplane ride cost three dollars, Gurney recalled. "It was an enterprise of close margins; close on time; close on profit. Hurry to get the passengers out of the front cockpit and two new ones in. A dozen flights to a filling of gasoline and three quarts of Mobil B. No time to really taste the noonday sandwich or the quick swig of soda pop while passengers were lined up and waiting." Later that year, Lindbergh joined an enterprising pilot-promoter named Wray Vaughn in Colorado, passing out business cards that stated, "We specialize in Fair and Carnival Exhibition Work, Offering Plane Change in Midair, Wing Walking, Parachute Jumping, Breakaways, Night Fireworks, Smoke Trails, and Deaf Flights." Lindbergh's days were filled with stunts and short hops, catering to the whims of Vaughn and any paying customer. On deaf flights—a new fad—he climbed several thousand feet and then dropped into a dizzying ear-popping spin, all in the advertised effort to cure the passenger's hearing. He delivered a groom to his mid-air wedding while Vaughn carried the bride and preacher in the accompanying plane. He satisfied the desire of one customer who wanted nothing more than to fly over a certain town—and urinate on it. It was a long way from the juvenile romance of "Tam o' the Scoots," but it was a living.

In the fall of 1925, Washington awarded the first Contract Air Mail routes. CAM-2, the Chicago-to-St. Louis run, went to the Robertson brothers, Frank and William. The Robertsons immediately hired Lindbergh, widely regarded as one of the finest pilots at Lambert Field, for one of the best jobs in civil aviation: flying the mail as the $300-a-month chief pilot of Robertson Aircraft Corporation. Over the next several months he helped lay out the 285-mile run, establishing nine primitive airfields in towns along the way. In each case the "airport" was little more than a pasture with a wind sock and access to a nearby telephone. Each of Robertson's three pilots flew a rebuilt De Havilland biplane with a 400-horsepower Liberty engine, a war-surplus aircraft disconcertingly known in aviation circles as "the flying coffin."

One April afternoon in 1926, two hundred people at Lambert Field watched the first sacks of mail ceremoniously loaded into the front cockpit of Lindbergh's silver-and-maroon two-seater as Robertson Aircraft inaugurated mail service between Chicago and St. Louis. "It took me two and three-quarters hours to reach St. Louis, including stops at Peoria and Springfield, Illinois," Lindbergh recalled. "Hurtling through the air at ninety miles an hour behind my mail sacks, I thought of the two-mile-an-hour oxcart travel of my father's boyhood." The daily round trips became more challenging in the autumn and winter months, when daylight was at a premium. Unpredictable weather and the lack of accurate meteorological information added to the peril, though an expanding network of beacons and emergency airfields was helping to lower the risk. Generally speaking, airmail pilots flew as far as they could until poor visibility—fog, rain, snow, nightfall—forced them to find a place to land. If it happened to be at one of the intermediary stops, the mail was taken off the plane and put onto the next train.

Lindbergh made two more emergency jumps as an airmail pilot. On the evening of September 16, 1926, he was caught in a fog northeast of Peoria. After spending nearly two hours circling in the soupy mix and draining his main and reserve gas tanks, Lindbergh maneuvered his plane over open country and then bailed out. He neglected to cut the fuel switch before exiting. As he was floating to safety, the falling plane unexpectedly coughed back to life, leveling out and passing too close for comfort before man and machine made their separate landings in a cornfield. This was excitement, of a sort, but flying the same route, day after day, soon bored Lindbergh, as he had expected it would. He was the kind of person who not only welcomed new challenges but also thrived on them. He had been promoted to captain in the Missouri National Guard, with his superiors describing him as "purposeful, quick of reaction, alert, congenial, intelligent and conscientious." Despite these and other glowing remarks in his service jacket, as well as his experience in flying a wide range of civilian and military aircraft, he'd had no luck in obtaining a regular army commission or in securing a spot on one of the various aerial expeditions being formed. During uneventful flights he let his mind wander. His thoughts increasingly centered on the new single-winged plane in the news, the Wright-Bellanca. Trade publications were touting it as the most efficient plane yet built, capable of setting all sorts of endurance and distance records. He mused about how far he might be able to fly such a beauty.

On November 3, 1926, an unexpected squall forced Lindbergh, after hours of trying to locate a landing spot through the fog, to bail out of his De Havilland at thirteen thousand feet somewhere between Springfield and Peoria. This time he landed on a barbed-wire fence. A nickname he would soon come to hate, "Lucky Lindy," didn't originate here, but it could have. Not only was he unhurt, he also didn't even suffer a tear in his flying suit. Gathering up his chute and tucking the wadded silk under his arm, Lindbergh started hiking down the muddy, potholed roads. A short while later he walked out of the gloom and into the warmth of a general store in Covell, where a small group of men looked up from their card game. A young farmer offered to drive the stranger to the nearby train station in his Model T. The men made small talk along the way. Mention was made of the possibility of a flight between New York and Paris. "It can be done," Lindbergh said, as the car bumped along in the darkness, "and I'm thinking of trying it."

6

Giuseppe, the Gypsy, and the Junk Man

We not only wanted to develop the plane so that we could take
Mr. Orteig's money away from him, but we knew that a plane that was
capable of doing that would make a wonderful commercial plane to
follow up the flight.

—Clarence Chamberlin

Toward the end of November 1926, Charles Lindbergh took the
train from St. Louis to New York to see some men about a plane.
This was no ordinary aircraft. The Bellanca high-wing monoplane
that Lindbergh coveted had won thirteen speed and efficiency com-
petitions in just a short period of time, including two trophies at the
recently concluded National Air Races in Philadelphia. It was capable
of zipping along at a cruising speed of 110 miles per hour and could
reach a top speed of 130 miles an hour. The Bellanca was a prototype created specifically to showcase the nine-cylinder Wright J-5
Whirlwind, a lightweight air-cooled radial engine built by the Wright
Aeronautical Corporation of Paterson, New Jersey. The engine, which
produced 220 horsepower and averaged 9,000 miles between failures,
was a perfect complement to the wondrously configured plane it
propelled.

Veteran journalist Richard Montague began covering aviation for the *New York Post* in the 1920s. In *Oceans, Poles and Airmen*, a memoir recalling the distinctive personalities and flying machines he encountered during this period, he explained what made the Bellanca so special and desirable.

> The *Columbia*, as this machine came to be called, was more efficient than her rivals because the wing struts as well as the fuselage were designed to augment the lift afforded by the wing....The struts on the *Columbia*, which extended from the bottom of the fuselage out to the wing, acted not only as braces. Each of them—there were two on either side—exerted a lift, for they were formed like airfoils. That is, they were like little wings which still exerted a lift, even though they were not horizontal like the wings but slanted up to them. The struts also tended to stabilize the plane, for when the machine canted over, the struts on the downward side were closer to the horizontal than those on the upward side, and thus exerted more lift than the others. Additional lift was provided by the *Columbia*'s fuselage, whose top side curved down behind the cabin a bit more sharply than the fuselages of other planes. Thus, because of the strut and fuselage design, as well as masterly wing contours, the *Columbia* had more lift per unit of horsepower than other contemporary aircraft.

Lindbergh was the only pilot to seriously consider making the Paris flight alone in a single-engine plane. Most believed that a multiengine plane offered a better chance for crossing the ocean safely, but even in the case of a single-engine craft the conventional wisdom was that there should be a second crew member aboard. In Lindbergh's view, the trimotor planes favored by some contenders only tripled the chance of engine failure; a hobbled aircraft might be able to land safely, but it would be unlikely to reach its intended destination running on two engines. The idea of an expanded crew was predicated on the assumption that even if one person could handle the twin chores of navigation and piloting the craft, he could not possibly stay awake for the entire duration of the flight. Lindbergh figured the risks of flying alone were offset by the benefits: less weight, which meant increased range, and no worrying over the opinions or welfare of somebody else. As was often the case throughout his life, Lindbergh preferred going solo.

Guiseppe Bellanca and his namesake monoplane.

He pinned his hopes on buying the spectacularly successful Bellanca, which he felt certain could carry him safely to Paris. Never a clothes-horse and always thrifty, he nonetheless spent a hundred dollars for a new suit, overcoat, scarf, and fedora for the meetings. He had not "the slightest use for them," he confessed. "I hate to do things just to make an impression. But right now that may be as essential to my Paris flight as a plane itself will become later."

A Bellanca had already crossed the Atlantic. In 1911, twenty-five-year-old Giuseppe Mario Bellanca, armed with mathematics and engineering degrees, left his native Sicily for Brooklyn, New York. Having built two planes in the Old World without actually taking to the air, he constructed a third in his new country and taught himself to fly it. For several years afterward he operated a flying school, with one of his students being Fiorello LaGuardia, future mayor of New York. Bellanca, a gentle but shrewd man barely five feet tall, found his greatest satisfaction in designing small planes. In 1924 he went to work for the Wright factory, where he developed the first single-engine monoplanes with enclosed cabins.

Bellanca's most ardent supporter was part-time Wright test pilot Clarence D. Chamberlin, a plainspoken speed imp from the American heartland. Chamberlin was a pure seat-of-his-pants pilot. He admitted he "never learned to fly by instruments for the same reason that I never learned how to milk a cow: for fear that I might have to do it some-day." Born November 11, 1893, in Denison, Iowa, he had the unremark-able looks of a small-town store clerk, which is precisely the occupation his father, who operated a local jewelry store, was grooming him for. Chamberlin sought more exciting outlets. First it was motorcycles, which he learned to tear down, reassemble, and race. Then it was Stateside air service during World War I and barnstorming and racing afterward.

Augustus Post described Chamberlin as "a 'gypsy flyer,' the picturesque phrase for a picaresque way of life. The gypsy flyer owns his plane and picks up a living by it however and whenever he can; taking up passengers, buying and selling second-hand machines, taking photographs, and espe-cially stunt-flying at fairs or other open air assemblies. The gypsy flyer has been quite naturally looked down upon by the profession as a sort of aerial acrobat and camp follower, but he furnishes some of the most interesting and significant types of young Americans." By the time Chamberlin was in his early thirties he had survived at least ten crashes. Once he ran out of fuel and was forced to land inside the walls of a penitentiary; after gassing

Clarence Chamberlin in 1927.

up, he deftly flew out despite a tight takeoff space and high walls. Elzie Chamberlin said her son always was a bit of a daredevil. "We are always worrying about him," she admitted.

In the spring of 1926, Chamberlin was vice president of the Aeronautical Club of New Jersey when the organization pledged to raise $50,000 to help underwrite the transatlantic attempt of one of its members, Noel Davis. Two days after that announcement, Chamberlin—naturally competitive and his pride a bit ruffled—issued his own statement to the press. He, too, would be going after the Orteig Prize, a challenge that he and Bellanca had been thinking about since the two had first met in 1920. Chamberlin made no mention of who was going to finance the expedition because he had no idea. He did, however, know what designer he would turn to. Bellanca "was convinced he could build a plane that would do the job," Chamberlin said. "It was my dream to fly it."

Lindbergh met with a Wright executive on November 29, 1926. He was told the company's original plan was to manufacture Bellanca monoplanes fitted with Whirlwinds, but it was decided such a move would put the firm in direct competition with the planemakers they were selling their motors to. Thus, the company had already severed its connections with Giuseppe Bellanca when Lindbergh showed up. It was suggested that the lanky visitor in the spiffy new clothes talk to the designer himself, and the following day Lindbergh did just that. He and Bellanca spent an hour at the Waldorf-Astoria, and Lindbergh came away impressed with the designer's "genius, capability, confidence." Bellanca believed his monoplane, fitted with extra tanks, could stay in the air continuously for fifty hours, easily enough time to reach Paris. Unfortunately, in the limbo Bellanca presently found himself in regarding the rights to his prototype, there was little he could do but offer Lindbergh encouragement.

Lindbergh returned to St. Louis, where his focus over the winter shifted to trying to raise money. He had $2,000 in the bank, but obviously needed much more. Earlier, when he spoke with a Fokker representative about the costs of mounting an ocean expedition that included buying one of the firm's trimotor planes, he was told the craft alone would cost $90,000. "You should plan on over $100,000 for such a project," the salesman said. "In fact, you should have almost unlimited financial backing." Lindbergh was astonished and discouraged, but not to the point of giving up. He had already approached his uncle, longtime Detroit politician John C. Lodge, about using his connections to garner support, but Lodge—who never learned how to drive an automobile—was even less enthusiastic about aviation. He considered a solo flight to Paris to be a suicide mission. So did the editor of the *St. Louis Post-Dispatch*, who quickly shot down the idea of a sponsorship. "We have our reputation to consider," he said. "We couldn't possibly be associated with such a venture!"

Fortunately for Lindbergh, as an occasional flight instructor at Lambert Field he had become acquainted with several of St. Louis's leading businessmen. One by one, a coalition of civic-minded aviation buffs, many of whom were private pilots, was assembled.

Earl C. Thompson, a wealthy insurance executive, was the first to pledge support. Next were Major A. B. Lambert and his brother, Wooster. Harry Hall Knight, a partner of a brokerage house and president of the local flying club, not only came on board, he also introduced Lindbergh to the influential Harold M. Bixby, a banker and the head of the chamber of commerce. Bixby initially was willing to provide the bulk of the funds until his wife interceded. "Oh, no!" she said. "I don't want you to give him that money, because he's going to kill himself." Knight's father, Harry F. Knight; Lindbergh's bosses, William and Frank Robertson; and E. Lansing Ray, owner of the *St. Louis Globe-Democrat*, also came in.

In early February, Lindbergh received a cable from Giuseppe Bellanca, informing him that he was now associated with a new enterprise called the Columbia Aircraft Corporation. The firm had acquired the rights to the Wright-Bellanca and would consider selling the plane to him. Lindbergh hurried to New York, where the company had opened an office in the Woolworth Building. There he was introduced to the chairman of Columbia Aircraft, a short, stocky, balding, fascinatingly abrasive man who shared Lindbergh's initials—C.A.L.—but had little else in common with him.

Charles A. Levine would emerge as the most polarizing figure in the story of the Orteig Prize. Born on March 17, 1897, in North Adams, Massachusetts, he grew up in the Williamsburg section of Brooklyn. The early twentieth century was the golden era of Jewish boxing, with such fighters as Abe "the Little Hebrew" Attell inspiring undersize youngsters to learn how to use their fists in neighborhood gyms. Consequently, Levine's method of conflict resolution often owed more to the likes of Battling Levinsky than to the local rabbi espousing the wisdom of Psalm 34 ("Seek peace and pursue it"). The pugnacious Levine sought wealth and status and pursued both ardently. He quit school in his early teens. Between stints at his father's scrapyard he also worked as an apprentice mechanic at an aviation company on Long Island. When he was eighteen he went into business for his own, making a tidy profit by buying and selling used automobiles. Two years later he married Grace Nova, a local beauty contest winner known as "the Belle of Williamsburg."

Levine was twenty-four when he organized the Columbia Salvage Corporation, contracting with the War Department to buy surplus shell casings and ammunition. The scrapping operation quickly made him rich. Among his indulgences were a trio of high-powered automobiles and a private plane that he occasionally took lessons in. It should have been a more than satisfying life, but the ordinariness of it ate at Levine. When the Argonauts were in the midst of preparations at Roosevelt Field, he offered the organization $25,000 for the privilege of coming along on the *New York–Paris*. If he couldn't fly the ocean himself, or be a member of the crew that did, he would settle for becoming history's first transatlantic passenger. It didn't seem to matter to him that, at the time, his pregnant wife was stuck inside their Belle Harbor home, on the verge of delivering their second daughter. Levine's proposal was promptly turned down, a rejection that did nothing to dampen his appetite to be something bigger in the eyes of the world than a millionaire junk man with lifts in his shoes.

In early 1927, Levine organized the Columbia Aircraft Corporation, with an initial capitalization of $50,000. Bellanca was named president, and Chamberlin was retained as chief pilot. Levine paid Wright $15,500 for all rights to Bellanca's monoplane, which he planned to manufacture for the New York-to-Chicago airmail route he was bidding on as well as for sale to the general public. Bellanca thought that his plane could make the New York-to-Paris flight, and Chamberlin naturally wanted to be part of any such attempt, but for the time being the plane's new owner resisted. A failure would be a public-relations disaster for a start-up aircraft company. Better to develop a new three-engine plane or a flying boat for a try at the Orteig Prize. Meanwhile, he remained open to offers for the prototype.

"So," Levine said at the start of his meeting with Lindbergh, "you want to buy our Bellanca?" Assured that Lindbergh had a syndicate backing him, Levine told him he could have the plane for $15,000, a markdown from the $25,000 he said the only existing Wright-Bellanca actually was worth. The difference in price would represent Columbia Aircraft's contribution to the project. Lindbergh returned to St. Louis to see if his backers would agree to the price. He explained that the plane needed little more than to be fitted with fuel tanks and run through a few tests before tackling the Atlantic.

The syndicate quickly raised the money. "What would you think of naming it the *Spirit of St. Louis*?" asked Harold Bixby. Bixby was thinking of Louis IX, the only French king ever to be canonized. The benevolent thirteenth-century monarch was the patron saint of Paris. Lindbergh had no objections. In fact, he had earlier entertained the idea of a public subscription, asking the citizens of St. Louis to donate $10 apiece to buy a plane with the city's name emblazoned on its fuselage. "All right," Lindbergh agreed, "let's call it the *Spirit of St. Louis*."

On February 19, Lindbergh arrived at Levine's office, a cashier's check for $15,000 in hand. Instead of taking possession of the prized Bellanca, however, he had a bombshell dropped on him. As a condition of the sale, Levine insisted on being able to select the crew that would fly it to Paris. That would be Chamberlin and another top pilot still to be chosen. "You understand we cannot let just anybody pilot our airplane across the ocean," Levine said. Lindbergh was speechless.

"We know better than anybody else how to fly the Bellanca, how to take care of it," Levine continued. "It would be wise for you to let us manage the flight to Paris. You should think it over." As Lindbergh picked up his check and started walking out the door, Levine told him to call him the next morning at eleven. When Lindbergh did, Levine asked, "Well, have you changed your mind?" Lindbergh slammed the receiver down.

Lindbergh was livid. Time and money had been wasted pursuing the Bellanca. The press was reporting that several teams in the United States and Europe had already been formed to compete for the Orteig Prize; more were on the way. He fell back on his plan of having a plane built to his specifications, though only one of the manufacturers he had contacted over the winter had agreed to work with someone with his limited resources and lack of reputation. That was the Ryan Aircraft Corporation, a small, financially struggling firm headquartered in a nondescript building on the San Diego waterfront.

At the end of February, Lindbergh went to California to meet with president Frank Mahoney and chief designer Donald Hall. After a few days of discussing the project and how to custom-fit a plane to meet Lindbergh's special requirements, the parties came to terms on price and delivery on February 28. For $10,850 (including a $1,000 deposit at signing), Ryan would build a plane capable of getting Lindbergh to Paris and deliver it within sixty days. The price of the airframe was $6,000. It would be equipped with a Wright Whirlwind and the latest in instrumentation (all provided at cost), including an earth inductor compass (an extra expenditure also provided at cost) that would make it easier for Lindbergh to hold a course during the projected day-and-a-half-long flight. That evening Mahoney phoned Wright sales manager Joe Hartson in New Jersey to place an order for a new $4,000 engine. "I want this one as quickly as possible," he said, "because the chap that's buying the first of my planes is going to fly it to Paris."

"Suffering cats!" exclaimed Hartson, who went on to explain why his company could not fulfill the order. "Listen, Franklin, we don't want to let you have the engine for that purpose. We've discouraged that flight, because we think it's sure to fail in a single-engine ship and then what a black eye we'd get! As well as feeling we'd done the youngster dirt by selling him something that would lead him into trouble."

After some vigorous discussion, Mahoney played his trump card. He had a sales agreement for six Whirlwinds that was awaiting his signature. "Well, Joe," he said at last, "I'm going to sign your blank contract and what can you do but give me an engine?"

7

Revving Up

Paris in the twenties was an icon of joyous freedom. So was flying. The long-unclaimed Orteig Prize blended the two images into a single romantic dream, and as springtime came to America's eastern seaboard in 1927, the few muddy airfields dotting Long Island became magnets for fliers eager to cross the Atlantic.

—Lisle A. Rose, *Explorer*

On February 28, the day Charles Lindbergh filed an entry for the Orteig Prize and work on his Ryan monoplane began, there were two naval expeditions with a clear jump on the young, unknown pilot whose name appeared in some brief newspaper items as "Linberg" or "Lindenburgh." One was headed by Commander Richard Evelyn Byrd, recent conqueror of the North Pole and an unparalleled organization man whose pedigree, bearing, looks, and squeaky-clean image made him an almost impossibly perfect hero. The other was Lieutenant Commander Noel Davis, a straight-talking westerner whose bulldog persistence offset some of the advantages of Byrd's name recognition when it came to acquiring backing for his flight. "Both Byrd and Davis are excellent navigators, both have unusual records in the navy," observed the *New York Times*. "Their aides are distinguished not only for their flying ability, but for their resourcefulness and calmness in an emergency."

Byrd descended from an old Virginia family with a long record of distinguished service in politics and the military. A brother, Harry Flood

Byrd, was the Democratic governor and would go on to a lengthy career in the U.S. Senate. Born October 25, 1888, the future aviator and polar explorer was only twelve years old when he traveled alone to the Philippines to visit his father's friend, a judge, and wound up spending a year. He saw volcanoes erupt and men hanged, and eventually returned home, crossing the Atlantic on a British tramp steamer. The wiry, worldly "Dickie" acquired an education at Virginia Military Institute and the U.S. Naval Academy, from where he graduated in 1912. He played quarterback on the football team and was a member of the gymnastics squad, but two broken legs cut short his athletic career and caused him to be placed on inactive duty just as America entered the war. Undaunted, Byrd talked his way into flight school at Pensacola, surviving a head-on crash in the process of winning his wings.

Byrd displayed a knack for mathematics. He developed different navigational techniques, including drift indicators and bubble sextants. In 1919 he was assigned the task of planning the flight path for the squad of Nancy flying boats attempting to cross the Atlantic, but was greatly disappointed when he was not named to one of the four crews. A couple of years later, while in England, he unsuccessfully tried to join the group flying the British dirigible *R-38* to America. Once again he was disappointed—until news came that the airship had exploded, killing forty-five men, including several friends.

From the mid-1920s on, Byrd's closest friend and confidant was clear-eyed, low-key, and utterly dependable Floyd Bennett. Bennett grew up on his aunt's farm in Warrensburg, New York, and worked for several years as a mechanic before joining the navy in 1917 at age twenty-seven. Warranted as a machinist, he attended flight school and became an accomplished pilot. Bennett first impressed Byrd during an aerial survey of Greenland in 1925. When the oil in an engine on the amphibian they were flying overheated, threatening to cause the oil tank to explode and force the craft down, Bennett daringly crawled out to the tank and removed the cap, relieving the pressure. As one newspaper noted, "crawling out of the fuselage in a plane bouncing around in an Arctic gale, with the temperature below zero, is not an enviable occupation." According to Byrd biographer Edwin P. Hoyt, Bennett was "the ideal second-spot man to Byrd. Totally without personal ambition, he was willing to have Byrd make all the speeches and take the lion's share of the glory, while he, Bennett, stayed in the background. When it came to pondering the problems, solving them, and displaying expert knowledge of the planes they were flying, Bennett had no peer. Byrd was pilot, commander and navigator. Bennett was pilot, engineer and mechanic. The two men complemented one another perfectly in temperament and training; the experience one lacked the other possessed, and both were well endowed with brains and courage."

In 1926, Byrd led his first polar expedition, looking to accomplish the first overflight of the North Pole. Bennett's fearlessness and cool competence put him at the controls of the *Josephine Ford*, a trimotor Fokker named for the daughter of one of the expedition's principal backers, industrialist Edsel Ford. At the same time, Norwegian explorer Roald Amundsen was hoping to fly over the pole in the *Norge*, an Italian-built dirigible. On May 9, 1926, Byrd, Bennett, and two other crew members set off from the Norwegian island of Spitsbergen. Several hours into the flight, oil started leaking from a reserve tank, affecting the starboard motor. Bennett babied the throttle. "For the next hour and thirty-five minutes Commander Byrd was busy with his sun compass, sextant, drift indicators and cameras," Bennett later wrote in *Aero Digest*. "Suddenly he came forward and shook hands with me. We had reached the pole!"

But had they? Skeptics, especially in Europe, pointed out that the *Josephine Ford*, flying along at 85 miles per hour (and limping along at some points at 65 miles per hour), could not have possibly made the 1,520-mile round trip in the 15½ hours the plane had been in the air. Doubting voices were drowned out by the cheers of unquestioning Americans. The National Geographic Society examined the explorer's charts, sextant, and other data and pronounced its satisfaction that Byrd had indeed been the first to conquer the North Pole by air. He was awarded the society's Hubbard Medal, only the sixth man to receive the honor.

As Byrd and Bennett basked in the public acclaim, they quietly made plans to tackle another colossal challenge: a nonstop New York-to-Paris flight. This time their financial backer would be Philadelphia retail merchant Rodman Wanamaker, inside whose department stores the storied Fokker was displayed for customers to admire. Wanamaker, a philanthropic supporter of various cultural and scientific causes and a devoted Francophile, had previously backed Glenn Curtiss's aborted bid to win the *Daily Mail* prize. For all his expensive interests as a bibliophile, antiques collector, and historical preservationist, Wanamaker was a futurist. It was said that the longest gangplank in the world ran between New York and Paris, with several liners making the five-day trip between the bustling piers in Manhattan and Le Havre each week. His father, John Wanamaker, the firm's founder, had crossed the ocean forty-four times before dying in 1922, which meant eight months of his life had been spent just traveling on a boat between the United States and France. It was unthinkable to most maritime men of the era that the airway would one day supplant the seaway. "People who amuse themselves with speculations as to the time when steamers will no longer plough the oceans and when all our overseas transportation will be done by airmen in air machines," said one skeptic in 1925, "are in the happy company of those who still pursue the pleasures of alchemy." But Wanamaker knew that such a time was coming, and he wanted to have a role in its arrival. His America Trans-Oceanic Company ultimately plunged an estimated $150,000 into Byrd's bid to bridge the Atlantic.

On February 25, 1927, in a ceremony at the White House, President Calvin Coolidge presented the Medal of Honor to Byrd and Bennett. By

President Calvin Coolidge awards Floyd Bennett the Medal of Honor on February 25, 1927. Richard Byrd, whose medal was accompanied by a promotion to commander, stands at left. The pair were honored for the 1926 expedition to the North Pole.

then work was well under way on an improved version of the trimotor Fokker they'd flown across the Arctic ice. This craft, like Curtiss's 1914 aeroboat, would carry the name *America*. At the time, Anthony H. G. Fokker was the largest airplane manufacturer in the world, with operations in New Jersey, Germany, and his native Holland. The tempestuous thirty-seven-year-old "Flying Dutchman" was considered a design genius, his contributions during the war including the Fokker triplane that Baron von Richthofen flew and the synchronization device that allowed machine gun bullets to be fired through a spinning propeller. Fokker had moved to the States in 1922 and established the Atlantic Aircraft Company, whose sales jumped in the wake of Byrd's polar flight.

To cross the Atlantic, Byrd "stuck to the type which had successfully carried Bennett and me over the Pole, only we planned a bigger plane," he said. Like the *Josephine Ford*, the new Fokker would be powered by three Wright engines. This time there would be special catwalks installed so a malfunctioning motor could be serviced in flight. The wing, built in Holland, was increased from 63 to 71 feet. The extra surface would help the plane lift 3,000 more pounds than the *Josephine Ford* had been able to. "The extra capacity would permit us to take fuel for our very long flight and 800 pounds of equipment over and above that which was absolutely necessary," Byrd explained. "We wanted to show that some pay load could be carried across the Atlantic." Byrd planned to bring along a special radio set, two rubber boats, and a variety of emergency food and equipment.

Work on the Fokker began in January. Over the following weeks Byrd's organization also sprang into shape. He established headquarters at the McAlpin Hotel in Manhattan; there, he and Bennett spent long hours discussing the innumerable details and decisions that were a part of any long-distance flight. A well-equipped hangar was rented at Roosevelt Field, offering mechanics and journalists every tool and convenience, and the shabby runway was lengthened and leveled at considerable cost. In addition, an earthen takeoff ramp was built that provided the equivalent of another 500 feet of runway. Byrd, emphasizing the scientific nature of the flight, convinced the Naval Research Laboratory to outfit his plane with the latest wireless technology. The equipment weighed 800 pounds and featured a kite-flown antenna. Byrd, along with Noel Davis, also persuaded the Department of Agriculture to instruct the

U.S. Weather Bureau to more methodically monitor conditions over the Atlantic. The president of the Radio Corporation of America, James G. Harbord, chaired the Orteig Prize board of trustees. At his direction a system was established whereby ships at sea regularly reported weather data to the bureau's New York office, which used it to issue timelier and more accurate forecasts.

In addition to Byrd, Bennett, and George Noville, it was possible that the final crew would include a still-to-be-decided fourth member, "to demonstrate that passengers could even now be taken across the Atlantic." Fokker wanted that man to be his chief test pilot, Bernt Balchen, a Norwegian whose twenty-seven years had been packed with adventure. After studying forestry engineering, he had served in the French Foreign Legion and the Norwegian army during the war. He then joined the volunteers helping Finland in its fight with Russia and was badly wounded during a cavalry charge. The rugged outdoorsman, who excelled as a skier, a marksman, and a boxer, abandoned his bid to be on the 1920 Olympic team upon being accepted into the Royal Norwegian Naval Air Service. Balchen was a member of Amundsen's ground party during the 1926 Arctic expedition, but he also lent some critical assistance to Byrd, supervising the repair of the *Josephine Ford*'s aircraft skis, which had been damaged while trying to take off from the ice. Tough, intelligent, and resourceful, the handsome young airman would be an asset to any expedition, but the flight's sponsor, Rodman Wanamaker, said no. The *America* was to be crewed entirely by Americans.

Noel Davis was a man who believed in luck. He was "shot with it," he boasted. Born near Nephi, Utah, on Christmas Day in 1891 (hence his name), Davis grew up poor and with a sketchy education. Nonetheless, he had a nimble and insatiably curious mind, learning the practical aspects of engineering as a ranch hand and reading books on mathematics in his spare time. The largely self-taught cowpuncher applied to the U.S. Naval Academy and scored miserably on the entrance exam. "I didn't know any history, geography, grammar or literature," he said, "but the mathematical problems were pie." To his astonishment, he was accepted. Given this unexpected break, the short, muscular cadet finished third in his class and went on to distinguish himself during the war, supervising the laying of anti-submarine mines between Scotland and Norway and then sweeping them up after the Armistice. After this hazardous task he earned his wings at Pensacola, wrote widely on aerodynamics and other technical subjects, and took a leave of absence to study law at Harvard. While in Boston he managed the local reserve flying field, doing such a commendable job that he was appointed to Washington to oversee all Naval Reserve aviation activities. Somehow he found time to create the Davis aircraft sextant. Its first real test would come on the Paris flight that he had been seriously pondering since 1925.

Davis knew a lot of people in Washington, and he approached more than a few of them for advice and support as he used his organizational skills to build an expedition. In the latter part of 1926, Major General Mason M. Patrick, chief of the Army Air Service, suggested he get in touch with Thomas Huff and Elliot Daland, who had been building planes for the army for several years. Huff-Daland Airplanes (which would change its name to Keystone Aircraft Corporation on March 8, 1927) was in the process of designing a civilian transport version of its standard biplane bomber at its plant in Bristol, Pennsylvania. The ten-passenger proto-type, known as the Keystone K-47 Pathfinder, was 45 feet long, had a 67-foot wingspan, and could be modified for Davis's use—assuming he found financing. Davis needed as much as $100,000. Serendipitously, the American Legion, of which Davis was a member, was planning to hold its annual convention in Paris in September 1927. As a publicity gimmick, the veterans organization agreed to help underwrite the flight. The national commander saw the plane—to be painted yellow with black trim and called the *American Legion*—as the herald of a second American Expeditionary Force, an army comprised this time of an anticipated 30,000 merrymaking conventioneers. "You lead the way," he said, "we follow."

Under Davis's direction, the Pathfinder's two water-cooled Liberty engines were replaced with a trio of lighter and more efficient Wright Whirlwinds. One motor was placed in the nose and the other two were mounted in nacelles on the lower wing. The craft was fitted with several fuel tanks totaling 1,500 gallons, five times its normal capacity. As with all ocean planes, compromises had to be made. The placement of the tanks in the fuselage meant crew members would have to use a catwalk to move between the cockpit and the back of the plane when it was in flight. In late March, the big craft came out of the factory and was taken on a couple of short hops. On April 10, as 1,500 spectators at Bristol cheered,

The *American Legion* was a trimotor Keystone bomber modified to cross the Atlantic.

Davis got behind the controls for the first time to give the plane its first extended trial: a flight to Langley Field in Virginia with a stopover in Washington, D.C. There several new instruments were installed and top Pentagon officials were given an up-close look at the "yellow giant."

Davis's flying partner was Lieutenant Stanton "Bob" Wooster. A light-hearted Connecticut native and Annapolis graduate who had served on the battleship *Nebraska* during the war before earning his wings at Pensacola, the thirty-two-year-old aviator was known for having a deft touch with large aircraft. He also was unflappable in an emergency. While on duty in Panama, he once found himself boxed in by mountains. Unable to climb over them, he gently crashed his plane and spent the next four days walking out of the jungle. More often than not, Wooster was at the controls of the *American Legion* as it went through a myriad of technical tests and cross-country jumps over the coming weeks.

With little fanfare, Davis took the lead in preparations for a Paris flight. Byrd's plane still was not finished, whereas the *American Legion* was already showing itself to be a legitimate contender for transatlantic honors. "She is a perfect ship!" exclaimed Rear Admiral William A. Moffett, the head of naval aviation. "I am confident they will succeed!" To Davis, who on March 2 had filed a new, second entry for the Orteig Prize, the award money was unimportant. Should he win, he planned on donating it to some aviation cause. His motive was patriotism, pure and simple. "A few years ago we held all the aviation records," he said. "We have lost nearly all of them. We make as good planes and motors as any country in the world, and we have as good pilots. I want to see some prestige in the air return to our country."

Charlie Levine remained undecided about a Paris try. For now, it was far less risky to attempt to break the duration record, held for almost two years by the Frenchmen Drouhin and Landry. The goal was fifty straight hours in the air—a nice, round number for the headlines and excellent training for a possible transatlantic flight. A giant 320-gallon tank was fitted into the fuselage directly behind the cockpit. Smaller tanks were placed in the wing roots. Levine had originally retained Leigh Wade to accompany Clarence Chamberlin; however, the former army world flier dropped out on April 8, citing the "stunt character" of the flight. Taking his place was Bert Acosta, a burly free spirit who "liked his wine, women and song," recalled a fellow aviator. The thirty-two-year-old self-taught pilot had tested army planes during the war, helped map out the first airmail routes, and won the 1921 National Air Races. He was considered one of the top commercial pilots on the East Coast, his specialties including the tricky art of skywriting. Acosta's legend was writ nearly as large as the mile-high letters his plane coughed out in the sky above New York. George Dade, a young-ster befriended by many Long Island pilots, remembered one occasion when "Acosta was hanging around a bar and nobody knew what time it was. He jumped in his plane, flew a circle around the Metropolitan Life Clock Tower in Manhattan, and flew back to the bar to give a re-port. A few years later I was bringing him cigarettes at the county jail where he was cooling off for a few days."

At 9:30 a.m. on April 12, the silver and yellow Bellanca, carrying 375 gallons of fuel, took off from Roosevelt Field. With Acosta and Chamberlin alternating piloting duties and the occasional catnap, the Bellanca officially droned through 51 hours, 11 minutes, and 25 sec-onds of flight over Long Island. Most of their time aloft was spent circling around in poor weather and in a terrible thirst. (An over-heated oil storage tank had ruined most of the milk, soup, and drink-ing water they had brought along.) The parched and "oil-blobbed" fliers brought the plane down at 12:42 p.m. on April 14, having bettered the old endurance mark by six hours. In the process they had covered 4,080 miles, enough to reach Paris with a comfortable cushion. Despite some wear, the Wright engine behaved wonderfully. "I did not believe that in the first test that motor would do the trick," admitted C. G. Patterson, a Wright official. "I couldn't help but feel that some little thing might go wrong just enough to spoil the attempt. I knew, of course, that we could build a motor that would do it, but I didn't think that this one would. It has already done about 30,000 miles, and except for new rings and pistons had not been built over." Levine was now convinced that the Bellanca could literally go the distance in the Orteig sweepstakes.

Acosta and Chamberlin had to fight their way through a jubilant crowd of three thousand people. The euphoria was short-lived. "Bert and I had won a record," Chamberlin later wrote, "but we had not won the right to fly the Bellanca to Paris."

After the flight, Levine announced that either Acosta or Chamberlin would be replaced on any Paris flight by Lloyd W. Bertaud, a thirty-one-year-old airmail pilot and expert navigator. Levine added that the choice of who would accompany Bertaud would be decided by tossing a coin just before takeoff. Privately, Levine thought Acosta and Bertaud would be the better pairing. The problem was not Chamberlin's piloting; it was his plain looks and slender physique. Levine was concerned that Chamberlin would appear less than heroic on the screen. It was better to have two tall and well-built pilots such as Acosta and Bertaud representing America, Columbia Aircraft, and Charles A. Levine to the world.

Giuseppe Bellanca was having none of it, however. He sent an ultimatum to Levine by registered mail. He would quit if Chamberlin was not part of a Paris flight.

8

Against the Prevailing Winds

Both shores of the Atlantic buzzed last week with the activities of men determined to fly between New York and Paris. The standing offer of Raymond C. Orteig, Manhattan hotel man, of $25,000 to be the first successful performer . . . would hardly pay interest on the total investments involved. Fame, promotions, cinema and press contracts, above all Adventure—were the real stimulants.

—*Time*, April 25, 1927

Aperitifs in New York! To Paul Tarascon and François Coli, the Prohibition laws in America were far less daunting than the immense and unruly body of water they resolutely intended to cross in the late autumn of 1926. A year after the crash of their Potez, and close on the heels of René Fonck's fiery disaster, the two airmen—now backed by a new sponsor—declared that all was nearly ready with their Bernard 18T. The large monoplane, the prototype of an eight-passenger transport, featured a high elliptical wing, a 420-horsepower Gnome & Rhone Jupiter motor, and a watertight hull that would keep them afloat in the unfortunate event that they dropped into the ocean somewhere between the shores of France and America. One Paris newspaper, recognizing the "beautiful bravery" of their undertaking, commented, "Let us hope that the tragedy of *New York–Paris* will not be renewed!"

It was not. The Bernard remained grounded in La Courneuve as the Société Industrielle des Métaux et du Bois, the small company that built

it, went bankrupt. The Paris–New York Committee, a group of sportsmen organized for the sole purpose of seeing Tarascon and Coli win the
Orteig Prize, lacked the resources to come to the rescue. Carl Schory
grew frustrated in his attempts to get back the $250 entry fee George
Burleigh had advanced the Tarascon team. "These Frenchmen," Schory
grumbled, "seem to be a hard lot to deal with."

A policy of fiscal restraint had been ushered in by the new government
of Raymond Poincaré in the summer of 1926, and most of France was
feeling the pinch. By the spring of 1927 the franc had doubled in value
against the dollar. But private money continued to be tight, and most
government spending went to the pensions of disabled veterans and war
widows, the never-ending reconstruction of shelled-out communities,
the massive ongoing reorganization of the army (the greatest in half a
century), and the building of a complex series of fortifications known as
the Maginot Line. There had been a thaw in Franco-German relations,
with Germany being admitted into the League of Nations in 1926 and
regular passenger and cargo service being inaugurated between the two
countries. But France's need to always keep one eye trained on its historic
foe included maintaining Europe's largest air force. With most generals
convinced of the inevitability of another Franco-German war—the third
since 1870—the government remained heavily focused on military projects at the expense of *grands raids* (spectacular long-distance flights).
Inside the heavily guarded Blériot shops in Suresnes, for example, great
resources were being expended in building a top-secret bomber and a
new fighter plane even as ocean-minded airmen scrambled for technical
and financial assistance. The firm's namesake was one of many respected
members of the French aviation community who saw little practical value
in rushing a plane to New York. "A non-stop flight across the Atlantic is
quite possible," said Louis Blériot, "but in the present state of aeronautical science its accomplishment can only be regarded as a sporting exploit.
The idea of a commercial airway between the two great cities, I believe,
is still in the realm of dreams."

French aviation was in decline, hampered by institutional conserva-
tism. Commercial carriers were heavily subsidized, and the air service
was under the control of hidebound career types, a system guaranteed
to discourage risk and dampen innovation. In contrast to American and
German aviation, which stressed "experimentation in all its forms" and
methodically gathering experience "without worrying too much about

immediate practical results," the French had "an absolute horror of experience," claimed General Henri Duval. "Our learned officials pride themselves on their knowledge of pure science, and in their arrogance they make calculations on paper . . . they never stimulate new thinking, rarely collaborate, and usually slow things down." The welded-steel tubing being used in the construction of Charles Lindbergh's new Ryan plane, for example, was not permitted under French aeronautical guidelines.

Caution had come to characterize the nation's aviation policy, just as it had its fiscal doctrine. Maurice Bokanowski was minister of commerce and aviation in Poincaré's cabinet. The man in charge of all French aviation was not a pilot and personally disliked flying, though he often traveled by air to provide the public with an example of confidence. "Flying is means of locomotion for people in a hurry," he told his brother while forbidding him to ever step foot in a plane. Any transatlantic attempt launched from France ultimately required the air minister's official blessing, but Bokanowski refused to grant permission until he was satisfied that any such flight met sufficient expectations of success and safety. Likely influenced by a harrowing wartime experience—he had spent half a day clinging to flotsam after the ship he was sailing on was sunk by a German torpedo—he insisted that all transoceanic craft either be a hydroplane or, if a land plane, retrofitted to make it seaworthy in case of a ditching. Tragically, Bokanowski's private apprehensions about flying would prove justified. During a short routine flight in 1928, his plane caught fire and plunged to earth, incinerating everybody on board.

On February 26, 1927, Jean Sapene, the intensely nationalistic managing director of *Le Matin*, offered 30,000 francs toward the creation of a trophy to be given the first all-French crew and plane to jump the Atlantic. Sculptors, artists, and jewelers were all invited to submit designs. "It is certain that this flight will soon be accomplished," the newspaper announced. "Will it be a plane flying from New York to Paris or one bearing the tricolor from Paris to New York that will succeed? In the hope that it will be a French crew which wins this international contest, preparing this year, the Matin creates a trophy for a transatlantic plane of French make with a French motor and a French crew."

There were a number of ongoing efforts, some less advanced than others. There was Lucien Bossoutrot, who had left Farman in 1926 to throw in his lot with Louis de Monge, an innovative Belgian designer whose "flying wing" aircraft was being built in stages at the Dyle and

Bacalan shipyard at Bordeaux. In Marseilles, one of aviation's true pioneers, Louis Paulhan, was constructing an all-metal seaplane that he planned to outfit with twin 650-horsepower engines. Paulhan had been the first to fly above the Pacific Ocean, skimming Los Angeles Harbor in a Farman biplane during the first U.S. air show in 1910. Lieutenant Dieudonné Costés, a decorated fighter ace and now a test pilot for Bréguet, could claim a feat of more recent vintage. In October 1926, he and Captain Jean Rignot set a new nonstop distance record with a 3,353-mile flight between Paris and Persia. The two pilots did it in a Bréguet 19, a converted light bomber they hoped to fly to New York, assuming the military and the manufacturer allowed it.

At Toussus-le-Noble, Maurice Drouhin was handling a mammoth new Farman craft. The F-180 was the prototype of a twenty-four-passenger airliner that would go into service in 1928. The giant biplane was named *Oiseau Bleu* (*Blue Bird*), and its bottom wing stood six feet off the ground. The wingspan was 85 feet, while the fuselage was extended to 54 feet to help accommodate a dozen fuel tanks. It employed a pair of 500-horsepower motors mounted in tandem on the top wing. The forward "tractor" engine pulled the plane, while the rear "pusher" engine—its four-blade

Farman test pilot Maurice Drouhin was one of several French aspirants for the Orteig Prize.

propeller facing backward—shoved it along. The push-pull configuration was designed to reduce the effects of either engine failing in flight. Joseph Le Brix, a seasoned airman recently decorated for his service in Morocco, also explored the possibility of organizing his own expedition before ultimately signing on as Drouhin's copilot and navigator.

The Tarascon-Coli attempt refused to die. Potez had built a second ocean plane for the expedition in 1926 but then sold it, after which the pilots joined forces with the ill-fated Société Industrielle des Métaux et du Bois. The failed constructor was revived in early 1927 as the Société des Avions Bernard under founder Adolphe Bernard. The firm's chief designer, Jean Hubert, was building a derivative of the original Bernard 18T prototype. This new monoplane, nominally a ten-seat airliner and designated the 18GR, would be filled with enough fuel tanks to give it an anticipated range of 4,100 miles. It also would be fitted with an undercarriage that would be dropped after takeoff. The Bernard, which when finished was painted a glossy yellow and christened the *Oiseau Tango* (*Tango Bird*), was not expected to be ready until summer.

In aviation circles it was generally accepted that headwinds made a Paris-to-New York flight at least 20 percent more difficult than crossing in the opposite direction. "There does not seem much likelihood that any successful attempt to fly over the Atlantic will be made from Paris this year," Percy J. Philip, an overseas correspondent for the *New York Times*, observed in late March. "This is not any lack of ambition among pilots. There are a dozen, at least, eager to try and capable of making the flight, but money wherewith to finance it is lacking."

That same day, war hero Charles Nungesser announced to Paris reporters that he and a certain one-eyed navigator aimed to buck the winds—and the odds.

The war literally was Charles Nungesser's calling card. One of the French ace's postwar business cards listed his thirty-nine decorations and seventeen wounds, a compilation that left one marveling that there was enough left of the man to wear all the hardware awarded him. In four years of fighting he had suffered a fractured skull and a brain concussion. His upper jaw was broken five times and his lower jaw twice. Nearly all of his teeth had been knocked out. He'd been shot in the mouth and the ear and had a chunk of shrapnel embedded in his right arm. He had dislocated his clavicle, wrist, ankle, and both knees, and the tendons and muscles in his legs had atrophied. Among his many honors were the Croix de Guerre with thirty palms. He was made an officer of the Legion of Honor in 1918, his citation noting his "arrogant contempt for death" and his fame as "the most feared adversary for German aviation." In a country that so conspicuously honored and cared for *les mutilés de guerre*—the legions of veterans with missing limbs and featureless faces—the mangled but seemingly invincible Nungesser was widely admired. His recklessness and bad-boy persona added to his appeal.

Nungesser was born on March 15, 1892, in Paris and spent his early boyhood in his mother's hometown of Valenciennes. His parents divorced and he was sent to live with an aunt when he was ten. He was an indifferent student, though he displayed an aptitude for mechanics and excelled in swimming, boxing, and other competitive sports. When he was sixteen he sailed to South America, spending much of the next six years working as a mechanic and a gaucho in Argentina. He had thick blond hair, bright blue eyes, and a head that seemed too large for his five-foot, nine-inch 150-pound frame. He was only a teenager when he first flew, "borrowing" a Blériot and teaching himself the controls. He was fearless, racing cars and performing aerial acrobatics in his free time, but it was as a member of a French Hussar regiment that he galloped off to war in 1914. He distinguished himself in the opening weeks of fighting by ambushing a German staff car, killing its occupants, then driving pell-mell through gunfire by both armies to deliver two French infantrymen and a cache of captured enemy documents to headquarters. For this he was awarded the Médaille Militaire, France's highest award for enlisted men. He also got to keep the bullet-riddled Mors.

Nungesser soon secured a transfer to the air service, flying Voisins on bombing missions before moving into a fighter unit. The victories quickly added up, though at times he was so crippled by wounds and injuries he had to be hoisted into the cockpit of his Nieuport. An officer once asked Nungesser about his tactics. *"Mon Général,"* he replied, "when I am behind the adversary and believe that I have his airplane well and truly centered in front of my machine guns, I close my eyes and open fire. When I open them again, sometimes I see my opponent hurtling through space, and at other times I find myself in a hospital bed." Nungesser didn't limit his many crashes to airplanes. One October evening in 1917, his longtime mechanic drove the speeding Mors into a tree as they were on their way to a good time in Paris. His friend was killed instantly and Nungesser spent two months in the hospital.

Nungesser was as responsible as anyone for creating the enduring image of the dashing, reckless "fighter jock," regularly being reprimanded for disobeying orders, guzzling champagne between missions, and crawling out of hospital beds to battle the Hun and falling into beds with a bevy of beautiful women. One of his conquests reportedly was the notorious Dutch spy Mata Hari. Some of his exploits were apocryphal, but it hardly mattered. All were widely publicized. By war's end Nungesser had forty-five victories, making him France's third-leading ace.

Lieutenant Nungesser returned to peacetime with two rows of gold teeth; a platinum jaw, knee, and foot; and adrenaline still pumping through his veins. He opened a short-lived flying school in Orly, which attracted some rich friends but few other students. He set his eyes on conquering America, and for a while he was successful. He put on barnstorming exhibitions across the States and engaged in mock combat for the movie *Sky Raiders*, filmed at Roosevelt Field. He married nineteen-year-old Manhattan heiress Conseulo Hatmaker in Paris in 1923, but three years

Charles Nungesser and his American wife, Consuelo Hatmaker, circa 1924.

later she divorced him, citing incompatibility. "I still love her devotedly," he said. "It is still a question of my work taking up all my time. I work 17 hours daily and can't very well give over 10 hours daily to pleasure." His principal project, designing an amphibian plane, went nowhere.

Nungesser came back to France in 1926, just ahead of a $5,017 judgment rendered against him in a New York court for money owed the American Express Company. Approaching his thirty-fifth birthday, the still jaunty Nungesser was viewed in some quarters as a dissipated failure, his heroic status notwithstanding. Talk of private debts and indiscretions was kept out of the newspapers but circulated as gossip. "Good young friends had benefited from my departure to the United States to freely attack me," he told a trusted journalist upon his return. "Before too long, I will undertake an adventure which will fill the entire world with wonder." The correspondent asked if this astounding feat involved flying the Atlantic. "Perhaps," he said with a smile.

Nungesser wasn't being coy, just careful. For one thing, he didn't want to tip his hand. For another, he wasn't sure he could find support for such an adventure. He made the rounds of important people and came up empty until he visited Pierre Levasseur, whose firm built aircraft for the French Navy. "I want a plane to fly across the Atlantic from east to west," Nungesser told him.

"Oh, you do, do you?" replied Levasseur, who told him he'd think it over.

"There's not much time for that," Nungesser said. "I need the plane within, say, three months at the outside."

"Three months!"

"Yes, at the outside. The Americans are getting ready now and I don't want them to get in first."

Levasseur was intrigued. He told his visitor about an ongoing contract he had to build "certain special machines" for the navy. The PL.8 was a biplane based on an earlier model, the PL.4 reconnaissance plane. It wasn't exactly an amphibian craft, but its fuselage was designed to float if the plane came down in water. Levasseur was convinced he could custom-build a plane with enough range to make it to New York. Best of all, he could do it quickly and relatively cheaply.

Work began on their maritime biplane on February 28 under the supervision of Levasseur, chief engineer Émile Farret, and factory manager Albert Longelot. "Fuel comes first," Nungesser stressed. "Everything must be sacrificed to that." The two forward cockpits were ripped out to help make room for three enormous fuel tanks. The remaining cockpit was widened to accommodate two pilots, with the navigator's seat positioned adjacent to and slightly behind Nungesser's. The 32-foot-long fuselage, deep and watertight, was strengthened with additional plywood and bracing. Because it was meant to land on water, the bottom of the fuselage was planed. To lift the additional weight the span of both wings was expanded to 48 feet. The wheeled undercarriage would be released shortly after takeoff, diminishing weight and wind resistance and improving the craft's speed and range.

Nungesser initially planned on flying alone. But when Levasseur told him it would be impossible to handle the piloting and navigating by himself, Nungesser expressed interest in bringing along François Coli, who over the years had collected a large amount of technical data relating to a transatlantic flight. However, the one-eyed aviator was contractually attached to Paul Tarascon's expedition. Coli, knowing the Levasseur plane would be oceanworthy long before the *Tango Bird*, asked Tarascon to release him from his contract, and his old friend graciously did. Coli left open the possibility that he would accompany Tarascon on future flights. On March 26, a month after work had quietly started on his plane, Nungesser publicly announced that he and Coli were planning an Atlantic flight.

As work continued inside the Levasseur shops, Nungesser took courses in meteorology, wireless navigation, and other subjects while Coli continued to study weather maps, tables, and charts while plotting the best routes. One day both men were looking over the machine that was to take them to America when Coli suggested it needed a name.

"I suppose she ought," Nungesser said. "They're going to paint her white, so that she'll be easier to find if we have to come down in the sea."

Coli was inspired. Why not call it the *Oiseau Blanc*—the *White Bird*?

"Good idea," Nungesser said.

The government refused to either endorse or prohibit the expedition. "In the fear that such a project would seem too audacious, the official air service has lent nothing to this enterprise except unofficial patronage," observed *Le Figaro*. However, the fliers were allowed to adorn the *White Bird* with the insignias of French naval planes: a tricolored cockade and roped anchor.

Betting was under way in Paris. Early on, Drouhin's *Blue Bird* was viewed by some handicappers as the leading favorite, but progress in improving the big plane's range was frustratingly slow. With a projected takeoff weight of twelve tons and headwinds to consider, Farman

Maurice Drouhin's giant Farman, the *Blue Bird*. The name of the plane's builder and the expedition's goal, "Paris–New York," were prominently featured on the fuselage.

engineers were still unable to squeeze enough mileage out of it to send it to New York with an adequate cushion. In mid-April, Drouhin suggested he might try to cross the Atlantic in stages. He would fly from Ireland to Newfoundland—basically tracing Alcock and Brown's 1919 flight in reverse—and then continue to New York. Assuming everything went according to plan, he said, he would wait ten days before embarking for Paris, the expected tailwinds boosting the *Blue Bird*'s range to what was required to reach France and win the Orteig Prize. From any number of standpoints—logistical, technological, meteorological, and financial—this itinerary was as ambitious—many would say unrealistic— as one could imagine.

Compared to some of the American expeditions under way, there was less talk among French pilots of advancing the cause of science. Most saw "the big jump" as a straight grab for glory—and nobody fit the role of conquering hero better than Nungesser, who quickly emerged as the front-runner and sentimental favorite in the Paris press. *Le Matin* thought his and Coli's combined experience gave the *White Bird* the edge over everybody else in the race. "Coli understands the sea even better than the air, for he spent many years in the merchant marine," the paper observed in late April, "while Nungesser is more at home in the air than on the ground and knows all the ins and outs of flying. With two such admirably equipped airmen France should be the first to gain the honor."

9

Come to Earth

Other stories are told of men who tried to fly with wings shaped like the wings of birds strapped to their shoulders. It was their practice to leap from some high buildings with wings outspread to catch the wind and break their fall. Sometimes, they did manage to cover some slight distance before they came to earth, but all of them, sooner or later, made one jump too many and did themselves some injury.

—Robert J. Hoare, *Wings Over the Atlantic*

April 16 was the day before Easter, but anticipation caused Richard Byrd to treat it almost as the night before Christmas. That Saturday afternoon the *America* was rolled out of the Fokker factory, and Byrd, along with Floyd Bennett and George Noville, eagerly traveled to Teterboro, New Jersey, to get a firsthand look at the machine that had been built specifically to carry them over the ocean. Although Tony Fokker preferred to take the big plane up by himself the first time out, he acquiesced to their request to come along. "Some of my friends tried to dissuade me from the flight," Byrd said. "The plane was brand new and had not been in the air yet. But I did not want to accept the plane without personally observing its performance."

With Fokker at the controls, Bennett in the copilot's seat, and Byrd and Noville crouching behind them, the *America* lifted off in fine fashion. Fokker put it through its paces for a half-hour or so, flying with one engine off, then two. With all three motors off, Byrd noticed Bennett licking his lips—a sure sign that he was nervous. The new plane was dangerously nose-heavy, the result of an unbalanced load. The 1,300-gallon main tank in the middle of the fuselage was practically empty, affecting the plane's center of gravity, and its placement prevented any of the passengers from moving aft to provide counterweight.

Fokker aborted the first landing attempt, then had everyone aboard brace themselves for a second approach. "There came a terrific crash," Byrd recalled. "It sounded as if every inch of the plane were being crushed to kindling." The *America* hit the ground at 60 miles an hour, pancaking and then flipping over onto its back. Noville was sent hurtling into Byrd, snapping the commander's wrist and momentarily knocking him unconscious. The center engine crushed the cockpit, pinning Bennett into his seat. "Look out for fire," he said weakly. Noville, remembering the men incinerated in the Fonck disaster, wildly punched an exit through the cloth fuselage and stumbled out, screaming. Byrd followed. When it was apparent that the *America* would not turn into a torch, Byrd rushed into the wreckage. He found Bennett drenched in oil and blood.

"Guess I'm done for, Commander," Bennett said. "I'm all broken up. I can't see and I have no feeling in my left arm."

"Nonsense, old man," Byrd responded. But his good friend was in critical shape.

Fokker, seated nearest the hatch, had managed to escape without injury. Byrd suffered a broken wrist. Noville spent a week in the hospital, recovering from torn groin muscles and shock and undergoing an operation to remove a blood clot. Bennett was the worst off. His right thigh, his collarbone, and a rib were broken, and he had suffered severe facial injuries. To add to his stress, his wife, Cora, was seriously ill in the hospital with pneumonia and was unable to see him for almost two weeks. Gloom settled over the *America*'s camp. The plane and its crew would be on the mend for weeks. Bennett, who would need months to recover, was out of the flight for good.

Byrd put on an optimistic face, minimizing the damage to the plane while growing more determined to make a successful transatlantic flight as a way of assuaging public phobia. "I felt like making a plea to the people of the country then not to let such pioneering accidents hurt the advancement of commercial aviation," he wrote. "Such an accident had nothing to do with regular commercial flights. The country was not yet sufficiently air-minded to distinguish the great difference."

On the same day that Byrd's Fokker came to grief, Noel Davis and Bob Wooster left Langley Field in the *American Legion*, bound for the plane's christening ceremony at Long Island's Mitchel Field, three hundred miles away. They flew at 2,000 feet through the overcast, averaging 92 miles per hour. Considering the load—nine people plus the new radio equipment designed to keep the plane in regular contact with ships and shore—this was a sprightly pace. However, the Pathfinder had already proved it could exceed 125 miles per hour with its throttle wide open and could fly with one of its motors off.

A reporter along for the ride recorded his impressions. "The roar of the three motors made one so deaf that it became a monotonous clashing overtone that drowned everything," he observed. "At first one's whole system fought against the noise, and then came a sleepy hypnosis and finally a nonchalance that made flying over the ocean seem the most commonplace thing in the world. There was no connection with the earth, merely riding on a whirlwind of sound, a piece of steel-braced framework hurtling through the air with the pull of three powerful motors, a bit of flying mechanism which it seemed nothing could down." He was amazed at how nonchalantly the pilots and the technicians on board crawled along the catwalk between the cockpit and the aft section (where the wireless and the navigator's work station were located), their faces comically distorted by the driving windstream. Only a safety belt attached to a three-inch-high railing kept a man from being blown off into space.

Also on board was Davis's wife. Mary Merritt Davis was a member of a prominent Pensacola family. She enjoyed flying; for a time there even was talk that she would accompany her husband on the Paris flight. However, there was their one-year-old son to consider when weighing the risk of such an adventure, and Mary decided her place was at home. She was still part of the team, preparing a week's worth of emergency rations—bacon, peanut butter, and dried beef sandwiches, packed in watertight tins—in case her favorite airmen fell into the ocean.

Based on the *American Legion*'s performance on this overcast Saturday, such a possibility seemed more remote than ever. The big ship was fast

U.S. Navy officers Noel Davis (left) and Bob Wooster crewed the *American Legion*.

and it was responsive, with Wooster bringing the plane "down on the field so easily that it wouldn't have overturned a glass of water on the calculating table." The naming ceremony followed. Assorted dignitaries gave brief speeches, then watched as Mary Davis climbed a ladder and broke a bottle of ginger ale over the spindle of the nose engine. "The contents spurted out over her coat and into her face," the *New York Times* reported, "and she came down smiling ruefully, while Commander Davis helped her, laughing heartily at her shower."

Neither Byrd's setback nor the *American Legion*'s front-runner status deterred others from throwing their flying helmets into the ring. The number of American and European pilots announcing plans to go after the Orteig Prize seemed to grow almost by the day, though the cost of mounting such an expedition was generally in the range of $50,000 to $150,000. This put it out of the reach of aspirants such as Leigh Wade, who told of his plans to build a "mystery machine"—the real mystery being who would bankroll it. "If someone will back me financially," he said hopefully, "I'll be ready to start in six weeks."

Six weeks, of course, fell short of the sixty-day waiting period required of all contenders. But it wasn't just flights of fancy that were cavalierly disregarding the prize rules. Many of the leading contenders had not formally submitted entries, either. There seemed to be a general assumption that the Orteig Prize committee would have little choice but to award the prize to the first crew to make the big jump between New York and Paris, even if the winning airmen hadn't officially entered the contest or had left early. At the same time, additional incentives were being offered. Bartlett Arkell, president of the Beech-Nut Packing Company, promised to present a silver cup and $5,000 to Noel Davis should the *American Legion* reach Paris. Ralph Jonas, president of the Brooklyn Chamber of Commerce, announced a $15,000 cash prize if Charlie Levine's Bellanca did the same.

On April 18, Winston W. Ehrgott, a second lieutenant in the New York National Guard, wrote to the NAA in Washington. The impressive stationery bore the letterhead "The American Non-Stop Trans-Atlantic Flight" and carried the address of the Liberty National Bank on West Fifty-seventh Street. "I wish to notify you of the desire of this crew to compete for the Orteig Prize," Ehrgott began. "However, we would not wish to bind ourselves to wait until the expiration of a specified length of time before making our attempt."

Ehrgott elaborated on the organization's plans at a press conference the following day. Standing alongside him was John H. Stelling, a local businessman and president of the Aircraft Corporation of America. The concern evidently had yet to build its first plane, but no matter. The organization was jumping into the race and hoped to be off to Paris within six weeks. In addition to Ehrgott, the announced four-man crew included pilots Lieutenant George R. Pond, a naval reserve officer, and Major Thomas Lanphier of the U.S. Army Air Corps. Recently retired navy commander J. H. Klein would serve as navigator. They planned to fly a twin-engine amphibian being built for them at the new Sikorsky plant in College Point, Long Island. Although he wasn't an aviator, Ehrgott made it clear that he was the expedition commander. (He also would tend the radio as they flew the ocean.) Members of the flight committee included a local congressman, a banker, and two high-ranking officers of his National Guard unit. The governor of Connecticut also was supporting the effort, Ehrgott said, though not in a financial way.

What to make of this newest entrant? Tall, lanky, and energetic, the twenty-three-year-old Ehrgott was described in the press as "having accompanied the Byrd polar expedition as far as Spitsbergen in a minor capacity." That was one way of phrasing it. Ehrgott, twice a cadet at West Point without ever graduating, had been discovered as a stowaway on Byrd's steamer *Chantier* just before it left New York for the Arctic. Faced with being tossed off the boat, Ehrgott accepted a position as a coal passer in the boiler room. A hapless seeker of adventure—in the 1930s he would flee Cuba after being involved in some murky scheme, possibly gunrunning—Erhgott considered himself, like Byrd, more of a producer or a general contractor, someone able to envision the big picture while others attended to most of the operational details. Alas, the American Non-Stop Trans-Atlantic Flight organization failed to accomplish much beyond ordering stationery and holding a press conference. Sikorsky officials told reporters that they were unaware of any plans to build a plane for Ehrgott and Stelling; meanwhile, others said to be involved distanced themselves from the project. Ehrgott did offer the novel idea of having all competitors hold off until the summer, when everybody would then start for Paris using a system of handicaps. "Leaders of other projected flights showed no disposition to endorse Lieutenant Ehrgott's proposal for delay," reported the *New York Times*.

As aspirants continued preparations on both sides of the ocean and interest mushroomed, most of the pilots downplayed any notion of an actual race. "What do you think we are? Racehorses lined up at the gate?" René Fonck, in the midst of organizing a second attempt, said testily. "We're going to fly the Atlantic, that's all. Whoever's ready first will start first—and good luck to him. It won't make the job any less difficult for those who start after him—or less important." Byrd's mantra remained the same. His goal was the advancement of aeronautical science, not personal glory. Byrd, who claimed to be uneasy with "this hero business," later complained that he "had been projected into what was euphemistically called by the press the 'Great 1927 New York-to-Paris Air Derby.' I admit it would have been gratifying to be first across; but that was only a secondary consideration with us. So we repeatedly said we were in no race, though the public insisted that we were."

The public's attitude was understandable. Press coverage of the "contest" between Byrd and Amundsen to be the first to fly over the

North Pole had whetted the appetite for another international rivalry. In a decade where spectator sports exploded in popularity, framing in sporting terms what most pilots habitually referred to as an "expedition" appealed to the average person's sense of competitiveness and easily stirred one's patriotism. "It is a matter of great satisfaction," President Coolidge had said when word reached the White House that Byrd had "beaten" Amundsen to the pole, "that this record has been made by an American." The flag-waving throngs who had turned out for Byrd's ticker-tape parade up Broadway obviously shared Coolidge's national chauvinism. Members of the scientific community might consider the notion of a race unseemly—a third "competitor," Australian explorer George Wilkins, had purposely removed himself from the story by concentrating his activities elsewhere in the Arctic—but with large financial investments, personal ambition, and a country's prestige all in the mix, the urge to be first was hard to resist. Somewhat perversely, the crash of Fonck's giant Sikorsky a few weeks after Byrd's triumphant return had further heightened public interest in the Orteig Prize by demonstrating just how truly dangerous such aerial adventures were. Despite the perils and his own misgivings, Byrd conceded that "spectacular flights" were needed to seize the imagination of the people and to accelerate scientific advancement. "Sensational flights," he said, "are the italics in the story of aviation's progress."

On April 24, the Bellanca was christened the *Columbia* in a brief ceremony at Curtiss Field. Levine's nine-year-old daughter, Eloyse, broke a bottle of ginger ale over the propeller. Afterward, Chamberlin took Eloyse and Jonas's teenage daughter Grace for a short pleasure flight. Also on board was Bellanca's chief mechanic, John Carisi. However, unbeknownst to Chamberlin, during takeoff a pin in the left shock absorber broke, causing the front strut to fall out of its fuselage fitting. As the *Columbia* embarked on its innocent Sunday afternoon excursion, the left wheel hung useless. Any attempt at a normal landing would end in disaster.

Looking to head off calamity, a couple of men grabbed a spare wheel and quickly took to the air in a biplane. As the pilot maneuvered alongside the *Columbia*, the mechanic in the front cockpit kept gesturing with the wheel in his hand and pointing to the Bellanca's damaged undercarriage. Chamberlin, who at first thought they wanted to race, finally got the connection. He began by lightening his load, dropping the sandbags being carried as ballast, one by one, as he circled low over the field. "An energetic motorcycle cop, who seemed very anxious to help, caused me more worry than any other part of my predicament," Chamberlin recalled. "He saw the sand bags falling and got the idea I was dropping messages to the people on the ground. He steamed over to pick up the notes and would dash from one sand bag to another like a dog chasing sticks. I was afraid one of them would fall on him and break his neck, but somehow I managed to keep him from guessing just where the next one would drop. They told me later he came back with a manufacturer's 'O.K.' tag, which a factory inspector had fastened on one of the bags, and assured the anxious crowd that everything was all right."

But it clearly wasn't. Carisi, thinking he might be able to fix the strut, hung upside down out the open cabin door as Chamberlin gripped him with one hand and flew with the other. This was to no avail. For an hour the *Columbia* continued to circle the field at treetop level as the sky around it filled with planes and the crowd swelled into the thousands. All were helpless to do anything. Carisi and Grace Jonas became airsick from the constant circling. Then a plane flew up with a message hastily painted on its fuselage: "Land at Mitchel." This made sense. The nearby military field was less crowded and offered a smoother surface for an emergency landing. An ambulance and fire truck sped there. "To hell with the Paris flight," a visibly distraught Giuseppe Bellanca said as he jumped into his car and joined the pack racing to Mitchel. "If only those girls and those boys come back safely."

Chamberlin's superior airmanship prevailed. As he brought the *Columbia* down, he banked it to the right so that the right wheel, right wingtip, and tailskid made for an unconventional three-point landing. The wingtip dug into the wet grass, acting as an anchor as the Bellanca "ground-looped" and settled on the crippled left wheel. Chamberlin had prepared all on board for a possibly violent crash, but scant damage was done to the plane. The fabric on the wings didn't even tear as the plane slid to a halt. Everyone emerged unscathed. Bellanca rushed to embrace Chamberlin, while the girls politely thanked the pilot for their adventurous ride. The post surgeon at Mitchel Field approached, but Chamberlin waved him aside. "Thanks, doc," he said, "but I won't need you this time."

As the *Columbia*'s ordeal grabbed headlines in Monday's papers, Noel Davis and Bob Wooster were readying a final load test for the *American Legion* in Virginia. Weeks of meticulous testing and a series of cross-country flights under various conditions had gone so smoothly that the big yellow plane was now widely considered the leading contender for Orteig Prize honors. "I think we have licked all our troubles and I guess we will be in Paris as soon as the rest of them," Davis told a reporter Monday night. "It looks pretty good." Already the Paris post of the American Legion was coordinating preparations with the French government for their eventual arrival, which many now believed could happen in the first week of May, weather permitting.

The following morning, April 26, was a clear and calm Tuesday. Aviators, ground crew, and observers gathered at Langley Field. Also on hand were Wooster's fiancée and Mary Davis with little Noel Jr. The pilots were upbeat, confident. The preflight checks showed that everything was working perfectly. Just this one last test flight, then it would be on to New York to prepare for the final assault on the Atlantic. Several officers, sensing history being made, wanted to come along, but each passenger request was denied. With its gas tanks topped off for the first time, the *American Legion* was already severely bloated. Its wings were being asked to lift a load of 17,000 pounds, half of it fuel. This was 4,000 pounds more than it had ever attempted before. Wooster, at the controls, knew he might need every inch of the mile-long runway to get airborne with 8 ½ tons of deadweight.

Its three Wright motors singing harmoniously, the *American Legion* started down the runway, its tail beginning to lift as it picked up speed. Mechanics timing the takeoff glanced nervously at their stopwatches. Ten seconds passed . . . then fifteen . . . then twenty . . . and still the wheels had not left the ground. Another ten seconds passed as the large craft continued to gather momentum, and then it began to rise—slowly, fitfully, like an old man laboring to get out of bed. It headed toward a thicket of pine trees, a hazard it had easily cleared in previous tests with lighter loads, still straining to climb. Davis was concerned. With the altimeter showing the *American Legion* 50 feet lower than it should be, and the line of trees approaching, he told Wooster to bank right. The intention was to circle back to Langley, ending the mission. However, the maneuver caused the plane to lose flying speed. It began a long, drooping glide to earth.

It was clear to those watching on the ground that the *American Legion* was in serious trouble. It flew over Back River, a stream at the northern edge of Langley Field. As the aircraft passed over marshland adjacent to the river, Davis and Wooster switched off the engines and the fuel lines, coolly preparing for an emergency landing. The plane dipped lower and lower until its wheels skimmed the scummy surface. There was a huge splash. The *American Legion* plowed through the swamp, skidding for more than a hundred feet before it struck a bank on the far side of a large pond. The impact dislodged the center motor and crumpled the nose, but despite some leaking fuel and the smoldering engines there was no explosion or fire.

Fishermen in the Back River dropped their nets and rushed to help. Langley personnel commandeered a rowboat. Several men tied a rope

The *American Legion* crashed into a Virginia swamp on April 26, 1927, killing its two-man crew and eliminating a leading contender for the Orteig Prize.

around the tail section and tried to right the plane, but the rope snapped. A second, stronger rope was found, but that also broke. Some men attempted to dig through the muck in a desperate effort to reach the pilots. When rescuers finally got to Davis and Wooster, they found their lifeless bodies hanging upside down, still buckled into their seats. "I don't think either of the men knew what happened to them," said Lieutenant Commander D. H. Vance, who headed the board of inquiry into the accident. "The impact was enough to render them unconscious if not to break their necks, and even had the shock not killed them, the fumes from gasoline would have, for one of the tanks became loosened in the crash and gasoline poured into the cockpit." The naval board did not order a postmortem examination of the victims, calling it unnecessary. To those who recalled the crash of the giant Sikorsky at Roosevelt Field seven months earlier, the *real* cause of death had been a grossly overweight aircraft—again. For all of the soaring expectations, the *American Legion* had not gotten more than fifty feet off the ground.

Richard Byrd was shaken by the news of this latest catastrophe. He knew Davis and Wooster as "old friends," not as competitors. Each man was a "brilliant, courageous air pioneer," he said. "We were rooting for each other. I hoped that both would make Paris for the advancement of science. Only several days ago I wrote [Davis] offering what assistance he cared to ask of me, and his last message to me before taking off was to offer some good advice. It was this type of splendid American that aviation has lost . . . that makes one feel proud to strive for the same goal."

Wooster was buried with full military honors at Arlington National Cemetery. Davis was laid to rest in the family plot in Pensacola. The navy soon announced the creation of the Noel Davis Trophy, which continues to this day to be presented to the reserve squadron judged to be at the highest level of readiness. Meanwhile, the Orteig Prize contest committee quietly arranged for checks totaling $500.66—representing the two entry fees Davis had paid plus interest—to be sent to his widow.

10

Little Silver Plane

Everybody knows that when it is noon in the United States the sun is setting over France. If you could fly to France in one minute, you could go straight into the sunset, right from noon. Unfortunately, France is too far away for that. But on your tiny planet, my little prince, all you need do is move your chair a few steps. You can see the day end and the twilight falling whenever you like.

— Antoine de Saint-Exupéry, *Le Petit Prince*

On April 27, the day following the deaths of Davis and Wooster, Carl Schory responded to a letter from George Burleigh insisting on strict adherence to the prize rules. "In view of the tragic accident to the 'American Legion'. . . the sixty-day entrance requirement seems entirely justifiable if for no other reason than to discourage hasty preparations for a flight which requires the utmost perfection of equipment and plans," Schory wrote. "Mr. Charles A. Lindbergh is the only remaining entrant who has filed entry with the entrance fee as required by the regulations."

This would quickly change. That same day, the *France* docked in New York, and René Fonck clambered down the gangway. On hand to greet him was Robert L. Dodge, who wasted no time getting the French ace settled at the elegant Ritz Towers on Park Avenue. By day's end an entry form for the Orteig Prize had been filled out, notarized, and mailed to the contest committee. One line described the type of aircraft to be used: "Sikorsky type S-37 twin engined airplane or Sikorsky S-36 type

132

biplane." Once again, Igor Sikorsky had been hired to build a transatlantic plane and Fonck had agreed to fly it to Paris.

Their new backers had the smell of money about them, thanks to healthy international sales of such fragrances as Mes Fleurs and Ivresse d'Amour. Robert Dodge was the second husband of Lillian Sefton Thomas Dodge, president of the Harriet Hubbard Ayer Company, a Manhattan cosmetics firm she had run since the death of her first spouse. In January their newly formed venture, the American and Overseas Corporation, was incorporated with an initial capitalization of $150,000. The Dodges clearly could afford to underwrite the entire cost of the new Fonck-Sikorsky project, which included renting factory space in College Point and a hangar at Roosevelt Field. In 1930, Lillian Dodge would be penalized a record $213,286 by the U.S. Customs Service for trying to smuggle several trunks of undeclared Parisian goods off the *Île de France*, a staggering fine that the cosmetics queen paid as effortlessly as a bill from the milkman.

Sikorsky bemoaned the "deplorable" state of his company in the immediate wake of the *New York–Paris* disaster. He was broke, heavily in debt, and finding it hard to shake off criticism of his destroyed aircraft. The Dodges had just overseen one challenging project: a thirty-five-room Tudor mansion had been shipped over from England and then reassembled, brick by brick, on their estate in Mill Neck, Long Island. Similarly, the Dodges now gave Sikorsky the opportunity to rebuild his crumbled dream of a successful prototypical transatlantic airliner, one that offered all parties involved the potential for large profits with the inevitable introduction of overseas mail and passenger service.

Sikorsky's plan was to have a new twin-engine transport completed by summer. An elaborate schedule of graduated load and takeoff tests, the kind the planemaker had wanted performed the previous fall on the *New York–Paris*, would follow. With the *American Legion* tragically eliminated and Byrd's bid in jeopardy, Fonck immediately joined the shortened list of favorites for the Orteig Prize. As much as he craved the idea of a triumphal landing in Paris, the pilot echoed Sikorsky's plea for patience. "I shall not hurry my preparations because I do not wish to take any chances with the great undertaking until I am thoroughly prepared," he said. "I was surely prepared last year, but fate was against us." The flight would take place in September, when, in his judgment, the meteorological conditions were most favorable. "Of course I shall make the flight even if some other aviator wins the prize before I am ready to go. In that event I will try to beat his time."

On April 28, Charles Lindbergh climbed into his new Ryan monoplane for the first time. As promised, Frank Mahoney and Donald Hall had delivered the craft in exactly sixty days. On its gleaming silver wings was its government-mandated identification number: N-X 211. "N" was the international code letter for the United States, while "X" indicated that the plane was experimental. The manufacturer had designated it the Ryan NYP, the initials standing for "New York to Paris." The cowling had been elaborately burnished with a swirling pattern of overlapping circles, giving it a distinctive jeweled finish. Inscribed in black paint on each side of the cowling were the words *Spirit of St. Louis*.

Lacking the time to develop an entirely new design, Hall had created a strut-braced, high-winged monoplane out of two existing Ryan models, the Brougham and the M-2. The standard M-2 fuselage was extended 42 inches to produce an overall length of 27 feet, 8 inches, and the wingspan was expanded from 36 to 46 feet to help reduce stress on takeoff with a full load of fuel. The fuselage was treated fabric stretched over a tubular frame, while the wings consisted of fabric over wood spars. The *Spirit* had five tanks that held a collective 450 gallons. There was a forward tank (88 gallons), the main (209), and three wing tanks (153 total). Lindbergh chose to have the forward and main tanks installed in front of the enclosed cockpit, with the oil tank acting as a firewall. This not only improved the plane's center of gravity, but also in case of a crash he wouldn't be crushed between the engine and the tanks. Hall was concerned that the unusual positioning cut off all forward vision. This didn't bother Lindbergh, accustomed as he was to flying in the rear cockpit of his De Havilland with mail sacks in the front. When he wanted to see what was ahead, he could bank the plane slightly and look out either of the side windows. Just to be safe, a Ryan employee who had been a submariner in the navy fashioned a periscope out of a tube of sheet metal and a pair of mirrors.

The cockpit was a snug fit: just 3 feet wide and 51 inches high, with not even enough room for the lanky pilot to stretch his legs. The instrument panel included a tachometer, altimeter, airspeed indicator, bank and turn indicator, fuel pressure gauge, oil pressure and temperature gauges, a clock, and a liquid magnetic compass. The fact that the panel was far removed from the engine meant that the delicate instruments would be less susceptible to vibration and thus give more accurate readings. The plane also would carry an earth inductor compass, an innovative navigational tool that allowed a pilot to more accurately follow a predetermined path to his destination. This "aviator's eye" would be especially useful over the ocean, where there would be no visual checkpoints, as on land. Unlike the magnetic compass, the earth inductor compass was not affected by storms and other atmospheric disturbances. The large cylindrical generator needed to run the earth inductor compass was positioned on the roof of the fuselage a few feet back of the pilot's seat. In flight, a rotating wind-cup caused the shaft to spin, generating the necessary electrical current. It was necessary for a pilot to correct for deviation and wind speed every 100 miles, which in the case of the *Spirit of St. Louis* meant that Lindbergh would need to reset his course approximately every hour. The controller dial was positioned to the lower right of the instrument panel. "Once the course is set," explained Brice Goldsborough of the Pioneer Instrument Company, "the pilot has only to keep the plane so headed that the hand of the compass always remains on zero, and he will always be on the right course."

Assuming a cruising speed of roughly 100 miles per hour, with no help from a tailwind, the plane had a theoretical range of 4,100 miles—enough

The *Spirit of St. Louis* in an early test flight in San Diego.

to reach Paris with a reserve of 500 miles. To squeeze every last mile out
of the *Spirit*, Lindbergh planned to eliminate all unnecessary weight. He
decided against bringing along a radio (which he considered unreliable)
and a parachute (which he thought impractical). He also trimmed the
borders off maps, ripped pages out of his notebook, had his seat made of
wicker, and even turned down a stamp collector's $1,000 offer to carry a
pound of souvenir letters to Paris—anything to save a couple of pounds
here and a few ounces there. Although he had little faith that he would
survive an emergency ditch into the ocean, he did allow for an inflatable
raft, flares, army rations, and an Armbrust cup, a device that could turn
condensed moisture from his breath into drinking water.

Lindbergh's major concern was his navigation skills. He had never
flown more than five hundred miles nonstop and had no experience
flying over great bodies of water. Celestial navigation—steering by the
moon and the stars, as mariners had done for centuries—was problem-
atic. No pilot flying alone could hold a sextant steady enough to get
an accurate reading of the longitude and latitude while simultaneously
working the plane's controls. This meant he would depend on dead reckoning: determining his position from an hourly log showing the course
flown, the distance made, and the estimated drift. Working in a small
second-floor office at the Ryan factory, the air a pungent comingling of
airplane varnish and rotting fish from the nearby wharves, he read navigation books borrowed from the local library, studied maps and charts,
and plotted his Great Circle course from New York to Paris. He divided
his charted route into thirty-six separate segments. Each segment represented 100 miles, or roughly an hour's flying time. At each interval
he marked down the distance from New York and the magnetic course
to the next change in angle. "It's fascinating," he thought, looking with
satisfaction at his completed chart, "that curving, polygonic line, cutting fearlessly over thousands of miles of continent and ocean. . . . It
curves gracefully northward through New England, Nova Scotia, and
Newfoundland, eastward over the Atlantic, down past the southern tip
of Ireland, across a narrow strip of England, until at last it ends sharply
at the little dot inside of France marked 'Paris.'"

With builder and pilot preferring to keep a low profile, most Ryan
employees initially were kept in the dark as to what they were working on. Fred Magula helped fabricate the main tank. "I thought it was
a gas tank for a doggone fishing boat," he recalled. "It was a mammoth

thing. They didn't want a scratch on it because they figured vibrations would set in and create a leak." Such attention to detail was laudable but occasionally frustrating, even as the purpose of everyone's labor became clear. A worker once complained, "Why does this damn thing have to be so perfect?"

"Two reasons," Lindbergh replied. "The first is I'm not a good swimmer!"

Lindbergh always considered himself fortunate to have hooked up with Ryan. He liked Mahoney's enthusiasm, admired Hall's dedication, and enjoyed the camaraderie of company workers. The firm wasn't going to make any money on this job. But with the plane builder's reputation riding along with Lindbergh, Ryan employees—most of whom made 35 to 65 cents an hour—willingly worked long hours of unpaid overtime to get the *Spirit* out on schedule. Hall himself averaged 86-hour weeks, at one point putting in 36 straight hours at the drafting table. All told, the company spent 3,850 man-hours designing and building the *Spirit of St. Louis.*

Among those who worked on the plane was a young metal finisher named Douglas Corrigan, who eleven years later would become

Charles Lindbergh (third from right), shortly before leaving San Diego. Donald Hall, who designed and built the *Spirit of St. Louis*, stands second from right.

celebrated as "Wrong-Way" Corrigan for flying from New York to Ireland when his intended destination was Los Angeles. (Some would consider his misadventure a planned stunt and not a spectacular mistake.) It was Corrigan who pulled the wheel chocks when Lindbergh taxied the *Spirit of St. Louis* onto the field at Dutch Flats, a couple of miles from the Ryan facility, for its inaugural flight on April 28. "We yelled, slapped each other on the back, kissed all the girls, then stood there rather awkwardly but proudly, watching him circle overhead," recalled chief mechanic John Van der Linde. Lindbergh flew over the factory, the harbor, and the nearby naval station, putting the *Spirit* through its paces. "A Navy Hawk fighter plane dropped down to nose up to this rather strange silver bird and Lindbergh rolled over in a bank to dogfight with him," Van der Linde said. "The Hawk had more speed, but Slim cut inside him over and over. Then he brought her back to earth."

Lindbergh's first flight in the *Spirit of St. Louis* lasted twenty minutes. "I've never felt a plane accelerate so fast before," he marveled. "The tires are off ground before they roll a hundred yards." He was pleased to see the indicator climb to 128 miles an hour at full throttle, a tad faster than expected. There were minor adjustments to be made, but overall the craft handled beautifully.

A week of speed and load tests, preparatory to leaving for the East, followed. All the while he half-expected one of the contenders to take off and successfully cross the Atlantic. He had settled on a contingency plan should that happen. He would attempt a transpacific flight by way of the Hawaiian Islands or maybe try to fly around the world. In some ways either option was a riskier proposition than flying to Paris. But Lindbergh felt that with the *Spirit of St. Louis*, he now had a plane that he could do extraordinary things with.

11

Paris au Printemps

Because Americans are optimistic, they are better equipped than the French for the battle of life. But the price of this advantage is a source of weakness, a diseased pride. At every page of their history crops up a childish belief that Americans are the chosen people.

—André Tardieu, *France and America* (1927)

It was turning out to be a pleasant spring in Paris. The first stretch of warm and sunny weather arrived in mid-April, just in time for the Easter holiday. The fashion shows had unveiled several new colors for 1927 to brighten the cafés, boulevards, theaters, and horse shows, including red banana, silver gray, and a light shade of green called *vert d'eur*. Paris was "a beautiful, alluring, satisfying city," remembered Janet Flanner, who began contributing her weekly "Letter from Paris" to the *New Yorker* in 1925. "It was a city of charm and enticement, to foreigners and even to the French themselves. Its charm lay in its being no way international—not as yet. There were no skyscrapers. The charm still came from the démodé eighteenth- and nineteenth-century architecture that marked the façades of the private dwellings and the old-fashioned apartment houses." Flanner was part of the colony of American expatriates settled into the cheap flats and legendary bars of Montparnasse, most notably a literary avant-garde whose ranks included Ernest Hemingway, James Joyce, Gertrude Stein, and F. Scott Fitzgerald. Negroes found unaccustomed freedom in Paris, with the ultimate expression of licentious liberty being the frenetic cabaret star Josephine Baker in her banana skirt and slicked-back hair. "When spring came, even the false spring," Hemingway would later write of this time and place, "there were no problems except where to be happiest."

Although France resented the United States' growing domination in political, financial, cultural, and economic affairs, it could not escape American influence. "France dances to American jazz," Percy Philip observed in a 1927 dispatch to the *New York Times*. "Paris urchins whistle Irving Berlin's latest tunes. The French peasant plows, sows and reaps with American machinery. The French business man uses the American bank more and more freely." The French were alternately fascinated and repulsed by the immensity of America. France might be the largest country in western Europe, but the entire nation could be fitted comfortably within the borders of Texas. Parisians could claim the tallest structure on Earth in the Eiffel Tower, but residents of the otherwise low-slung city—where building restrictions capped new construction at seven stories—were astonished by the cloud-scrapers America threw up with such ease and regularity. By the end of the 1920s "Imperial New York" could boast 188 buildings more than twenty stories high. More were on the way, including the Chrysler Building, a shimmering Art Moderne masterpiece that would surpass the Eiffel Tower's record height when it was completed. To many, New York's skyscrapers were the very symbol of all that was great and decadent about America: its wealth, its energy, its optimism, its audacity, its brutish reach, its single-minded focus on the business at hand.

The "Great Franco-American Air Race," as some Paris papers had come to call the Orteig competition, was playing out during a time of ticklish relations between the two countries. The French were outraged that "Uncle Shylock" had insisted on its former ally repaying its war debts in full even as the country was teetering on bankruptcy in 1926. There were isolated instances of Americans being booed on the street and of stones being thrown at tourist buses. Warm memories of the doughboys of 1918 evaporated as free-spending Americans arrived in record numbers in 1927. "It was a curious thing," observed journalist Bill Shirer, who had left Iowa to work at the Paris bureau of the *Chicago Tribune*, "but an American who blew into Paris as a tourist, his pockets stuffed with traveler's checks, his mind emptied of whatever had filled it at home, his manners—if he ever had any—forgotten, became at once a simpleton and a barbarian: loud, vulgar, inane, and insensitive to the French, who after all were his hosts. He couldn't have been that bad back home. While the wife (whom he invariably called 'Mother' or 'Mama') made for the Louvre and some 'culture' and then for the fashionable couturier shops for new clothes, he made for the nearest bar and soon was blotto, a condition in which he remained until the end of his stay and friends poured him onto a departing boat train." Bilateral relations were further strained by the highly politicized case of Ferdinando Sacco and Bartolomeo Vanzetti, Italian immigrants and anarchists convicted of a double murder during a 1920 armed robbery in Massachusetts. In Paris, Communists and Socialists routinely ginned up anger outside the U.S. embassy and inside the Chamber of Deputies. In the spring of 1927, Ambassador Myron T. Herrick was being guarded around the clock in response to threats to avenge Sacco and Vanzetti's impending executions. Herrick knew to take such threats seriously. Six years earlier, an anarchist's bomb intended for him had exploded inside the American embassy, nearly killing his valet.

Charles Nungesser had no quarrel with America. Indeed, he had enjoyed his extended stay in the States and aspired to return there as quickly as possible, this time with François Coli in the *White Bird*. On

A French postcard of Nungesser, Coli, and the *Oiseau Blanc* (*White Bird*), the favorite of Paris newspapers and oddsmakers to be the first to New York.

April 16, the newly finished *White Bird* was transported from the factory at Chalais-Meudon to the military field at Villacoublay, where access was severely restricted. The next day the first trial flight took place, using one of the three water-cooled twelve-cylinder engines Lorraine-Dietrich provided. (Two were used in the factory and flight trials, while the third was reserved for the actual flight.) The modified large-bore, slow-turning engine was successfully block-tested for forty-three straight hours and had a peak power setting of 550 horsepower. To take advantage of this power, various types of oversize propellers were tested. Although metal airscrews produced a slight vibration and wooden ones did not, ultimately a 12½-foot two-bladed propeller made of forged duralumin was chosen. The giant prop—which had a ground clearance of just 8 inches—could be locked in a horizontal position for alighting on water. Tests would show that the *White Bird* had a top speed of 125 miles per hour and a cruising speed of about 100 miles an hour when fully loaded and flying in calm winds.

Aside from Nungesser's endurance at the controls and the engine's durability, nothing was more critical to a successful outcome than Coli's navigational skills. With his compass, sextant, chronometer, and wind-drift indicator, "Coli will certainly not control the elements: winds, clouds, and fog, but his scientific understanding will enable him to predict their traps and avoid them," observed *Le Matin*.

> For three years, Coli has studied the problem of this "Great Exploit," and . . . he has collected an impressive amount of documentation including all the weather reports about the north Atlantic for the past twenty years. He knows the conditions favorable to his flight through interpretation of barometric readings taken over different points in the ocean. He knows that if the clouds have a particular appearance, it means good weather, and that if the sky is a particular color, which to the eyes of the ordinary person appears insignificant, a storm is brewing. The brilliance of coastal lights holds no secrets from him. Flying by day over the sea when no land is visible on the horizon is the equivalent of flying at night, and for a sailor the night is more revealing, since instead of there simply being a single sun in the sky, with the aid of a sextant a myriad of stars can lead you to port. And during this flight from France to America, which could last anywhere between 30 and

42 hours, for a long stretch Nungesser and Coli will only have what they can read in the sky to guide them.

Coli traced his route on his maritime map long ago—an immense curve ... made up of a collection of twenty or so straight lines, making oblique angles, from which the skilled aerial navigator put together his marching plan, according to the speed, hour by hour, of the plane. Each side of this polygon, which the plane will trace in the air, must be covered in so many hours and so many minutes, after which Coli, as if he were on the bridge of his steamship, will indicate to his helmsman, Nungesser, what new compass heading to take. In the olden days, for example, one would have ordered a heading of north 45 west; now a new set of rules has been put in place, where one counts 360 degrees on the compass starting from the north, turning in the direction of the needles on a dial and absolute west becomes a simple 270 degrees. If at that moment, Coli is unsure of his exact position, he will take a reading with his sextant using the sun as much as possible, when it seems to be at the highest point of its course in relation to the place they are flying over. If the observation takes place at night, the star being used obviously will no longer be the sun but, for example, the pole star, which will be especially high on the horizon, as the plane heads more towards the north.

Coli intended to follow the Great Circle course. After crossing the English Channel, the *White Bird* would bisect the southwestern parts of England and Ireland before heading out over the Atlantic. It would roughly follow the fifty-fourth parallel until reaching Newfoundland, after which it would head south down the coastline to New York. Coli knew that adverse winds would be a constant challenge. "The old windjammers managed it, all the same," he said. "They tacked, didn't they? Well, so will we."

On Long Island, the *Columbia* had the field all to itself, though work continued apace on Byrd's *America*, and news items described other fledgling expeditions, most of them illusory and none of which posed an immediate threat to the Bellanca. The crew had been finalized with the abrupt resignation—or dismissal—of Bert Acosta on April 25. Acosta's unconvincing explanation was that the plane's range and chances of success would be significantly enhanced by not carrying his 210 pounds of body weight—50 pounds more than Clarence Chamberlin—all the way to Paris. Some speculated that Acosta had finally decided that any organization that would select a pilot for such an onerous undertaking by picking straws or flipping a coin was not one he cared to be part of. However, the press didn't know that Charlie Levine had recently submitted Acosta's required paperwork and entry fee to the Orteig Prize committee, which hadn't even had a chance to act on it before Levine instructed that Acosta's entry be yanked. The timing of Acosta's departure—coming the day after Chamberlin had demonstrated his flying chops with his one-wheeled landing of the stricken Bellanca at Mitchel Field—suggests that Levine may have simply changed his mind about who was the more capable pilot. There also was the possibility that Acosta's legendary debauchery was somehow involved in some behind-the-scenes decision-making. In any event, the *Columbia*'s crew now was Chamberlin and Lloyd Bertaud, though like most things involving the mercurial Levine, this was subject to change.

In the aftermath of the *American Legion* tragedy, the New York press began to warm up to the idea of an actual race, one that offered the proven ingredients of a good story: peril, uncertainty, courage, death. National pride suddenly was at stake. Levine was cocky, telling reporters that "prize or no prize, we will be the first to land in Paris. Our plane is ready now. If any other machine starts, we will start after her. We'll give any of them a three-hour handicap if necessary and be at the finish first." In terms of pure drama—and newsstand sales—nothing could be better than an American plane and a French plane leaving their respective shores simultaneously, maybe even crossing paths at the ocean's midpoint while millions waited in unbearable anticipation. "Possibly the *Columbia* from New York and these French flyers from Paris will take off at about the same time," the *Brooklyn Eagle* suggested on May 1, "and then the air race of the century—of the centuries—will be on." While such a scenario was unlikely, the horse-racing season had just started, and the prospect of some flier winning by a nose over his rivals stirred the sporting blood of many.

The Paris press was growing dangerously overheated. *Le Matin* ran front-page stories every day beginning in late April. It also announced a cash incentive of 25,000 francs (about $1,000) on top of Raymond Orteig's prize money. *Le Temps* offered its own prize of 10,000 francs ($400). *Le Figaro* assigned its nationally known sports editor, former

Olympic rugby player Frantz Reichel, to cover the race, giving over a chunk of its front page each day to his reportage and impressions. At *Le Petit Journal*, respected aviation journalist and biographer Jacques Mortane did the same. *Le Petit Parisien*, its two-million circulation reportedly the greatest of any newspaper in the world, dressed up its page-one coverage with aviation-related cartoons. One, titled "Anticipation," foresaw the Atlantic in the year 2000, by which time the air between the New and Old worlds buzzed with flying taxis, and the mighty ocean had been tamed to accommodate floating apartment houses and casual fishermen. Another cartoon, "*Paris–New York en Avion . . .* ," pictured an officer chatting with a pilot alongside his biplane. "It would be very funny that you cannot land in America because of the floods and that you are obliged to return," the officer said, making reference to the devastating Mississippi floods then capturing headlines. *L'Auto*, a sports periodical, resorted to the hoary gimmick of asking a psychic to peer into the future. After putting herself into a trance, the seer predicted that there would be several close calls but no more tragic accidents. "There will be many attempts from both sides of the Atlantic this year," she said. "Several will fall into the water, others will crash, but a handsome young Frenchman will finally be the one to triumph, after a delay now unforeseen."

Nungesser was unhappy with the escalating pressure from the press and the public. "Every place I go all I hear is 'Are you ready?' 'Are you going?' 'Will you make it?'" he complained. "I really don't know when I shall leave but what I do know is that all this talk has created an atmosphere of nervousness which is not at all helpful. Now, one does not fly across the Atlantic in the same manner in which these countless questions are asked. I am aware that each night in well-known Paris bars numerous aviators successfully cross the Atlantic between cocktails. But so far as I am concerned I have been carefully preparing for three years and do not intend to take off until I am certain of my plane and as certain of the weather as it is physically possible to be."

On Sunday, May 1, Parisians observed a favorite spring ritual. Lilies of the valley were sold on the streets, and during the next few days it was hard to find anyone not wearing a spray of the fragrant bell-shaped flowers as a boutonnière. According to Christian tradition, the Virgin Mary's tears turned into lilies of the valley at the death of her son. They were a symbol of resurrection, of hope and renewal, of man's ability to visualize a better future. The dashing Nungesser loved flowers.

There were several British and German teams in various stages of preparation for a westerly crossing of the Atlantic in the spring of 1927, but these expeditions were not planning departures from French soil and thus were ineligible for the Orteig Prize. However, there were some European fliers who were planning to use Paris as their springboard to New York. Belgian army lieutenants George Medaets and Jean Verhaegen, who the previous April had completed a round trip between Brussels and the Congo in a Bréguet 19, were readying an improved version of their long-distance craft and were due to arrive at Le Bourget in early May. At the same time, a battle-tested veteran of the Polish air force, Captain Ludwik Idzikowski, was in the process of obtaining an Amiot biplane bomber and a navigator, Major Kasimir Kubala, for a flight to America. There were any number of French hopefuls mentioned in Paris papers, but aside from such established candidates as Nungesser, Maurice Drouhin, Dieudonné Costés, and Paul Tarascon, most simply lacked the resources to be taken seriously. When it came to ocean flying, personal ambition and élan could carry a pilot only so far.

A pair of leading contenders in the "Great Franco-American Air Race," Dieudonné Costés and Maurice Drouhin, grace the cover of a Paris sporting magazine in 1927.

Drouhin's team futilely worked to keep pace with the steady progress being enjoyed by Nungesser and Coli. In late April there were a myriad of detailed tests: flying the *Blue Bird* on one engine, then the other . . . measuring fuel and oil consumption at different power settings . . . experimenting with various propellers . . . examining the water, oil, and fuel pumps and verifying the information on the gauges. There still was a radio system to install, and that meant even more testing of receiving and transmitting capabilities. Farman understood that "nothing can be left to chance," *Le Matin* observed, "if this great transatlantic flight is to succeed."

Farman had just put the finishing touches on a similar transatlantic aircraft, the *Paris–Amérique Latine*. Captain Pierre de Saint-Roman intended to become the first to jump the South Atlantic in a single bound. The planned flight from St. Louis, Senegal, to Pernambuco, Brazil (covering roughly half the distance of a Paris-to-New York hop), would be followed by a goodwill tour of fifty-two South American cities designed to promote business and cultural ties. The expedition was financed in part by the Latin American Society of Paris, with Farman agreeing to provide one of its Goliaths and Lorraine-Dietrich two of its motors.

In April, Drouhin flew the *Paris–Amérique Latine* from Le Bourget to St. Raphael in the south of France, where, to satisfy the government, the plane was fitted with floats. Drouhin then successfully conducted full-load takeoffs at a lagoon near Marseilles before delivering the craft to de Saint-Roman. There were concerns about de Saint-Roman's experience and judgment. The former infantry officer had only one fifth the number of hours in the air of his young navigator, Commander Hervé Mouneyres. When de Saint-Roman damaged the plane's pontoons while attempting to take off from Casablanca to Senegal, he decided to put the original wheels back on the Farman and fly it as a land plane. Upon hearing of this, the government revoked the plane's certificate of airworthiness and tried to quash the flight, causing a mechanic and a journalist to leave the expedition. Defections and official rebukes did not bother de Saint-Roman, who added a mechanic named Louis Petit to the crew. "If I succeed there can be no complaint," de Saint-Roman said. "If I fail a reprimand will never reach me." In the midst of the controversy, Drouhin announced that Mouneyres would be his navigator when the *Blue Bird* left for New York, a departure now pushed back to June at the earliest.

The *Paris–Amérique Latine* left St. Louis in fine weather on the morning of May 5. Radio transmissions were picked up until 11:35 a.m.—and then there was silence. By the following morning the plane was several hours overdue. There had been an unconfirmed sighting of the craft within two hundred miles of Brazil, but nothing more. Vessels passing through the area where the plane may have gone down found no sign of the plane or the crew. The Cape Verde Islands, south of the starting point, were searched, as were islands off the Brazilian coast. Some thought the French government dragged its feet in trying to find the recalcitrant Captain de Saint-Roman. According to a high official in the Foreign Office in Rio de Janeiro, the government of Brazil had "taken no measures to search for the aviators because, since the flight was made against its wishes, the French authorities had made no such request."

An Associated Press reporter filed that dispatch on May 10. By then attention was centered on the disappearance of another French plane over the vast, gray stretches of the Atlantic.

12

A Stout Heart Does
Not Fear Death

"Now, I talked to you about winning this thing, Charlie, and I'm sure
you will. But have I talked to you about losing? Have you thought
about what will happen if you fail?"

"I'll be dead.". . .

"You may be. You may be." Tuttle brushed it aside with a sweep of
his palm. "But what about if you come down just outside New York, say.
Ten miles out, and some trawler picks you up. You're all right but the
plane's gone and you don't get the prize. What then?"

Halifax shrugged. "The impact, Will. I doubt—"

"*If.* I said if. Play the game with me, Charlie. If you lose the race,
people are going to put as much energy into forgetting about you as
they'll put into remembering you if you win."

—Paul Watkins, *In the Blue Light of African Dreams*

Charles Nungesser was untroubled by the series of catastrophes suffered by his American rivals or by the disappearance of the *Paris–
Amérique Latine*. His supreme self-confidence was buttressed by a strong
belief in the capabilities of his plane and his flying companion, as well as
an unshakable conviction in his own good luck. He felt he owed the latter
to the macabre personal insignia that had decorated all of his aircraft

149

since during the war and now adorned the fuselage of the *White Bird*: a
skull and crossbones, a coffin, and a pair of candles, all arranged within
the borders of a black heart. Nungesser explained the symbolism to an
inquiring reporter. "A stout heart," he said, "has no fear of even the most
hideous aspects of death."

Over the objections of Levasseur's chief engineer, Nungesser eschewed
a radio for the *White Bird*, preferring to carry its equivalent weight in fuel
to increase the plane's range. "My dear Farret," he said, "I'm thinking of
flying to New York, not of saving my skin. You fly with petrol, not with
wireless sets." The only communication would be a crude electric signal
fitted to the bottom of the fuselage: an automobile lamp that throughout the flight would flash the Morse code signal for the letter "N."
Lighthouses and sea vessels would be advised of the plane's departure
and asked to pass on word of any sightings.

As the *White Bird* continued to be fine-tuned in early May, meteorological matters took center stage. All ocean fliers knew that when
it came to predicting the weather and plotting a course based on the
forecast, there were no guarantees. There were no real-time data, and the

François Coli and Charles Nungesser
stand inside the cockpit of the *Oiseau
Blanc* (the *White Bird*). Nungesser's
mocking death's-head symbol adorns
the fuselage.

information available was typically incomplete or outdated. The French had long envisaged an organized national weather bureau that would maintain boats stationed between Ireland and Newfoundland, but lack of funding made such a system unattainable. The best forecasters could do on either side of the Atlantic was offer an educated prognosis based on historical patterns and scattered observations.

Théophile Moreux, director of the respected Bourges Observatory, gave his predictions on the probable weather awaiting any French attempt. In Moreux's view, May historically was "one of the most disturbed months of the year," and an early drift of icebergs indicated a "troubled period" ahead. Generally speaking, the end of June was much better, though he admitted "even then one would not know whether or not to throw one's self into the adventure." Statistics from the National Weather Bureau indicated that for the period of April through June, fliers leaving Paris had only a 22 percent chance of encountering calm or favorable winds. *Le Matin* stressed that "pilots absolutely cannot use one drop of petrol fighting against the wind or to take the slightest detour because of the weather." As Nungesser and Coli continued to be "occupied by a million and one details," the paper's meteorologist, Gabriel Guilbert, described what would constitute the "right moment" for the crossing.

First of all, there should be an area of high pressure over northwestern Europe, Iceland, the English Channel, and as much as possible across the breadth of Ireland. This is an essential condition. There must also be good weather and favorable winds from the east for the departure. Because of its load of fuel, the plane will be very heavy on take-off, and it will be impossible for the pilot to get high enough to find favorable winds. He will have to navigate with surface winds, thus they must be favorable to him. He should never count on continuous east winds for his whole trip to America. That would be unprecedented luck. The largest area of high pressure, if it predominates, from Iceland to Ireland and over the Channel, will barely cover half the ocean. Beyond the high pressure system, the low pressure system will reclaim its rights, and the pilot should expect rain and fairly violent, swirling surface winds. But the closer he gets to his goal, the lighter his plane will become, which will allow him to gain altitude. This is the real way to deal with storms. Climb, climb, and climb again ever higher.

Neither Nungesser nor Coli filed an entry for the Orteig Prize. Officially, they were attempting to break the distance record owned by Costés and Rignot. "Both of them, bravest of the brave, are making their attempt simply for the glory of French wings," Le Figaro said of the White Bird's crew. Glory and adventure aside, these middle-aged pilots with creaky joints and few assets naturally intended to exploit a successful flight. Their supporters included men of means and influence, such as General Adolphe Girod, chairman of the French cabinet's Army Committee and head of an ad hoc committee of sportsmen assisting the expedition; Pierre Levasseur, who made an outright gift of the White Bird (valued at $54,000 or 1.35 million francs) to the airmen; and Jean Sapene, who in addition to being the hands-on director of Le Matin also was the most important film figure in Europe. Sapéne's credo as head of Pathé-Cineromans—where he had made his young wife into a screen star—was Vaincre ou mourir (Conquer or die). Nungesser and Coli knew there was a world of opportunities out there for conquering heroes. But first the pilots had to cross the Atlantic before anybody else.

They kept close tabs on developments on Long Island, where the crew of the Columbia was said to have practically wrapped up its tests and now waited only on favorable weather before getting under way. The Americans seemed unconcerned, unhurried. Maurice Drouhin, for one, couldn't understand their attitude. "If I were trying to fly from New York to Paris," he said on Monday, May 2, "I would have left by now." Nungesser did his best not to feel rushed. "It is impossible to say when Coli and I will leave," he said on May 3, the day a large crowd gathered at Villacoublay as the White Bird made a round trip to Chartres. "The tests are not completely finished, and nothing obliges us to hurry them." He stressed that the "smallest negligence, the smallest fault, the smallest impatience, can cause everything to fail." It was a prescient observation. In the wee hours of May 4, the White Bird narrowly avoided being destroyed inside its hangar when the bulb in an overhead lamp fell to the floor and broke, igniting several tins of gasoline. Alert mechanics doused the fire, but not before it had scorched the underside of the wing.

As the damaged fabric was replaced, news reports indicated that a Columbia flight was imminent. U.S. military attachés in Paris had completed all preparations to assist the American fliers, including agreements by the French to light up airfields and the Paris-to-London airway. The brand-new beacon at Mont Valérien outside Paris—its billion-candlepower beam so powerful it could be picked up more than a hundred miles away—also would be switched on to assist the American airmen. Welcoming committees of high officials had been organized, with the president of the International League of Aviators declaring he would fly midway out over the ocean to greet and then guide the *Columbia* into Paris. However, on Thursday, May 5, a storm over the Atlantic caused the Bellanca team to postpone departure indefinitely. Both camps now seemed resigned to waiting until the week of May 14–20, when a full moon and improved meteorological conditions were forecast.

Nungesser and Coli spent much of Thursday and Friday in the air, going over every control and instrument. The compass was swung, and a wheeled undercarriage strong enough to handle the plane's final five-ton load was attached. The Frenchmen appeared fit, confident, and anxious. There was a palpable mood of expectation in the air, with a steady stream of Parisians making the pilgrimage to the airfield. On Saturday, May 7, *Le Matin* predicted that an area of low pressure over the ocean would keep all attempts grounded for several days. But early that evening, Coli met with the head of the National Weather Bureau and got unexpected news. Conditions were "excessively favorable," the director said: a tailwind for the first 1,200 or so miles, a stretch of bad weather upon approaching Nova Scotia, but then apparently agreeable conditions afterward. "It seems to me that you won't find the same atmospheric conditions for some time to come. Now it's up to you to decide."

Coli didn't hesitate. "I will take the responsibility for our departure," he said, just as Nungesser arrived.

"We're leaving," Coli told him.

Nungesser took a moment to digest the news. "Is everything ready?" he asked. "Is everything prepared? Have you absolutely made up your mind?"

"Yes."

"Okay, then it's agreed." The two airmen stood there for a long while, warmly shaking hands. *La grande exploit* had begun.

To great cheers from onlookers at Villacoublay, they flew the *White Bird* to Le Bourget, chosen for its longer two-mile runway. Over the next several hours, as a light rain fell and occasional flashes of lightning illuminated the sky, the men oversaw final preparations, squeezed in a nap, and had a massage. Nungesser received a caffeine injection. Before donning their bright yellow leather flying togs, the men emptied their pockets of all miscellaneous and nonessential items. This included coins and paper money. Nungesser hesitated over his pocket comb. "I'll take it after all," he decided, sliding it into a gusset in his suit.

Dawn was approaching. It was Sunday, May 8. The rain had stopped, but some thunder and lightning continued in the distance. Farewells were said inside the hangar as soldiers kept the growing crowd at bay. André Bellot, an intimate friend who had to leave early to prepare one of the four chase planes, could barely speak. "Come, my friend," Coli said, comforting the man. "Don't worry." Bellot then gave Nungesser "a brotherly kiss on each cheek, while two hands squeezed his arms, as if with this embrace the friend wanted to transmit to him his enormous desire for Nungesser's victory," said an observer of the emotional scene. Soon the pilots got into the backseat of an open car to be driven out to "the crate," as the *White Bird*, rolled out of its hangar and parked on the damp field, was jocularly called. There were shouts of *"Vive Nungesser!," "Vive Coli!,"* and *"Vive la France!"* A young lady threw a rose. Nungesser caught it and blew her a kiss.

Throughout the warm night, several thousand people had descended on Le Bourget: friends, celebrities, midnight revelers, and ordinary folks. Notables included entertainers Maurice Chevalier and Mistinguett, prizefighter Georges Carpentier, and playwright Tristan Bernard, but only two ministers—a comment, perhaps, on the government's view of their chances. As always, the spectators included a small number of *seaux d'ordures* (garbage pails), sensation-seekers who were more interested in the pyrotechnics of a fiery crash than the quiet heroism of a successful takeoff. There was a good chance that they wouldn't be disappointed. The *White Bird* was carrying its complement of 880 gallons of high-octane aviation fuel for the first time. During the past few days Nungesser had decided against practicing takeoffs with a full load, figuring he needed to be successful only once. Either the plane would get off the ground or it wouldn't. "It's no use challenging the gods," he said.

Coli was embraced by his wife. Tears rolled down her cheeks. There was a flurry of last-minute handshakes; then the pilots climbed a ladder and settled into their cramped positions inside the cockpit. The powerful Lorraine-Dietrich engine roared to life. "The moment was absolutely gripping," Frantz Reichel wrote in *Le Figaro*. "Everyone was quiet, faces

A last view from a chase plane of the *White Bird* as it heads for the English Channel on May 8, 1927. It has already dropped its temporary wheel carriage somewhere over the French countryside.

anxious. Nungesser accelerated little by little, gave a last wave, then returned his hand to the plane. The *White Bird* shook, taxied slowly, then accelerated second by second and as she passed by we all took off our hats. She tested the air once, twice, she went faster and faster. And suddenly she took off! It was 5:21. The silence was immediately broken. Cheers erupted, rising with the magnificent plane."

Nungesser expertly threaded the low-flying plane through the hilly countryside, dropping the temporary wheel carriage over a field along the way. Pierre Carniaux, Levasseur's chief test pilot, was in one of the escorts that accompanied the *White Bird* as far as the English Channel. The *White Bird*, moving at a clip of about 105 miles an hour, cleared the French coast at Étretat at 6:48 a.m. Then the aircraft was "lost to view," observed Carniaux, "far away between the water and the sky."

News of Nungesser's departure caught the *Columbia* camp by surprise. "Well, we wish him the best of luck and hope he is successful in his flight," said Giuseppe Bellanca, who added that they would "do nothing until we see whether Nungesser gets here safely." Clarence Chamberlin was skeptical of the Frenchmen's chances, saying, "I don't see how Nungesser can make it." He was referring to a revised weather report whose disturbing forecast included icy rain, snow squalls, and twenty-five-mile-per-hour headwinds off Newfoundland.

In San Diego, Charles Lindbergh had just finished a week's worth of load tests at Camp Kearney, an abandoned army post. He was waiting on a break in the weather before heading east, but word that the *White Bird* had left Paris caused him to study charts he had assembled for a possible Pacific flight. "That's the first time a plane loaded for the New York–Paris flight has actually taken off the ground," he thought. "Nungesser and Coli are in the air with full tanks. They're experienced men. They should land in New York tomorrow."

Monday, May 9, dawned in France with no word of Nungesser and Coli. This was not unexpected. Barring a sighting from a ship at sea, the *White Bird* would be cut off from the rest of the world for the twenty or so hours needed to bridge the coasts of Ireland and Newfoundland. The religious lit candles and said prayers. Those who trusted technology talked up the soundness of the plane and the engine. Whether one put their faith in a divinity or the gods of science, the human part of the equation was the most gripping. "What is happening out there?" one Paris-based correspondent wondered. "They cannot change position. In their little cockpit they cannot stand up, they cannot move more than a few inches to obtain relief for cramped limb or aching nerve. On and on—that is all they may think of, all they can feel."

Throughout France, people guardedly discussed the fliers' chances. Could they possibly make it? Crowds formed outside newspaper offices, awaiting the latest update. Newspapers were an extremely competitive business in Paris, which reputedly had more publishers per capita than anywhere else in the world. It was said that the typical Parisian bought three to five papers on a normal day, a number that could easily double on an occasion such as this. *Le Petit Parisien* was among the most widely read. On its front page, Maurice Prax, the son and grandson of French generals, wrote of the fliers' special type of valor as they flew somewhere over the rolling Atlantic.

> We have new fashions, new customs, new manias, and we also have a new kind of courage, an entirely modern and special

courage. This courage is sporting courage ... sometimes a little slovenly, sometimes a little careless, with its own slang and grease stains. But it's a tough courage. Do we really understand that the attempt to cross the Atlantic represents this kind of courage— the new sporting and mechanical courage? What kind of hearts must the men who left have? What hearts! What souls and what cold and clear will! They did not boast, get carried away or dragged along. They are not surrounded by that collective enthusiasm, that animated passion, which at certain times whips up crowds and nations. They are alone, they are separate from other men.

It was about 11 a.m. in New York when the first unconfirmed sightings of the *White Bird* began coming in. Reports said it had been spotted by a U.S. destroyer at 9 a.m. over St. Pierre-Miquelon, a group of small islands southwest of Newfoundland, and then at 10:10 off Cape Race, Newfoundland. As the plane continued its journey down the North American coastline, the sightings multiplied. At 2:53 p.m., the Boston Navy Yard reported that the *White Bird* had passed Portland, Maine, "headed south and flying very fast." Ten minutes later the Navy Yard at Portsmouth, New Hampshire, issued a bulletin: "Nungesser sighted off the Isle of Shoals."

Before leaving, Nungesser had stated his intention to land in New York Harbor between the Statue of Liberty and Pier 57 of the French Line. Plans to greet the incoming fliers had been hastily arranged. A welcoming committee included Richard Byrd, Leigh Wade, Homer Berry, Mayor Walker, and Robert Nungesser, the flier's brother, who worked as a tinsmith in Washington, D.C. They were aboard the mayor's flag-bedecked yacht. A suite was reserved on the French liner *De Grasse* for the official reception. It was a rainy, foggy day. Clarence Chamberlin and Lloyd Bertaud were among those waiting to fly out into the mist and escort the *White Bird* in. "You've got to hand it to those Frenchmen," said Bertaud. "They're real men and fliers."

Parisians were waiting to uncork their bottled-up emotions. Inside the offices of *La Presse* on Rue Montmartre, editors of the afternoon paper were poised to run with a story based on the *White Bird*'s stated itinerary and employing the kind of "creative license" common to journalism of the era. Sometime between five and six o'clock, based on what the publisher later insisted was information "from a usually reliable source," *La Presse* gave the antsy public the news it had been waiting for. Its headline roared, *L'ATLANTIQUE EST CONQUIS!*

The Atlantic had been conquered! Nungesser and Coli had succeeded, and suddenly it was hard to find anyone in the cheering mobs who would admit to ever doubting the airmen's chances. At such a moment, nobody would dispute that these were indeed "the golden hours of French aviation," as *La Presse* proclaimed. *L'Intransigeant*, *Paris-Soir*, and other evening papers followed *La Presse*'s lead, rushing *éditions spéciales* into the hands of readers. "The two pilots reached New York Harbor," *La Liberté* announced. "Flying over the port and landing on the water without incident to the acclamations of the crowd." There was a feel-good authenticity to the story of the *White Bird*'s splashdown, a narrative readers wanted to believe. "Then they both rose out of their seats and embraced," *La Presse* reported. "A motor boat pulled up alongside the fuselage of the plane and led Nungesser and Coli to shore. A huge crowd awaited them. . . . Nungesser did not make any statement on his voyage; he simply said that he was happy to have succeeded and that he was in a hurry to rest." There was no mention of tears streaming down Miss Liberty's patina face, but that seems merely an oversight by the chain-smoking wordsmiths banging away at typewriters inside newsrooms thousands of miles from the fraternal tableaux they were artfully describing.

The reactions of the fliers' mothers were reported. "Luck has always been with my son," said Mme. Nungesser, reached at her top-floor flat on the Boulevard du Temple. In Marseilles, Mme. Coli said, "I knew my son would make it because he told me he would. He's been in many tight spots in his career and always he has come out safely." Levasseur officials sent a congratulatory telegram to the airmen, care of the French consul in New York, expressing "indescribable joy and profound admiration" over their feat.

Celebrations broke out in Le Havre, Marseilles, Lyon, and Bordeaux, but nothing on the scale of Paris. Many thought it the greatest spontaneous merrymaking since the Armistice. "I knew Nungesser could do it," exclaimed one veteran who wore his old medals for the occasion. "I served with him during the war. That was a fellow, I can tell you!" Bill Shirer, who had interviewed the heroes of the moment at Le Bourget, waded into the happy, champagne-guzzling throngs. "Parisians snake-danced through the streets," he remembered. "Offices and stores shut down. I joined in the celebration. To have watched those two brave

Parisians gather outside the offices of *Le Matin*, anxious for the latest word of Nungesser and Coli.

Frenchmen set off so confidently on so hazardous a flight and then to know they had succeeded filled you with pride in men."

Paris-American newspapers were noticeably restrained—not because of jealousy over France apparently winning the transatlantic derby, but because there still was no reliable, independent verification of what a nation full of celebrants believed to be true. At the offices of the *Herald* on the Avenue de l'Opéra, an employee put up a notice in the street-front window where it normally posted news bulletins: "The *Herald* has no confirmation of the arrival of Nungesser and Coli in America."

"That did it," managing editor Eric Hawkins later wrote. "Elderly gentlemen began brandishing canes, men in blue berets shook their fists in our direction." As the situation threatened to escalate, police were called to the scene. Hawkins explained the paper's position to a police official, who listened skeptically. "But really, monsieur, all Paris knows about it," he said. "Can't you just put up a notice that your cables have been delayed?" It wasn't until the *Herald*'s advertising manager addressed the crowd in fluent French that passions finally subsided outside the paper's office.

13

Limbo

Since this imperious thing exists
That desires that we should go into the skies
France is the country of mothers with sad eyes

—Edmond Rostand, "Le Cantique de l'Aile" (The Song of the Wing)

Robert Nungesser stood on a New York pier and peered into the grainy distance, unwilling to believe that the bulky white biplane carrying his brother and Captain Coli would not at any moment suddenly break into view. It was eight o'clock on Monday night, May 9, and the *White Bird* still had not arrived. The tugs carrying scores of newsmen and photographers had left, as had the flotilla of pleasure craft and the small air armada that had circled for hours overhead. Among the group sharing Nungesser's somber vigil were a couple of members of the prize committee and two of Raymond Orteig's sons. The prize donor was not among them; he was on vacation with his wife when the *White Bird* unexpectedly left Le Bourget.

It was well past midnight in France, where bulletins that the *White Bird* had *not* landed in New York—that it was, in fact, dangerously overdue and that the fate of its crew was unknown—had been met with incredulity and then outrage. Thousands protested outside Paris newspaper offices, claiming a deliberate fraud had been foisted on them. Papers were piled and burned. People lashed out at publishers, at the government, at the United States.

There were conflicting accounts on Tuesday regarding the size and intensity of anti-American fervor. Reportedly some rowdies in a large crowd that had gathered outside *Le Matin*'s offices demanded that an American flag be torn down, but newspaper officials denied the incident. Rumors circulated accusing the United States of providing false weather information to lure the French pilots to their doom. Ambassador Herrick, recognizing that "we were in one of those periods of petulant nagging and quarreling between the French and ourselves which have flared up and died down more than once since the Armistice," cabled the U.S. State Department in Washington, warning against antagonizing the French by sending an American plane their way. That same day a telegram from the Paris chapter of the NAA was forwarded to Carl Schory, who was due to arrive on Long Island to officially seal the barometers of any departing plane. It read: DUE TO DEPTH OF FRENCH FEELING OVER LOSS OF NUNGESSER AND COLI STRONGLY ADVISE AGAINST ANY AMERICAN TRANSATLANTIC FLIGHT UNTIL FRENCH FLYERS HAVE BEEN ACCOUNTED FOR AND SUITABLE PERIOD ELAPSED.

Richard Byrd, whose damaged Fokker was almost ready to return to the race, said his thoughts were with the missing fliers, not a Paris flight. However, Charlie Levine said his plans would not be affected. Last-minute preparations continued on the *Columbia*. Wright field service engineer Ken "Spoons" Boedecker gave the Whirlwind a thorough going-over, checking valve clearances, replacing the spark plugs, and declaring the engine fit for flight. "Other mechanics went over every joint in the steel-tubed frame of the fuselage and every spar of the struts and wings," the *New York Times* reported. "Every square inch of the fabric covering the wings and fuselage and the stabilizer, elevators and rudder were examined for the most minute flaws." The original brass-tipped wooden propeller was replaced with a duraluminum airscrew, and the wheels were painted red, white, and blue. Only bad weather, not French public opinion, would keep the Bellanca grounded.

Meanwhile, debate raged inside and outside the Chamber of Deputies. Maurice Bokanowski, the air minister, absolved the French government of all blame in the sequence of false sightings and unsubstantiated reports that he called "a phenomenon of collective illusion." It was "not surprising that in the fog, generous hearts mistook their hopes for reality." The defense minister specified that the military was not involved in the flight's preparations, had been skeptical of the reports of its success, and could not be held accountable for events. The director of the National Weather Bureau took responsibility for the meteorological data that had informed the fliers' decision-making, but ultimately it was up to Nungesser and Coli as to whether they should stay or go. Nobody dared criticize the fliers directly, though Théophile Moreux of the Bourges Observatory, who had earlier warned about May's volatile weather, would later describe their decision to leave as "very poorly chosen."

Many felt that a distorted sense of nationalism was at the root of the tragedy. The cranky Marxist deputy Paul Vaillant-Couturier published a page-one rant in *L'Humanité*. "Taking the perpetual brainwashers at their word, Paris spent the whole day delirious with joy over a victory trumpeted by the bourgeois press, only to learn at about 11 o'clock last night that in fact that there was no news of Nungesser and Coli," he wrote.

"A National Victory" cried yesterday's press, like a flock of stupid, conceited chickens. Stupidity! The airplane, cinema, radio, all this incredible machinery arising from capitalism, the machinery of speed, repudiates the motherland. And it is absurd to try and confine an exploit, which at once enlarges humanity and makes the world smaller, to pride of ownership or to the narrow ledger of national borders, like a monstrous pumpkin or a giant prize-winning beetroot.

General Henri Duval was a close friend of the fliers. "These men died for nothing," he angrily declared on the front page of *Le Figaro*. "What they tried to do is neither good for sport nor does it serve in any way the progress of aviation." Duval continued, "That the crowds of two continents should be passionately roused into a fever of excitement by the possibility of whether the airman is to succeed and live, or fail and die, is both immoral and shameful. Every sport takes into account the possibility and risk of accident. But that the death of brave men is the almost inevitable consequence of failure is a barbarian competition of sport which takes us back to the days of the gladiators."

The German press, while expressing proper concern, found it hard to suppress their self-admiration. Throughout the Orteig Prize competition the Germans regularly dropped reminders that they had already conquered the Atlantic with the crossing of the *ZR-3* in 1924 and were making great progress on a Berlin-to-New York flight with their own long-range aircraft. "This case was not about a simple sporting exploit, but the French wanted to prove that the plane is at least equal to the Zeppelin for transatlantic flights, and perhaps even better because of its speed," said *Tägliche Rundschau*. "However, the Zeppelin will remain the most appropriate means of aerial transport for flights over such significant distances for a long time to come."

The scope of America's generosity and the sincerity of its grief heartened France. President Coolidge immediately ordered navy and coast guard vessels to conduct far-ranging searches, while philanthropists Rodman Wanamaker and Daniel Guggenheim soon offered separate $25,000 rewards for the recovery of the crew, dead or alive. But where to look? It seemed most likely that the plane went down between midocean and the coast of Newfoundland, but also it was possible it had survived the icy rain and high winds only to crash in the wilds of Maine or Canada. Just before leaving, Coli received the latest weather bulletin and told Pierre Levasseur that the low-pressure system in the mid-Atlantic would cause them to fly slightly north of their projected course. "If I should find cloudy weather over Newfoundland," Coli said, "I'll abandon the idea of going to New York and will head for the Canadian interior. If possible, I'll head to St. Lawrence and will come into New York from the south. They'll be pretty surprised, since they'll expect me to arrive on the other side. If that's also impossible, I'll land on one of the great lakes. So don't worry, you might not have news of us for several weeks." The pilots had brought along two weeks' worth of provisions, including cognac, bananas, caviar, and Kola, a French food supplement. They had fishing lines and hooks and signal flares.

Another of Nungesser's brothers, Léon, who lived in France, speculated that the *White Bird* may not have gotten very far into its journey before being forced down. "I have a feeling that my brother Charles is alive," he said, "that he landed Sunday off Étretat and is still floating on the sea." Such a scenario was unlikely. The plane may have fallen into the Channel or somewhere off the Irish coast, but the weight of its fuel would have caused it to sink immediately. Even if the fliers had successfully used the dump valve before ditching, the plane would have been broken apart by a rough landing or by moderately heavy seas. There was no raft; they had decided to save weight by not bringing one.

The *White Bird* had carried enough fuel for roughly forty hours' flying time, but the storm blowing off Newfoundland would have drastically pared its projected airspeed and reduced its range. As reports came in, authorities struggled to determine which ones were credible and which ones sprang from an overactive imagination. In Newfoundland, several people claimed to have heard strange noises overhead on the morning of May 9. An old woman in Otterbury said she thought it was geese winging through the murk before recognizing it as the same sound she had heard eight years earlier when one of the *Daily Mail* competitors had flown over her village. A couple of trappers in Labrador said they heard a loud crash in the woods. Scattered reports came in from Maine. Two schooners reported seeing a plane a hundred miles northeast of Boston. The steamship *Belleplaine* spotted what appeared to be wreckage floating in the vicinity, but the debris sank before it could be retrieved. There were rumors that rum smugglers had shot down the plane. Bottled messages began to wash up. As newspaper and radio coverage continued, people who had paid scant attention to the transatlantic air derby now found themselves absorbed with the ongoing saga of Nungesser and Coli. "No wonder they never made it," said a man in Stonington, Maine. "One of them is all wired together and the other has only got one eye."

In the Chestnut Hill section of Philadelphia, a society girl named Mary Fanning Wickham Porcher composed "To Nungesser," a poem that borrowed the meter of Percy Bysshe Shelley's famous ode "To a Skylark." Porcher's widely published verse underscored the tremendous public interest in the wayward *White Bird*.

Hail to you, brave spirit!
Bird you tried to be,
Flying to heaven, or near it,
In your ecstasy.
To conquer air and leap across the sea!
But are you lost, Nungesser?
Are you still onward bound,
Aerial aggressor,
And scorner of the ground?
Oh, every heart hopes you may yet be found!

Coli left behind a mother, wife, and three daughters to agonize over his uncertain fate. Nungesser had the two principal women in his life keeping a vigil for him. One was Consuelo Hatmaker, with whom he had regularly been seen around the airfield. There had been rumors that he and his ex-wife would reconcile after he landed in New York. Normally very socially active, she would not be seen in public for almost two weeks after his disappearance. The other was Laure Nungesser, who remained optimistic about her son's return. "Just look at the miraculous escapes Charles had during the war," she said. "If he has not been able to get to New York, I am certain he and Captain Coli will be picked up safe and sound somewhere in the Atlantic. I shall pray all night, and in the morning I know I shall have good news."

In San Diego, Charles Lindbergh readied the *Spirit of St. Louis* for departure to its namesake city. It was Tuesday, May 10. His plan was a 1,550-mile shakedown flight over the Rockies that would test his and the plane's abilities. After an overnight stay in St. Louis, the second leg of his transcontinental hop would take him over the Alleghenies and on to Long Island—the starting gate for Orteig hopefuls. "Send us a wire when you get to Paris," a Ryan employee yelled at Lindbergh as he said his good-byes.

Flying entirely by compass, Lindbergh made a beeline for St. Louis, crossing Arizona, upper New Mexico, the Oklahoma panhandle, Kansas, and Missouri. At one point he took the *Spirit of St. Louis* up to 13,000 feet over the moonlit mountains. At higher altitudes the engine started missing, causing him to contemplate a forced landing, but once he had cleared the peaks and dropped to a lower altitude the coughing ceased. He figured the problem was the engine temperature, which could be corrected by having an intake heater installed when he got to New York.

On Wednesday morning, fourteen hours and twenty-five minutes after leaving California, Lindbergh touched down at Lambert Field. This was a record time, but as the hungry pilot made his way with friends to Louie's Shack for breakfast, he was more interested in the latest developments in the transatlantic race. Was there any news of Nungesser and Coli? Had the Bellanca taken off yet? He was told of the admonition to American fliers not to start for Paris. It was just a warning, though, not a government edict. "What do you think you'll do, Slim?" someone asked.

Lindbergh wasn't sure. "I'll go through to New York at least," he said. "If Nungesser and Coli are lost, it seems to me it's up to the rest of us to carry on what they attempted."

As Lindbergh dug into his eggs and ham, some of his financial backers dropped in to talk about the plane, the flight from San Diego, and several upcoming dinner invitations and official dedication ceremonies. Lindbergh, afraid of the Bellanca getting the jump on him, asked if he could continue on to New York as quickly as possible.

Harry Knight understood. "It's going to disappoint a lot of people," he said, "but you're right. Now that we're really in the running, we're not going to let a couple of dinners hold us down." Lindbergh spent the evening at Knight's house. By eight-fifteen the following morning he was back in the air, winging toward Long Island. It was Thursday, May 12. A low-pressure system east of New York was keeping the Bellanca grounded, but for how long? If Lindbergh knew how deeply superstitious Charlie Levine was, he would have realized that there was no way the *Columbia* would take off for Paris on Friday, the thirteenth.

At Curtiss Field, Lindbergh's destination, the wives of the *Columbia*'s crew reacted to one newspaper's recommendation that all New York–Paris flights be permanently banned. "I think it is just horrid to suggest such a thing," Helen Bertaud said. Wylda Chamberlin nodded in approval. "I wouldn't love my husband if he didn't make the attempt," said Wylda, who didn't mention that Clarence's lucky number had always been thirteen.

Dueling superstitions were the least of the problems in the discordant Bellanca camp. A major point of contention was whether or not a radio should be carried on the flight. Lloyd Bertaud and Levine favored a wireless for safety reasons; the plane would automatically transmit an intermittent signal to ships at sea. If the signals stopped, nearby vessels could proceed to the area of the presumed crash. However, because of the radio's 125-mile range, the *Columbia* would have to follow a course close to the shipping lanes, south of the shorter Great Circle course that Chamberlin preferred. Giuseppe Bellanca was fiercely opposed to having a radio on board. It meant a longer flight and less margin for error, particularly since the radio's generator, which was attached to the strut, would trim five miles an hour off the plane's airspeed and affect the plane's unique lift capabilities. As the debate continued, the apparatus was installed and removed several times, causing technicians to swear under their breath. Levine was unhappy as well, since with each change of heart the compasses had to be compensated all over again, an expensive procedure. The final compromise was for the

Charlie Levine (center) flanked by Lloyd Bertaud (left) and Clarence Chamberlin.

plane to carry a small battery-powered set that could send distress calls 25 miles.

Although Chamberlin and Bertaud didn't agree on many issues—most notably the radio and Bertaud's plotting of a southern course—they shared legitimate concerns. One was the absence of life insurance for their families should they die during the flight. Rodman Wanamaker was providing insurance for the crew of the *America*. Why not Levine? The answer, of course, was money. The premiums on a pair of $50,000 policies for ocean fliers would be somewhere in the low five figures. Then there was the unresolved matter of compensation. The pilots were risking their necks, yet Levine stood to garner most of the financial rewards. Levine and Bertaud butted heads when each separately approached the North American Newspaper Alliance about purchasing the exclusive rights to the flight's story, a battle Levine won. "Mr. Levine's insistence upon having whoever made the flight under his 'management' amounted almost to a passion," Chamberlin would later write, "and might be compared to the ambition of a man who 'discovers' a fighter to have the credit of developing him into a world champion." Unlike Bertaud, Chamberlin was willing to swallow a lot of guff in order to make the flight. Fresh in his mind was the memory of approaching the *Chicago Tribune* in 1924, and again in 1925, for $10,000 to underwrite his and Bellanca's dream of capturing the Orteig Prize, only to be rejected as a crackbrain each time. "No one had listened to me in the past and I wasn't going to let slip an opportunity to vindicate myself and the plane," he explained. "I wanted to be able to say 'I told you so,' to those who had refused to finance me when they had a chance."

Amid the ceaseless bickering, the *Columbia*'s owner seemed to be enjoying his elevated profile among the reporters, photographers, and spectators swarming the flying fields in early May. Levine—described as "this drab little man" by the *Boston Post*—began showing up with a seductive thirty-two-year-old socialite named Mabel Boll at his side. Boll, a saloonkeeper's daughter and a former showgirl, was addicted to melodrama, much of it self-produced. The short and slender dark-eyed blonde married at least four times during her lifetime (there were rumors of a fifth husband), her charms once causing a much younger (and poorer) admirer to shoot himself in the garden of her French villa because of unrequited love. Dripping with as much as $400,000 worth of jewelry, including a 46.6-carat emerald-cut diamond given to her by her second husband, a Columbian coffee mogul, she told the press, "There is no pleasure in the world comparable to the possession of diamonds." Boll refused to say whether any of the gems were gifts from Levine. However, the "Queen of Diamonds" did admit to a burning desire to fly the ocean to Paris, the site of three of her weddings.

Soaring high above the dissonance and the conceit was the *Spirit of St. Louis*, which on Thursday afternoon gracefully circled Curtiss Field after completing the second stage of its record hop across the United States. "It swooped lower and lower," a correspondent wrote, "and finally came to a perfect landing and taxied across the grass. Spectators rushed to it from all sides. A window opened and the smiling face of a man who seemed little more than a boy appeared. His pink cheeks, dancing eyes and merry grin seemed to say: 'Hello, folks. Here I am and all ready to go.'"

14

Hunting Dragons

Charles was not born just anywhere, he was born on this planet. He knows why he is in the world and why the world is there. He has no concept of death: his blood is too strong.

—A. J.-M. Franck, "Lindbergh et Ma Vie" (Lindbergh and My Life)

Charles Lindbergh was accustomed to flying in and out of bad weather, but the storm he encountered at Curtiss Field on May 12 was like nothing he had ever experienced. He landed at 5:33 p.m. local time, having flown from San Diego to New York in two hops in an elapsed time of twenty-one hours and twenty minutes, shattering the old transcontinental mark by five and a half hours. He barely had a chance to climb out of the *Spirit of St. Louis* before he was surrounded by a mob of aggressive reporters and photographers, all demanding a posed smile or a quote. "Look this way, will ya!" "Shake hands with somebody!" "Say something!"

In the midst of the clamor somebody yelled, "Look! There's the *America*." Overhead, Bernt Balchen was delivering Richard Byrd's giant three-engine craft from the Fokker factory in New Jersey, where it had undergone two weeks of repairs, to the plane's hangar at Roosevelt Field. The nearly simultaneous arrival of Byrd's plane and the previously unheralded Lindbergh injected fresh excitement into the Orteig sweepstakes. Suddenly it was a three-cornered race among Byrd, Clarence Chamberlin in the *Columbia*, and the dark horse the press dubbed the "Kid Flyer." "What promises to be the most spectacular race ever held—3,600 miles over open sea to Paris—may start tomorrow," the *New York Times* declared on Friday. "Three transatlantic planes are on Curtiss and Roosevelt fields, within a short distance of each other, ready to take to the air."

As Lindbergh got his plane settled into a hangar, Clarence Chamberlin made a neighborly visit to size up his new competitor. Photographers shouted for the obligatory "grip-and-grin," and the two pilots self-consciously shook hands. "May the best man win!" someone in the crowd shouted.

"I guess that goes both ways," Lindbergh said, smiling.

"You bet it does," responded Chamberlin.

Inside the Bellanca hangar, workmen were seeing to a rush of last-minute details. It was expected that the *Columbia* would be the first to get under way, quite likely on Saturday morning, May 14. On Friday evening, Chamberlin and Lloyd Bertaud were preoccupied with their preparations when Charlie Levine approached them. In his hand were contracts, freshly drawn up by his lawyer, that outlined the pilots' compensation. Each man was to receive $150 a week for a year from the date of the flight, during which time Levine would act as their "manager." In that capacity he would determine which vaudeville, motion picture, and other commercial opportunities the pilots would pursue. He would collect all revenue and issue "bonuses" as he saw fit. Levine also was to get half of all the prize money from the flight, including newspaper rights and the hefty cash awards offered by various manufacturers for the use of their products. There were no provisions for life insurance for the fliers' families.

"You can sign it or not, just as you please," Levine said, "but if you don't sign, you don't fly."

Levine was "a shrewd psychologist," Chamberlin admitted. "We were a pair of pilots on the brink of our greatest adventure, our minds occupied with a thousand and one details which might mean the difference between success and failure. What was to happen to us during the next year seemed of little consequence; our chief concern was for the next forty-eight hours." After discussing the matter privately, the pilots signed, with the thought that they would decide later whether to actually go through with its provisions. "No one could cheat us then of being the first to fly without a stop from New York to Paris," Chamberlin reasoned. "Not very ethical, perhaps, but amply justified by the circumstances. My

motto then, and always, was: 'Fly first and fight afterward—if necessary.'"
However, bad weather kept the *Columbia* grounded—a delay that gave
Bertaud time to stew over Levine's power play.

Lindbergh meanwhile spent his first full day on the ground getting
acquainted with the various technical representatives assigned to his
plane while also trying to satisfy the incessant demands of cameramen
and the public. The Wright Aeronautical Corporation had hired two
public relations professionals, Dick Blythe and Harry Bruno, to assist
him, and they did their best to keep the distractions at bay. It was difficult, for the "handsome and smiling young Westerner" in his "odd plane"
was "easily the favorite of the crowd," observed the *Brooklyn Eagle*. "It is
safe to say that all of the 10,000 visitors at the field sought him out, but
this likable young man is shy and spent most of his day resting at the
Garden City Hotel. Lindbergh revealed, however, that he is perfectly
willing for bad weather to postpone his start until his mother arrives here
from Detroit to see him off."

Reporters had tracked down Evangeline Lindbergh in Detroit and were
harassing her at home and at school. They emphasized the dangerous
aspects of her son's "suicidal" flight to the point that on Friday she caught
an overnight train to Garden City to have her suddenly magnified concerns
smoothed over in person. Once on Long Island, mother and son were sub-
jected to a fresh barrage of popping flashbulbs and inane questions.

"Was your son a good boy?" one reporter asked.

"Just look at him," she replied.

"Kiss him, so we can get a good-bye picture," demanded a photog-
rapher at the train station as the Lindberghs wrapped up their brief
reunion. She refused. "I wouldn't mind if we were used to that," she said,
"but we come of an undemonstrative Nordic race."

The following day the *Graphic*, which had once famously published a
photograph of screen idol Rudolph Valentino being greeted into heaven
by Italian tenor Enrico Caruso, gave its readers a scenario nearly as
improbable: Lindbergh and his mother exchanging a buss in public. The
composite photo had been created by pasting the Lindberghs' heads on
the bodies of two posed models.

Lindbergh was galled by these and other fabrications that appeared
in print over the following days. "When I enter the cockpit," one paper
quoted him as saying, "it's like going into the death chamber. When I step
out at Paris it will be like getting a pardon from the governor." Another

Evangeline Land Lindbergh
and her aviator son, at Curtiss
Field, May 13, 1927.

paper had him exclaiming, "Boys, she's ready and rarin' to go!" as he
hopped out of his plane. "These fellows must think I'm a cowpuncher,
just transferred to aviation," he complained.

Lindbergh spent his first few days at Curtiss Field overseeing work
on his plane. A carburetor heater was installed, a cracked spinner was
replaced, and the compasses were swung. Meanwhile, the number of
visitors swelled to an estimated thirty thousand on Sunday, May 15.
Strangers, reading in the papers of how "Lucky Lindy" had survived
multiple crashes and parachute jumps, rushed up to touch him and
his plane, hoping some of his luck would rub off on them. The "mirror girl," an elusive footnote to the Lindbergh story, appeared at this
time. Part of a crowd gathered outside the roped-off hangar door, she
overheard the flier discussing with mechanics the need for a small
mirror to keep in view his new liquid magnetic compass. Because of
the lack of space, the compass had been installed on the cabin's ceiling, inches above Lindbergh's head. "It will give you a more accurate

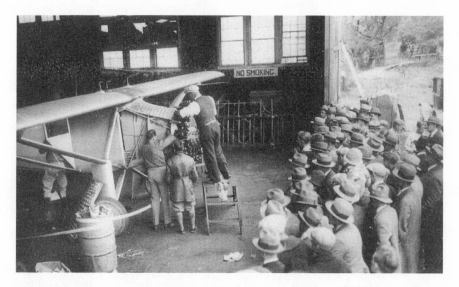

A crowd forms outside the hangar housing the *Spirit of St. Louis* as the Atlantic race heats up.

indication up there than any other place we can find," he was told. "It will swing less in rough air. You sure haven't any extra room in here."

"I don't mind reading it through a mirror," replied Lindbergh. "The most important thing is to have it accurate and steady." The men inside the hangar looked around for a suitably sized mirror. Then a young, well-groomed woman stepped forward. "Will this do?" she asked, pulling a compact mirror out of her handbag. It was about two inches round. The size was perfect. It was temporarily attached to the instrument panel with a wad of chewing gum. The mirror would remain there, reflecting Lindbergh's course all the way to Paris.

As a way of thanking the donor, the rope was lifted and she was given a look inside the cockpit. Lindbergh never learned her name and never saw her again. Many years later, he was still wondering about her intentions. "Was she among the few who maintained unreasoned confidence in my success," he wrote, "or was hers a gesture of compassion toward a man about to die?"

Sometime that summer, after the Orteig Prize had finally been won, the Bar-Zim Toy Company of New York would come out with its

New York To Paris Aero Race palm puzzle. The pocket game gave dexterous youngsters a fun opportunity to relive recent history. It featured three colored beans: red for Lindbergh, white for Chamberlin, and blue for Byrd. The idea was to start with all three "planes" in their hangars at New York and then, by adroitly jiggling the beans inside the glass-encased puzzle, land them in their corresponding hangars at Paris. According to the toymaker's instructions, "This NEW CAPTIVATING GAME can be played by several people at one time. Each player is furnished with one game. The player who lands all three planes first shouts 'PARIS' and is declared the WINNER."

If only it were that simple. In the real world, the obstacles were imposing. Getting an overloaded plane off the ground and then managing to stay airborne were formidable feats in themselves, as evidenced by the fiery takeoff of the *New York–Paris* and the fatal stall of the *American Legion*. There also was the risk of engine failure over an unprecedented distance, which may have been the cause of the *White Bird*'s disappearance. All three American contenders featured Wright engines, and success depended on them performing flawlessly. This would be the most strenuous test yet for the Whirlwind, whose cylinders would be required to make 14,472,000 explosions during the planned thirty-six-hour flight. And weather forecasting remained more guesswork than science, as evidenced by James "Doc" Kimball's response when one pilot asked him what he could expect over the Atlantic. "You want to know what the weather is going to be 4,000 miles away and 48 hours in advance?" said the head of the New York Weather Bureau. "I can't tell you for sure whether it's going to rain here tomorrow."

By Monday, May 16, Lindbergh felt that he and the *Spirit of St. Louis* were ready to go the moment conditions were reported to have improved over the Atlantic, but storms and fog stubbornly covered the path to Paris. He didn't know about his rivals' plans; the papers were filled with conflicting stories and rumors. "The newspapers have kept us on edge about it all," he grumbled, "and it's difficult to pull out any plums of fact from the hot cake of fiction that they print." After just a few days in New York, Lindbergh's relationship with the press had deteriorated along with the weather. Initially, publicity was part of his overall plan to draw attention to his flight. "It would increase my personal influence and earning capacity," he explained. "I found it exhilarating to see my name in print on the front pages of America's greatest newspapers, and I enjoyed reading the words of praise." He respected certain New York dailies, such as the *Times*, the *Post*, and the *World*, as well as the monthly *Aero Digest*, but most of the media were a distracting nuisance. Photographers tried to get him to pose with publicity-seeking actresses and once stormed into his hotel room, hoping to snap a picture of him in his pajamas. The reporters milling around his hangar or camped inside the Garden City Hotel (where all the pilots stayed) pestered him with insipid questions: "Do you carry a rabbit's foot? Do you have a girlfriend? What's your favorite kind of pie?" Their simplistic stories often portrayed him as some kind of aw-shucks hayseed or a death-defying stunt pilot (the "Flying Fool") instead of as an experienced aviator who had soberly calculated his chances and was meticulously preparing for his flight. On one occasion Lindbergh narrowly avoided striking some cameramen foolishly running toward him as he came in for a landing, damaging the *Spirit*'s tailskid in the process.

The media drumbeat grew more intense. It seemed as if all of America had become infected with what the press called "Atlantic fever" or "ocean fever." On the night of May 14, for example, several thousand people responded to rumors of an impending "surprise" departure by descending on Curtiss Field. Roads were jammed, the hangar areas were overrun, and a small metal building collapsed when a group of people climbed on its roof to catch a glimpse of the *Spirit of St. Louis*. In the chaos a spectator was hit by a car. "These have been the most extraordinary days I've ever spent," Lindbergh reflected, "and I can't call them very pleasant. Life has become too strange and hectic. The attention of the entire country is centered on the flight to Paris, and most of all on me—because I'm going alone, because I'm young, because I'm a 'dark horse.' Papers in every city and village are head-lining my name and writing articles about me. Newspaper, radio, and motion-picture publicity has brought people crowding out to Curtiss and Roosevelt Fields until the Nassau County police are faced with a major traffic problem." Harry Guggenheim was one of several aviation luminaries drawn to Curtiss Field to meet the new name in the news. While openly encouraging to Lindbergh, Guggenheim was privately dismayed that he probably would never see the promising and hand-some young flier again. "This fellow will never make it," he thought after looking inside the cockpit of the *Spirit of St. Louis*. "He's doomed."

For all of the attention lavished on Lindbergh, the favorite among many handicappers remained the *Columbia*, if only the Bellanca organization could pull its act together. The Bellanca was considered a superior plane to the Ryan, and Chamberlin was regarded as being a more experienced pilot than Lindbergh. But where Lindbergh's remarkably supportive backers never interfered with his plans and decisions, the Bellanca camp was hobbled by Charlie Levine's constant meddling and uneven temperament.

Levine sparred with Lloyd Bertaud, who decided he didn't care for the contract he had just been strong-armed into signing. As Chamberlin phrased it, Bertaud "looked on the flight promoter's plan as a pure money-making scheme with us as the cat's paws that were to fork out the chestnuts." His anger mounted when Levine publicly lied, telling newspapermen that "every nickel of the prize money" would go to the *Columbia*'s pilots.

A lengthy conference was held at the Garden City Hotel on May 15, with all parties and their lawyers trying to hash out a new agreement behind closed doors. Also attending were the president and one of the directors of the Brooklyn Chamber of Commerce. Levine, who was openly criticized, finally agreed to draw up a new contract that guaranteed the pilots all of the flight's prize money and provided insurance for their wives. But by the following day, he'd had a change of heart. Bertaud, recognizing opportunity slipping away, publicly declared that he would donate his share of the prize money to the families of the airmen killed in the crash of the *American Legion*, then followed up that announcement with an offer to buy the *Columbia*. Levine continued to stall, whereupon Bertaud's attorney followed through on his threat of legal action. On May 18, Judge Mitchell May of the New York State Supreme Court in Brooklyn signed a temporary injunction prohibiting the Columbia Aircraft Corporation from sending the Bellanca on a transatlantic flight without Bertaud. It was returnable for judgment before Judge May at 1 p.m. on Friday, May 20. Levine's behavior didn't surprise Chamberlin. The "tendency which all men have to resent being forced into doing anything is developed to an unusually high degree in Mr. Levine," he said. "It is almost so strong that, if anyone were to try to make him do something he really wanted to do, he would thereupon start figuring out how he could do something else."

In the midst of the Bertaud-Levine row, a former member of the dysfunctional Bellanca family, Bert Acosta, had joined the crew of the *America*. Although Richard Byrd and George Noville had healed from their injuries of April 16, Floyd Bennett faced a long recovery. Acosta would replace him in the pilot's chair.

The Byrd expedition reeked of money, organization, and order. Despite this, of the three contenders the *America* was the least prepared to hop off. "I felt it important to go through a full series of scientific tests of plane and equipment, fuel and engine, in order that we should know exactly what our machine would do," Byrd said. "To hasten this laboratory work for the sake of notoriety was to undermine the scientific character of our expedition."

The capabilities of single-engine planes such as the *Columbia* and the *Spirit of St. Louis* were already known, but nobody knew just what a three-engine craft the size of the *America* could accomplish. Ascertaining its lifting capacity, cruising speed, and other data would take time—more time than those critics who knew nothing of performance curves were willing to give. "Coward," read one of the hundreds of derogatory letters Byrd received. "I am sick of seeing your name. You are a disgrace to America. You never had any idea of flying across the Atlantic." Even the plane's builder stopped just short of questioning Byrd's courage. "I could never understand why he did not take off before Lindbergh," Tony Fokker wrote in his 1931 autobiography. "There had been the most interminable series of test flights it has ever been my grief to witness. They dragged on for days. It seemed to me that every possible excuse for delay was seized on. I began to wonder whether Byrd really wanted to make the transatlantic flight, which was basically hardly more than an elaborate advertisement." The *America* was indeed an elaborate advertisement—for U.S. aeronautics, for the Wanamaker department store—and Rodman Wanamaker was insistent that every last precaution be taken.

Russell Owen, a respected journalist who was one of the few reporters to make a serious effort to understand both the technological and the psychological aspects of manned flight, thoughts the swipes at Byrd were unfair. Owen knew the airmen waiting out the weather on Long Island to be brave if unsentimental fatalists. "Aviators seem to have no nerves," he wrote in that week's issue of the *New Yorker*.

When disaster threatens the flyer may strain every mental resource to bring about that perfect coordination of knowledge and instinct—or whatever it may be—on which his life depends. But when it is over there is no trace of the emotional letdown which overcomes so many men. . . . When the airmen talk, as they rarely do, you discern something that sets them as a race apart. They actually live in another world. Gradually you understand that it is *necessary* for these men to attempt the impossible. It is a necessity as impelling as that of breathing. They must see if they and their planes can do it. And each one of them thinks that failure, death even, of the other man was due to some mistake on his part: he didn't have quite so good a plane, or he went west because his time had come. Something inside them drives them on. Hundreds of years ago they would have hunted dragons or looked for the biggest knight with the biggest axe in Christendom, just for the joy of trying to lick him. To them, the bright face of danger is the sun of their peculiar universe.

On Thursday, May 19, Lindbergh and several companions drove into New York to see the Broadway musical *Rio Rita*. It was a dreary evening. Rain fell, and the tops of Manhattan's skyscrapers were lost in fog. The group was driving down Forty-second Street when it was decided to pull over and make a final perfunctory phone call to the weather bureau. The new forecast caused an immediate change in plans. After a solid week of bad weather, the front over the North Atlantic was lifting. With that the group hurried back to Long Island to get the *Spirit of St. Louis* ready for takeoff at first light.

En route, they stopped at Queensboro Plaza for a quick meal. "You'd better prepare yourself for some unpleasantness in France," a friend told Lindbergh as they sat eating. "I was talking to a fellow who just came back from Europe last week. He says the feeling over there isn't very friendly toward Americans. He thinks our embassy in Paris is right—that no American ought to make the flight so soon after Nungesser and Coli have been lost. It won't be like Curtiss Field when you land; but I don't think you'll have any serious trouble." The French press had picked up the "Flying Fool" nickname, occasionally referring to Lindbergh as *le*

Fou-Volant (which was somewhat gentler than the alternative translation of *l'imbécile de vol*).

As Ryan's Frank Mahoney supervised the *Spirit*'s preparation inside its floodlit Curtiss Field hangar, Lindbergh crossed to Roosevelt Field. He expected to find Byrd, who would have been privy to the same weather information, getting the *America* into shape for a dawn departure. To his surprise, Byrd—evidently influenced by the steady rain—was nowhere in sight. There was no activity in the *Columbia* camp either, though Chamberlin was spotted in the hotel lobby, waiting anxiously for word that the court order grounding the plane had been lifted. As an experienced bad-weather pilot, Lindbergh knew the downpour was inconsequential. What really mattered was what lay beyond this local system. And the weather updates continued to report clearing skies over the North Atlantic.

At about midnight Lindbergh returned to his hotel room, hoping to catch at least a couple of hours of desperately needed sleep. Lieutenant George Stumpf, a member of Lindbergh's National Guard unit, was posted at the door with strict instructions to keep intruders out. Just as Lindbergh was dozing off, Stumpf unaccountably walked into the room, sat on the edge of the bed, and asked, "Slim, what am I going to do when you're gone?" His sleep ruined, Lindbergh got dressed and returned to Curtiss Field at 3 a.m. There he helped with last-minute adjustments to the *Spirit of St. Louis*.

Shortly after four o'clock, the rain slackened and the *Spirit of St. Louis* was moved by truck from its hangar at Curtiss Field to the runway at Roosevelt Field. Lindbergh was far from inspired by the sight of his plane, shrouded and dripping, being towed through the gloom. He thought it looked "more like a funeral procession than the beginning of a flight to Paris."

Although the press had all along played up the competitive aspects of the great Atlantic air race, Lindbergh's rivals wished him the best and came to see him off. Byrd offered updated weather information and the use of his ramp at the east end of Roosevelt Field. Lindbergh would have used it, but what little wind existed was blowing in the wrong direction. The *Spirit of St. Louis* was placed at the west end of the field. Over the next three hours it was slowly filled with 451 gallons of fuel filtered through cheesecloth to remove any impurities that might affect the engine's performance. Carl Schory arrived to install the barograph and seal the tanks, requirements for any record attempt.

While this was taking place, well-wishers tried to force a variety of good-luck charms on Lindbergh. But the only talisman he carried on the flight was a St. Christopher medal that a local woman, Katie Butler, had taken from around her neck and handed to a policeman to give to him. Lindbergh, his mind focused on more important matters, distractedly pocketed the gift. Many hours later, over the Atlantic, he would be surprised to discover it inside his flying suit.

As an airmail pilot, Lindbergh was used to traveling light. His few supplies on this flight included a match safe (to keep matches dry), two flashlights, a ball of string and a ball of cord, a hunting knife, a large needle (for repairing canvas), a hacksaw blade, four flares, an air raft, and two floatable cushions. He also had an Armbruster cup, a device for turning the moisture in one's breath into water. In addition to five cans of army emergency rations, he brought along a sack of sandwiches—two beef, two ham, and an egg salad—and two canteens of water.

Charles Lindbergh pulls on his flying suit in the misty early morning hours of May 20, 1927, just prior to climbing into the cockpit of the *Spirit of St. Louis*.

It was Friday morning, May 20. At seven-forty, Lindbergh shook hands with Byrd and settled himself into the cockpit. Under his brown flight suit he was wearing a white shirt, with a red-and-blue striped tie knotted at the collar, an Abercrombie & Fitch flight jacket, and army-issue breeches and ankle boots. On his head was a wool-lined leather helmet; he also wore lined gloves and goggles to protect him from the elements. He carried a $500 bank draft, his passport, and letters of introduction from Colonel Theodore Roosevelt Jr., whom he had visited at Oyster Bay earlier in the week.

Takeoff was the most dangerous part of the flight. Lindbergh was at the controls of what the tabloids termed a "flying coffin." Mechanics had done everything they could think of to save weight, even replacing the grease in the wheels with lubricating oil. Nonetheless, the 2,750 pounds of gasoline boosted the overall weight of the plane to 5,250 pounds. This was a thousand pounds more than the *Spirit of St. Louis* had ever carried before. To make the launch more challenging, there now was a slight tailwind. Of greater concern was the high humidity, which was causing the engine to turn at thirty revolutions lower than maximum capacity. Assuming Lindbergh got airborne, would he then have enough power to clear the telephone wires rising menacingly at the end of the runway?

"It's the weather," a mechanic said, trying to sound encouraging. "They never rev up on a day like this."

Lindbergh saw the apprehension in the man's face. He looked down the wet, soft runway. Because of the mist, there was no horizon; the strip stretched into a hazy nothingness. Unbeknownst to him, Tony Fokker had earlier barged into the *America*'s hangar, shouting to sleeping mechanics, "Get up! Get me quick some fire extinguishers. That young fool is getting ready to take off. Maybe he will have trouble!" Now Fokker and Frank Mahoney were stationed at runway's end, fire extinguishers at the ready.

Lindbergh continued to sit, engine and mind idling as one, pondering whether he should cut the switch or open the throttle. He was accustomed to balancing such variables as wind, weather, power, and load. "Now, the intangible elements of flight—experience, instinct, intuition—must make the final judgment, place their weight upon the scales," he thought. Entering into the equation—perhaps the persuasive factor—was the solitary nature of his endeavor. There had been nobody to consult before making the decision to prepare his plane for takeoff, nobody to influence

The *Spirit of St. Louis* is lined up for takeoff on muddy Roosevelt Field.

his judgment one way or the other as he contemplated his next move, nobody's welfare to consider should his choice turn out catastrophic. He was independent, alone.

It was just a few minutes before eight o'clock. Finally he decided. He would go. The chocks were removed and the plane started creeping forward, over the same strip of earth that the *New York–Paris* had rumbled down. "If the *Spirit of St. Louis* gathers speed too slowly; if the wheels hug the ground too tightly; if the controls feel too loose and logy, I can pull back the throttle and stop—that is, I can stop if I don't wait too long," he thought. "If I wait too long—a few seconds will decide—well, another transatlantic plane crashed and burned at the end of this same runway. Only a few yards away, two of Fonck's crew met their death in flames."

Among the 150 or so people present were ten-year-old William Johnke of Garden City and his father, who had been tipped off by a family friend, *New York Times* reporter John Frogge. "A group of about six or seven men lined up behind the main struts," recalled Johnke, who squeezed his father's hand throughout. "They began shoving the airplane and then running while pushing to help the plane get rolling through the soft earth. The plane left them behind as it gathered speed. It seemed to bounce off a bump. Two more times it looked like the plane got off the ground for a moment but couldn't stay up." Frogge later called the takeoff "the most breathless thing I've ever seen." He remembered the tailskid catching weeds, "and they'd hold him back. A bunch would fall off, and more of them would catch on. He must have known something was holding him back."

But the rushing, bouncing plane quickly found its stride. It lifted off, strongly and surely. Lindbergh later estimated that on a dry field, the craft could have shouldered another five hundred pounds into the air. There was one last obstacle. "You could see the telephone wires at the end of the field," Frogge said. "You knew the plane would not break through those wires, and he would go down. Finally he pulled over them. I know from the pictures that he cleared those wires by two, three feet, but from that distance it looked like an inch."

Dipping a wing, the *Spirit of St. Louis* slipped through the morning mist and eased into a northeasterly course. "There was no cheer," Frogge remembered. "Everybody was just holding their breath. We knew he was over the first hump, but it was still three thousand miles. No motor had ever gone that far, pulling an airplane."

15

We Two

Now it is not much farther, and we must pull ourselves together, we two. Have you enough oil? Do you think you need more gasoline? . . . It is not much farther. Here comes Ireland, and then Paris. Will we really make it, we two?

—*Lindberghflug* (Lindbergh's Flight)

Lindbergh flew low along the north shore of Long Island before pointing the *Spirit of St. Louis* across Long Island Sound toward Connecticut. Crossing thirty-five miles of water in a heavily fuel-laden plane was a new and slightly unsettling experience. Until gas consumption made the *Spirit of St. Louis* lighter, it was especially vulnerable to the waves of turbulence it was now encountering. Lindbergh warily watched the wingtips bend with the strain of each new shock as he slowly climbed through the haze. A thousand feet over the sound, the choppy air suddenly turned calm. Pilot and plane settled down.

Shortly before nine o'clock, an hour into his flight, Lindbergh filled out the first of his hourly logs. With his goggles pushed back on his head, he meticulously recorded speed, altitude, visibility, wind velocity and direction, true course, and compass variation. He carefully noted oil temperature and pressure, fuel pressure and mixture, and engine RPMs. Below the instrument panel was a complicated array of fourteen valves controlling the five fuel tanks. He regularly switched tanks—every fifteen minutes in the beginning, then hourly afterward—manipulating the petcocks to ensure a balanced load. He hugged the New England coastline north, maintaining a steady speed of 105 miles per hour and an altitude of 200 feet, until reaching Plymouth, Massachusetts. There he headed out over the Atlantic. His next landmark, Nova Scotia, was more than two hours away.

This was the moment of truth—or supreme arrogance, as he later described it. Who was he, a pilot accustomed to using roads, railroad tracks, and other visible landmarks on the ground to guide him, to think that he could successfully navigate over such an immense and uninviting expanse of water and find, in succession, Nova Scotia, Newfoundland, Ireland, and Paris? Everything depended upon his having plotted the Great Circle course correctly, and then using his compasses and the wind-blown chart he struggled to spread over his knees to make the necessary adjustments along the way. Lloyd's of London, which had been handicapping each entrant in the Atlantic derby, certainly didn't think much of his chances. The firm refused even to post odds, believing the risk of one man flying a single-engine plane too great.

Lindbergh flew the *Spirit of St. Louis* a mere fifty feet above sea level from Massachusetts to Nova Scotia. In this era of uncrowded skies, a midair collision with another plane was highly unlikely, but he was careful to periodically use his periscope to make sure there were no smokestacks or ships' masts in his path. He made St. Mary's Bay on the northwest end of the Canadian province and discovered to his satisfaction that after more than four hours of flying, he was only two degrees—six miles—off course. So far, his navigating had been solid.

During much of the next three hours, the time it took him to traverse the craggy Nova Scotia countryside, he had to contend with fog and heavy rain that forced him to make several detours. He emerged from the squalls still on course and slightly refreshed, the buffeting and the cold, wet weather momentarily reviving his dulled senses. However, fatigue was becoming as big a concern as bad weather. He had been without any real sleep for nearly thirty hours, with the lion's share of the flight still to come. Despite the chill, he decided against inserting the plastic windows he had brought along. He figured they would make the cockpit too warm and cozy, too conducive to a fatal sleep. He crossed Cape Breton Island in clear skies and headed toward Newfoundland, two hundred miles distant. Once again he was over the ocean.

At 4:52 p.m., nearing Newfoundland and entering his tenth hour of flight, he filled out his hourly log. He was at 150 feet, flying 95 miles per hour, with the engine purring at 1,600 revolutions per minute. He continued his straight-line flying, checking his charts at every 100-mile point and adjusting his course accordingly.

Soon he was winging past the rugged, granite mountains of the Burin Peninsula on the south coast of Newfoundland. The craggy landscape and ice fields passing under his wing caused him to consider the fate of Nungesser and Coli, now missing almost two weeks, and what their odds for survival would be if the *White Bird* had gone down in such an inhospitable environment. Searches had yet to turn up any trace of the Frenchmen. It was "a hopeless hunt" over tens of thousands of square miles of wilderness and sea, thought Lindbergh, who believed a sleet storm had most likely caused the plane to crash. "With no accurate clue to follow, searching was only a gesture, the payment of a debt felt by living men to their lost brothers who, by some miracle, might not be dead. When a plane is missing, you may convince yourself by logic that all hope for the crew is gone, yet the vision of injured and starving men haunts you into action, regardless of how futile it may be." Lindbergh had once seen Nungesser put on an exhibition in his pursuit plane at Lambert Field. "I stood nearby, watching the great French ace, thinking of his deadly combats, of the enemies he'd killed, of the clashes from which he had so narrowly escaped. I wonder if *he* concluded that flying the ocean was less dangerous than, say, a single combat in the air."

During this first phase of the flight, his thoughts also turned to his mother. She was teaching science classes in Detroit, doing her best to "curtain off in her mind a pilot and his plane." After a hectic day of dealing with antsy students and prying reporters, Evangeline locked herself into the house she shared with her bachelor brother. She disconnected her phone and refused to see anybody. By the following evening she would know whether her boy had made it—or disappeared into the same black maw that had swallowed Nungesser and Coli.

Lindbergh veered ninety miles off his Great Circle course to fly over St. John's. The harbor town on the easternmost tip of Newfoundland would be his last contact with land before heading out over the ocean and the last human settlement for some 1,900 miles. He wanted to fix his position and set his course for Ireland, but he also wanted people to know that he had made it this far in case he later went down at sea and a search mission was launched. He knew that news of his sighting would be relayed over the radio and word would reach his mother.

Lindbergh checked his watch, which he kept set to Eastern Standard Time (EST). It was 7:15 p.m. Friday. He had now covered more than 1,100 miles in a little over eleven hours. Yet the most daunting part of the flight was still in front of him: the long hop across the wild, frigid expanses of the North Atlantic to Ireland. There would be no more charting his position by landmarks; nothing but open sea lay ahead. The sun was setting over the horizon; blackness lay ahead and below. Lindbergh plunged into the gathering darkness, a last few shards of light reflecting off the giant cakes of ice floating beneath him.

Within an hour he was flying through a driving storm. "The sleet began to stick to my plane," he wrote later. "I made several detours trying to get out of snow and sleet, but in vain. I dropped down to ten feet above the water, but it was even worse there and I was on instruments entirely. So I gave my engine full power and climbed through the clouds to a height of ten thousand feet." As the embattled young flier maneuvered the *Spirit of St. Louis* through the biting cold two miles above the Atlantic, the first of many Lindy-inspired songs to come was being performed inside the studios of WJZ radio in New York by a trio called the Bonnie Laddies.

Captain Lindbergh, we're with you
Won't you, please, come smilin' through?
Keep her going, give her the steam
You'll soon be reaching the land of your dream.

On and off throughout the flight, storms and fog would force Lindbergh to resort to instrument flying, sometimes for long stretches at a time. The concentration required of a fully rested pilot to fly strictly by instruments in such disorienting, claustrophobic conditions is considerable; for a sleep-addled pilot, the effort is excruciating. Every time the *Spirit of St. Louis* tunneled sightlessly through thick weather, Lindbergh had to keep his eyes glued to the instrument board. He had to stay especially focused on the turn and bank indicator, to keep the plane from tipping to either side, and the inclinometer, to prevent the nose from rising or falling. "With these instruments any tendency of the plane to turn right or left, up or down, or to bank can be instantly detected," he explained. "But it is a strange fact that on a long flight a pilot becomes

The cramped cockpit of the *Spirit of St. Louis* was just slightly more than three feet wide and four feet high. Lindbergh spent 33½ hours seated in a wicker chair in front of the instrument panel.

so weary that his instruments appear to be deceiving him. He feels that he is stalling or turning when actually he is in straight, level flight, and his instruments so indicate."

As the *Spirit of St. Louis* continued to perform majestically, monotonously, over the sawtooth waves of the Atlantic, Lindbergh did everything he could think of to fight off the overpowering urge to nestle his head into a passing cloud and fall into a deep and immediate sleep. He stamped his feet. He propped his eyelids open with his fingers. He dove to within a few feet of the ocean's choppy surface to allow the cold spray to hit him in the face. He didn't eat anything for fear that a meal would relax him. The *Spirit of St. Louis* was an intentionally temperamental plane, requiring his constant attention to stay on course. Whenever he dozed off for even a second or two, he could feel it pulling away from him, and he would instantly be jarred back to his senses. He flew on, dulled by fatigue and cramped muscles and repeating to himself that he had to stay awake or die. "Every cell of my being is on strike, sulking in protest, claiming that nothing, nothing in the world, could be worth such effort; that man's tissue was never made for such abuse."

Suspense over the young flier's progress carried through Friday evening and into the wee hours of Saturday. People who a few days earlier had never heard of Charles Lindbergh now tuned in to radio bulletins and prayed for his safety. "I think half of America stayed home, glued to radios," aviatrix Elinor Smith Sullivan, then a fifteen-year-old girl living in New York, recalled years later. "You kind of held your breath. Where is he now? And what's happening? Can he possibly make it?" With no radio on board the *Spirit of St. Louis* and no sightings from ships at sea, Lindbergh was as alone and as incommunicado as any modern adventurer had ever been. For millions, the ongoing story of Lindbergh's flight was more gripping than any novel, its outcome more agonizing to wait on than any newspaper or film serial. "As Saturday dawned over the vast Atlantic," reporter George Hicks of WJZ radio informed listeners, "the Lindbergh plane is unreported since passing Newfoundland early last night."

Scant hours after the *Spirit of St. Louis* left Roosevelt Field, a decision by Judge Mitchell May in the New York State Supreme Court in Brooklyn paved the way for the *Columbia* to follow. May vacated the temporary injunction that had been granted Lloyd Bertaud against the Bellanca plane taking off without him. The country did not care who owned or flew the plane, May said: "Its successful flight is the great concern."

Clarence Chamberlin and Charlie Levine were all for the *Columbia* leaving for Paris as soon as possible—"as a purely sporting proposition," they said—but Giuseppe Bellanca considered it to be in poor taste and an unnecessary risk of life as long as Lindbergh's fate remained unknown. "If Lindbergh is successful," Bellanca said, "then there is no need for the feat to be duplicated. At the best it is merely a stunt and there are plenty of opportunities for the *Columbia* plane and its pilots."

But who *were* its pilots? While Bertaud returned to Cleveland to resume his airmail career, Levine was coy about who would replace him. Rumors swirled that Chamberlin's cockpit companion would be Walter Hinton, who had copiloted the *NC-4* across the Atlantic in 1919; or Bill Kline, who flew mail between New York and Boston; or Bernt Balchen. "He is known only to three persons," Levine said. "The three are the man himself, Chamberlin and myself." To add to the intrigue, the mystery airman would not be named until just before departure.

The *Columbia* was ordered prepped as soon as Bertaud's writ was tossed. The plane was loaded with fresh oil and fuel. Charts, navigating instruments, emergency gear, and provisions were put in place. As work continued, bulletins came in describing foul weather over Newfoundland. For a while there was a general belief that Lindbergh would have to return. "I feel very sorry for the boy," Chamberlin told reporters. "I think he will turn back—as he should turn back. If he's running into bad weather it's the only sensible thing to do." Lindbergh actually did contemplate turning around at that point, the only time during the entire flight when he seriously considered doing so. "But then I figured it was probably just as bad behind me as in front of me," he explained, "so I kept on toward Paris."

Just before midnight, sixteen hours after the *Spirit of St. Louis* lifted off, Levine declared that the *Columbia* would leave at daybreak on Saturday. Chamberlin and Balchen walked over the runway at Roosevelt Field, checking its condition. There was a palpable air of expectancy, with reporters and mechanics from other hangars sticking around to see what would happen. Nothing did. A new weather bulletin reported a northwesterly wind, meaning the *Columbia* would face headwinds all the way to Newfoundland. At 1:30 a.m., Chamberlin announced that the takeoff had been delayed. By then Lindbergh had just passed the midway mark of his flight. He was now closer to Ireland than to the North American coast. From here on out there would be no turning back, even if he wanted to.

In Paris, where the clocks were five hours ahead of those in New York, it was Friday afternoon when most people first heard of Lindbergh's departure. After midnight, following word that he had been spotted over Newfoundland and was now headed out over the Atlantic, they had cheered his name and argued his chances in places such as Jed Kiley's Montmartre nightclub. There, wealthy Americans belted out "Give My Regards to Broadway" and "La Marseillaise" while the French clientele and waiters applauded appreciatively and the jazz band guzzled free champagne. Inside the nearby Chez Florence, "big ebony Harvey" sang "Mademoiselle from Armentières" and Mary Lewis, a young, golden-haired soprano, performed "California, Here I Come," recalled newspaperman Hank Wales, a regular patron: "Everybody in the place was making the flight with Lindbergh, marking his course over the sea on the tablecloths with lipsticks and burnt matches." Lindbergh had seized the French imagination like no American since the war. "His calm courage and his quiet and efficient preparation, unaccompanied by fiery publicity, recalls to French minds that picture of 'a real American' they found among the doughboys of the Marne, St. Mihiel and the Argonne and had, for sundry causes, almost forgotten since," observed one Paris correspondent. However, French admiration was imbued with considerable skepticism that the flight would end well. The recent losses of the *Oiseau Blanc* and the *Paris-Amérique Latine* were fresh wounds in the national psyche. *Paris-Soir* warned that it was "considered doubtful by the experts that a single flier can stay awake and alert long enough to challenge successfully the dark forces waiting to do battle with him over the Atlantic." At the Ritz Bar on the Rue Cambon, where wagering was brisk, legendary barkeeper Frank Meier set odds of ten to one against Lindbergh making it. Some thought the odds too low.

Saturday morning arrived in Paris with no new word of Lindbergh coming in overnight. "It was a lovely, not too warm, sunny day, with the chestnut trees in full bloom and their scent filling the balmy air," Bill Shirer remembered. "Paris in late spring was always at its loveliest and this was one of the finest days we had yet had." Thousands of tennis fans crowded into the Stade Français in St. Cloud to watch the Davis Cup doubles match between America's "Big Bill" Tilden and Francis Hunter and France's Jacques Brugnon and Jean Borotra. Others flocked to verdant spots in the Bois de Boulogne and Champs-Élysées for dining and dancing. The cafés were jammed. Curious Parisians snatched up copies of their favorite papers, trying to stay abreast of developments in the unfolding saga of *le Fou-Volant* and *l'Esprit de Saint-Louis*. "It will be two weeks tomorrow that Nungesser and Coli took off from Le Bourget in the gray dawn, and boldly committed themselves to the immense ocean," *Le Petit Parisien* reminded its readers.

> Since then we have been living in the most anxious times. And even today, we want to hope. But the heroes' hearts do not allow themselves to be weakened by the direst catastrophes. Nungesser and Coli . . . fell while attacking the staggering task that is crossing the Atlantic: but that did not chill the ardor of those who intended to conquer the ocean, and yesterday, another

hero was found to launch himself into the infinite, the American, Lindbergh. Lindbergh departed alone with magnificent bravery in his monoplane, the tiniest of the planes that have been prepared for this great crossing. We'll be waiting for Lindbergh this evening at Le Bourget. And if, as we most passionately hope, he does arrive, we don't doubt that Paris and France will know how to acclaim him.

La Liberté, arguably the most nationalistic of all French newspapers, dismissed any suggestion that the country was rooting against the American flier.

Paris, which carries in its heart mourning for Nungesser and Coli, is preparing to receive the brave American aviator. We shall give to him the same welcome America would have given our heroic pilots had they succeeded. Facts will answer the stupid reports that the public opinion of Paris was hatefully unloosed against America when it found out all the telegrams announcing Nungesser's success were lies. . . . If Lindbergh should disappear in the immensity of the ocean, we shall think of his mother and join in the same pious thought—mother of Lindbergh, mother of Nungesser, mother of Coli.

Somewhere over the Atlantic, Lindbergh, oblivious to the escalating public fascination with his flight on both sides of the ocean, pressed on in his trancelike state. Because he was racing toward the sun, he experienced a much shorter night than if he had been stationary—slightly less than four hours of darkness instead of seven. At that it was still a jeopardous night. "There was no moon and it was very dark," he recalled. "The tops of some of the storm clouds were several thousand feet above me, and at one time, when I attempted to fly through one of the larger clouds, ice started to collect on the plane, and I was forced to turn around and get back to clear air immediately and then fly around any clouds which I could not get over."

He continued burrowing through the towering walls of cumulus. Fog, coupled with exhaustion, prevented him from taking accurate readings. Without making regular adjustments, it was possible that he had drifted hundreds of miles off course. He dove close to the ocean's choppy surface, trying to estimate drift and direction by the way the foam flew off the whitecaps. Breaking into clearer skies, deception crept into his fatigued mind. "Numerous shorelines appeared," he remembered, "with trees perfectly outlined against the horizon. In fact, the mirages were so natural that, had I not been in mid-Atlantic and known that no land existed along my route, I would have taken them to be actual islands."

After more than a full day in the air, and two days without sleep, he was halfway between sleep and consciousness, sharing an ethereal no-man's-land with a platoon of phantoms. As he later described it, the figures appeared "suddenly in the tail of the fuselage while I was flying through fog. I saw them clearly although my eyes were staring straight ahead. Transparent, mist-like, with semi-human form, they moved in and out of the fabric walls at will. One or two of them would come forward to converse with me and then rejoin the group behind."

Lindbergh's ability to stay awake for more than two days straight was one of the most remarkable aspects of his flight, especially since he didn't bring along coffee, tea, chocolate, or tobacco, the standard stimulants carried on endurance flights. Augustus Post, an experienced long-distance aeronaut, insisted that adrenaline and youthful vigor alone could keep a pilot awake for the time needed to cross the ocean, but not everybody agreed. A popular explanation for Lindbergh's stamina was that he had trained himself to stay awake while in San Diego, gradually increasing his hours of sleeplessness. He "used to take long walks out into the country, fighting off sleep for 30 hours or more," one variation of the story went. "A week before he took off for St. Louis he put himself to his most grueling test. One of his friends, who was driving an automobile, saw him plodding along a lonely road one morning and offered to give him a 'lift' into town. Lindbergh thanked him and declined the offer. On that occasion he remained awake for 49 hours on a stretch." Some speculated that Lindbergh must have had some kind of pharmaceutical support—most likely Benzedrine, a popular stimulant used to increase alertness and ward off fatigue, especially among military pilots. "There was this doctor in Garden City we used to see when we wanted to get pills to stay awake," recalled John Frogge, the *New York Times* reporter assigned to shadow Lindbergh at Curtiss Field. "He was the only doctor who would prescribe them. About two days before [taking off] some deputy sheriff told me Lindbergh had gone to see this doctor. Lindbergh always claimed he never took any pills, but how are you going to stay awake that long without something?" Amphetamines might explain the "ghosts" aboard the *Spirit of St. Louis* and the usually voracious pilot's lack of hunger during the long flight, as the drug's side effects can include hallucinations and suppressed appetite.

But there were no special exercises or magic pills, Lindbergh insisted, just as there was no relief pilot or navigator to lend the dozy pilot in the wicker chair a helping hand on the way to Paris. It was simply a superhuman effort by a healthy young man focused on a goal and desperate to stay alive—an effort Lindbergh would later doubt he could ever replicate.

The *Spirit of St. Louis* droned on. Porpoises leaped in play, providing a welcome diversion. Then, during Lindbergh's twenty-sixth hour in flight, he unaccountably emerged from his stupor. Something or somebody had given him a reprieve, and he felt a sharpening of his senses. He spotted seabirds, a sign that he must be approaching land. Then occurred what he later called the most exciting moment of the entire flight: seeing several fishing boats rocking gently in the swells below him. Surely a harbor could not be far off, but in which direction? He throttled back the engine and swooped down to within fifty feet of the water. As the *Spirit of St. Louis* glided like a giant gull around one of the vessels, Lindbergh leaned out and shouted at the top of his lungs, "Which way is Ireland?"

There was no answer. He circled a second trawler, but the only response he got to his continued shouts was an expressionless face staring at him through a porthole. Several passes failed to bring anybody up on deck. Finally, seeing that he was wasting his two most precious commodities, fuel and daylight, he climbed away in disgust. It was now early Saturday afternoon. He had no way of knowing for sure how far off course he was.

Before another hour passed, Lindbergh had the answer to his question. Where was Ireland? It was directly in front of him, its welcoming presence signaled by high mountain walls and lush emerald fields. Sixteen hours after leaving the last landfall, Newfoundland, and two hours ahead of schedule, thanks to a healthy tailwind, he had reached Valentia and Dingle Bay on the southwest coast of Ireland. Villagers craned their necks in curiosity. Some waved. Lindbergh was filled with emotion. It was like emerging from a long, dark tunnel. After spending a small eternity cut off from the mortal world and sharing the ride with phantoms, he was back among the living. "Here are human beings," he thought. "Here's a human welcome. Not a single detail is wrong. I've never seen such beauty before—fields so green, people so human, a village so attractive, mountains and rocks so mountainous and rocklike."

Equally heartening was finding that his dead reckoning had put him only three miles off course. Assuming no mechanical malfunctions, adverse weather, or pilot error, he could expect to be in Paris within another six hours.

A wireless message that the *Spirit of St. Louis* had been sighted five hundred miles from Ireland was sent at 12:10 p.m. Greenwich Mean Time (8:10 a.m. EST) by an unknown ship at sea. The message, transmitted in German, was intercepted by the Dutch steamer *Hilversum*, which in turn relayed it to stations on land. The unconfirmed report reached America early Saturday morning. That was followed nearly two and a half hours later by a London Press Association dispatch saying that Lindbergh was spotted just a hundred miles off the Irish coast. By late morning reports were coming in of sightings over Valentia. Premature shouts of celebration were outweighed by sober calls for cautious optimism. Lindbergh still had to make England and then France. Who knew what might go wrong? Nonetheless, with every subsequent sighting of the *Spirit of St. Louis*, the frenzy was cranked up a notch. Groups of men, women, and children hung around newsstands, waiting for the latest extra edition, or bunched around radios, handicapping Lucky Lindy's chances between bulletins. "In the subway no one minded anyone else looking at his paper to see how the flight was coming," reported the *Brooklyn Eagle*. "Even hard-boiled subway guards asked each new crowd: 'What's the latest dope on the kid flier?'"

Jimmy Stewart, who turned nineteen the day Lindbergh left for Paris, would grow up to know something of drama, of both the genuine and theatrical kind. For now, though, the Oscar-winning actor and highly decorated bomber pilot of the future was just one more ordinary American obsessed with the unfolding story of Lindbergh's flight. For years he had been building model airplanes for fun, but this time he outdid himself. On a large piece of beaverboard he drew a map of the North Atlantic, with New York's Woolworth Building and the Eiffel Tower at opposite ends. To illustrate the curvature of the Earth, he bent the beaverboard in a semicircle. On Friday evening, he put the display in the window of the family hardware store in Indiana, Pennsylvania, with a note saying that the following day he would track the flier's progress by placing his handcarved model of the *Spirit of St. Louis* at the appropriate spot on the map and updating the position each hour.

The store opened Saturday morning, and Stewart soon "moved the plane to the southern tip of Ireland, where he had just been reported," he later recalled. "As other stores opened for business and farmers began coming to town for weekend shopping, people gathered in front of my display as though it were a World Series scoreboard. By noon you couldn't fight your way into my father's store. I imagine my father lost a lot of business that day, but he never said a word to me about it."

Lindbergh, a virtual unknown two weeks ago, was now in the thoughts of millions. Everywhere, the conversation invariably turned to the young flier: his current whereabouts, his chances of success. Inside a restaurant in Brooklyn, a waitress took a customer's order: "Corn beef hash, did you say, sir—where is Lindbergh now?"

"Oh, he's just crossed the English Channel—all right, bring along the hash."

The *New York Times* was inundated with ten thousand phone calls asking for the latest update, while an emergency crew of switchboard operators at the *Detroit Free Press* was instructed to preemptively ask each caller, "Is this about Lindbergh?" Morning papers reported on the distracted fight crowd that had attended Friday evening's heavyweight bout between Jack Sharkey and Jim Maloney at Yankee Stadium. Before the fight, ring announcer Joe Humphreys had implored the crowd to "rise to your feet and think about a boy up there tonight who is carrying the hopes of all true-blooded Americans. Say a little prayer for Charles Lindbergh." Observed the *Times*, "Forty thousand persons put Lindbergh first and Sharkey and Maloney second. . . . The remarkable thing about last night's fight crowd was that they were all wondering how the transatlantic flight would come out and not who would be knocked out."

"Lindbergh Flies Alone," a piece written by Harold M. Anderson for the *New York Sun*, was already on its way to becoming the most widely reprinted editorial since Francis P. Church's "Yes, Virginia, There Is a Santa" appeared in the same newspaper thirty years earlier:

Alone?

Is he alone at whose right side rides Courage, with Skill within the cockpit and Faith upon the left? Does solitude surround the brave when Adventure leads the way and Ambition reads the dials? Is there no company with him for whom the air is cleft by Daring and the darkness made light by Emprise?

True, the fragile bodies of his fellows do not weigh down his plane; true, the fretful minds of weaker men are lacking from his crowded cabin; but as his airship keeps her course he holds communion with those rarer spirits that inspire to intrepidity and by their sustaining potency give strength to arm, resource to mind, content to soul.

Alone? With what other companions would that man fly to whom the choice were given?

Alone, but carrying the hopes of millions, Lindbergh roared across the English Channel during his thirty-first hour, reaching the port city of Cherbourg just as the sun was setting over the French coast. Townspeople raised a cheer as the *Spirit of St. Louis* passed overhead.

Despite having been awake for the better part of two and a half days, sleep was no longer a concern. Euphoria had taken over. At 9:20 p.m. local time, Lindbergh unwrapped a sandwich, his first bite of food since leaving Roosevelt Field. It tasted stale, though, and he had to wash down each mouthful with a slug of water from his canteen. He balled up the wax paper and prepared to toss it out the window, then thought better of it. He didn't want to be an ugly American, littering the French countryside minutes into his first visit. To his pleasant surprise he saw beacons blinking dimly in the distance, marking the airway between London and Paris. The City of Light, sprawling and sparkling and little more than half an hour away, would be impossible to miss. "From now on," he thought, "everything will be as simple as flying into Chicago on a clear night."

In Paris, a cadre of newspapermen scrambled to cover what promised to be the biggest story since the war. "Sometime in the afternoon the word came that Lindbergh had been sighted over Ireland," recalled Eric Hawkins of the *Herald*. "Immediately the French air and navy ministries alerted all Normandy and Channel ports to be on the lookout. Each new development sent fresh crowds of Parisians toward Le Bourget. The field was feebly lighted, but this was normal, and the runways were well marked. It was a fine clear night with a bright moon. A little after dark the word was flashed that Lindbergh had passed over Cherbourg, and from that moment on all of us knew he couldn't miss."

By sunset the road leading to Le Bourget was filled with taxis, buses, bicycles, and pedestrians. There were tens of thousands of Americans in Paris—expatriates, students, tourists, businessmen, and journalists—and an unknown number of them joined the swarms heading north out of the city. Among them were Massachusetts schoolteacher Dicky Richards and his wife, Julia, whose brother had been a pilot in the war. The middle-aged couple was on vacation with two of their children. On Friday morning they had bought theater tickets for Saturday night, a decision they quickly regretted. "That fellow Lindbergh has started," Dicky told Julia, "and if he should make it, it would be rather interesting to see him land." On Saturday afternoon, the Richardses were at the Café de la Paix on the Place de l'Opéra when they read the giant letters sliding by on the electronic sign atop the Selfridge Building. Lindbergh had been spotted off the Irish coast and was headed their way! With that the couple rushed to change their tickets and clothes, scooped up their children, and dashed off to Le Bourget. Once there, they managed to squeeze onto the stairs of an iron staircase. "As we waited," Julia later wrote her brother, "the last lingering fingers of daylight dissolved into darkness, and one by one the searchlights were turned on, making the field stand out so brightly that it almost hurt one's eyes. . . . At intervals rockets roared up into the air, and the excitement caused by the slowly descending lighted parachutes kept the crowd amused and patient."

Lindbergh followed the Seine as the slow-flowing river wound its way through the picturesque countryside to Paris. With the end in sight, pilot, plane, and power plant continued to work together flawlessly. The *Spirit of St. Louis* whisked along at 105 miles per hour, covering 1¾ miles every minute, 154 feet each second, the Wright engine firing rhythmically on all nine cylinders. Lindbergh's appreciation for his machine turned into affectionate animism. "The *Spirit of St. Louis* is a wonderful plane," he thought. "It's like a living creature, gliding along smoothly, happily, as though a successful flight means as much to it as to me, as though we shared our experiences together, each feeling beauty, life, and death as keenly, each dependent on the other's loyalty. *We* have made this flight across the ocean, not *I* or *it*."

In the past, when he had idly imagined what would happen upon reaching his destination, he always pictured a small delegation of civil and aviation officials greeting him, maybe escorting him to a hangar or airport office for some sort of simple ceremony. He would answer reporters' questions, see to the proper care and storage of his plane, then check into a nearby hotel. He would get up the next morning after a good night's rest, have a hearty meal, tend to some business, and then see a bit of the city while planning his next move. He had brought along letters of introduction. After all, he knew nobody in France, and nobody knew him.

It was just a few minutes before ten o'clock when Lindbergh spotted the Eiffel Tower, all lit up. He circled it at 4,000 feet, trying to get his bearings. He had been told Le Bourget lay about a dozen miles northeast of the city. Despite being assured beforehand that it was a big airfield and easy to find, he missed it on his first go-round and after several miles had to turn back. Looking out the window of the *Spirit of St. Louis*, he spotted a large black patch with a curiously irregular lighting pattern. One end was floodlit, while the other was alive with crawling lights—car lamps, he finally determined.

Armand Deutsch, a teenager from a well-to-do Chicago family, was lucky enough to be in Paris that long-ago spring evening. He had joined the throngs streaming toward the airport, an impromptu welcoming committee that ultimately numbered between 100,000 and 250,000 people, depending on whose estimate one believed. Many had been merrily sharing bottles of wine and champagne for hours. They stood on the tops of cars, filled the roofs of airport buildings, and jostled each other behind the guarded iron fences separating them from the field. As viewed by Lindbergh from a thousand feet up in the sky, this massive assemblage was a dark, jellylike blob.

"Suddenly," recalled Deutsch, "you could hear this small noise. And it grew a little louder . . . a little louder. And suddenly this small plane, caught in a shaft of light from the ground at Le Bourget, came into the view of all these people."

After several passes, each of which heightened the anticipation of the hordes below, the slightly puzzled Lindbergh decided that this was probably the right place and prepared for his final approach. As the crowd surged forward in rising excitement, he executed a perfect sideslip landing on the east end of the field, taxiing the *Spirit of St. Louis* near some civilian hangars and cutting the engine just in time. His journey suddenly over, unaware of what was about to wash over him, he had but a few brief moments to sort out his emotions. The euphoria he felt was leavened with a certain sadness that the great adventure had actually ended. It was 10:24 p.m. local time on Saturday, May 21, 1927. He had flown nonstop 3,635 statute miles (5,850 kilometers) from New York to Paris in an official time of 33 hours, 30 minutes, and 30 seconds—and still had enough gas and stamina, he later insisted, to continue at least another thousand miles if he had wished. It was a shame to land, he reflected, "with the night so clear and so much fuel in my tanks."

For now, though, he and the *Spirit of St. Louis* were going nowhere. In an almost frightening demonstration of unbridled adoration, people exploded en masse past the barriers and guards and rushed toward the plane, shouting, "Lindbergh! Lindbergh!" Many of the policemen joined the celebrants in their mad dash. "One second I was gazing transfixed at that unbelievable ship drifting softly down its lighted way," Julia Richards recalled, "the next I was gazing at a sheer black wall of humanity trying to fight its way up and over a six-foot fence. Two seconds later the fence gave way, and the black wave broke over and swept forward like the Mississippi floods." The reaction of the crowd, said Deutsch, "was one of jubilation and disbelief, the likes of which I can't conceive of happening today about anything." In the forefront of the thundering herd was Karl Arhendt, a twenty-three-year-old music student from Ohio, who, "yelling and out of breath . . . just went dippy with joy." Arhendt described the bedlam in a letter to his father: "In a few seconds we found ourselves in the midst of a seething mob, helpless to get closer than fifteen or twenty feet from the plane. . . . Lindbergh hadn't even had a chance to get out of his machine. With the mob shouting, 'en triomphe,' it started for the exit, shoving the plane along. For a few seconds Lindbergh was carried on the shoulders of those nearest him, then suddenly he disappeared and no one knew where he was."

In New York, Lowell Thomas informed his radio audience, "He made it! Charles A. Lindbergh, 'Lucky Lindy' as they call him, landed at Le Bourget airport, Paris, at five twenty-four this afternoon." All across the country, factory whistles blew, church bells rang, car horns honked, and newsboys hawked special editions. Ball games, vaudeville shows, movies,

Police at Le Bourget try to cordon off the *Spirit of St. Louis* from mobs of enthusiastic admirers.

and meals were interrupted. Fire engines raced through streets, their sirens screaming. Orchestras struck up "The Star-Spangled Banner" and "La Marseillaise." At Coney Island, two hundred thousand people sang, burned a barge, and staged impromptu parades along Surf Avenue. In Times Square, reservists from two stations attempted to settle down an estimated ten thousand revelers.

The drawn-out drama of Lindbergh's crossing of the Atlantic, capped by his tumultuous touchdown in Paris, became one of those shared national experiences that binds a generation until its last member dies. In Cleveland, sixteen-year-old Margo Behan listened to the radio and kept up her diary: "Mr. Bruhn called over that Lindy had crossed the channel so we tuned in Detroit and followed the flight till . . . he landed at Le Bourget at Paris. Detroit went mad, in fact we all did. Hooray for Lindy!" In Mill Valley, California, fifteen-year-old Flora Reynolds got the word from her language teacher. "I'm probably the only living person who heard that Lindbergh had crossed the ocean—in Latin!" she said with a laugh more than seventy years later. "I remember something about *navigabat per aerem*. That's how I got the news." In San Francisco, seven-year-old Harry Miles Muheim learned a new word. "Before Lindbergh, I had no idea at all of what a hero was," he recalled. "I'm not even sure I'd ever heard the word. But when the *San Francisco Chronicle* reported on his stupendous feat and when the crystal set on our back porch crackled the news into our headphones, the whole idea of heroism got to me. I now understood what a hero was. And I had one. Lindy. Lucky Lindy!" Inside Long Island's Glen Cove Community Hospital, newborn Charles Lindbergh Hurley became the first of many babies across the country to be named after the heroic flier. In Chicago's Chinatown, Mr. and Mrs. Lee Long also wished to honor the boy wonder; after much discussion, they decided to name their infant One Long Hop.

Newspaper publishers everywhere enjoyed booming newsstand sales; pressmen were kept busy printing run after run. Demand in New York was so strong that a reader in Central Park was mugged for his paper and one vendor resorted to "renting" his last remaining copies to customers at the rate of a dollar per thirty minutes. Given the intensely competitive nature of the Orteig Prize in its final stages, it was not surprising that many headline writers treated Lindbergh's crossing as they would a sporting event. The *St. Paul Dispatch* declared: LINDBERGH IS VICTORIOUS! The entire front page of the *Philadelphia Daily News* was given over to a photo of the flier and three bold-faced words: THE KID WINS! The excitement proved too much for one man in Washington State, who fell dead while grabbing an extra edition of the *Aberdeen Daily World*.

Amid the backslapping, bonfires, and screeching headlines, there was a perceptible sense of relief that the nerve-racking ordeal was finally over. "People became restless," observed the *Brooklyn Eagle*. "The relief from nervous tension was marked." Hotel and restaurant patrons "seemed to want to walk, not in any particular direction, but just walk." Churches appeared "unusually crowded. It seemed as if thousands, finding a need of relief from strain and desiring to show 'the Celestial Pilot' their thanks for Lindbergh's safety, hurried to places of quiet and refuge." Even the cynical and the unsanctified, those stock characters of the Jazz Age, were briefly moved to introspection. "A young Minnesotan who seemed to have had nothing to do with his generation did a heroic thing," F. Scott Fitzgerald would later write, "and for a moment people set down their glasses in country clubs and speakeasies and thought of their old best dreams."

It was late Saturday afternoon in New York when Lindbergh touched down in Paris. A couple of thousand people had gathered at Roosevelt

Field in a public ceremony intended to honor Rodman Wanamaker and officially christen the *America*. As with all Byrd productions, this one was planned down to the last detail and dripped with patriotic symbolism. The hangar and speakers' stand were decorated with the national colors of the United States and France. Bottles of water were brought in from the stretch of the Delaware River that George Washington had famously crossed during the American Revolution. Wanamaker's daughters—one born in the States and the other in France—broke them over the center engine's spindle. A trio of military planes flew overhead, dropping little weighted American flags that fell, trembling, over the grounds. Then, just as Byrd was getting ready to give his speech, he received word of Lindbergh's arrival.

Byrd, his expedition suddenly rendered irrelevant in the eyes of many in the crowd, did his best to rescue an awkward situation by turning the festivities into "a celebration of Lindbergh's safety and success." If his spirits were sagging, he didn't show it. He ditched his prepared remarks and heaped genuine praise on the young flier. He didn't mention his own contributions to Lindbergh's triumph, notably the creation of a transatlantic weather reporting service and the free use of the runway he'd had built for the *America*. "I could of course think of nothing else but his magnificent feat," he wrote later. "I realized what it meant to aviation and to international good-fellowship. I had seen enough of Lindbergh to know that he would make an ideal representative of our country. I knew also that his flight would create far more enthusiasm for aviation than ours could possibly do." Those who had lost money betting on Byrd were not nearly as gracious. Telegrams and letters criticizing the commander's perceived timidity poured in. "I just want you to know what you may not realize," cabled a man in North Carolina, "that you are the world's prize boob to get left at the switch as you did."

Clarence Chamberlin, a man fully capable of piloting the first plane from New York to Paris, and Charlie Levine, whose meddling had prevented it from happening, issued statements congratulating Lindbergh's feat. Both were sorely disappointed. Throughout Saturday, even as it became apparent that Lindbergh was going to succeed, they had scrambled to arrange a follow-up flight. Levine announced that the *Columbia* would leave for Paris at eight o'clock that evening. However, a prolonged argument occurred when members of the *Columbia* team were denied access to the runway at Roosevelt Field. The standing policy was a six-hour notice by anyone requesting its use to allow time for arranging police protection, but the grounds were still filled with people milling around after the Byrd ceremonies. Tempers got hot and fists briefly flew. Adding to the confusion, NAA secretary Carl Schory, who had left for Washington, could not be found to officially install the sealed barograph required for all record attempts. Then Giuseppe Bellanca—who had waited for word of Lindbergh's safe arrival in Paris before acting on his long-simmering contempt for Levine—announced he was severing all ties with his business partner. He had decided "two characters such as Levine and myself should not continue in the same enterprise."

Levine, stung, released a statement: "Due to the crowning blow of Mr. Bellanca's resignation, the plane will be placed in the hangar. Mr. Bellanca's resignation causes us to abandon plans for the New York–Paris flight for the present." Chamberlin was flustered and near tears over this latest postponement. "Yes, it's off," he said. "When and if we fly, we'll fly somewhere else than Paris—perhaps Honolulu."

16

"Vive l'Amérique!"

You were strong, Lindbergh, but you also had soul. And it's your soul that has conquered the French soul, which exists in each of us, the French soul that has saved us so many times. For, you should know this: you have placed us in a state of grace.

—Pierre Weiss, *La Bataille de l'Atlantique* (The Battle of the Atlantic)

Charles Lindbergh cut the engine of the *Spirit of St. Louis* and sat helplessly inside his cockpit, tugging the cotton wool out of his ears. History cannot agree on his first words in France. Several Paris papers reported the following exchange:

"I am Lindbergh. Where am I?"

"In Paris."

"Well!"

A variation had the beaming pilot emerging from his plane, doffing his cap, and declaring, "I am Charles Lindbergh!" Some reports insisted he had said, "Here I am; I have done it." Others had him asking, "Is this Paris?" Told that it was, he responded, "Good. Now help me out of this box!" A wire service correspondent described him as calmly saying, "Well, here we are. I'm very happy." Lindbergh himself gave conflicting versions of his first utterance, telling *Le Matin* that it had indeed been, "I am Charles Lindbergh." "I was afraid they might think I was somebody else," he said. Later he remembered his opening line as a shouted query: "Are there any mechanics here?" This was quickly followed by "Does anyone here speak English?"

Whatever Lindbergh's first words, it's certain they were issued in a state of near panic and utter astonishment over the burst dam of humanity who washed over him and his plane. The pandemonium, never mind the language barrier and Lindbergh's muffled hearing—the result of sitting less than ten feet from a roaring engine for nearly a day and a half without respite—made communication impossible. Clutching hands tore at him and ripped pieces of fabric off the *Spirit of St. Louis*. Amid shouts of "Viva l'Amérique!" and "Cette fois, ça va!" ("This time, it's done!"), he was pulled from the plane and hoisted onto the shoulders of the crowd, where he bobbed for a spell before being rescued by a pair of resourceful French fliers. A young pilot named Michael Détroyat yanked off Lindbergh's leather flying helmet and jammed it on the head of a blond American later identified as Henry Wheeler, a vacationing student from Brown University, diverting the crowd's attention, while a civilian aviator named George "Toto" Delage threw a coat over Lindbergh's shoulders. As the protesting Wheeler was hauled before a hastily assembled official reception committee on the upper floor of the administrative building, the real hero was whisked into a hangar on the darkened end of the field. Major Pierre Weiss offered the weary American a cot, but he was too wound up to sleep. Lindbergh innocently asked if he could expect trouble for not having a visa, a question that gave his custodians a good laugh. Willy Coppens, the Belgian air attaché, was struck by the young man's self-possession; his face "conveyed no emotion whatsoever, neither joy nor enthusiasm." Meanwhile, thousands of people, some wearing evening gowns and tuxedos, continued to pour into Le Bourget, running head-on into the multitudes trying to leave.

To Lindbergh's relief, police had wrested his plane from the frenzied crowd and moved it into a hangar for safekeeping. He was shocked by the condition of the suddenly sorry-looking *Spirit* and dismayed to find that someone had made off with his flight log. (The theft of this historical treasure would years later force him to rely on his memory and contemporary news items to reconstruct an hour-by-hour account of the flight for his prize-winning book, *The Spirit of St. Louis*.) At about one o'clock in the morning, after being examined by a physician, introduced to Ambassador Herrick, and persuaded that his plane's damage could be easily repaired, Lindbergh crowded into Delage's Renault for the surreptitious ride into Paris. The French pilots took back roads to avoid the unprecedented traffic jam around the airfield. It was a wild, unforgettable night. A torrent of celebratory champagne flowed, revelers danced in the Place de l'Opéra, and news vendors shouted, "Bonnes nouvelles! The American has arrived!"

As Parisians and ex-pats partied into the wee hours, Lindbergh was driven to the U.S. embassy, but not before his escorts made his first stop in France a brief visit to the Tomb of the Unknown Soldier. Herrick had invited Lindbergh to stay with him and his family, an offer he gratefully accepted. He ate a small meal—an egg and some bouillon—then took a bath, all the while marveling over the servants who scrambled to meet his every need. With the press demanding time with the man of the moment, Herrick acquiesced to a quick press conference. It took place on the stairway leading up to the second floor and lasted eight minutes. Lindbergh then went to bed for the first time in sixty-three hours, wearing a pair of borrowed pajamas. He woke up early Sunday morning to find himself no longer an obscure airmail pilot from the Midwest. Bold-faced headlines in a thousand different newspapers were shouting his name. The *Detroit Free Press* trumpeted his new status: LINDBERGH, IN PARIS, ACCLAIMED WORLD HERO. The French press was uniformly effusive. "A young man, almost a child . . . has just conquered, with rushing wings and heroic audacity, immortality," proclaimed the Paris daily *Excelsior*. "The admirable and splendid effort of intelligent willpower made French and American hearts beat as one during the long hours of waiting, hope and anguish, while millions and millions of people followed the crossing in their imaginations," *Comoedia* editorialized. "Courage deserves a respectful salute, and heroism commands admiration even when the exploit seems humanly impossible to repeat." Paul Painlevé released a statement calling Lindbergh "this daring human bird" and his victory a "magnificent human triumph." He added, "Some heroes die, and others, coming after them, succeed. Those who die are not sacrificed in vain. Lindbergh has triumphed in the great flight undertaken by Nungesser and Coli. All honor to Lindbergh!"

Publications on the left emphasized the universality of his achievement. "There is glory for all of humanity in such a titanic exploit!" Gustave Hervé, a great admirer of Benito Mussolini's air-minded policies in Italy, declared in the fascist publication *Victoire*. "It is the courage of all aviators from all countries, expended gloriously and in obscurity for twenty years, in peace as well as war, which today reached its crowning achievement in the person of Lindbergh!" "In Lindbergh we salute A MAN, of the highest caliber," Paul Vaillant-Couturier wrote in *L'Humanité*, which had displayed contempt for the "bourgeois" organizations behind other attempts. "Exceptional guts, miraculous success, favorable conditions. We could expatiate endlessly on this

Lindbergh's arrival in Paris, as pictured on the cover of a special number of *Le Petit Journal Illustré*.

fantastic journey. What will remain is that we have reached a new stage in the history of speed. Two continents are closer together. Today, millions and millions of men on both sides of the ocean are going to feel more neighborly towards each other, more like brothers. And that is a revolutionary victory." *L'Oeuvre*, a Paris paper with socialist tendencies, also focused on the ecumenical quality of Lindbergh's triumph, with Jean Piot writing that "we do not wish to see in Lindbergh's victory a purely American victory. It is a victory for the human race. By this act of pulling himself from one continent to the other by the force of his will . . . Lindbergh transcended nationality and rose to the level of citizen of the world." "The victory of Lindbergh is, above all, a moral victory," Claude Francueil would observe a few days later in a special number of *Le Petit Journal*. "He succeeded as much with his soul as with his muscles . . . he proved that any undertaking, no matter how crazy it seems at first, must succeed if it is conducted by a man with an ideal."

The fascination with Lindbergh had no borders. In Buenos Aires, a mistaken report that there had been a kitten aboard the *Spirit of St. Louis* "tickled the fancy of the Argentinians," with hundreds harrying newspaper offices for the latest details of the flier and his pet. Congratulatory cables came in from Japan, Guatemala, Poland, Cuba, and all other corners of the globe. In Rome, Mussolini composed a personal letter, describing the "enthusiastic admiration which rises in this moment from the hearts of the entire Italian people," and Pope Pius XI also sent praise. In Budapest, Michael Lorant—"the champion stenographer of Hungary"—was already busy transforming piles of newspaper clippings into *The Hero of the Ocean*, a soon-to-be-published novel "so realistic that the reader soon feels well acquainted with Colonel Lindbergh and his mother, and is in love with 'the slender, blond Daisy,' evidently a character created by the author's romantic imagination." In New York, noted architect Francis Keally was letting his imagination soar, conceptualizing a monument dubbed the "Lindbergh light," a 500-foot-high marble shaft whose beacon would serve as a guide for airmen. In Belfast, members of the Linen Merchants Association had a humbler tribute in mind, hoping to present the clean-cut American a gift of handkerchiefs made from the finest Irish linen. The world that suddenly was obsessed with Lindbergh "is a cockleshell, with live coals inside it, upon which we spin about in a big universe," observed columnist Heywood Broun. "And we are small and fragile and, as some would have it, miserable sinners." But Lindbergh had "put the angry sea in its place," proving the human race still had the right stuff. "Whoa floods and quakes and fogs and oceans! Listen to us. This is our world and we can mount and manage. Man is a really notable creation. Don't let 'em tell you different."

The next few days were a head-spinning blur as Lindbergh was feted from one end of Paris to the other. Parisians displayed American flags everywhere in his honor and launched cheers of *"Vive Lindbergh! Vive l'Amérique!"* in his presence. He won them over with his modesty, magnanimity, and simple grace, and grew in their esteem whenever he invoked the names of famous French aviators, which was often. His capable guide was Herrick. The ambassador's counsel and tact were immense helps to Lindbergh, who forged a lifetime friendship with the courtly old diplomat and his family.

That first day in France, Herrick arranged for a complicated three-way telephone hookup so Lindbergh could speak with his mother in Detroit. Evangeline Land Lindbergh had been stoic throughout her son's flight, rarely giving even a hint of emotion. She stayed true to her nature during the brief, static-filled conversation, which was routed through an interlocutor in London. She had just turned down an offer from the *New York Daily News* to travel to Paris at their expense. She was "grateful to the French people for being so wonderful to him, but I'll be patient and wait to greet him when he lands in New York."

There initially was a strain of disappointment in France's acclamation of Lindbergh. The regret seeped through in conversation and in print. "We'd have preferred it had been a Frenchman—*mais qu'est-ce-que tu veux?*" said some who had witnessed Lindbergh's arrival at Le Bourget. Major Pierre Weiss later wrote that his cheering countrymen were thinking, "What a shame he isn't one of ours!" As if to lessen the sting, much of the early French commentary about Lindbergh made sure there was room in the *Spirit of St. Louis* for a pair of ghosts named Nungesser and Coli. Forgotten was the fact that the worldly Nungesser had been casually dismissive of the youngster in the race. He and Coli were in their final stages of preparation when somebody mentioned that Lindbergh was ready to leave San Diego for St. Louis, en route to New York. "Cable him to stay in St. Louis," Nungesser said. "We will tell him all about it when we come there on our tour." Whether Lindbergh was aware of the remark or not, throughout his stay in Paris he tactfully invoked the names of the missing French aces in his public comments, almost to the point of obsequiousness.

Lindbergh's first stop after talking with his mother was at the modest flat of Mme. Nungesser. A reporter for *Le Petit Journal* described the mob scene around the Place de la République when the flier arrived with Herrick at 5:30 p.m.

> A great shout erupted! From the terraces of neighboring cafés, from balconies . . . it was only one cry that arose. He stopped for a moment. He looked, his tall body a bit stooped, as if under the weight of a victory too heavy for his young shoulders. He smiled a fresh and somewhat amazed smile. This smile conquered the throngs once and for all, who cheered him even more frenziedly. The crowd surged forward and the barriers threatened to give way under the weight of the flood. Lindbergh was hustled to the building's entrance. The tenants grouped on the porch continued the crowd's applause. Some women, always a little superstitious, touched Lindbergh's clothes, saying, "This will bring me luck!" A

mother held out her baby to him, and the pilot's blond hair mingled with the infant's as he kissed him. Finally we could go up. Reaching Mme. Nungesser's sixth-floor apartment took a while, since on every landing there were young girls with pens and postcards in hand waiting for the hero to sign his autograph after they kissed him. Moved and amused, the American aviator continued to smile.

Lindbergh stood self-consciously inside the cramped dining room where, just a couple of weeks before, Nungesser and his mother had said their good-byes. "I wanted to make my first call on the mother of my valiant friend, Captain Nungesser," he started. Mme. Nungesser, her eyes brimming with tears, nodded slowly as the flier's words were translated. "I knew Charles in New York and admired his spirit," Lindbergh continued. "I have high hope that he will be found. I want you to have confidence that he will be found. My own mother was confident that I would be safe at the end of my journey. With the whole American people I regret that the searches made for Charles and his companion, the brave Coli, up to now have been unfruitful, but I want you to keep on hoping." "I am a mother, that is all," she responded sadly, placing her hands on her visitor's shoulders. "I have not lost hope of seeing my son again. The heart of a French woman knows how to support suffering and anxiety." At that she broke down and wept. Lindbergh consoled her with some awkward pats and more words about the strong bonds between him and his mother. He gave her the small bouquet of white and pink flowers that a young female admirer had thrust into his hands as he arrived. "Let them be my lucky charm!" Mme. Nungesser said as she kissed the flowers. The visit ended with an embrace at the door.

Lindbergh's gesture "pleased the sentimental crowd," said the reporter for *Le Petit Journal*. "'That's very decent of him!' we heard people saying all around us." But that was just the beginning of Paris's love affair with Lindbergh. The next day, at the Aéro Club of France, he made his first speech—praising Nungesser and Coli—and responded to chants of *"Au balcon! Au balcon!"* by walking out onto the balcony and waving a pair of flags, French and American, to the delight of the hordes below. He accepted a gold medal but politely turned down the accompanying gift of 150,000 francs (about $6,000), suggesting that the money be donated to a fund that had been created to help care for the families of fallen French pilots. "Who can say, after seeing this boy here land his little plane almost on the same spot where Nungesser and Coli took off—who can say after seeing the great welcome that the people of France are giving this young son of Uncle Sam—that the magnificent friendship that has existed for 150 years between America and France is not an eternal, indestructible and genuine feeling?" asked Herrick. The theme of eternal bilateral relations continued after the reception, when Herrick and Lindbergh drove to the Ministry of Finance. "This feat of yours," Raymond Poincaré told Lindbergh, "will bring together France and the United States as nothing else could have done."

And so it continued for the rest of the week. "We followed Lindbergh through a succession of presentations of awards, official receptions, banquets, and laudatory speeches, reporting word after banal word," remembered correspondent Waverly Root. "Never in human history had the name of Lafayette been so frequently brandished." Like the souvenir hunters who had partially dismantled the *Spirit of St. Louis* (now being repaired inside a guarded hangar), everybody wanted a piece of him. *L'Humanité* skewered the men in monocles and top hats who "grabbed him and still haven't let him go—dragging him to official receptions, forcing the same old speeches

The world's newest hero waves the U.S. and French flags during a function at the Aéro Club of France, to the delight of cheering Parisians.

down his throat. We no longer see this simple solitary figure of a boy . . . unless he's flanked by the official grimaces of all those who 'have nothing to do,' the officials, ministers, presidents . . . wanting to take their share of these crazy acclamations, which are for Lindbergh alone. He's certainly a hero, but he's surrounded by official clowns."

Lindbergh was obliging to the verge of exhaustion as he was hustled from one event to the next. "From the moment I woke in the morning to that when I fell asleep late at night, every hour was scheduled," he remembered. Parisians rioted to get closer to him. He was embarrassed when strangers insisted on kissing his hand, startled when women rushed up to peck him on the cheek, and humbled when Louis Blériot, the father of French aviation, called him "the prophet of a new era." A respected graphologist examined his signature and determined that the way he dotted his *i* indicated idealism, even mysticism. "All the signs I have been able to discover are proofs of superiority," Dr. Camille Streletski concluded. "But what astonishes me are the sensibility, intellectualism and cerebralism which are clearly expressed." All the while, a team of secretaries tried in vain to put a dent in the tens of thousands of letters, telegrams, and packages that poured into the embassy.

Thursday, May 26, was Ascension Day in France. Upward of a million people turned out for Paris's official tribute to Lindbergh. At City Hall he was seated like royalty in a golden chair and presented with a specially designed medal and the key to the city. Major Pierre Weiss, one of the airmen who had saved him from the crowd and then driven him to the embassy, thought the tousle-haired American possessed all the authentic qualities one would wish in a hero: "How sad it would have been to see emerge from the *Spirit of St. Louis* a second-class hero, with a cigarette hanging from his mouth! And what satisfaction . . . that glory should have gone to this gentleman with light-blue eyes." Weiss imagined the seventeenth-century poet Jean Racine describing Lindbergh in "eternal verses" as "Young, charming, attracting all hearts toward him." Those hearts were beating inside the chests of countless female admirers. "Have you seen him?" a highly perfumed society lady asked a fellow guest at one of the receptions. "But he's charming! Much better than the photos!"

Raymond Orteig and his wife had been in Pau when Raymond Jr. cabled them that Lindbergh was on his way. The hotelier rushed to reach Paris by train, arriving a few minutes before the *Spirit of St. Louis* landed. But he was stuck in the crush of the mob, unable to "move an inch," he said. The following day, at the American embassy, the donor of the Orteig Prize was finally able to greet the exhausted and exalted young man who had just claimed it. Coincidentally, it was May 22, eight years to the day that Orteig had first offered the $25,000 incentive in a letter to the Aero Club of America.

"Well, Mr. Orteig," said Lindbergh, who towered over the plumpish hotelier, "you certainly started something." When Orteig expressed mild surprise that the flier would remember him after the rush of events, Lindbergh smiled. "Well," he said, "I've good reason for remembering you."

It was difficult for Orteig to dismiss hope for Lindbergh's vanished rivals. "I knew Coli particularly well," he told the French press. "The pilot Tarascon introduced us, and I met Nungesser in New York. We went through such anguish when we learned of these brave men's departure, and then heard the false reports of their landing in front of the Statue of Liberty, then the great mystery of their disappearance. It is my earnest wish that we may learn in the coming days—let us continue in this hope—that they have been found somewhere in Labrador."

Orteig, for all his honest concern, was not the type to dwell in morbidity. Yes, several brave men had been lost or nearly killed in pursuit of his prize, but any psychological encumbrances melted away in the glow of Lindbergh's magnificent flight and the flier's splendid mien. Someone asked Orteig how he felt.

"I feel a lot lighter," he said.

"About $25,000 lighter?"

"No," he responded. "I mean my spirits feel lighter at the thought of what this man has done."

On Thursday evening, Orteig and his wife attended a private dinner at the embassy with the ambassador, his family, and the world's newest celebrity. Orteig was able to enjoy "a most cordial heart-to-heart talk" with Lindbergh, a conversation that gave him the opportunity to appreciate his "sterling qualities." Part of the conversation involved the flier's desire to drop a message of thanks to the people of Paris when he left in a couple of days for Belgium, honoring a request to appear before King Albert and his queen, both enthusiastic pilots. Orteig, who was staying

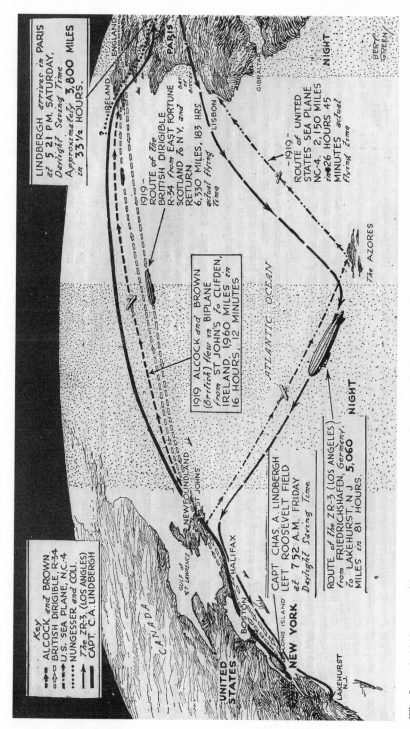

The June 4, 1927, issue of *Literary Digest* included a map illustrating the conquest of the North Atlantic from the first successful crossings in 1919 through the recent attempts of Nungesser and Lindbergh.

215

at the Hotel Crillon, coyly suggested that he drop it near the ancient Egyptian obelisk on the Place de la Concorde so he might have a chance at retrieving it as a souvenir.

Early Saturday afternoon, following a final slate of receptions and public duties, Lindbergh left Le Bourget in the *Spirit of St. Louis*. He circled the Eiffel Tower and performed several aerial acrobatics for the huge crowds gathered below. He then flew over the public square and expertly aimed his parting gift at the base of the obelisk. The message was attached to a French flag, weighted with a small sack of sand, and tied with red, white, and blue ribbons. Orteig was at the prearranged spot, but his effort to catch the falling trophy was frustrated by a dozen others battling to do the same. A war veteran named Howard Darrin ultimately emerged from the scrum with it. A friend of Orteig's told Darrin the package had been intended for the prize donor.

"Are you Mr. Orteig?" Darrin asked the hotelier.

"Yes, sir."

"Well, here it is," he said, handing it over. The flier's handwritten farewell read, "Good-bye! Dear Paris. Ten thousand thanks for your kindness to me. Charles A. Lindbergh." The message was delivered to Paris officials while the national colors were brought back to New York by Orteig, who for years proudly displayed them on the wall of the Lafayette.

Lindbergh made the airfield at Evere, Belgium, in a little over two hours. With five thousand armed soldiers keeping a crowd ten times that number at bay, the greeting was considerably less raucous than the one he had experienced a week earlier at Le Bourget, but no less warm. He spent the weekend being feted at a series of private and public receptions, gathering a handful of decorations and awards in the process.

Then it was on to England. On Sunday, May 29, he crossed the English Channel and made for the Croydon aerodrome outside London. To his horror, the storied British reserve was nowhere to be found in the mob of 150,000 people swarming over the field. Fearful of a disaster, he aborted his landing and circled the airport for several minutes while an overmatched army of bobbies tried to clear out a path. Upon his second touchdown the crushing mass of admirers damaged the *Spirit of St. Louis* and just barely missed getting to Lindbergh, who was snatched away in an automobile by

The *Spirit of St. Louis* is mobbed at the Croydon aerodrome outside London, where an estimated 150,000 people turned out to greet Lindbergh.

members of the Royal Air Club. The chaos caused the official welcome to be canceled, but the balance of the next few days' events went on as planned.

He had a congenial meeting with Teddy Brown—eight years removed from history's first nonstop transatlantic flight—who called the American "a marvelous young chap." Another highlight was a private session with King George V. "Now tell me, Captain Lindbergh," he asked at one point. "There is one thing I want to know. How did you pee?" Lindbergh explained that he had a hole in the seat of his wicker chair, which allowed him to urinate through a funnel into an aluminum container. He had disposed of the corked container somewhere over the French countryside.

Lindbergh's original plan to see a bit of Europe and possibly make a flight to the Orient also was tossed aside as America clamored for his return. Even his commander in chief, President Coolidge, postponed his summer vacation in order to be in Washington for Lindbergh's expected arrival. Lindbergh later jested that he had "found that it didn't make much difference whether I wanted to stay or not; and while I was informed that it was not necessarily an order to come back home, there was a battleship waiting for me." Actually, the USS *Memphis*, which Coolidge dispatched to bring him home, was a cruiser, but to judge by the way Lindbergh was being deified in the press, some idolaters saw no need for a vessel of any size. He could walk back across the Atlantic.

17

"Lindbergh Is Our Elijah"

The Nation is glad to know that Lindbergh is home again. It will acclaim him wherever he goes. He numbers his friends by tens of millions. The good that he can do is beyond imagination. He has directed the thoughts of the country from sickly and morbid sensations, and has taught American youth to lift up its eyes to the heavens.

—*Washington Post* editorial, June 12, 1927

For reasons that were not always that easy to articulate, Lindbergh's flight had captured the popular imagination like none other. Journalists, jitterbugs, and gewgaw makers all worked themselves into a lather. On the day he touched down in Paris the *New York World* alone sold an extra 114,000 copies, with most readers agreeing with the paper's assessment of the flight as "the greatest feat of a solitary man in the records of the human race." At the Savoy Ballroom in Harlem, dance-happy patrons shouted "Lindy's done it!" and created a variation of the Charleston called the Lindy Hop. It became the dance craze of the nation. And the first wave of what would become a tsunami of Lindbergh-inspired merchandise, everything from sheet music to quickie biographies, rolled into stores.

While the city fathers of Washington, New York, St. Louis, and Detroit planned elaborate civic receptions, offers of all types continued to pour in. At least three proposals involved flying a rocket ship to the moon. A self-described "biologist" suggested a scheme to graft wings onto monkeys, an intermediate step until the procedure could be performed on humans: "If you will sit down and talk with me, you will see that the idea is not nearly so fantastic as it sounds." But there also were plenty of serious propositions on the table: motion picture contracts, book and lecture deals, vaudeville tours, and product endorsements. Manhattan attorney Dudley Field Malone could tell Lindbergh all about the "hero business." His clients included Gertrude "Trudy" Ederle (he had financed her feat of being the first woman to swim the English Channel) and heavyweight champion Gene Tunney. Malone had made sure both celebrities cashed in on their ephemeral fame; they in turn publicly encouraged Lindbergh to do likewise. "Lindbergh had better get the money now; later on it may be too late," Ederle told the press. Tunney's advice to the flier was to "commercialize his stunt for every cent that's in it, for in a year from now he will be forgotten."

Collectively, somewhere between $5 million and $10 million in legitimate offers were waved under the young man's nose. Lindbergh, who was sailing back with publicity men Dick Blythe and Harry Bruno, repeatedly said no. The flier's refusal to capitalize on his fame only added to his mystery as the *Memphis* steamed closer to home. "Who *is* this Lindbergh?" wondered a country grown accustomed to the bald opportunism and vaporous notoriety of a succession of flagpole-sitters and marathon dancers. The excitement surrounding his return continued to mount. "You are in for it now," Blythe warned. "You're the great American idol. Your time is no longer your own."

"I don't know about the idol part," Lindbergh responded. "But I do know I'm in a terrible mess."

The *Memphis*, accompanied by an escort of vessels and airships and awash in an ear-splitting stew of sirens, bells, whistles, cannonades, and cheers, docked at the Washington Navy Yard on June 11. It was a muggy Saturday in the nation's capital. As high-ranking members of the government and the military waited respectfully but anxiously, Lindbergh enjoyed a private reunion with his mother aboard ship. Then the clean-cut wonder boy who had braved the Atlantic walked down the gangplank into the public's embrace. Life would never again be the same.

Hundreds of thousands of people lined the parade route while a record radio audience listened to the proceedings. The procession that took Lindbergh to a specially constructed reception stand at the foot of the Washington Monument included a truck carrying 55,000 telegrams of congratulations; meanwhile, ten messenger boys struggled with a giant scroll that constituted a single telegram from Minneapolis bearing 17,500 signatures. President Coolidge delivered the opening remarks, making the already common allusions to Columbus, the Pilgrims, and Lindbergh's "Viking ancestors," after which the surprisingly verbose "Silent Cal" pinned the Distinguished Flying Cross on the guest of honor's lapel. Lindbergh also received a promotion to colonel in the reserves. There was an every-man quality to the hero, who had been talked out of wearing his army uniform by Blythe in favor of a blue serge suit. After several minutes of cheering, the object of all this adulation finally stepped to the microphone.

"On the evening of May 21," Lindbergh said, "I arrived at Le Bourget, France. I was in Paris for one week, in Belgium for a day, and was in London and in England for several days. Everywhere I went, at every meeting I attended, I was requested to bring a message home to you. Always the message was the same.

"'You have seen,' the message was, 'the affection of the people of France for the people of America demonstrated to you. When you return to America, take back that message to the people of the United States from the people of France and of Europe.'

"I thank you."

Unprepared for the brevity of the speech, the crowd waited a few seconds before bursting into applause. At 106 words, Lindbergh showed that he could economize words as expertly as he rationed fuel. If nothing else, he needed to conserve his strength for the whirlwind of receptions to follow.

After a blurry succession of high-level banquets and medal-awarding ceremonies in Washington, it was on to New York for more of the same. On June 13, Lindbergh was transferred from a seaplane to a police launch to Mayor Jimmy Walker's yacht for final delivery to the southern tip of Manhattan. There were 300,000 people jammed into the Battery, but more than ten times that number were uptown, corralled behind police barricades or hanging out of windows. The entire city had shut down for Lindbergh Day. Elinor Sullivan Smith was one of the estimated four million people—which amounted to two out of every three New Yorkers—who turned out in welcome. "The parade that went down Broadway, the people went wild," she recalled years later. "They were throwing things out windows. Telephone books. Why half the people weren't hit in the head and killed, I don't know." It took an hour for the procession, which included 10,000 soldiers and sailors, to crawl the

New York City goes wild for Lindbergh.

one mile from Battery Park to City Hall. There, robed trumpeters and grandstands stuffed with 3,000 city officials awaited his arrival. "Colonel Lindbergh," said Mayor Walker, pinning an elaborately designed medal on his lapel, "New York City is yours. I don't give it to you. You won it."

Lindbergh Day concluded with yet another medal ceremony, in Central Park, this time Governor Al Smith draping the state's Medal of Valor—designed by Tiffany—around his neck. Afterward Lindbergh and his mother retired to a Park Avenue apartment for some rest before leaving for a private banquet at the mansion of New York social lion Clarence Mackay, president of the Postal Telegraph Company. Several more days of receptions, both great and small, followed. The grandest was the official dinner of the City of New York at the Hotel Commodore, which at 3,700 guests was publicized as the largest banquet ever given an individual in the country's history. That evening, former U.S. Supreme Court justice Charles Evans Hughes was his usual eloquent self. "We measure heroes as we do ships, by their displacement," he said. "Colonel Lindbergh has displaced everything."

On Thursday, June 16, Brooklyn celebrated its own Charles Lindbergh Day, with nearly 750,000 men, women, and children lining the twenty-two-mile parade route. Afterward it was back to Manhattan for a six-o'clock tea at the Hotel Breevort. There a scroll, a medal, and an ornately designed check for $25,000 were presented to the flier. Hundreds of invited guests crowded into the flag-bedecked dining room to witness the brief ceremony, which seemed almost anticlimactic in the wake of the mass delirium of the previous weeks.

Colonel Walter Scott introduced Raymond Orteig, who spoke of his reasons for creating the prize. He'd had "two thoughts in mind: first, to stimulate aviation and long-distance flying and, second, to strengthen the friendly relations between the United States and France. Thanks to you, Colonel Lindbergh, my aspirations have materialized beyond all expectations."

Orteig then thanked Lindbergh for his recent thoughtfulness in Paris. "I shall never forget the thrilling moment on the Place de la Concorde, when, as you were leaving for Belgium, you dropped your message of farewell to Paris," he said. "It is with great pride that I brought back to America the colors of the two great countries, to which the message was attached. By your wonderful achievement, you have won the great crown of glory that I hoped would be yours. The trustees having acknowledged your winning of the prize, I take the greatest pleasure in handing you this check, insignificant as it may be when compared with the magnitude of the feat accomplished."

Lindbergh's remarks were characteristically short.

"I have often been asked what it was that first directed my attention to the flight from New York to Paris," he said. "I believe Mr. Orteig's offer directed the attention of aviators to that flight. The offer was nothing more nor less than a challenge to pilots and engineers in aeronautics to see whether they could build and fly a plane from New York to Paris. I do not believe that any such challenge, within reason, will ever go unanswered."

Then it was off to another reception, another dinner, and another party, the latter featuring Mayor Walker, silent-screen legend Charlie Chaplin, and publisher William Randolph Hearst. Everybody, it seemed, wanted to meet the fellow whom Cardinal Hayes had greeted as "the first and finest American boy of his day."

Preferring to be known as nothing more than a first-rate pilot who, through skill and diligent preparation, had accomplished one of the

On June 16, 1927, Lindbergh officially received the Orteig Prize in a ceremony at the Brevoort Hotel. From left: George Burleigh, Lindbergh, Raymond Orteig, Walter Scott, Franklin Q. Brown, and Orteig's sons, Evariste and Jean. Burleigh, Scott, and Brown were among the trustees of the prize.

great feats in aviation, Colonel Charles A. Lindbergh was to his eternal dismay transfigured into that newest of modern creatures: a celebrity. Thanks to advances in radio, newsreels, photojournalism, and other instruments of mass communications during the 1920s, that insidious accompaniment of fame cynically known as "ballyhoo" reached a level never seen before and rarely matched since.

If image wasn't quite yet everything in 1927, the expansion of the cult of personality—fueled by the growing and converging fields of advertising, public relations, and electronic media—was nonetheless well under way in American life. In no time at all, Lindbergh the hero was overshadowed by Lindbergh the celebrity. The fact that he was such big news made him even *more* newsworthy. Even the normally staid *New York Times* devoted its first sixteen pages to coverage of his New York welcome. His fame grew exponentially with the overwhelming media coverage of all the subsequent pseudo-events: parades, banquets, medal ceremonies, and grip-and-grins with a dizzying procession of dignitaries. The levelheaded Lindbergh realized the absurdity of a fame that fed on itself. "I was so filled up with this hero guff," he told Dick Blythe after they left New York for yet another round of celebrations in St. Louis, "I was ready to shout murder."

Despite his protestations, in looks and demeanor Lindbergh was made to order for his assigned role as public hero. He was young, brave, movie-star handsome, modest almost to a fault, and obviously considered his mother his best girl. Lots of women were trying to change that, however, as evidenced by the ten thousand marriage proposals he received. In St. Louis, a group of starry-eyed ladies engaged in a free-for-all over the half-eaten cob of corn he left on his plate. He was remarkably photo-genic. An estimated 7.4 million feet of newsreel film were shot of him by the time the last flakes of confetti had fallen in New York. Meanwhile, newspaper and magazine photographers took thousands upon thousands of pictures of him. Whenever a camera caught him frowning, editors charitably labeled the expression of displeasure "Lindbergh's flying face." Nothing could tarnish the young man's image. "Colonel Lindbergh is a messenger from God," insisted the St. Louis man who offered to guard Lindbergh's growing pile of gifts and trophies for free.

Within a few weeks of his flight Lindbergh received an astonish-ing four million letters, cards, cables, and parcels. "Fair-haired Apollo," began one flowery missive, "your meteoric traverse of the sea, your tran-scendent victory over boundless space, shall thunder down the avenue of time!" Recognizing a good thing, Western Union offered the public twenty different preformatted telegrams. One canned message read, "It's the most glorious individual achievement in the history of the human race. Welcome home." Another boilerplate telegram required the sender to fill in a couple of blanks: "The _____ Club of _____ sends greetings. In the good old American way you put it over and now we're glad to have you home again."

The *Providence Journal* doubted that "any man of any age in the world's history has ever been the recipient of such adulation." Those commentators not comparing him to George Washington (who, like Lindbergh, was "first in the hearts of his countrymen") or a Norse god trotted out analogies to such historical figures as Napoleon and Julius Caesar. Lindbergh was embarrassed by the comparisons. He was no king, certainly no god, but in his admirable unpretentiousness he attracted perhaps even more acolytes than if he had been. "The stiff military bear-ing of the others, that touch of dramatic superiority which can suggest so much in the air of a military victor, was totally lacking in Lindbergh," wrote Fitzhugh Green, covering the Washington welcome for the *New York Times*. "His hair was mussed; his stance awkward. But it was a mussiness and an awkwardness that made men cheer and women weep to see." Green noted that one radio broadcaster, affected by Lindbergh's unexpected genuineness, cried unashamedly on the air at the conclusion of his speech.

The power of radio in fueling Lindy mania cannot be overstated. In fact, Lindbergh was the first national radio celebrity. Thirty million Americans—a quarter of the nation's population—listened to his clipped, high-pitched voice carry over the airwaves from Washington. "Americans had known national figures before—political leaders, military heroes, even athletes—but with Lindbergh national radio networks began to demonstrate their ability to turn persons of accomplishment into celebrities by transmitting the sound of their voice as well as information about them," historian David Kyvig wrote. "Hundreds of thousands of people who would never come close to Lindbergh could feel that they knew him as well as they knew a neighbor."

Journalists, intellectuals, and social commentators were almost desperate to analyze the flier's fame and to understand the mania to which they were all contributing. "The popularity of Lindbergh is due to the fact that he has chosen to achieve an aim the whole world can understand and admire," Philip Whitwell Wilson observed in the *New York Times*. "Every era has its allotted evangel. . . . Our faith is locomotion. . . . To fly is thus a supreme mysticism. To fly across an ocean is the beatific vision. Charles A. Lindbergh is our Elijah."

Lindbergh's "pureness" took on near-mythic proportions. He was exalted in the pulpit ("He has roused a planet's soul," exclaimed one minister) and lauded by the Cleanliness Institute, which urged christening every bathtub "The Spirit of Colonel Charles Lindbergh" to encourage boys to bathe more often. Lindbergh "has shown us that we are not rotten to the core," Mary B. Mullett wrote hopefully in *American Magazine*, "but morally sound and sweet and good." A stock example of his incorruptibility was his change of heart over the $500,000 contract he had signed with William Randolph Hearst to star in a movie about aviation. After arguing Hearst's motives with Harry Guggenheim, a fabulously rich ex-navy pilot whose father had endowed the Daniel Guggenheim Fund for the Promotion of Aeronautics, Lindbergh came to agree with his new friend and adviser that Hearst was more interested in using the film as a vehicle to promote the career of his mistress, actress Marion Davies, than aeronautics. At Lindbergh's request, Hearst tore up the agreement. The media mogul was impressed enough to send the reluctant leading man a pair of nearly priceless seventeenth-century silver globes—one celestial, the other terrestrial— that Lindbergh had admired inside Hearst's New York apartment.

One measure of Lindbergh's celebrity was the more than two hundred songs—some silly, many sentimental, all celebratory—that were written in the aftermath of his flight. Throughout America, such titles as "Plucky Lindy (We're Proud of You)," "Dreamt We Heard a Lindy-Bird," and "Like an Angel You Flew into Everyone's Heart" were played on parlor pianos and listened to on living-room Victrolas. Most were marches ("Spirit of St. Louis March"), fox-trots ("Lindy, Youth with the Heart of Gold"), and waltzes ("Over the Ocean Waltz"), but the mix also included stomps, two-steps, and a mazurka. Musical tributes appeared in France ("Les Vainqueurs du Ciel," "L'Aigle de L'Atlantique Hommage à Lindbergh"), Sweden ("Lycko Lindbergh"), the Netherlands ("Vijf dagen naar Parijs"), and several other countries. One of the most popular numbers in this flood of sheet music and 78-rpm recordings was "Lindbergh (The Eagle of the USA)," the product of famous Tin Pan Alley songwriters Howard Johnson and Al Sherman. It was hurried into circulation before its namesake had even returned to the United States. "For Lindbergh, oh what a Wonder Boy is he," people sang. "Lindbergh, his name will live in history." Lindy-related merchandise was rushed into stores and would continue to be produced for several more years: board games, dolls, bookends, hats, shoes, calendars, rulers, pocket knives, ink pens, pennants, lapel pins, pedal planes, straight razors, postcards, watches, letter openers, paperweights, tapestries, poker chips, decanters, cast-metal toys, model kits, ashtrays, cigars, and commemorative plates and spoons. A number of hastily written biographies hit the shelves, all uniformly hagiographic and inspirational.

The excesses of Lindy mania did not go unrecognized. One person wrote of his disgust with the "ostentatious display of pomp" in a letter to the *New York World*. Even Lindbergh—a fellow "bored to distraction" as he rode up Fifth Avenue—would have approved of using the money spent on his parade to aid the victims of the Mississippi floods, the reader insisted. Another *World* reader expressed "the greatest pity for young Lindbergh. This fame was not of his seeking, at least, not in the monstrous form which it is now assuming. A daring, modest young fellow, he performed a bold feat which thrilled even me as nothing since the war has done. But why must his exploit be exaggerated and repeated and harped upon until one loathes the sound of his name?" The *New Yorker*, with such writers as Robert Benchley and E. B. White tossing darts, spoke for the smart set with its regular cynical takes on Lindbergh's fame: "Sooner or later he will leave the ways of a god, resume the ways of a man. This will not be so much disillusion as simple bathos, which is almost as terrible."

There was little chance "the celestial Viking" would be reduced to human scale anytime soon. Many who had never written verse before were impelled to explore the lyrical possibilities of his epic flight. Newspapers and magazines were bombarded with their offerings, nearly all of it heart-felt slush. The *New York Times* alone received two thousand unsolicited poems. Another five thousand were sent directly to Lindbergh. A New York publisher held a competition to select the best Lindbergh-inspired poems and in short order was deluged with four thousand entries from around the world. Such lines as "Thus you, O Sky-man, in your sun-bright youth" and "Viking Lief to the sunrise racing" found their way into the published book of finalists.

Lindbergh, nearly suffocated by the demands of ballyhoo, was able to escape to a familiar sanctuary: the cockpit of the *Spirit of St. Louis*. Having become friends with Harry Guggenheim, Lindbergh undertook a three-month "goodwill" tour of all forty-eight states. The idea was to use his fame to spread the gospel of aviation to engineers, politicians, and average citizens, but the flying ambassador was just as happy for the opportunity to leave the maddening crowds behind, if only for a few hours at a time.

The tour began on July 20 and ended on October 23. During these three months he covered 22,350 miles in the *Spirit of St. Louis*, making stops in Boston, Cleveland, Detroit (where he gave Henry and Edsel Ford their first airplane rides), Tulsa, Salt Lake City, Los Angeles, and 72 other major cities. He gave 147 speeches and dropped 192 messages onto communities he could not visit. He "tried to convince everyone who would listen that aviation had a brilliant future, in which America should lead," he said. Politicians and airport officials at every stop were moved to action. But newspaper editors knew that the average person hurrying to the local airfield for a glimpse of the world's greatest celebrity and his famous plane really cared little about the wonders of the earth inductor compass. So, just as they had before the flight to Paris, reporters often peppered the "apostle of aeronautics" with questions readers wanted asked but that the flier considered inane.

"Is it true, Colonel, that girls don't interest you at all?" he was asked at one stop.

"If you can show me what that has to do with aviation," he snapped, "I'll be glad to answer you."

These occasional displays of irritation did nothing to harm Lindbergh's immaculate image as he flew in and out of cities across the country. People couldn't get enough of him. Everybody wanted a souvenir, no matter how intangible the connection. Laundry workers stole his underwear, maids rummaged through his wastebaskets for scraps of paper, people scrambled to grab a pencil or a fork he had used. Donald Keyhoe, a pilot who accompanied Lindbergh on his tour, remembered one time when, having just settled into a hotel suite, they heard a loud hammering on the door.

"They must be afraid we'll escape," Lindbergh said. "That sounds as though they were nailing us in."

Keyhoe opened the door and a large brass plaque hit the floor. The inscription on it declared Colonel Charles A. Lindbergh had occupied the room on this particular day.

"Well," said Lindbergh, "they don't believe in wasting any time."

In the hero's wake, streets, parks, bridges—even railroad cars and a viaduct—were named after him. So were a town in Wyoming, a lake in Montana, and a mountain peak in Colorado. By year's end the publisher of *Time* magazine had created its "Man of the Year" award specifically for him and the newest of several schools bearing the Lindbergh name was under construction in Dearborn, Michigan.

The new year found him in the midst of a second goodwill tour. It started in mid-December with a twenty-seven-hour nonstop flight between Washington, D.C., and Mexico City, then continued through fifteen Latin American countries. Upon his return in early 1928, he retired the *Spirit of St. Louis* to the Smithsonian Institution, where it has been on display ever since. He also received the Medal of Honor from President Coolidge, the nation's highest award for bravery. An unintended consequence of this high-profile globetrotting was to keep throwing logs on the fire of Lindy mania. His flying ambassadorship kept him in the news daily, so much so that Paris papers were criticized for

sacrificing coverage of developments in French aviation in favor of publishing the latest word on the American's activities. The tours also added
to the glut of gifts and decorations: trophies, loving cups, proclamations,
keys, portraits, honorary degrees, testimonials, resolutions, certificates
of membership, addresses of welcome, bound scrapbooks, medals, busts,
and good luck charms of every type. In all, Lindbergh received more
than fifteen thousand presents from sixty-nine countries and every state
in the union. There were expensive silver portrait busts and a simple
collection of flies ("Flies for a Flyer") from the Bug House of America
in Butte, Montana. There were corsets, cigarette cases, cocktail shakers,
and a pouch of chewing tobacco. With no place to store this eclectic
collection (conservatively estimated to be worth about $2 million), he
eventually donated it to the Missouri Historical Society.

Money remained a secondary consideration to Lindbergh as he
weighed his options. His life's work would be aviation—of that he was
absolutely certain. Still, a man had to make a living. According to Harry
Bruno, Lindbergh was "never averse to cashing in on his flight. Once he
realized how everyone was reacting to it, he resolved a plan to make it
solve his financial problems, and made sure that he was never short of
a dollar again. But that doesn't mean to say he gave us carte blanche to
endorse anything in his name. Just the opposite. He kept a tight hold on
everything we were doing for him, and made sure that the only recom-
mendations he made were for articles or projects directly associated with
his flight or his interests. But for those we were to ask as much as the
market would bear."

Lindbergh endorsed such products as Champion spark plugs, Vacuum
motor oil, Waterman fountain pens, and the Bulova timepiece he wore
during his flight. He accepted a high-powered Franklin touring car, his
first automobile, and posed in ads with the car and the *Spirit of St. Louis*.
The pairing of Lindbergh and his plane was a natural one, for the two
had become inseparable in the public mind. The marriage was reinforced
by his habit of using the pronoun "we" when speaking of his flight. He
actually was referring to his syndicate of St. Louis backers, but most
people didn't know or care enough to make that distinction.

To Lindbergh's disappointment, *"We"* became the title of a book that
was hurriedly produced in the period between the end of his New York
homecoming and the start of his national goodwill tour. He had signed
a contract with New York publisher George Putnam before the Paris

flight. The original manuscript was ghostwritten in a first-person format by *New York Times* reporter Carlisle MacDonald. This common literary device struck Lindbergh as being mildly deceptive. Contributing to the author's dissatisfaction was MacDonald's bombastic style, so unlike his own. As Lindbergh went line by line through the finished manuscript, he finally decided that the book, if it was to carry his byline, needed to be almost completely rewritten. So, as Putnam and bookstores nervously waited, he holed himself up inside Harry Guggenheim's mansion and wrote forty thousand words of straightforward prose in three weeks. The book was rushed to the printer and was in the hands of eager readers by the middle of July.

"*We*" was an instant best seller. At the end of its first month in print, it had sold nearly 200,000 copies. It went through scores of editions, was published in several languages, and within a year of its release had earned its author roughly $250,000 in royalties. Lindbergh's bank account swelled with his book proceeds and the various cash prizes and syndication fees he collected, including $50,000 from the Guggenheim Fund for his national tour and $50,000 from the *New York Times* for the exclusive rights to the story of his Latin American tour. Various endorsements brought him $10,000 to $25,000 apiece. These were not inconsiderable sums. The salary of New York Yankees first baseman Lou Gehrig, for example, was $7,500 in 1927, a year in which he was named the American League's Most Valuable Player.

Lindbergh's personal worth quickly grew with the salaries and stock options he received as chief consultant to two airline companies. Within three years of his flight to Paris, the once financially strapped airmail pilot would be close to being a millionaire—at a time when the term still meant something. If Lindbergh did not court his enormous fame, he indeed capitalized on it. Unlike less dignified members of America's celebrity culture, however, the Lone Eagle did not feather his nest with nearly as many dollar bills as he could have. It was one reason why a fickle public would not sour on him when the decade of ballyhoo drew to a close.

Concurrent with the secular canonization of Lindbergh was the growing acceptance that Nungesser and Coli had entered whatever spiritual realm awaits lost airmen. Common sense said that the Frenchmen, if

not killed outright in a crash, would have perished of drowning, expo-
sure, starvation, or untreated injuries. Still, it was hard for some to let
go. When *Time* mentioned the "late" François Coli in a July issue, a
reader in Québec scolded the magazine for its presumptuousness. "This
is more of your self-sureness, of your typically American wish to be
ahead of others—for I well know that you do not know (because no one
knows) that François Coli is dead," Marie Jeanne Saval wrote. "When
some funeral has been held for these heroes, when the beautiful custom
of strewing rose leaves on the water has taken place, then you can write
of Coli as late—not till then!"

Such protestations could not alter the reality that all rational belief
in the airmen's survival had evaporated on both sides of the Atlantic.
The French newsweekly *L'Illustration* ran a full-page aerial photo of the
rugged and inhospitable part of Maine where some thought the *White
Bird* had gone down in. The magazine's correspondent described the
fruitless search:

> They flew over the forest so close that they almost brushed
> the tips of the trees, coming, going, scrutinizing the clearings
> in the forest, the lakes, the rivers—disseminating thousands
> of leaflets intended to inform the troubled, possibly wounded.
> They even sent fur trappers into the dense forest, to look, always
> look. Toward mid-June, glimmers had been perceived, strange
> glimmers that one could neither define, nor localize. No longer
> hoping to solve it, they waited impatiently for the Indians,
> coming back from their six to eight months of hunting in the
> regions up north. We saw them camping, these Indians, under
> their tents, on the shores of Lake Saint-Jean, carrying a very nice
> spoil from the hunt, but no news.

The mysterious and much-discussed "glimmers" were actually the
lights of the aurora borealis, not signals from the downed airmen. On
June 15, banjo-eyed Broadway star Eddie Cantor emceed a gala benefit at
the Roxy Theater for the families of the missing Frenchmen. Lindbergh,
Raymond Orteig, and six thousand other guests raised nearly $40,000
that night. Eventually some $110,000 in donations came in from around
the country, a windfall that was divided between Mme. Coli, who shared
a Marseilles apartment with her three children and her parents, and

Mme. Nungesser. At about this time an oddly constructed raft was discovered by fishermen along an isolated stretch of Brazilian coastline. It was made of two spoked wheels and a large section of fabric stretched over a frame. The debris was sent to France, where Farman officials ultimately concluded that the parts had come from the *Paris–Amérique Latine*. Their examination indicated that the wheels had been removed with a tool after a normal landing, not violently shorn off by a crash. But what of de Saint-Roman and his two companions? The raft had been found more than a thousand miles north of their intended destination. However, the plane hadn't carried enough fuel to enable it to stray that far off course, suggesting that the raft had drifted a considerable distance. The makeshift device was regarded as too small to hold three men, leading to speculation that not all of the crew had survived to build it, or that it had been constructed and set adrift in an attempt to alert rescuers. Searches were launched, but no traces of the men or other pieces of wreckage were ever found.

Public interest in these "other" missing French airmen quickly waned. One reason, perhaps, is that de Saint-Roman's flight was widely regarded by his contemporaries as being foolhardy, not heroic. Apart from whatever catastrophe befell the crew either in the sea, on the shore, or inside the Amazon jungle, their chief misfortune, as far as history is concerned, was simply bad timing. In the summer of 1927 the public was consumed with the triumph of Lindbergh, the tragedy of Nungesser and Coli, and the excitement over a flurry of ocean attempts.

18

Two More Across

Now that three American planes have in a month been flown over the
Atlantic . . . there seems to be no limit to what it is hoped to achieve in
the air. Lindbergh, Chamberlin and Byrd have given to aviation a new
impetus. Nothing seems impossible.

—*New York Times* editorial, July 5, 1927

On Saturday morning, June 4, two weeks after the wheels of the
Spirit of St. Louis touched down on the worn grass of Le Bourget,
the *Columbia* was fully gassed and positioned for takeoff at Roosevelt
Field. Clarence Chamberlin was in the cockpit. "Why don't you tell
us the name of the second pilot?" a reporter asked as Charlie Levine,
nattily dressed in a suit and leather vest, climbed in. "We have to have his
obituary all written, you know, and he may not even get off the ground.
Remember the two fellows in Fonck's plane?"

Levine not only remembered, but also his enthusiasm to be part of history had almost placed him in the same inferno that had consumed Charles
Clavier and Jacob Islamov. Levine had been so eager to fly the Atlantic that
he had offered the Argonauts $25,000 for a seat on the *New York–Paris*, a
proposition Igor Sikorsky rejected. Considering that he would have been
seated in the back of the plane along with the victims when it crashed,
Sikorsky's refusal had undoubtedly saved his life.

Now, on the same field nine months later, Grace Levine was growing
nervous as she and thousands of spectators waited for the "mystery

233

airman" to dramatically appear and join Chamberlin in the launch of the
Columbia Aircraft Corporation's long-delayed ocean adventure. "What's
with all this foolishness of Charles getting into the plane?" she asked.

"It's all right," said chief mechanic John Carisi, who was not quite sure
what to make of it himself. "It's only a test run."

It appeared that way as the *Columbia* started down the runway, then
turned off the course after going several hundred yards. Carisi ran over
to the idling plane. "What are you doing, Mr. Levine?" he asked. "Your
wife is going out of her mind! She has got the idea that you are going to
Europe in that plane!"

Chamberlin had aborted the takeoff and turned around because he
was afraid of hitting some bystanders. With the path now cleared by
police, he started down the runway a second time. Carisi fell away from
the moving craft, which picked up speed and—as Mrs. Levine looked
on in wide-eyed astonishment—was quickly airborne. "He isn't really
going!" she cried out. "He isn't really going!"

But he was. Unbeknownst except to a select few, Levine had been
planning for this moment for some time. One evening in late May, in the
midst of his row with Lloyd Bertaud, he made Chamberlin a proposition: "If you'll take me along with you on this flight to Europe instead of
another pilot or navigator, I'll give you a $25,000 'prize' myself and you
needn't count on Orteig's money at all. I'll also put up $50,000 insur-
ance for Mrs. Chamberlin before we start." Levine also promised him
a weekly salary of $150 and a share of any commercial proceeds arising
from the flight.

Chamberlin was agreeable. He really didn't mesh with Bertaud, and
any reservations he had about sharing the cabin with the inexperi-
enced Levine weren't enough to overcome his intense competitiveness.
Chamberlin burned to jump the Atlantic, to show that years of talking
about flying to Europe were not just empty words. Although Lindbergh
had beaten him to Paris, he knew that the *Columbia* could outdistance
the *Spirit of St. Louis* point to point. To prove it, he'd fly with a mongoose
if he had to.

Levine had purposely kept the *Columbia*'s destination a mystery to
the public and the press. After Lindbergh's flight the word "Paris" on
the fuselage had been painted over. Now it simply read "New York–,"
leaving the blank to be filled in by one's imagination. All Chamberlin told
newsmen prior to taking off was that he would fly the Bellanca as far as it

could go until it ran out of gas. Secretly, he and Levine settled on Berlin as their destination. Reaching it would mean setting a new distance mark. They also would be welcomed by a major city still smarting from being passed over during Lindbergh's tour of European capitals.

The *Columbia* started on its way to Germany at 6:20 a.m., with Chamberlin following a course laid out for him during a late-night session with Bernt Balchen at the Garden City Hotel. Levine slipped into the flying suit he had hidden on board. Early in the flight, engine vibration broke the gauge needle of the earth inductor compass, meaning they would have to depend on the less-reliable magnetic compass. Chamberlin's suggestion to turn back to have the instrument repaired was met with incredulity by Levine: "And meet my wife?!" He'd rather confront the dark, serried waves of the ocean than a hysterical Grace Levine. The *Columbia* pressed on, with Levine regularly cursing the now useless compass, which had cost him $1,125. Chamberlin, who carried all of $11.44 in his pockets, could empathize.

"Passenger Levine" was not quite the novice he later was made out to be. The Bellanca was equipped with dual controls. He had taken flying lessons with Bert Acosta and flown several times with Chamberlin to familiarize himself with the instruments. He could take an occasional turn at the controls in stable weather. For now, he made himself useful,

June 4, 1927: The *Columbia* flies into the mist, bound for Germany. In the right foreground is Byrd's *America*.

regularly refueling the main tank from the stock of five-gallon tin cans stuffed into the cabin. Chamberlin strived to keep the *Columbia* above the towering clouds. On other occasions he flew under the fog, close to the ocean's roiling surface. The weather bureau's forecast proved accurate: headwinds for the first thousand or so miles, then a strong tailwind halfway over the Atlantic. The hours passed.

Late Sunday morning, the men sighted a passenger liner that "appeared to have sprung out of the sea by magic," Chamberlin recalled. It was the Cunard liner *Mauretania*, and among the passengers cheering the plane as it circled its deck was Raymond Orteig, returning home from a hectic stay in Paris. "The noise of your propeller brought me on my feet," Orteig later told Chamberlin. "The sight of the *Columbia*, which seemed to be playing with us, filled my heart with joy, as you were adding another link between Europe and the U.S.A."

Chamberlin was more than playing; he was using the *Mauretania* to figure the *Columbia*'s position and fix course. Using the shipping notices from a newspaper they'd brought along, he estimated that the vessel was about 350 miles out of Cherbourg. Chamberlin used the liner as a check on the course he had been following. He "pointed the Bellanca straight over the center of the big liner and on back through the middle of her wake," he later explained. "This path, I knew, led straight past the Scilly Islands and Land's End into the English Channel and so on to Germany. . . . this gave me exactly what I wanted—the compass reading, with corrections already made, that would bring me to my destination."

As the fliers intended, the *Mauretania* reported its sighting of the *Columbia* to an anxiously waiting world. After a day and a night of flight, all appeared well with the little plane. England, and then continental Europe, were within its reach. The fliers' families and supporters were ecstatic when news broke. "Charlie's is a greater feat than Lindbergh's!" Levine's father, Isaac, declared to reporters. "Well, it was Lindbergh's business to fly," the proud papa explained. "He sort of had to go. But Charlie didn't have to. He just went!"

Half an hour later, another ship came into view. It was the *Memphis*, carrying Lindbergh back to America. Levine wanted Chamberlin to "jazz her up," but the pilot shook his head. There was no sense in burning up more gas and time fooling around over the Atlantic.

The sun was beginning to set when Chamberlin made out some cliffs in the twilight. It was Land's End, England, the first solid ground they had seen since leaving Newfoundland twenty-one and a half hours earlier. The good weather the fliers had enjoyed soon ended. Chamberlin took the *Columbia* up to its ceiling of 20,000 feet and still found it difficult to get above the great mountains of fog. Finally, he decided to skirt the edge of the cloud range, nursing the motor to preserve fuel until daylight and better visibility arrived. The strain of flying, aggravated by the thin air, made Chamberlin dangerously light-headed. He had not slept for forty hours. "See what you can do with her for a while," he said, turning the controls over to Levine before stretching out on the shelf atop the fuselage tank for a quick restorative nap. A few minutes later, he was jolted awake by the sensation of the *Columbia* spiraling out of control. Levine had lost his bearings completely—and possibly his mind. He was laughing as the rudder bar vibrated violently and the airspeed indicator shot past 160 miles per hour. It took everything Chamberlin had learned in a lifetime of flying to pull the *Columbia* out of its free fall. By the time he was able to get the plane under control again, they had plunged more than three miles toward the ocean. "Never in my life have I felt that death was so close or been so badly scared," he later confessed.

Chamberlin, shocked out of his lethargy, kept the plane on an easterly course throughout the night. His calculations showed that they were somewhere over Germany. Signal flares shot into the sky as they approached the airfield at Dortmund. Some men on the ground waved at them. Chamberlin throttled down to quiet the motor, then circled low above them, yelling, *"Nach Berlin? Nach Berlin?"* The men pointed, and Chamberlin headed in that direction.

There was no gas gauge on the *Columbia*, leaving Chamberlin to judge how much gas was left by banging on the tank. In his estimation, they were now down to the last little bit of fuel—not enough to reach Berlin. Presently, the spluttering Wright engine signaled that it was time to find a safe place to put down. Chamberlin picked out a wheat field and brought the Bellanca to a rough but successful dead-stick landing. It was a few minutes past six o'clock, Monday morning, June 6. They were outside Mansfeldt, roughly 110 miles short of their destination. The *Columbia* had flown 3,911 miles, breaking Lindbergh's nonstop distance record. They had been continually aloft for 42 hours, 45 minutes. Chamberlin emerged from the plane, weary and rubber-legged from the long flight, while Levine, elated, skipped about like a schoolboy at recess. The two unshaved foreigners scared off the first locals to approach them, but by and by a boy was sent to fetch gasoline from nearby Eisleben so they could continue on their way to Berlin. Soon a truck bearing twenty gallons of fuel arrived. With no hose available, Chamberlin was forced to transfer the gas into the *Columbia*'s tank using a coffee pot with a curved spout, one quart at a time. By midmorning they were back in the air. Unable to find Berlin in the fog, they once again flew until their gas ran out. This time Chamberlin brought the plane down on a field a few miles outside the thousand-year-old city of Kottbus. The wheels sank into the muddy ground and the plane nosed over, breaking the propeller. The burgomaster of Kottbus, resplendent in striped trousers and formal morning coat, hustled out to meet the fliers, who were fed, sheltered, and smothered with attention while a new propeller was found and fitted onto the Bellanca. The Americans were invited to sign the city's *Goldenes Buch* (Golden Book) of distinguished visitors. The following afternoon the pair flew to Berlin, finally reaching their original destination. One hundred thousand people jammed Templehof Field for a glimpse of the heralded *Ozeanflieger*. Chamberlin, still dressed in the grubby golf knickers and argyle socks he had worn under his flying suit, and Levine, wearing a stained pinstripe suit, were personally received by President Paul von Hindenburg and later honored at a formal banquet at the U.S. embassy.

The flight of the *Columbia* was hailed around the globe. Telegrams of congratulations and various offers poured into the embassy. Charles Lindbergh was still sailing home on the *Memphis*, so there was plenty of ink to spill on the second American crossing of the Atlantic in less than three weeks. For several days practically every move and utterance by Chamberlin and Levine enjoyed page-one coverage, though some European papers either didn't mention Levine's name or barely acknowledged his presence on the flight. Levine's brio was evident in the cable he sent to the Hearst press: "Lindbergh was lucky and we were not. If we had one-tenth of Lindbergh's luck, we would have done much better." Then Lindbergh arrived in the States, and the American press shifted to blanket coverage of the Lone Eagle's return.

After being feted in Berlin, Chamberlin and Levine spent the rest of June flying around Europe. They visited Munich; Vienna; Budapest; Prague; Warsaw; and Berne, Switzerland. Wylda Chamberlin and Grace Levine hastily booked passage to Bremerhaven to join them, traveling between cities by train while their celebrated husbands kept to the air. Charlie Levine clearly enjoyed the adulation and talked incessantly of

The *Columbia*, with Clarence Chamberlin at the controls and Charles Levine leaning out the window, arrives in Paris on June 30, 1927. At that moment Byrd's *America* was headed for France.

his plans to fly back to America and to create a transatlantic airline, in which he planned to invest $2 million of his own money. Chamberlin quickly grew tired of the ballyhoo and seemed to be distancing himself from his flying partner and his schemes. "The fact of the matter was that I knew only too well what a hazardous thing a trans-Atlantic flight in a single-motored land plane is, and did not care to ride my luck too hard by attempting to fly back," he later wrote.

Although it was not his intention, Levine became a symbol in a way that Chamberlin could not. Jews everywhere were sharing in his triumph. "The anti-Semites in Germany and the anti-Semites around the world will have to take their hats off to Levine, the Jew, no less than they would for the 'Nordic' Lindbergh and Chamberlin," declared an editorial in New York's Yiddish daily *Der Tog*. Eddie Cantor—born Israel Iskowitz—was moved to record "Levine and His Flying Machine." The uptempo ditty was the most popular of several musical homages to the flier. "*Levin, levin, bist der held yetst fun yisroel, Levin, levin, vi di oves fun amol,*" residents of the Lower East Side sang in Yiddish and English.

Levine, Levine, you're the hero of your race
Levine, Levine, you're the greatest Hebrew ace

We got a thrill when Chamberlin flew
But you were right there too, we're proud of you
Levine, Levine, just an ordinary name
But you brought it everlasting fame
We welcome you home from over the foam
Levine with your flying machine

Jewish leaders, who in the summer of 1927 pried a remarkable public apology from industrialist Henry Ford for his anti-Semitism, were sensitive to any slights. *Der Tog* blasted President Coolidge for omitting Levine's name when he cabled congratulations to Chamberlin in care of the U.S. embassy in Berlin. It was pointed out that adding three words—"Charles A. Levine"—would have cost taxpayers just 66 cents. "Are the pennies worth that much," the paper demanded to know, "or is it just a coincidence that the pioneer is named Levine?" Levine, far from devout, also came in for some criticism. An influential rabbi at a Hassidic synagogue expressed his displeasure that, in choosing to start his flight on a Saturday, Levine had "spurned the holiness of the Sabbath before the whole world." And his refusal to grant a separate interview to the Yiddish press in Warsaw—saying, "I am here as an American, not as a Jew"—caused him to be portrayed in many ethnic papers as a Jew who denied his race. Nonetheless, Levine was widely admired, particularly by immigrant Jews eager to enter the American mainstream.

To the French, it wasn't about where Levine came from, but where he and Chamberlin went. On the morning after the *Columbia* landed in Germany, *New York Times* correspondent Edwin "Jimmy" James was leaving his Paris hotel when he idly asked the concierge his thoughts about American aviators.

"Lindbergh is a fine fellow," he replied.

"But there are two other American aviators who have gone much further—who have gone to Germany," James pointed out.

"Yes," the concierge said, "but Lindbergh came to Paris."

The Atlantic was shrinking, and it soon got even smaller. On June 29, following a stretch of on-again, off-again rain, Commander Richard Byrd's *America* got under way at last. Shortly after midnight, Byrd was informed that weather conditions, while not ideal, were about as good as they were going to get. "I had determined not to wait," he explained, "because I felt that the trans-Atlantic plane of the future could not wait for *ideal* conditions. Moreover, we probably could gain more scientific and practical knowledge if we met some adverse weather." Influencing Byrd's decision was the mounting frustration by expedition members over the innumerable delays. The commander seemed to be in no hurry to get to Paris. One day he was off accepting an honorary degree at Yale University; another day he was being sworn in as the first official U.S. transatlantic airmail pilot. The word "Peace" was painted on the fuselage of the *America*, but plane builder Tony Fokker wasn't in a pacific state of mind. He confronted Byrd: "If you don't get going I will buy the ship back and get going myself! Instead of taking the first good weather, you seem to use every possible excuse to stall it off. I am sick and tired of it. It is a damned shame!"

On this drizzly Wednesday morning, the four-man crew settled into their positions inside the craft, but not before Byrd did some last-minute housecleaning to pare its takeoff weight to its allotted 17,261 pounds. Among the items tossed were a pair of moccasins and a thermos of tea. The big Fokker was perched on Byrd's specially built ramp at Roosevelt Field. With its three engines revving and a thick rope holding it back,

The *America* anchored on the small earthworks ramp Byrd built at Roosevelt Field to assist the plane's takeoff.

the craft quivered like a guard dog on a leash. Suddenly, unexpectedly, the rope broke and the *America* slid down the runway. Bert Acosta, at the controls, had to make a split-second decision: kill the engines, which were not fully warmed up and thus put the plane at risk of stalling once it was airborne, or continue accelerating. He chose to keep going, but kept one arm in the air, ready to signal George Noville to hit the dump valves if a crash appeared imminent. The plane picked up speed as it trundled over the mile-long runway. A row of hangars stood at the end. After forty seconds the plane was approaching 80 miles an hour and still hugging the packed earth. It didn't look like Acosta could get the eight and a half tons off the ground, but within another few seconds the wheels of the *America* finally became unglued and the craft began climbing. Bernt Balchen, who a few days earlier had been officially added to the "all-American" crew after taking out U.S. citizenship papers, let out a whoop.

The *America*, which was following essentially the same course that Lindbergh and Chamberlin had, made for Nova Scotia at 100 miles an hour, flying through rain and mist. By the time it reached Newfoundland it was plowing through thick fog and the pilots were flying wholly by instruments, a situation that would last almost until hitting Europe. "Above the ocean at night, bitterly cold, lost in storm clouds, so dark that we couldn't see our hands before our faces. . . . It was a strain I must admit," Byrd later wrote. "Only an aviator knows what it means to fly 2,000 miles without seeing the ground or water beneath." Flying nearly two miles high, the *America*'s radio provided a lifeline to the outside world that Lindbergh and Chamberlin had not enjoyed during their flights.

It was Thursday afternoon when the *America* passed over Brest. Byrd and company had been in the air for more than thirty hours. They were two hundred miles off course, having planned to enter France at Le Havre. Paris was three hours away, if they followed the railway from Brest to the capital, as Balchen, who was very familiar with northern France, suggested. However, Byrd—who had never been to France before—insisted on flying northeast along the coast to Le Havre, then following the Seine River into Paris, a route that added two hours to the flight. By then the plane's earth inductor compass had malfunctioned and the craft was being tossed about in a storm, its beleaguered crew trying to locate Paris in the inky darkness. Two revolving searchlights crisscrossed the sky and rockets were fired, all in a vain attempt to guide the big ship to Le Bourget. Some in the wet crowd that had gathered thought they heard the faint sound of motors, but then it petered out. SOS signals were intermittently received by ground operators, and then all radio communications stopped. One English-language paper headlined its final edition: BYRD VANISHES IN STORM SOMEWHERE NEAR PARIS. The bulletins were confusing and frightening. Nobody knew exactly where the *America* was—including, for the longest time, the crew itself.

For hours the *America* had been roaming blindly in the murk, desperate to visually locate any landmark. Expecting to find Le Bourget, the crew instead found themselves somewhere over the Normandy coast. Byrd was running out of fuel and options. Landing on or close to the beach was out of the question, as the shore was lined with rocks and fishing vessels were pulled onto the sand. He decided the best choice was to bring the plane down at sea. With Balchen at the controls, the rest of the men braced themselves for a landing that all assumed was very likely to end in their deaths.

Balchen was attempting a first. Nobody had ever ditched a three-engine plane before, not even in daylight. Guided by three flares tossed onto the dark surface, he eased the throttles back to just above stalling speed, then deftly dropped the *America* into the water. Waves sheared off the undercarriage and the plane quickly sank up to its wings, but the craft kept together. Battered, dazed, and deaf from listening to the unremitting roar of the engines for forty-two straight hours, the men managed

The *America* crash-landed in the sea near the French fishing village of Ver-sur-Mer.

to inflate a rubber raft and paddle to shore. They had landed near the village of Ver-sur-Mer, whose wide beach would be the site of D-Day landings by British troops seventeen years later.

It was the predawn hours of Friday, July 1. The soaked, exhausted fliers were taken in and cared for by local residents. It was a few more hours before the rest of the world learned of the *America*'s fate. The plane, though ravaged by the crash and souvenir hunters (who stripped the fabric off the fuselage and tried to carry away an engine), was soon salvaged, crated, and returned to the States. A group of reporters interviewed the fliers inside the assistant mayor's modest stone house, where they were enjoying a meal after thirteen hours of sleep. The strain of their ordeal was evident in their freshly shaved faces. Acosta, who had broken his collarbone, appeared especially worn down. Byrd greeted the newsmen with a simple query: "Do you think we failed?"

Byrd need not have worried. There was worldwide acclaim for him and for American aviation in general. To think, three transatlantic jumps in six weeks! The flight of the *America*, like those of the *Columbia* and the *Spirit of St. Louis*, was an impressive feat that contributed to the mushrooming public interest in flying. Moreover, it carried enormous commercial implications. "Fifteen years ago only dreamers talked of a passenger service from New York to Paris," editorialized the *New York Times*. "Today it seems to be a matter of a few years." The *America*'s suspenseful story appealed to the French people, who crowded railway stations and threw flowers as the crew made their way to Paris. The aviators were treated like visiting royalty during their stay, with Byrd being made an officer of the Legion of Honor. Some ascribed mystical healing powers to the commander, who was visiting the Hotel des Invalides, home to the country's wounded veterans, when a paralyzed aviator dramatically rose from his wheelchair and took several steps for the first time since his legs had been shredded by machine-gun fire nine years earlier. "Your courage gave me courage to try to walk again," the crippled flier told Byrd.

On July 4, the combined crews of the *America* and the *Columbia* participated in a series of patriotic events, culminating with an elaborate banquet at the Hôtel Palais d'Orsay, with Marshal Ferdinand Foch attending. Soon, after a week's worth of activities that included visits to the Tomb of the Unknown Soldier, the French Aéro Club, and Mme. Nungesser's apartment, it was time to go home. Levine remained in

The crew of the *America* appeared on the cover of the July 9, 1927, issue of the newsweekly *L'Illustration*. From left: George Noville, Richard Byrd, Bert Acosta, and Bernt Balchen.

Paris as the others boarded the *Leviathan*. A fresh round of ceremonial events awaited the triumphant airmen, including a ticker-tape parade in New York on July 18. Drizzle didn't dampen the city's enthusiasm. "This seems to be my weather," said Byrd, his words carried into millions of homes via a national radio hookup. "It rained when we started, it rained when we reached France, and now look at what it's done!"

The French, meanwhile, weathered a storm of self-criticism. To some, Byrd's flight was the latest reminder of American technological ascension—and, by implication, French decline. As Henri Bouché observed in *L'Illustration*, "This third American success, obtained under such hard conditions, made some in France say and write: 'And us?'"

19

The Atlantic No Longer Exists

We will go to the . . . country of eternal blue skies; it is unalterable calm; it is darkness without night. We will fly in limitless space the color of dark sapphire. We will have left behind storms, tempests, stupid human divisions; they will all be far away beneath our feet. We will produce our oxygen as we go, smelling it like a flower, like a flask of perfume. Time will have been so shortened that if we leave Paris at 9 in the morning, we'll be able to come to lunch at your house in New York.

—Princess Bibesco, "Lindbergh et l'Océan"
(Lindbergh and the Ocean)

The standard view of the "world's greatest air race" was that it ended with Lindbergh's landing in Paris. The French saw things differently. Raymond Orteig's prize had indeed been claimed, and in a most electrifying way, but the competition to complete the circuit by being the first to fly from Paris to New York only intensified. For proud and ambitious French pilots eager to emulate Lindbergh, there still was national glory and riches to be won. *Le Matin* estimated that the first Paris-to-New York flight was worth more than $2 million in prizes, endorsements, and other opportunities. Much of it, perhaps half, would go to American and French taxes. But whatever remained was more than enough to set someone up in very fine style for the rest of his days.

Among the front-runners were Maurice Drouhin in his lumbering Goliath, *Blue Bird*; Paul Tarascon in his chunky Bernard machine,

Tango Bird; and Dieudonné Costés in his well-traveled Bréguet. The chief obstacles, other than meteorological, remained the same: a sclerotic government-run aviation industry and the lack of aircraft capable of going the distance. The "Americans succeeded because they had the man, that's understood, but also because they had the plane," General Henri Duval observed in *Le Figaro*. "We had the men, but we didn't have the plane." There was an embarrassing situation in the aftermath of Lindbergh's flight. The Bréguet factory had built a special long-distance machine, with gasoline and oil tanks occupying almost the entire plane. Such reservoir planes were known as a *bidon* ("can"). The factory sold it to the Belgian pilots Medaets and Verhaegen, who refused to sell it back after they scrubbed their own Paris-to-New York plans and returned to Brussels. Costés was forced to experiment with a special-mixture combustible that he hoped would increase the range of his existing Bréguet.

On July 7, 1927, a few days before Clarence Chamberlin, Richard Byrd, and the crew of the *America* left Paris for the States, French national pride took a hit when Charlie Levine injected himself and the *Columbia* into the race. After approaching Costés and other top pilots about pairing up with him on a Paris-to-New York bid, Levine was able to convince Drouhin to ditch his longtime employer with the promise of a more airworthy plane and a bundle of francs.

French contenders for the first Paris-to-New York flight continue their tests in the summer of 1927. On the ground is Paul Tarascon's Bernard monoplane *Oiseau Tango* (*Tango Bird*), while the *Oiseau Bleu* (*Blue Bird*) approaches for a landing.

Most of Paris howled. "For six months we have been preparing him to make the flight from Paris to New York," Henry Farman said of Drouhin. "We have trained him to use the charts and taught him all he should know for making a flight of this importance. Today everything is ready and Mr. Levine takes him away." Gallic pride was badly stung. "We must declare emphatically that however flattering Levine's proposition is for our aviators, it will not satisfy French public opinion," *L'Echo* editorialized. "We know that German aviators are preparing for a Berlin–New York flight with a German crew in a German plane with German engines. The Paris–New York flight must be accomplished by French aviators in a French plane with French engines. It is up to the French government to do its duty. The national interest is at stake." Farman replaced Drouhin with Léon Givon, an experienced commercial pilot who insisted that the *Blue Bird* would beat the *Columbia* into the air.

The Levine-Drouhin partnership quickly deteriorated. Neither man spoke the other's language. A French engineer named Mathis translated, but before too long communication began passing through lawyers. The same problems at the core of Levine's contentious relationship with Lloyd Bertaud—his backpedaling on promises of compensation and insurance, his threats to hire a new pilot, his indecisiveness and egotism—cropped up again. Drouhin, worn down by the constant bickering and wanting only to fly the ocean, ultimately agreed to a contract that guaranteed him a minimum of 100,000 francs (roughly $5,000), to be paid in installments. Meanwhile, Levine was once again seen in the company of Mabel Boll, who had a mansion in the Bois de Boulogne. The Queen of Diamonds offered to pay up to $50,000 for a seat on the next flight across the Atlantic. Her only requirement was that she be allowed to wear a sweater fashioned of tiny gold links and a platinum collar that was created by a famous jeweler of the Rue de la Paix.

Outfitted with a new engine and propeller, bigger tanks, and improved instruments, the *Columbia* was practically ready to go by early August. But there were endless delays, some caused by a long summer of Atlantic storms, others the result of Levine's quirkiness. Drouhin wanted to leave on August 13, but the superstitious Levine said no, disappointing the large expectant crowd that had turned out at Le Bourget. Soon there was no trust left between the parties. Drouhin, concerned that Levine might take off with another pilot or "the girl in the golden sweater," obtained an injunction preventing the *Columbia* from being flown by anybody except him. Levine, hammered in Paris papers, grew more prickly. A stranger made a wisecrack near the opera house, and the two wound up in a fistfight. "He had the kind of face you love to take a smack at," Levine later said of his opponent in the press-hyped "battle of the boulevard." The next day, the still feisty Levine nearly came to blows with Drouhin when the French pilot refused to fly him to Deauville to see the Grand Prix. Drouhin said he had been engaged to fly the Atlantic, not serve as his personal chauffeur.

The following day, August 29, Levine conspired to kidnap his own plane. He bribed a mechanic to wheel the *Columbia* out of the hangar so he could conduct some taxi tests. Moments later he was shooting down the runway and into the air. Two of Drouhin's friends climbed into an army plane and gave chase, but the *Columbia* was too fast for them. Levine, who had no license, passport, or maps, knew England was somewhere to the north, so he kept the plane pointed in that direction. Soon he was crossing the Channel and trying to find Croyden, the world's busiest airport. He saw a large field and, running low on fuel, decided that was it. "Then the fun began," remembered Levine, who had never landed an airplane before. As sirens screamed and the sky was cleared of traffic, he repeatedly tried to touch down, each time narrowly avoiding catastrophe. The *Times* of London described the scene: civil aviation officers, airport staff, and pilots "stood there helpless while Mr. Levine committed every possible error, any one of which might have cost him his life." Levine finally leveled off the speed and angle of his approach, but not enough. The *Columbia's* wheels hit the ground so hard the plane bounced thirty feet into the air. It came down and shot right back up, after which Levine was able to gradually bring the leapfrogging Bellanca to a halt.

Most agreed it was the damnedest piece of flying they had ever seen. On his first solo, Levine and his flying machine had jeopardized lives and property and broken air regulations and customs laws in two countries. He was dressed down by authorities, but all in all, the Brits thought it had been a jolly good show. While Levine was toasted in London, Drouhin seethed in Paris. "I am not going to chase Levine over to London because if I saw him I would feel like killing him and then the English would put me in jail," he said. Grace Levine wrote Drouhin a check for the balance due on his contract, but the pilot remained despondent. "It was not Levine's money that tempted me," he said tearfully, "but the prospect of being the first Frenchman to make the big jump. Now I have no plane and little hope of getting one."

The Farman that Drouhin had spent so much time learning to master was now in the hands of Léon Givon and co-pilot Pierre Corbu, who were ready to go the moment their employer and the weather bureau gave their blessings. At daybreak on September 2, the *Blue Bird* left Le Bourget. The large craft, struggling under its weight of fuel, flew ungainly into the mist. Ninety miles out, the Farman had yet to rise more than a thousand feet while encountering thick fog and angry headwinds. Givon's commonsensical decision to spray the plane's fuel over the countryside and return after just four hours in the air was applauded in air circles, but this latest failure of French aviation didn't set well with everyone. Two days later, Givon got into an altercation with a gang of scornful young men who called him "a flat tire" before pummeling him. By the end of September all French teams had canceled plans for the year.

Levine's public image also took a beating. His antics caused "the greatest Hebrew ace" to be rebranded as "the first real clown-hero." Dudley Field Malone, returning from Paris, suggested that in the interest of world peace, Washington should "send a battleship to Europe to bring back Mr. Levine." Grace Levine, who had sailed home alone and then suffered a nervous breakdown, pled for her husband's return. Charlie had other ideas. He attempted a flight to India with Walter Hinchliffe, the only one-eyed licensed pilot in England. After that excursion ended with a forced landing near Vienna, he moved on to Rome, wrangling personal audiences with Mussolini and Pope Pius XI. Finally, in mid-October, ongoing federal probes into Levine's business practices forced him to sail back to New York. The city, which had lavished $71,850 on Lindbergh's homecoming and $26,194 on the joint Byrd-Chamberlin parade, spent exactly $1,079.19 to greet Levine. A total of $400 went toward the scroll of honor he received from Mayor Walker on the steps of City Hall. It was a dismal day, with flags hanging limp in the rain. Few people lined the motorcade route. "You came back too late!" a policeman shouted.

Even when placed in the context of the feckless 1920s, it seems incomprehensible that something as dangerous and expensive as flying across an ocean could become a fad, but it did. Many a flier seeking instant celebrity was impelled "to hop off blindly for foreign shores in emulation of Lindbergh and be drowned," wrote Frederick Lewis Allen.

> The formula was simple. You got an airplane, some financial backing, and a press agent, and made the first non-stop flight from one place to another place (there were still plenty of places that nobody had flown between). You arranged in advance to sell your personal story to a syndicate if you were successful. . . . Having landed at your destination—and on the front pages—you promptly sold your book, your testimonials, your appearance in vaudeville, your appearance in the movies, or whatever else there was demand for. If you did not know how to pilot a plane you could still be a passenger; a woman passenger, in fact, had better news value than a male pilot.

There was a desperate quality to many of the pale imitators and heroic adventurers. The planes bore such names as the *Spirit of Los Angeles* and the *Dallas Spirit*. One pilot revealed his wish to be known as the "Lindbergh of the Pacific." Another later admitted to paying for his own "public" welcome-home banquet. From mid-August 1927 through the following March, at least sixteen aircraft attempted to hurdle the Atlantic from either side; all but two failed. Many turned back or ditched safely at sea. Five planes were lost, and thirteen people (including Lloyd Bertaud and Walter Hinchliffe) disappeared with them. The toll in the Pacific was more concentrated and thus had a greater impact on public opinion. James D. Dole, president of the Hawaiian Pineapple Company, offered a $25,000 prize for the first nonstop flight between the North American continent and Honolulu. The hastily arranged Dole Race in August 1927 (which Lloyd's of London refused to insure) was a debacle. Only two planes managed to finish. Several others crashed or were never seen again. Overall, ten lives were lost in the "pineapple derby" and the searches that followed. The victims included a young elementary school teacher, Mildred Doran, who was a passenger on the vanished *Miss Doran*.

An uproar ensued in the press over these "death flights," with concerned public officials urging Washington to ban them. Lindbergh and President Coolidge came out against any regulation. "During this experimental period of aviation," Lindbergh said, "we may expect casualties. Yet to totally restrict hazardous flights would be placing a ban on scientific progress. Such restriction would have the same effect on the future of transoceanic flying as the air mail would have experienced had it been abandoned by the government during the heavy casualty period of its pioneering days."

René Fonck approved of this hands-off approach. On September 3, he and Lieutenant Lawrence Curtin took Igor Sikorsky's new twin-engine ship for its first test flight. Sturdier and more graceful than the *New York–Paris*, the huge sesquiplane had a cruising speed of 120 miles per hour, could fly on one motor, and had a radius of 5,000 miles. A strengthened undercarriage and wider-set wheels allowed the plane to lift 21,000 pounds of fuel. The plane was outfitted with a radio compass and a radio beacon (a first for a transatlantic aircraft) and had the unprecedented ability to transmit on four wavelengths. Fonck intended to fly it to Paris and then, if conditions permitted, fly it back to New York. On September 8 at Roosevelt Field, the all-white plane was christened the *Ville de Paris* (*City of Paris*). However, the Navy Department—fed up with conducting extremely expensive searches for missing civilian aircraft—soon quashed Fonck's plans. Citing the "mounting toll of life," Acting Secretary T. Douglas Robinson revoked the extended leaves given to Curtin and Ensign Steve Edwards, the radio operator, and outlined new procedures. Going forward, navy personnel would only be considered for overwater expeditions involving seaplanes, not land planes. With these new restrictions, Fonck had no choice but to abandon the Paris flight. The *Ville de Paris* was crated and eventually sold to a South American airline.

Ever since the disappearance of the *Paris–Amérique Latine*, some had suggested that Captain de Saint-Roman may have made a forced landing on a Brazilian beach, far off course but still technically making the vanished Farman aircraft the first to jump the South Atlantic in a single bound. That hypothetical achievement was soon swept away by a greater and verifiable feat—this one with live heroes to cheer at the end.

On October 14, 1927, Dieudonné Costés and Joe Le Brix lifted off from St. Louis, Senegal, in their green-bodied Bréguet. Their objective was the same as de Saint-Roman's had been five months earlier. Twenty-one hours and fifteen minutes after leaving Africa, Costés touched down in Port Natal, Brazil. It was the first authenticated nonstop crossing of

THE ATLANTIC NO LONGER EXISTS   253

the South Atlantic by an airplane (as well as the first nonstop westerly flyover of the ocean by a heavier-than-air machine), and for a while Costés and Le Brix were the toasts of aviation. The French were understandably the most effusive in their praise. They put aside the memories of all the failures of the past year—the *New York–Paris*, the *White Bird*, and the *Paris–Amérique Latine*—and the men who had been lost. "French aviation had been in an extremely hard way, but it is once again in the forefront," declared *Le Matin*. "Once again sporting spirit, backed with scientific precision, has won out, and this great transatlantic victory of Costés and Le Brix is assured widespread acclaim."

Over the next several months, Costés and Le Brix continued their unprecedented aerial journey through Latin America and the United States. Lindbergh enthusiastically greeted them in Panama. Sentimental types couldn't help but be moved by the aviators' choice of name for their record-breaking Bréguet: the *Nungesser-Coli*. In New York, the celebrated fliers were Raymond Orteig's guests at the Brevoort while they planned the final leg of their amazing trip. Having already covered 39,944 miles in 338 hours of flying, they announced that they would fly to Paris in the spring of 1928, duplicating Lindbergh's feat. But the French government and the Bréguet factory weren't taking any chances. Costés and Le Brix were ordered to return home by liner. Cheering Parisians lined streets ten deep in a pouring rain to welcome them back.

German aviation had shown little interest in the Orteig Prize, but the first nonstop east-to-west crossing of the North Atlantic was a plum it desired. On April 12, 1928, a privately financed expedition consisting of two Germans and an Irishman departed Dublin in an all-metal Junkers, the *Bremen*, bound for New York. The single-engine monoplane battled fog, sleet, and headwinds for a day and a half, finally crash-landing on rugged, isolated Greenly Island. The *Bremen* had fallen short of its announced destination by a thousand miles, but the hair-raising flight still qualified as the first westerly crossing of the North Atlantic by an airplane. France, preoccupied with its homecoming for Costés and Le Brix, was a bit guarded in its praise. The *Bremen*'s crew had performed heroically, both in the air and in the wilderness. But an abbreviated hop between Ireland and Labrador, no matter how historic and suspenseful, still wasn't Paris to New York.

That honor remained up for grabs in 1928, with Costés and several other French pilots vying for it. Many were taken with the quiet effort of

Lieutenant Michael Détroyat, the only one planning a solo flight. The fearless stunt flier carefully patterned himself after Lindbergh, acquiring an all-metal Avimeta monoplane with a 220-horsepower Wright Whirlwind and devoting himself to meticulous preparation. Détroyat had "all the personal qualities to make him a great hero," observed one correspondent, "including modesty, youth and an engaging smile." However, it soon became apparent that Détroyat's underpowered plane would be no match for the strong air currents it would face. But the romantic image of a lone Frenchman returning Lindbergh's visit died slowly.

Maurice Drouhin jumped back into the transatlantic derby by joining forces with René Couzinet, a brilliant aeronautical engineer. Couzinet was only twenty-three when he completed the *Arc-en-Ciel* (*Rainbow*) in the spring of 1928. The thick-winged wooden monoplane featured an enormous 98-foot wingspan. Its driving power was provided by three Hispano-Suizas, including a 600-horsepower engine in the nose, each of which could be accessed via narrow passageways for in-flight repairs. Lending a storybook touch to the enterprise was that the monster plane had been paid for mostly through a public subscription, with donations ranging from 5 to 5,000 francs. In all, more than 2 million francs were raised. Although he had a wife and an infant daughter to support, Drouhin had invested the bulk of his payout from Levine in the *Arc-en-Ciel*. The riches would come when he crossed the ocean.

To that end the determined thirty-seven-year-old, who was on his third transatlantic team in a year's time, sat at the controls during a test flight at the Orly airfield on August 8. The *Arc-en-Ciel* was at two thousand feet when it suddenly began shuddering violently, suggesting a broken control. It nosed up, then plunged. Drouhin was able to right the plane just before hitting a hangar. A wing tore off, and the rest of the ship slid a couple of hundred feet before smashing into a brick incinerator. One of the four men aboard was crushed by an engine; the survivors were removed to a hospital. Drouhin's mangled leg was amputated, but the loss of blood was too great to save his life. "I would so much have liked to cross the Atlantic," he murmured before dying.

Paul Tarascon, another longtime aspirant, also saw his dreams dashed. The one-legged pilot, whose expedition was chronically underfinanced, was forced to drop out of the race when the *Tango Bird* was sold by its owners. That particular ship was replaced in the lineup of contenders by another speedy Bernard monoplane, the *France*. Captain Louis

Coudouret and Lieutenant Louis Demailly, both war aces, invested more than 1 million francs in their machine. The aristocratic Demailly—a count who owned a medieval castle—entertained his French friends by delivering in English a thank-you speech he had prepared for his arrival in New York. The crew of the *France* was rounded out by Captain Louis Mailloux, an experienced navigator whose identity was kept secret until the last moment so as not to worry his wife and four children.

Seventeen days after the crash of the *Arc-en-Ciel*, the *France* nearly met the same disastrous fate. In the predawn hours of August 25, the bright red plane was rolled out of its hangar at Le Bourget, loaded with 1,100 gallons of fuel, and readied for takeoff. The crew arrived, looking smart in their blue army uniforms with gold braid. It was the feast day of King Louis IX, a favorable omen for three men named Louis. But the *France* labored down almost the entire length of the runway before barely lifting off, smoke trailing. As the horrified crowd looked on, the plane dove under some telegraph wires, damaging its landing gear in the process. It circled back and—dumping fuel all the way—landed heavily but safely. It was a valiant effort by Coudouret, who would be killed when the *France* crashed in Spain the following year. The terrifying ten-minute ordeal was just the latest reminder of how hazardous the whole business of crossing the Atlantic was.

On September 14, 1928, Raymond Poincaré created France's first Air Ministry. Victor Laurent-Eynac, long active in aviation affairs, was appointed air minister. His first official act was to call for an indefinite halt to all transoceanic flights. This respite was intended to give the French aviation industry a chance to regroup from "ill-prepared and badly worked endeavors" and allow it to "redeem its prestige from widely advertised and often unsuccessful attempts." This coincided with tighter restrictions by the British Air Ministry, which now required the crew of any proposed transatlantic flight to provide adequate insurance for their dependents. Although the Brits did not ban Atlantic flights outright, the premiums—$80,000 for the mandated $250,000 of coverage—were prohibitive enough to dissuade hop-offs from English soil.

Amid the closer scrutiny of ocean flights, Charlie Levine had returned to Europe. Mabel Boll was his constant companion. The mercurial socialite informed reporters that she now wanted to be known as the "Queen of the Air," the name attached to the new $50,000 Junkers that she bought that summer. Levine had finally obtained a license and planned to serve

Charlie Levine (left) with Mabel Boll and Bert Acosta in 1928.

as the co-pilot to Bert Acosta on whatever headline-generating hop was decided upon. Boll thought flying "a man's job" and was content in her role as famous female passenger. Paris to New York was fine, but she didn't really care where they flew, as long as it was a "first." However, the late delivery of the *Queen of the Air* from the factory cut into the group's window of opportunity. Boll grew distraught as the flying season wound down. "I'm afraid the Frenchmen will beat us ... and I just can't stand another disappointment," she said. Levine, whose legal woes were mounting, was due back in a New York court. He left on a liner in September, just as the Junkers developed engine problems that snuffed out any hopes for the year. Boll was devastated. The uncrowned Queen of the Air would remain fixated on flying the ocean until 1936, when she claimed to be "mentally cured" of her obsession. She died in a New York asylum in 1949.

The first Paris-to-New York flight remained an elusive honor through 1929 and deep into 1930. Most Frenchmen were inclined to pin their hopes on Dieudonné Costés, Bréguet's chief test pilot, and his new shiny red machine, which had an enigmatic "?" painted on both sides of its fuselage. The Bréguet was officially known as the *Point d'Interrogation*, or the *Question Mark*.

The plane's name was a coy reference to its secret donor, François Coty. The famous but reclusive *parfumeur* was one of the richest men in France. One day in the spring of 1928, Coty invited the accomplished long-distance flier to a private meeting. "Would you be willing to attempt an Atlantic crossing," he asked, "if I give you the time and the means?"

"Certainly," said Costés. "I'll do it."

"I must insist that you resist all temptations, all excitement, and that you not leave unless you have every trump card in your hand," Coty continued.

"I promise I'll do it," Costés repeated.

Coty quietly paid the Bréguet works to build an upgraded version of the *Nungesser-Coli*. The new craft featured bigger tanks, a more powerful motor, and the latest instrumentation and radio equipment. The fuselage was now structured of metal instead of wood. Maurice Bellonte, a low-key veteran of the war and the Paris-to-London run with the Compagnie Air Union Aéronavale, joined Costés as navigator and wireless operator.

Costés was the French version of Commander Byrd: a national hero whose painstaking preparation and avoidance of unnecessary risks generated both admiration and criticism. Costés brusquely ignored the carpers. As he once put it, "An airman at the bottom of the Atlantic proves nothing." Meteorologists conceded that there really was no good time to fly the North Atlantic from east to west. The best one could hope for was a day when the air currents were less volatile than usual. Any successful westerly attempt would depend on the soundness of the aircraft and the superior judgment of the pilots.

Costés's judgment was put to the test when Ludwik Idzikowski and Kasimir Kubala left Paris for New York in the early hours of July 13, 1929. This was the second attempt by the popular Polish officers. The previous August they had passed the Azores when a cracked oil tank forced them to turn back and ditch the *Marshal Pilsudski* off the Spanish coast. A new Amiot biplane, the *White Eagle*, had been prepared for them. This time the Poles got off from Le Bourget in good style, and Costés and Bellonte followed forty-five minutes later in the *Question Mark*. Both planes took the southern route, bumping against headwinds that severely reduced their airspeed. After 1,600 arduous miles, Costés coolly

calculated that he would burn up his fuel just short of reaching New
York. He returned to France, having spent twenty-eight hours in the air.
Meanwhile, the *White Eagle* flew on a bit longer until a malfunctioning
engine caused the Poles to attempt an emergency landing on a small
island in the Azores. The plane hit a stone fence, flipped, and burst into
flames, killing Idzikowski. The twin failures demonstrated yet again the
immense challenge of a Paris-to-New York flight.

That September, Costés and Bellonte flew overland across Asia, setting
a new distance record of 4,910 miles between Paris and Manchuria.
Later they made the first Paris-to-Hanoi flight. Long hops such as these
allowed them to continually test new equipment and sharpen procedures
for their inevitable try at the Atlantic. Costés grew weary of people asking him when that was going to happen. "I'm attempting Paris-to-New
York," he exclaimed, "I'm not attempting Paris-to-Saint-Germain!"

Thanks to Coty, Costés was in charge of his own destiny. He owned
the plane and everything that went with it. Bréguet could not deny him
permission; neither could the engine's manufacturer. The Air Ministry,
while officially frowning on ocean attempts, had no choice but to issue
the country's greatest long-distance flier a permit and quietly await the

The *Question Mark* leaves Paris for New York on September 1, 1930.

results. If Costés failed, officials could cluck their tongues and say they had not endorsed the flight. But if Costés was successful, they would share in the glory.

It wasn't until the early hours of Monday, September 1, 1930, that Costés deemed that all was in place and the *Question Mark* was made ready. The weather outlook was unusually good over the North Atlantic, with the promise of favorable skies and a rare tailwind, though a localized system had produced a thick, cottony fog. The atmosphere at Le Bourget was different than in previous departures—more festive, less tense. "We'll start," Costés joked, "even if we have to go on foot!" Still, he delayed several hours, phoning weather bureaus throughout northern France for the latest bulletins.

At 10:54 a.m. the *Question Mark* finally lifted off. It was carrying seven tons, most of it fuel, but also cold chicken, hot soup, and champagne. Costés was confident they could maneuver their way through "a loophole" in the fog. Despite the load and temporarily adverse winds, the *Question Mark* made it over Valencia on the Irish coast at a sprightly clip of 125 miles an hour, breaking at last into clear skies. They saw the gray Atlantic rolling under them, marking the end of the Old World and the start of the long and jeopardous passage to the New.

The *Question Mark* had a range of 5,600 miles, which gave the Frenchmen plenty of leeway to play "hide-and-seek" with bad weather at various times over the ocean. They dodged three storms, adding 600 miles to their journey. Thrown off course, they deftly recovered each time, ably assisted by their levelheaded experience, more than thirty navigation instruments (some of which, for safety's sake, were duplicates), and a 100-watt radio with a 600-mile range. The pilots considered their wireless set as critical to their success as their 780-horsepower engine. From the time they left the French coast until hitting landfall the following day, the *Question Mark* was in constant touch with ships and coastal stations. Bellonte, with his hand on the key and two black discs in his ears, transmitted on the same wavelength used by all ships and ocean liners. The effect of the buzzes and whistles emanating from the heavy appliance was as much psychological as practical. Ensconced in an open cockpit, buffeted by wind, lashed by rain, and enveloped in gauzy mist far from other living beings, the airmen could still feel connected to the world they had fled. They could "talk" via key taps. If necessary, they could ask a ship to fix their position or send a warning should something go wrong; hopefully, help would arrive in time. While the two pilots placed their fate in the hands of the newest technology, some back home fell back on ritualistic piety to see them through their perilous passage over the broad Atlantic. They burned candles to St. Geneviève, the patron saint of Paris.

There were long stretches of monotony inside the *Question Mark*, with only "the song of the motor and the tedious watch of the instruments" to occupy their minds. Unable to be heard above the noise of the engine and the rushing wind, the men exchanged notes along the way. Costés would pass a query—"You recognize?"—and Bellonte would scribble a reply: "Yes." A few minutes later would come the scrawled observation: "Seagulls."

So it went, hour after hour. After dodging a storm while approaching Nova Scotia, they recovered and spotted the North American coast. Having reached landfall, they were determined not to lose sight of it. The *Question Mark* tore along the coast at top speed. The pilots' adrenaline was flowing. They were certain they had conquered the Atlantic. Parisians filled the Place de la Concorde and followed their countrymen's progress via the NBC radio broadcast, which was piped through loudspeakers.

Flying through fog and rain, the *Question Mark* was spotted over Norwich, Connecticut, at 6:45 p.m. local time. Twenty-seven minutes later, the glistening red plane was descending onto the damp surface of Curtiss Field. "He's taxiing down the field!" announcer Graham McNamee excitedly told the radio audience. Costés and Bellonte officially concluded their unprecedented and much-anticipated journey at 7:12 p.m. on September 2, 1930, 37 hours and 18 minutes after it had started. The fliers were hoisted on the shoulders of the crowd. Lindbergh was there to welcome them. "He said he never would have missed our landing," Bellonte recalled many years later. "He greeted us so warmly. He said Paris to New York was much more difficult than New York to Paris."

It was after midnight in Paris. Costés and Bellonte each spoke a few words into the microphone, their hoarse, disembodied voices echoing through the Place de la Concorde. The throngs shouted *"Vive Costés!"* Then a band at Curtiss Field played "La Marseillaise," and celebrants on both sides of the Atlantic either sang or hummed along. The triumphant pilots flew on to Dallas, winning an industrialist's $25,000 challenge as the first to complete a Paris-to-Dallas flight with one stopover. That was the start of a whirlwind tour that included visits or flyovers in more than a hundred cities in thirty states. On October 16, their final day in the States, they were feted at a Manhattan luncheon. "There is something about the air route between New York and Paris which sets it apart," said newspaper executive Louis Wiley, who presided over the affair. "The reason is easy to find. Our own young eagle, Colonel Charles A. Lindbergh, gave for us a special glory in the New York–Paris flight. As we followed his lone flight over the Atlantic . . . so we followed the bulletins of our gallant guests as they winged across the face of the waters to return, in their perfect French way, the visit of Colonel Lindbergh."

Costés and Bellonte sailed home with $100,000 in prize money and crates packed with trophies and souvenirs. The crowds in Paris were large but less demonstrative than those in the States. Bellonte, reflecting on the welcome Lindbergh had received three years earlier, suggested that his countrymen were far more enthusiastic spontaneously than when organized. Costés admitted, "I think we are about the last of the public's airmen heroes."

Dieudonné Costés (waving) and Maurice Bellonte receive a ticker-tape parade in New York after becoming the first to fly directly from Paris to New York.

The success of the *Question Mark* caused its anonymous benefactor to step forward. In a signed piece on the front page of *Le Figaro*, a paper he owned, François Coty explained his $100,000 involvement: "Like all Frenchmen, I was stunned and filled with wonder by Lindbergh's great achievement. . . . Knowing that government-run aviation was in no state to plan and carry out such a project, from that moment on I had only one ambition: to give France the means to accomplish the same feat, in the opposite direction, of course; an attempt which even the most daring considered impossible." Now the French pilots and their plane had "entered into History" and "brought back a universal victory" as well as renewed glory for France.

"Honor to Nungesser and Coli, unfortunate forerunners!" Coty declared in ending. "Thank you to Lindbergh!"

Costés and Bellonte proved that the New York-to-Paris corridor was no longer a one-way street. Direct flights in either direction were now possible, if still not anywhere close to being practical. The era of "spectacular flights," as far as the North Atlantic was concerned, was drawing to a close. Now came the demand for the charting of functional routes and the development of craft capable of safely and cost-efficiently transporting passengers, mail, and cargo—a challenge to surveyors, engineers, and constructors that diminished the need for heroics.

What would the future bring? On Lindbergh's first morning in France, he was asked if he thought regular transatlantic crossings were feasible. Yes, he answered, scheduled flights would surely come within five years. But only if there were "big mid-ocean landing fields. It is too big a jump without them." These artificial islands would serve as refueling stations. Engineers envisioned them rising a hundred feet above the ocean's surface, unaffected by the mightiest waves. Richard Byrd, quizzed about transoceanic travel after his flight to France, said it would take another twenty years for regular passenger service to arrive. Of paramount importance was lifting the veil of fog—the greatest impediment to safe flying—through improved instrumentation, radio, and radar. There also was a crucial need for coordinated meteorological services that could report rapidly changing weather patterns and offer accurate forecasts. Futurists predicted that airships would radically alter the look of cities such as New York and Paris. *Popular Science* anticipated airports on the sweeping flat tops of great apartment buildings, and massive, centrally located air docks for transatlantic liners. "These liners will probably be of two types—fast, passenger-carrying heavier-than-air machines, and huge dirigibles a quarter of a mile or more in length, to meet the need of slower passengers," the magazine said in its October 1927 issue. The sky would be brilliant with "the lights of airships and dirigibles, and the route markings and traffic signs of airways and landing stages." How fast could the airplanes of tomorrow possibly go? In 1927 test pilots were on the cusp of breaking the 300-mile-per-hour barrier. Richard J. Beamish, a journalist, historian, pilot, and Lindbergh biographer, sounded authoritative in offering an answer at the time: "Scientists and designers, basing conclusions on fixed formulae, set the absolute theoretical limit at 480 miles an hour, without consideration for such handicaps as fast landing speeds and controllability. They point out such a plane would resemble a winged projectile, with wings so short they would be only 9 square feet in area on either side." Costés foresaw passengers zipping between continents at 500 miles per hour, comfortably seated in an airtight cabin seven miles high.

Any such wonders existed in an aerocentric future that, thanks to Lindbergh, a once-wary public was keen on visiting. The *Spirit of St. Louis* had pulled along flocks of acolytes in its slipstream: applications for pilot licenses tripled in 1927, the number of licensed aircraft quadrupled, airport construction boomed, and public investment in aviation stock soared. On the first anniversary of his epochal flight, a leading trade publication neatly summarized Lindbergh's astonishing impact on the industry and the world at large. "Prior to Lindbergh's flight," observed *Aero Digest*, "the percentage of people who really appreciated the potentialities of aircraft was comparatively small. Consequently growth was slow. Then almost overnight the world became air-minded. The barriers of disbelief, the bugaboo of fear, the too skeptical attitude of capital which had retarded industrial growth of aviation for years were suddenly swept aside. One magnificent flight had accomplished in 33½ hours what hundreds of men had been trying to do for years."

Epilogue

Restless Spirits

New York to Paris—it seemed like a dream.

—Charles A. Lindbergh

After presenting the Orteig Prize to Charles Lindbergh, Raymond Orteig lived a dozen more years. To the very end he remained a man with two hearts beating in his chest, dying in French Hospital in New York on June 6, 1939, following a long illness. He was sixty-nine years old. Five hundred people attended his funeral. Lindbergh was not among them. A few days later, Pan American began the first commercial passenger flights across the Atlantic with a forty-ton Sikorsky flying boat named the *Yankee Clipper*.

It was the end of a remarkable journey for the erstwhile shepherd boy, whose role in creating the Lindbergh legend has never been fully appreciated. "You may, indeed, look back with pride upon your life's achievements," Gaston Tisné, president of the Alliance Française of New York, had said at a testimonial dinner given Orteig by his many friends in the fall of 1927.

It has been your fortune to live in a golden age, at a time when the whole world is exalted by great deeds, when life is a perpetual reaching for an ideal, when splendid dreams come true and cast as in a shadow the greatest things of yesterday. And, living in this

264

golden age, you have been one of those most eager to advance and to see the world advance, one of those who have believed, and who still believe, in the progress of mankind. . . . I lift my glass to you, my dear friend, with a feeling of affection which is not unmixed with envy. Your life has been a full and a happy one; and, surely, you can have no fault at all to find with your Destiny, you who have lived to see the two great nations close to your heart brought closer together by the ties of a common tribute, and in the midst of applause fairly earned and freely bestowed, could say to yourself that not only you contributed to the result but were the primary and efficient cause of the event.

By departing when he did, Orteig was not around to witness the devastation of another world war nor the denouement of many of the central figures from the great Atlantic air race.

René Fonck, twice thwarted in his attempt to fly the ocean, returned to France in October 1928. During the 1920s he had described Franco-German enmity as "perennial," but his opinion of the "eternal menace" would shift in the 1930s, when the Air Ministry promoted him to inspector of fighter aviation. On inspection tours he became friendly with Hermann Goering, the former German ace now masterminding the buildup of the Luftwaffe. After France fell to the Nazis in the spring of 1940, Fonck accepted a post in the Vichy government. Among his reported activities was encouraging French pilots to join the Luftwaffe to fight against their former British and American allies. Fonck was arrested as a collaborator after France was liberated, but he was never formally charged with a crime and was soon released. Later it was revealed that the Gestapo, questioning Fonck's loyalty to the Vichy regime, had briefly imprisoned him at the Drancy internment camp outside Paris. Fonck died of a stroke on June 18, 1953, in Paris. He was fifty-nine. At the time he was working as the manager of a chemical products firm and held the rank of retired colonel.

Dieudonné Costés, who rose to the rank of colonel in the reserves during the 1930s, had to contend with postwar allegations that he had spied for the Nazis. He was arrested in July 1947 and spent the next twenty months in prison before being tried for treason by a military court. Costés, facing a possible death sentence, contended that he had been a double agent, working for both the German and the American intelligence services. The United States provided proof of his value in capturing a French spy in New York in 1943, helping to offset incriminating material about the accused found in secret German files. Costés was acquitted by a single vote, but like Fonck, his image was tarnished. He died in Paris on May 18, 1973, after several surgeries and losing a leg to gangrene. He was eighty-one.

Paul Tarascon, the first aviator to post an entry in the Orteig sweepstakes, went on to invest 1.5 million francs in building a small airfield in Provence, a region whose natural splendor and superior climate acted like a balm on his scarred, battered body. It opened in 1931 and grew into what is today the Cannes-Mandelieu Airport, familiar to the international set arriving for their Riviera vacation or the Cannes Film Festival. Tarascon fought the Germans a second time as a colonel in the French Resistance and was once again decorated for bravery. Despite his many injuries and brushes with death, the popular warrior lived longer than most other airmen of the Great War. He died on June 11, 1977, during his ninety-fifth year.

Harold Hartney remained a familiar figure in aeronautical circles after the Argonauts disbanded, serving as a technical and legal consultant to various aviation concerns. His son, Harold Jr., a fighter pilot, was killed in action over Germany in 1944, a blow from which the senior Hartney never really recovered. He died on October 5, 1945, at his home in Washington, D.C. He was fifty-seven. He was buried with full military honors at Arlington National Cemetery, where he shares a grave with his son.

Fellow Argonaut Homer Berry was an accomplished test pilot before World War II and an instructor and staff officer in various Canadian, British, and American bomber units during it. At one time he also was the private pilot for Colonel Robert R. McCormick, the legendary owner of the *Chicago Tribune* (and, like Berry, a veteran of the fighting in Mexico and France). Berry, who retired a lieutenant colonel, was sixty-four when he passed away at a veterans' hospital in California on January 24, 1959.

Floyd Bennett slowly recuperated from the injuries he had received in the crash of the *America*. In the spring of 1928 he and Bernt Balchen flew a relief mission to the crew of the *Bremen*, stranded on Greenly Island after their historic westerly crossing of the Atlantic. Both men were getting over a bout of pneumonia, with Bennett collapsing upon reaching Québec. He died on April 25, 1928, in a Québec City hospital, with Richard Byrd by his bedside. Byrd, distraught over the loss of his closest companion, named the Ford Tri-Motor that Bennett was to have piloted on their upcoming South Pole expedition after him. Byrd mounted several expeditions to Antarctica, continuing in his role as public hero. On November 28–29, 1929, he flew the *Floyd Bennett* over the South Pole, with Balchen at the controls. Balchen went on to develop cold-weather survival skills and rescue techniques that saved an unknown number of airmen's lives during and after World War II. He retired as an air force colonel in 1956, believing his career was sabotaged by Byrd and his brother, Senator Harry Byrd. Asked once why Admiral Byrd would obstruct his advancement, Balchen replied, "Because he didn't fly over the North Pole and he knows I know it." According to Balchen, Bennett had admitted to him that the *Josephine Ford* had not reached the top of the world. Byrd, sixty-eight, passed away in his sleep at his Boston home on March 11, 1957, still one of the most famous men in the world. The following year Balchen released his memoirs, which criticized Byrd and maintained that his North Pole claims were bogus, but Byrd's powerful friends forced the publisher to destroy the entire first print run and replace it with a sanitized edition. Balchen died on October 17, 1973, a week shy of his seventy-fourth birthday. In 1996, the previously unavailable diary that Byrd had kept on the North Pole flight was closely examined for the first time. The pages were filled with erasures, alterations, and discrepancies that suggested the famous explorer knew full well that he had not reached the pole, yet chose to perpetuate what Richard Montague called "the biggest and most successful fraud in the history of polar exploration."

Clarence Chamberlin became involved in another New York-to-Paris air race in 1931, managing a young socialite named Ruth Nichols in her failed attempt to become the first woman to solo-fly the Atlantic. (Amelia Earhart would accomplish the feat the following year on the fifth anniversary of Lindbergh's flight.) His other activities through the years included lecturing, airport consulting, and operating a small airline and flying school. He divorced Wylda and in 1936 married a much younger woman, a former stewardess. Chamberlin eventually entered the real estate business in Florida and Connecticut. He was eighty-three when he died on October 30, 1976, after a long illness.

After battling charges that he had defrauded the U.S. government in his scrap-metal business and had illegally carried (and later sold) airmail on the *Columbia*'s flight to Germany, Charlie Levine lost much of his fortune in the stock market crash and several aviation ventures. Grace and the children left him. In Germany, the Nazis came to power and removed all mention of his name. One night in 1934, Levine turned on the gas jets inside the kitchen of the Brooklyn apartment at which he was staying, but his roommate was able to revive him. A suicide note asserted he had "taken it on the chin for the last time," but the pugnacious schemer still had a few adventures in him. He was married briefly a second time and involved in shadowy activities that caused him to be variously arrested for smuggling, forgery, and counterfeiting. In 1937 he was convicted of smuggling tungsten powder from Canada, was fined $5,000, and spent eighteen months in jail. Later he received a five-month sentence for bringing an illegal alien (actually a German Jew who had been denied a visa) into the United States from Mexico. When the FBI tracked Levine's postwar whereabouts, agents discovered he was in debt to practically everybody they interviewed. In 1955, Levine's brother said Charlie owed him $65,000 but that he hadn't seen him in twenty-five years. An agent who traced him to a seedy New York flophouse reported that the desk clerk "knew that he was a famous flyer at one time, but at the present time he looks very non-prosperous. . . . Levine lives alone and he knows of no one who calls on him." The Justice Department finally gave up trying to collect its money, though Levine, even as an old man, continued to run afoul of the law. In 1962 he was charged with illegally selling electronic equipment to the government of Venezuela. At about this time a woman who evidently either didn't know or didn't care about Levine's past took him in and cared for him for the rest of his life. He died at a hospital in Washington, D.C., on December 6, 1991, having lived ninety-four restless and eventful years.

In the shorthand of pop history, Lindbergh has come to be remembered as the first to fly the Atlantic—which, of course, he was not. Although the New York-to-Paris flight will always be the centerpiece of his fame, during his seventy-two years he lived a life remarkable for its breadth of physical and intellectual vigor. Among his many interests were rocketry, organ preservation, eugenics, and the development of an artificial heart pump. In 1929 he married Anne Morrow, the petite, bookish daughter of the U.S. ambassador to Mexico, and together "the first couple of the sky" spent much of the 1930s in a series of pioneering survey flights around the world. Anne, who would gain renown as a poet and diarist, had six children with Charles, but it was their firstborn whom history remembers best. In 1932, Charles Jr. was kidnapped and murdered. The sickening sensationalism that surrounded "the crime of the century" caused the Lindberghs to flee to Europe.

While overseas, Charles became impressed with the orderliness and technological advancements of Germany. Resigning his army commission so he could speak more freely, he became a key figure in the America First movement. Like his father before him, he saw no need for American involvement in a European war. His views were broadly criticized as being anti-Semitic, and he came under fire for refusing to return a medal given him by the Nazi government. As part of the backlash, the "Lindbergh flag" that Raymond Orteig had brought home from Paris in 1927 was taken down from its familiar spot on the Lafayette's wall. Everybody used to be proud of him, explained Jean Orteig. "But now he's talking politics."

Lindbergh, a patriot despite his principled stance as an isolationist, was refused active duty status by President Roosevelt after the Japanese attack on Pearl Harbor. Instead, he served as a technical consultant to Henry Ford, who was building bombers, and flew combat missions as a civilian adviser in the Pacific, once shooting down a Zero. After the war he was reinstated into the air force reserve as a brigadier general by President Eisenhower. In 1953, following many years of intermittent work, his best-selling account of the Paris flight was published. *The Spirit of St. Louis* received a Pulitzer Prize and was later made into a movie. The aging but wholesome Jimmy Stewart—who had plotted Lindbergh's flight in the window of the family hardware store thirty years earlier—played the lead role. The real Lindbergh spent little time at the family's Connecticut estate, tramping restlessly around the planet as a consultant to the air force and Pan Am and pursuing whatever interests caught his fancy. Evangeline Land Lindbergh passed away in Detroit in 1954. After her funeral Lindbergh never returned to the city of his birth, not even to visit his mother's gravesite.

By the time Lindbergh reached his sixties the "advance herald of the air age" had circled back. The postwar commercial airline industry had made flying safe, dull, and predictable. The poetry of imagination had taken a backseat to technological innovation. Soon the supersonic Concorde would zip between Paris and New York in three and a half hours. Far more troubling was aviation's devastating effect on the environment. Lindbergh regretted the part he had played in nature's despoiling. He devoted most of the balance of his life to conservation causes, protecting primitive societies in Africa and the Philippines and endangered species worldwide. He declined to participate in any of the anniversary celebrations of his Paris flight. "It's not that era any more," he said in 1967, "and I'm not that boy."

Lindbergh died of cancer on August 26, 1974. He was buried in a secluded mountain plot on the Hawaiian island of Maui. A wood coffin was built. It was snug, unadorned, and practical—a cockpit not unlike that of the *Spirit of St. Louis*, and one entirely appropriate for the Lone Eagle's final solo. "You know," Bud Gurney told an interviewer a few years later, "I'd like to tell you more about what Slim told me. I could tell you what Slim was really doing over there in Europe, and you'd have a different idea of him." Gurney, a retired United Airlines pilot, kept his friend's secret up to his own death in 1982. However, in 2003 it came to light that during the 1950s and 1960s, Lindbergh had fathered a total of seven children with three different women in Europe, including a pair of sisters in Bavaria. DNA tests validated the claims. Reeve Lindbergh, the youngest of his children with Anne, struggled with her father's hurtful hypocrisy, but she eventually came to terms with his secret, compartmentalized life. "He could not be completely open with anybody who loved him anywhere on earth," she concluded. What remains with her, she said, "is a sense of his unutterable loneliness."

And, finally, what of Charles Nungesser and François Coli? In the short term, the vanished airmen remained very much in the public's thoughts. "When shall the White Bird flash into sight?" Charles Prince plaintively asked in "Io Victis," published in the *Atlantic Monthly* four months after their disappearance.

> Questioning, doubting, waiting—in vain.
> Lost in the silence of sea and sky,
> No sound is caught from the White Bird again,
> No glimpse is given to mortal eye.
> Did they fail then, Coli and Nungesser?
> They cannot fail who ardently dare.

For years the anniversary of their disappearance brought a flurry of speculative articles. Bottled messages, all hoaxes, periodically washed up. Interest waned, then picked up again in 1980 when journalist Gunnar Hansen published a magazine article that threw new light on the old mystery. Hansen described how a reclusive woodsman named Anson Berry claimed to have heard an airplane fly overhead as he fished near Machias, Maine, on the overcast afternoon of May 9, 1927. Berry characterized the noise as erratic. A short while later he heard a crash somewhere off in the distance. It was raining hard, so he decided not to investigate. However, Berry (who died in 1936) shared his story with friends and neighbors, some of whom were still living decades later when Hansen began investigating. Through interviews and old reports, Hansen tracked a series of sightings that began at the top of Newfoundland and continued south through Nova Scotia and into Maine's coastal region. He learned of an engine found near Round Lake in 1950, within a mile of where Berry said he'd heard the plane pass. The motor was long gone. According to locals, it had been hauled away down a logging trail and used for scrap.

There were sixteen sightings in Newfoundland on May 9, some more credible than others. The biggest problem was timing, as they typically placed the *White Bird* more than seven hours behind schedule. Hansen

A stone monument commemorating the location of Nungesser and Coli's departure and Lindbergh's arrival was erected at Le Bourget in the spring of 1928. On it is inscribed: *"A ceux qui tentèrent et celui qui accomplit"* (To those who tried and one who succeeded).

speculated the plane was overdue because gale-force winds had cut its anticipated airspeed from 110 to 85 miles per hour and forced it into time-consuming detours. "What lends credence to the sightings is that, though officials sought information throughout Newfoundland, only persons in a line from Old Perlican to St. Lawrence reported hearing or seeing anything," he wrote. "And an airplane flying a course from Old Perlican to New York would have passed close enough to each of these locations to be heard or seen." According to Hansen's calculations, Nungesser and Coli flew over Berry's canoe sometime around 4:30 p.m. that day, which would have been during the plane's fortieth hour of flight, near the end of its projected flying time. The erratic sound Berry heard may have been a sputtering engine. If not an empty gas tank, then a malfunctioning motor or some other calamity may have brought the *White Bird* down into the wilderness near Round Lake. It was possible the plane sank into a bog, swallowing all trace of men and machine. As intriguing as Hansen's theory is, most experienced North Atlantic seamen at the time of the *White Bird*'s disappearance believed the plane never reached landfall, that it was driven into the seething Atlantic by sleet, snow, and high winds somewhere off Newfoundland. Captain S. J. Furneaux rode out the same storm on his steamship, the *Nova Scotia*. If the Frenchmen did fly into that squall, they never would have flown out, he insisted. "The frail plane could never have survived such a storm," aviation journalist Vern Hutchinson later wrote. "Of that the captain was certain."

The French government conducted an investigation in 1983. Based on an in-depth examination of contemporary news reports, eyewitness accounts, and technical bulletins, it concluded that Nungesser and Coli had probably reached North America, though no convincing physical evidence was offered. (If nothing else, this meant that the two French pilots, not the German-Irish crew of the *Bremen*, were the first airmen to successfully fly the Atlantic from east to west.) Clive Cussler, director of the National Underwater and Marine Agency, and Rick Gillespie, head of The International Group for Historic Aircraft Recovery, launched private expeditions, employing divers and even psychics in hopes of finding any clues to the fate of the *White Bird*. The results of their collective efforts were meager and inconclusive. This was not surprising; the plane was constructed largely of canvas and plywood, materials subject to rapid decay in such a harsh environment. However, fragments of metal, of a type not common to the United States or Canada in 1927, were found, leading to speculation that they could be from the instrument panel or the fuel tanks. The only part of the aircraft definitely known to exist—the undercarriage—never left France. It was dropped shortly after the start of the flight and returned to Pierre Levasseur after he issued a plea in the newspapers. Today it can be seen at the Musée de l'Air et de l'Espace in Paris.

A tantalizing question emerges. What if Nungesser and Coli had been able to make it all the way to New York? With Orteig's money won, there would have been no incentive for Charles Lindbergh to fly to Paris. He undoubtedly would have turned his sights to the Pacific—and perhaps *he* would have disappeared in the vast expanses of the ocean, his name surviving today as no more than a footnote. But that's not how events turned out. In French public memory, Nungesser, Coli, and Lindbergh remain a conjoined trinity of national heroes—two native, the other adopted. In the spring of 1928, a monument donated by Robert Jackson, one of the backers of the Argonauts, was unveiled at Le Bourget, near where the *White Bird* took off and the *Spirit of St. Louis* landed. The "figure of Lindbergh remains for us associated with particular emotion," a Paris paper once explained. "To receive him with the enthusiasm he deserved we had to shove aside the grief which the sacrifice of Nungesser and Coli caused us. Lindbergh remains for us the symbol of daring youth, of courage and of faith. He was sent to us from the sky and nothing shall soil his legend, which will remain for us as noble and pure as a page of Missal."

On October 24, 1940, Mme. Nungesser was crossing a Paris street when she was fatally struck by a cyclist. She was seventy-one years old and had never stopped believing that one day her son would show up at the door, medals jangling on his tunic, a cigarette hanging jauntily on his lower lip. "I am convinced that my son Charles still lives," she once said. "Something tells me that he will come back—perhaps in another month, perhaps not for a year. But I am sure I shall again clasp my son in my arms."

The mystery of Nungesser and Coli may never be solved. Setting aside all rational speculation, it does no harm to offer a more fanciful explanation of their fate, a tale in keeping with the soaring romance that caused airmen on both sides of the ocean to risk everything to chase a shepherd boy's dream. It borrows from the story French schoolchildren were told of the gallant Georges Guynemer, who disappeared into a cloud. One day, this particular version goes, two pilots climbed into their plane and set out for America. The winds pushed against them and the air was cold, but these men were very brave. On and on they flew, higher and ever higher into the sky—so high, they can never come back down.

Notes

The abbreviations below are used in the notes. These and other sources are listed in the bibliography. Unless otherwise indicated, all correspondence cited is from the Charles A. Lindbergh Orteig Prize Collection.

AOV	*Autobiography of Values* by Charles A. Lindbergh
CAL	Charles A. Lindbergh
LM	*Le Matin*
LOC	Library of Congress
LPJ	*Le Petit Journal*
LPP	*Le Petit Parisien*
NYT	*New York Times*
TSOSL	*The Spirit of St. Louis* by Charles A. Lindbergh
TD	*Testimonial Dinner Given to Mr. Raymond Orteig by His Friends*
WP	*Washington Post*

Prologue. Instant Fame—or Flaming Gasoline

1   *"The barrier was both"*   Vescey and Dade, 146.
2   *"It's less a decision"*   *TSOSL*, 185.
2   *"What do you say"*   Warren, "Before the Flight."
2   *"I think most of the"*   John Miller interview, "Heaven and Earth."
2   *"the greatest sporting event"*   *NYT*, May 6, 1927.
2   *instant fame*   Vescey and Dade, 153.

3   *"This transformation of geography"* Hoffman, 284.

4   *"a worthy son"* Telegram from Edith Scott Magna to Raymond Orteig, *TD*, 16.

4   *"A man is now living"* Post, "Columbus of the Air."

5   *"There was a great relief"* Anne Condelli interview, "Heaven and Earth."

5   *"We'll probably never see"* Miller interview.

1. "We've Come to Fly the Atlantic"

6   *"An aura of unreality"* Alcock and Brown, 86.

6   *"We've come"* Alcock quoted in Wallace, 158.

7   *"aeroplanes of enemy origin"* Northcliffe renewed the *Daily Mail* prize on July 17, 1918, but because of the war the Royal Aero Club put the challenge on hold until November 14, 1918, three days after the Armistice. The revised rules, posted on February 1, 1919, reflected the lingering animus between the Germans and British, particularly Northcliffe, whose effectiveness as minister of propaganda during the war caused German officials to refer to him as "General Northcliffe." "All persons, and the use of aeroplanes, of enemy origin are, by a resolution of the Royal Aero Club, with the approval of the Daily Mail, the donors, barred from taking part in the Daily Mail £10,000 prize for a cross-Atlantic flight" (*Flight*, February 6, 1919). The ban included all German, Austrian, Hungarian, Turkish, and Bulgarian pilots and craft.

8   *"The Atlantic race is pipped"* *NYT*, April 20, 1919. For the complete list of official entrants, including descriptions of the aircraft and names of crew members, see Allen, *The 91 before Lindbergh*, 36.

9   *"Everybody thought Newfoundland"* Wykes, 32.

11   *"Sir, do buck up"* Rowe, 82.

12   *"the two possible methods"* Hinton, "The First Trans-Atlantic Flight."

12   *"deflected glow"* Ibid.

13   *"Tell Raynham"* Rowe, p. 125.

15   *"the determined nature"* *Daily Mail*, May 26, 1919.

15   *"We are heartily proud"* Smith, 171.

15   *"We are safely"* Ibid.

15   *"danced many lazy figures"* *NYT*, June 1, 1919.

16   *"Nothing was further"* Ibid., July 13, 1921.

16   *"a jolly good effort"* Jablonski, 34. Hawker was planning an overland flight to Asia when he was killed on July 12, 1921.

17   *"showed us every kindness"* Alcock and Brown, 60.

17   *"The conditions seemed propitious"* Ibid., 39.

19   *"startlingly unpleasant"* Ibid., 94.

20   *"partly to take"* Ibid., 97.

20   *"What do you think"* Ibid., 173.

20   *"a terrible journey"* *Daily Mail*, June 17, 1919.

20   *"rattling like"* Alcock and Brown, 42.

21   *"I really do not know"* *Daily Mail*, June 21, 1919.
21   *"lesson of his fate"* *NYT*, December 20, 1919. After years of poor health, Brown died in his sleep on October 4, 1948, from an overdose of veronal. The British national hero had been despondent since his only son, Arthur, an RAF pilot, died in a mission over Holland on the night of June 5, 1944, just days before the twenty-fifth anniversary of his and Alcock's historic flight. See Rowe, 218–220, for Brown's melancholic life after 1919.

2. "Where Does France Come In?"
23   *"was deeply stirred"* Fife, 104–105.
23   *"I recall a little graveyard"* *NYT*, March 3, 1919. Rickenbacker led all U.S. aces in the war with twenty-six "kills."
25   "De l'eau" Lalanne, 117.
26   *"the gourmet's paradise"* *NYT*, August 14, 1938.
27   *"curiously European"* Brock, "When Hotels Mirrored New York's Life."
28   *"my cousin from Germany"* Lalanne, 160.
28   *"transplanted bits of France"* *NYT*, June 8, 1939. Two of Orteig's sisters married employees of the Lafayette.
29   *Orteig's offer* Ibid., May 30, 1919.
29   *"I had read so much"* Roseberry, *The Challenging Skies*, 26.
30–31 *Post and Orteig letters* *NYT*, May 30, 1919.
32   *"There will be no restriction"* Ibid., May 31, 1919.
32   *"If it is not won"* Roseberry, *The Challenging Skies*, 26.
34   *"a good thing"* Wykes, 51.

3. "The Ace with the Wooden Leg"
35   *"There is a strong possibility"* *LPJ*, April 30, 1925.
36   *"Records, yes"* Quoted in Roseberry, *The Challenging Skies*, 75.
36   *the South Atlantic was crossed* Hoare, 110–114.
37   *Two years after* The fliers and their craft were: flight commander Major Frederick L. Martin and Sergeant Alva Harvey in the *Seattle*; Lieutenant Leigh Wade and Sergeant Henry Ogden in the *Boston*; Lieutenant Lowell H. Smith and Lieutenant Leslie P. Arnold in the *Chicago*; and Lieutenant Erik H. Nelson and Lieutenant John Harding Jr. in the *New Orleans*. Only the crews of the *Chicago* and the *New Orleans*—Smith, Arnold, Nelson, and Harding—actually completed the entire circuit. The *Seattle* crashed in the Aleutians on April 30, 1924; it took eleven days for Martin and Harvey to walk out of the wilderness at Port Muller. With Martin missing, overall command of the mission passed to Smith. On August 4 the *Boston* was forced down by engine failure into the North Atlantic between the Orkney Islands and Iceland; Wade and Ogden were picked up by a cruiser, but the plane capsized and sank as it was being towed. Meanwhile, a replacement plane built by Donald Douglas—the *Boston II*—was delivered to Pictou,

Nova Scotia, where Wade and Ogden rejoined the flight on September 4 and finished the tour.

38   *"was black with people"*   Lieutenant Leslie P. Arnold, quoted in Thomas, *The First World Flight*, 147.

38   *"Lieutenant Leigh Wade"*   *NYT*, July 16, 1924.

40   *"These things must be borne"*   Ibid., January 19, 1919. Dinner patrons at the Brevoort regularly bought whiskey, cocktails, creme de menthe, and other liquor from waiters and bellboys in clear violation of the Volstead Act. In February 1926, following several months of undercover work, the U.S. Marshal's office presented its case against Sailors' Snug Harbor and its lessee, Raymond Orteig, Inc. Chagrined by the publicity and concerned about possibly losing his lease on the freshly remodeled property, Orteig decided not to contest the charges. On March 8, 1926, he consented to having the Brevoort's main dining rooms closed for six months—the first padlock action against a New York hotel since the start of Prohibition. Orteig issued a statement, saying any violations of the law at the Brevoort "were actuated more by a desire to satisfy the desires and wishes of a long-established patronage, rather than to obtain the profits that would naturally accrue to them." He promised no more liquor would be sold on the premises "until this pernicious and unpopular law is repealed." Ibid., March 9, 1926.

40   *The Orteig Prize also underwent*   George W. Burleigh to Godfrey L. Cabot, May 21, May 26, 1925; Burleigh to C. F. Schory, May 28, August 14, 1925; *TD*, 58–66.

41   *"You look like"*   Létourneau, "Fonck m'a dit."

43   *"the glorious risks"*   *LPJ*, September 4, 1921.

44   *"we will have"*   *NYT*, April 29, 1920.

44   *"French aviation loses"*   *Le Figaro*, September 1, 1921.

45   *"gallant, opinionated"*   *LM*, September 27, 1925.

45   *"I can still see"*   Funderbunk, 77–78.

49   *"Physical endurance proved superior"*   *NYT*, October 16, 1922.

49   *"I have been to America"*   Ibid.

50   *"If their flight had been"*   Ibid., Aug. 10, 1925. Farman was unique among French constructors in fitting the Goliath with its own twelve-cylinder "broad arrow" reduction-gear motor, "a technical feat of great importance." It reportedly was the first time since the very early days of aviation that a French planemaker had established a world record using one of its own engines. Bouché, "Vingt-quatre Records du Monde Deviennent Français."

50   *"Up to this point"*   Quoted in Burleigh to Howard F. Wehrle, August 12, 1925.

51   *"Just met Tarascon"*   Elbert Severance to Contest Committee, NAA, September 5, 1925.

51   *"Will you kindly"*   Burleigh to Schory, September 11, 1925.

51   *"we cannot do anything"*   The prototype Potez built for Tarascon's flight was officially designated 25.0 No. 01 by the planemaker. It has often been mistakenly stated that the zero was an "O" signifying "Océan."

52   *Tarascon crash*   *LM*, September 27, 1925; Cortet, 20–21. The September 27, 1925, edition of *LPP* has a map of the crash area and photos of the wreckage.

53   *"no reasons exist"*   Burleigh to Schory, September 28, 1925.

53   *"kindly send me"*   Harry G. Yerg to NAA, September 25, 1925.

53   *"They did not bring"*   *NYT*, August 22, 1925.

4. The Fortune of the Air

54   *"Flirting with danger"*   Fonck, *Ace of Aces*, 88.

56   *"calling each other Baron"*   "Emigré," *New Yorker*, August 28, 1926.

60   *"Death claimed him"*   Fonck, *Ace of Aces*, 91.

61   *"French are built"*   Ibid., 66–67.

61   *"I sent my bullets"*   Ibid., 123. Whether official or supposed, long-accepted "kill" figures are notoriously untrustworthy. "In dogfights, no one really knew for sure who had shot down what, and how many planes had fired on one enemy. Or how many 'kills' just dived out of battle and went home." Longstreet, 29.

62   *"perform those little coups"*   Longstreet, 156.

62   *"the tool of retribution"*   Ibid., 157. Most aviation historians have since discounted claims that Wissemann shot down Guynemer and that the German ace was later killed by Fonck.

62   *"He is not a truthful man"*   Ibid., 154. "Dismissing the entire concept of the Service Aéronautique confirmation system, Fonck claimed 127 victims, and he stuck with this figure until his death. . . . Why, then, was he not idolized like Guynemer and cheered like Nungesser? At bottom, it was because people not only demand that their heroes be magnificent in battle, but modest afterwards. Unfortunately, the chromosomes that nurture the first trait do not always coalesce to provide the second. However, coyness can sometimes be learned, but courage never." Mason, 148–149.

63   *"either fly or sink"*   *NYT*, May 5, 1926.

64   *"this organization"*   Harold E. Hartney to Schory, January 23, 1926. Hartney was a member of the Argonauts and the Orteig Prize flight committee, an obvious conflict of interest. "Colonel Hartney, on account of his direct connection with one of our entrants for the prize, should not be permitted to act as a member of the flight committee as a matter of ethics" (Schory to Burleigh, May 12, 1926). On May 14, 1926, Hartney was dropped from the committee.

64   *"the sensational recital"*   *Report of the Daniel Guggenheim Fund for the Promotion of Aeronautics*, 4.

64   *"I have taken the view"*   Harry F. Guggenheim to Orville Wright, July 19, 1926, Wright papers, LOC.

64   *"huge, elegant"*   Sikorsky, 171.

65   *"remained unsurpassed"*   Ibid., 173.

66   feel *"ashamed"*   "S-35," *Time*, August 23, 1926.

66   *"the quietest celebrity"*   "A Quiet Ace," *New Yorker*, August 21, 1926.

67   *"If a third pilot"*   *NYT*, August 29, 1926.

67   *"When I left"*   Ibid.

67   *"calls me an outsider"*   Ibid., August 30, 1926.

68   *"handled the giant"*   *New York Mirror*, February 5, 1941.

68   *"The best thing"*   *NYT*, August 31, 1926.

69   *"It is a big job"*   Ibid., March 25, 1926.

69   *"Why Not Make It"*   Unidentified 1926 clipping, Berry papers.

70   *"The New York to Paris flight"*   *NYT*, September 2, 1926.

71   *"My innermost wish"*   Unidentified September 1926 clipping, Berry papers.

72   *"The details of the Fonck flight"*   *NYT*, September 15, 1926.

72   *"even if it means"*   Ibid., September 19, 1926. Major Pierre Weiss, who had just completed a record 3,541-mile nonstop flight between Paris and Persia, contended that his message was sent in the spirit of camaraderie: "It is high time that a Frenchman crossed the pond. Fonck has risen magnificently to the challenge. He should leave! Our hearts are stretched out to him. And never mind if he dies at sea! It would be a beautiful end, and after all, death lies in wait for each of us." *LM*, September 20, 1926.

73   *"bubbling over"*   *NYT*, September 14, 1926.

73   *"I will never leave France"*   "Cartwheel," *Time*, October 4, 1926.

74   *"We'll be in Paris"*   *WP*, September 22, 1926.

74   *"René has always"*   *LPJ*, September 22, 1926.

76   *There were several long seconds*   Details of the accident and quotes are from *NYT*, September 22, 1926.

78   *"there was no team work"*   Ibid., September 25, 1926. Sidney B. Veit, the NAA's representative in Paris, refuted Hartney's charges: "Fonck has courage and competence; he has proved that. Don't think for a moment that he bluffed about his ability to pilot the ship. A man may bluff to attain glory and great pecuniary advantages, but he doesn't bluff when it comes to putting his life in danger." *WP*, September 26, 1926.

78   *Honneur gave no direct answer*   *NYT*, September 25, 1926.

79   *"The wheels were"*   *LM*, September 21, 1926.

79   *"It's finished"*   *L'Humanité*, September 22, 1926. Clavier's widow sued his employer, Radio des Industries, for damages, but in April 1930 a Paris court ruled that the technician's contract covered only trial flights and not the actual start for France.

79   *"an unfortunate accident"*   *WP*, September 28, 1926.

5. Slim

80   *"The life of an aviator"*   *AOV*, 63–64.

80   *"Had he demanded"*   *TSOSL*, 16.

80   *"It certainly doesn't take"*   Ibid.
81   *"Depending on which paper"*   Ibid., 161.
82   *"It was hot weather"*   Every and Tracy, 15.
82   *"Now, you have a head"*   Haines, 70.
83   *"He was an Apollo"*   Lodge, 7.
83   *"She made life miserable"*   Grace Lee Nute interview with Eva Lindbergh
     Christie, Lindbergh Family Papers, box 1. CAL's surviving half sister was
     described by C. A. Lindbergh's friend and biographer Lynn Haines as
     "a creature of cyclonic activity, with all the daring and independence of
     the Lindberghs" (Haines, 63). She graduated from Carleton College and
     worked as a schoolteacher and an aide in her father's Washington office
     before marrying journalist George W. Christie in 1916. Together they
     published the *Red Lake Falls Gazette*. She died on January 28, 1985, in
     Roseville, Minnesota, at ninety-two.
84   *"He'd let me walk"*   TSOSL, 377.
84   *"You and I can take hard knocks"*   CAL, Foreword in Larson, xiv.
84   *"I dreamed often"*   AOV, 63.
85   *"How wonderful"*   TSOSL, 244.
85   *"It was a price"*   AOV, 9.
85   *"My early flying"*   Ibid.
86   *"The actual flying"*   CAL to Richard Plummer, April 22, 1922, quoted in
     Berg, 65.
87   *"Ranchers, cowboys"*   TSOSL, 440.
87   *"The Army schools"*   Berg, 74.
88   *"it would be a worthwhile trade"*   TSOSL, 262.
89   *"He could make you feel"*   Mosley, 401.
89   *"It was an enterprise"*   St. Louis Post-Dispatch, May 21, 1967.
90   *"It took me"*   AOV, 67.
91   *"purposeful, quick of reaction"*   CAL's personnel records in the Militia
     Bureau of the War Department, quoted in NYT, June 5, 1927.
91   *"It can be done"*   McDermott, "Lindbergh History April 1926—November
     1926."

6. Giuseppe, the Gypsy, and the Junk Man
92   *"We not only wanted"*   TD, 24.
93   *"The Columbia"*   Montague, 38–39.
94   *"the slightest use"*   TSOSL, 46.
95   *"never learned to fly"*   "The Reminiscences of Clarence Chamberlin,"
     Aviation Project, Oral History Research Office, Columbia University.
95   *"a 'gypsy flyer'"*   Post, "Columbus of the Air."
96   *"We are always worrying"*   NYT, April 15, 1927.
96   *"was convinced he could build"*   Chamberlin, 15.
96   *"You should plan on"*   TSOSL, 28.
97   *"We have our reputation"*   Ibid., 34.

97   *"Oh, no!"*   McCarthy, "The Spirit of St. Louis."
98   *"So, you want to buy"*   TSOSL, 72.
99   *"What would you think"*   Ibid., 74.
99   *"You understand"*   Ibid., 75.
99   *"We know better"*   Ibid.
99   *"Well, have you"*   Ibid., 76.
100 *"I want this one"*   Ibid.

7. Revving Up

101 *"Paris in the twenties"*   Rose, 152.
101 *"Both Byrd and Davis"*   NYT, April 10, 1927.
102 *"crawling out of the fuselage"*   Ibid., April 26, 1928.
102 *"the ideal second-spot man"*   Hoyt, 157–158.
103 *"For the next hour and thirty-five minutes"*   Bennett, "Our Flight over the North Pole."
104 *"People who amuse themselves"*   Quoted in Brinnin, 460. The introduction of stricter U.S. immigration laws caused a jump in transatlantic leisure travel in the 1920s as steamship companies reconfigured third-class cabins into tourist class. During the summer of 1927, round-trip fares to France cost $177 to $200 for tourist class while first-class cabin rates ranged from $412 to $580, depending on the size of the liner. In his foreword to John Maxtone-Graham's *The Only Way to Cross*, an engaging history of the golden age of transatlantic ocean travel, Walter Lord succinctly traced how airplanes rapidly supplanted the great liners: "While plane travel steadily increased after World War II, ships continued to hold their own until the late 1950s. In fact, 1957 saw sea travel reach a new postwar peak, as 1,036,000 people sailed on some seventy steamers. In 1958 air passed sea for the first time, but the ships continued strong, with more than a dozen liners sailing from New York during a typical summer week. Then, on October 26, 1958, the first American commercial jet took off for Paris, and a whole new era was born. With flight time cut from twelve to less than seven hours, the lure was irresistible. By 1960 the jets had seventy percent of the business, and by the end of the decade only four of every hundred travelers still went to Europe by sea. White elephants almost overnight, the great liners were quickly taken out of service, or shifted to the bland pursuit of cruising."
105 *"stuck to the type"*   Byrd, Skyward, 225.
105 *"The extra capacity"*   Ibid., 227.
106 *"shot with it"*   NYT, April 17, 1927.
106 *"I didn't know any history"*   Ibid.
107 *"You lead the way"*   Ibid.
108 *"She is a perfect ship"*   WP, April 12, 1927.
109 *"A few years ago we held"*   NYT, April 27, 1927.
109 *"liked his wine, women and song"*   Bernt Balchen, quoted in Glines, 40.

110 *"I did not believe"* *NYT*, April 15, 1927.

110 *"Bert and I had won"* Chamberlin, 22. The endurance record stood less than four months. On August 3–5, 1927, a single-engine Junkers W 33 monoplane piloted by Johann Risztics and Cornelius Edzard stayed aloft for 52 hours, 22 minutes, and 32 seconds over Dessau, Germany.

8. Against the Prevailing Winds

111 *"Both shores of the Atlantic"* "Paris Preliminaries," *Time*, April 25, 1927.

111 *"beautiful bravery"* *LPJ*, October 6, 1926. Some press reports stated that Captain Maurice Noguès, a decorated veteran with experience piloting flying boats, would be a third crew member. In 1928 Noguès flew the first airmail from France to Lebanon and Syria.

112 *"These Frenchmen"* Schory to Colonel B. F. Castle, January 5, 1927.

112 *"A non-stop flight"* *NYT*, May 6, 1927.

112 *"experimentation in all its forms"* *Le Figaro*, June 3, 1927.

113 *"Flying is means of locomotion"* *NYT*, September 3, 1928.

113 *"It is certain"* *LM*, February 26, 1927.

115 *"There does not"* *NYT*, March 27, 1927.

116 *"arrogant contempt"* Franks and Bailey, *Over the Front*, 198.

116 "Mon Général" Mortane, *Nungesser*, 59.

118 *"I still love her"* "Milestones," *Time*, September 20, 1926.

118 *"Good young friends"* Mortane, *Nungesser*, 63–64.

118 *"I want a plane"* De la Croix, 60–61.

118 *"Fuel comes first"* Ibid., 63.

119 *"I suppose she ought"* Ibid., 65.

119 *"In the fear"* *Le Figaro*, May 4, 1927.

120 *"Coli understands the sea"* *LM*, April 22, 1927.

9. Come to Earth

121 *"Other stories are told"* Hoare, 9.

121 *"Some of my friends"* Byrd, *Skyward*, 235.

122 *"There came a terrific crash"* Ibid., 236.

122 *"Guess I'm done for"* Ibid., 237.

122 *"I felt like making"* Ibid., 238.

123 *"The roar of the three motors"* *NYT*, April 17, 1927.

124 *"down on the field"* Ibid.

124 *"The contents spurted out"* Ibid.

124 *"mystery machine"* Huttig, 13.

125 *"I wish to notify"* Winston W. Ehrgott to Secretary, NAA, April 18, 1927.

126 *"having accompanied"* *NYT*, April 20, 1927.

126 *"Leaders of other projected flights"* Ibid.

126 *"What do you think we are?"* De la Croix, 62.

126 *"had been projected into"* Byrd, *Skyward*, 232.

127 *"It is a matter of great satisfaction"* Montague, 15.

127 *"Sensational flights are the italics"* Byrd, *Skyward*, 298.

128 *"An energetic motorcycle cop"* Chamberlin, 31.

128 *"To hell with"* *Brooklyn Eagle*, April 25, 1927.

129 *"Thanks, doc"* Ibid.

129 *"I think we have"* *NYT*, April 27, 1927.

131 *"I don't think either"* Ibid., April 28, 1927.

131 *"brilliant, courageous"* Ibid., April 27, 1927. Keystone salvaged and sold the *American Legion*. The rebuilt plane was used for several years as a passenger airliner and freight carrier in Latin America.

10. Little Silver Plane

132 *"Everybody knows"* De Saint-Exupéry.

132 *"In view of the tragic accident"* Schory to Burleigh, April 27, 1927.

133 *"I shall not hurry"* *NYT*, April 28, 1927.

135 *"Once the course"* Goldsborough, "The Earth Inductor Compass."

136 *"It's fascinating"* *TSOSL*, 94.

136 *"It was a mammoth thing"* Cassagneres, *The Spirit of Ryan*, 48–49.

137 *"Why does this damn thing"* Wagner, 125.

138 *"We yelled, slapped"* Cassagneres, *The Spirit of Ryan*, 63–64. Ryan Aircraft employees signed the inside of the propeller spinner when the *Spirit of St. Louis* was completed. They also painted a left-facing Native American–style swastika—at the time, a popular symbol of good luck.

138 *"I've never felt"* *TSOSL*, 121.

11. Paris au Printemps

139 *"Because Americans are optimistic"* Tardieu, 56–57.

139 *"a beautiful, alluring"* Flanner, xxi.

140 *"When spring came"* Hemingway, 40.

140 *"France dances"* *NYT*, August 7, 1927.

140 *"It was a curious thing"* Shirer, 259–260. "Remember—you do not wish to be considered 'a Tourist,'" cautioned a popular 1927 guidebook. "Many Tourists in Paris are sneered at. They have given America a black eye. You want to be 'An American Gentleman.'" In order to be stamped an American gentleman, the reader was advised to tip liberally, speak softly, dress in a dignified manner, show respect for the French, demonstrate a knowledge of their language, and express a love of Paris. Bruce Reynolds, *Paris with the Lid Lifted*, 99.

142 *"Coli will certainly"* *LM*, April 28, 1927.

143 *"The old windjammers"* De la Croix, 68.

144 *"prize or no prize"* *Brooklyn Eagle*, May 1, 1927.

144 *"Possibly the* Columbia*"* Ibid.

145 *aviation-related cartoons* *LPP*, May 5, 7, 1927.

145 *"There will be"* *L'Auto*, quoted in *NYT*, May 6, 1927.

145 *"Every place I go"* Montague, 54.

147 *"nothing can be left"* LM, April 29, 1927.

147 *"If I succeed"* NYT, May 6, 1927.

148 *"taken no measures"* Ibid., May 11, 1927.

12. A Stout Heart Does Not Fear Death

149 *"Now, I talked"* Watkins, 275–276. The protagonist of Watkins's novel, Charlie Halifax, is modeled on Nungesser.

150 *"A stout heart"* LM, April 19, 1927.

150 *"My dear Farret"* De la Croix, 64.

151 *"troubled period"* LPJ, May 22, 1927.

151 *"pilots absolutely cannot"* LM, May 1, 1927.

151 *"occupied by a million"* Ibid., May 3, 1927.

151 *"First of all"* Ibid., May 5, 1927.

152 *"Both of them"* Le Figaro, May 4, 1927. Nungesser and Coli "are busy trying to find the best possible purchasers for their story of the flight and their impressions here before they start. The aviators appear to be well aware of the deep interest being taken by the American public and have fixed their price accordingly." NYT, April 26, 1927.

152 *"If I were trying"* LM, May 3, 1927.

152 *"It is impossible"* La Presse, May 4, 1927, quoted in Garreau, 38.

153 *"It seems to me"* LM, May 8, 1927.

154 *"I'll take it"* Ibid., May 9, 1927.

154 *"Come, my friend"* Ibid.

154 *"It's no use"* De la Croix, 66.

154 *"The moment was"* Le Figaro, May 9, 1927.

155 *"lost to view"* LPP, May 9, 1927. Footage of the White Bird taking off and heading for the English Channel is contained in the film Match pour l'Atlantique Nord, a copy of which can be found at the Musée de l'Air et de l'Espace.

155 *"Well, we wish"* NYT, May 8, 1927.

156 *"I don't see how"* Ibid.

156 *"That's the first time"* TSOSL, 129.

156 *"What is happening"* NYT, May 9, 1927.

156 *"We have new fashions"* LPP, May 9, 1927.

157 *"You've got to hand it"* Montague, 56–57.

158 *"usually reliable source"* Hamlen, 93.

158 *"The two pilots"* La Liberté, quoted in L'Humanité, May 10, 1927. The front pages of La Presse and Paris-Soir heralding the White Bird's arrival in New York are reproduced in Garreau, 100ff.

158 *"Then they both"* La Presse, May 9, 1927, quoted in Jullian, 179.

158 *"Luck has always"* Montague, 57.

158 *"I knew my son"* Ibid., 57–58.

158 *"indescribable joy"* Nevin, 82.

158 *"I knew Nungesser"* De la Croix, 72–73.

158   *"Parisians snake-danced"*   Shirer, 326–327.
159   *"That did it"*   Hawkins, 132.

13. Limbo
160   *"Since this imperious thing"*   Rostand, 5.
161   *"we were in"*   Mott, 352.
161   DUE TO DEPTH   NAA to Schory, May 10, 1927.
161   *"Other mechanics went over"*   *NYT*, May 11, 1927.
161   *"a phenomenon of collective illusion"*   *LPP*, May 11, 1927.
162   *"very poorly chosen"*   *LPJ*, May 22, 1927.
162   *"Taking the perpetual brainwashers"*   *L'Humanité*, May 10, 1927.
162   *"These men died"*   *Le Figaro*, May 16, 1927.
163   *"This case was not"*   *Tägliche Rundschau*, quoted in *LPP*, May 12, 1927.
       Germany was ahead of other countries in the developing field of rock-
       etry. An association of amateur rocket enthusiasts called the *Verein für
       Raumschiffahrt* (Society for Space Travel) was formed in 1927. Its members
       included fifteen-year-old Wernher von Braun (the future father of Nazi
       Germany's V-2 rockets and the U.S. Apollo moon program) and astrono-
       mer and inventor Max Valier, who described how passengers would soon
       cross the Atlantic in "rocket airplanes": "With a tremendous roar the
       rocket airplane races up an almost vertical runway, flings itself free, and
       heads straight into the upper air. At an altitude of fifty miles the pilot
       flattens his course; now he can put on full speed without any danger of
       burning up the craft like a meteor. Hardly more than an hour after leaving
       New York you are over Paris; the craft slows, and descends, and auxiliary
       rocket motors bring it gently to earth" ("To Europe by Rocket," *Popular
       Science*, September 1927). Rocketry and space travel were popular topics
       in the press as the race for the Orteig Prize helped focus public atten-
       tion on the expanding possibilities of manned flight. In early May 1927,
       Ivan Fedorof—a Russian mechanic and a member of the All-Inventors
       Vegetarian Club of Interplanetary Cosmopolitans—announced that in
       September he and Valier and three unnamed volunteers would be flying
       to the moon in a "moon machine" that was a cross between an airplane and
       a giant projectile. *Literary Digest* predicted that travel in a "space-ship" of
       the future would make transatlantic flight in conventional aircraft "look
       like the expedition of a snail across the street." "The Rocket-Ship of the
       Future," June 25, 1927.
163   *"If I should"*   *L'Humanité*, May 27, 1927.
163   *"I have a feeling"*   *LPP*, May 12, 1927.
164   *"No wonder they never"*   *WP*, August 13, 1972.
164   *"To Nungesser"*   *Philadelphia Inquirer*, May 19, 1927.
165   *"Just look at"*   Huttig, 27. France's largest-circulation Catholic newspaper
       noted that the airmen had left on the feast day of Joan of Arc, a national
       heroine: "Was it in her honor? Did they dream of invoking St. Joan of Arc?

Had they thought of the Lord of lords, of the Master of the elements, of He who holds the thunder in his hand, of the God of the sky and of the earth? Had they assisted in the mass? No paper has anything to tell us about these important things. Sport is the only god to which most journalists will sacrifice. They described down to the minutiae the preparations of the take-off scene, the form of the airplane, its force, its speed, the pounds it will carry, the proud allure of its aviators. Where in all of this is the place of God? We have the regret of not perceiving it. Ah! how a simple sign of the cross would have been good at the launch of such a perilous voyage. It's been said that the airplane was decorated with a symbol, not too happy in truth: a skull and crossbones. This grim emblem was, apparently, in the eyes of Nungesser, a bringer of good luck. Hopefully it wasn't a bringer of bad luck! Ah! I would have preferred, for the protection of his 'White Bird,' the image of St. Christopher, patron saint of automobilists and aviators! Whatever is the fate of these two heroes, let us offer them the gift of a prayer." *La Croix*, May 13, 1927.

165 *"Send us a wire"* TSOSL, 134.
165 *"What do you think"* Ibid., 146.
166 *"It's going to disappoint"* Ibid., 147.
166 *"I think it is"* *Brooklyn Eagle*, May 12, 1927.
167 *"Mr. Levine's insistence"* Chamberlin, 43.
168 *"No one had listened"* Ibid., 46.
168 *"this drab little man"* Quoted in "Uncle Sam's Second Flying Hop Across the Pond," *Literary Digest*, June 25, 1927.
168 *"There is no pleasure"* NYT, April 12, 1949.
168 *"It swooped lower"* Ibid., May 13, 1927.

14. Hunting Dragons
169 *"Charles was not born"* Franck, "Lindbergh et Ma Vie."
170 *"What promises to be"* NYT, May 13, 1927.
170 *"May the best man"* Ibid.
170 *"You can sign it"* Chamberlin, 37.
170 *"a shrewd psychologist"* Ibid., 37–38. Levine filed Chamberlin's Orteig Prize entry form on May 10 and asked for a waiver of the mandatory sixty-day waiting period, a request that was denied. "Under the circumstances, which involve Mr. Charles A. Lindbergh, who is eligible to start, and Captain René Fonck, who is eligible to start on June 26th, the Committee finds it impossible to waive the sixty-day entrance requirement as outlined under Article 7 of the Orteig regulations" (Schory to Charles A. Levine, May 12, 1927). To qualify for the $25,000 prize, Chamberlin could leave no sooner than July 9.
171 *"handsome and smiling"* *Brooklyn Eagle*, May 14, 1927.
171 *"Was your son"* *New York Herald Tribune*, May 15, 1927.
171 *"I wouldn't mind"* NYT, May 15, 1927.

171 *"When I enter"* Quoted in "Flight," *Time*, May 30, 1927.

172 *"Boys, she's ready"* TSOSL, 166.

172 *"mirror girl"* Ibid., 225–226. Aviation historian Ev Cassagneres, having spent years chasing down the mirror girl's identity, is satisfied that her name was Mrs. Loma Oliver, although everything else about her remains a mystery.

174 *"You want to know"* "The Reminiscences of Clarence Chamberlin."

174 *"The newspapers have kept"* TSOSL, 170.

174 *"It would increase"* AOV, 74.

175 *"These have been"* TSOSL, 165.

175 *"This fellow"* Lomask, 92.

176 *"looked on the flight promoter's plan"* Chamberlin, 38

176 *"every nickel"* Ibid., 39.

176 *"tendency which all men have"* Ibid.

177 *"I felt it important"* Byrd, *Skyward*, 239–240.

177 *"Coward," read one* Ibid., 239.

177 *"I could never understand"* Fokker and Gould, 260.

177 *"Aviators seem to have"* Owen, "The Dragon Hunters." Owen's take on courage is interesting in light of his experiences two years later as a *NYT* reporter attached to Byrd's Antarctic expedition. According to Byrd's most recent biographer, the slightly built, bespectacled reporter "was openly fearful, verbalizing his worries about disaster. But his besetting sin was that he would not work. . . . The reporter always seemed to be sick or ailing in some way" (Rose, 261). Despite being branded a misfit and a slacker, Owen returned to New York a hero in journalism circles and received a Pulitzer Prize for his dispatches from the South Pole.

178 *"You'd better prepare"* TSOSL, 172.

179 *"Slim, what am I"* Ibid., 175. At the time Lindbergh was under the impression that he was a few days short of the sixty-day waiting period required of Orteig Prize candidates, a misconception he repeated in many of his autobiographical writings. He had called Harry Knight earlier and explained that leaving jeopardized winning the $25,000 needed to pay back his investors. "To hell with the money," Knight responded. "When you're ready to take off, go ahead." However, the prize committee considered his application accepted as of February 28, 1927, the day his entry form was executed, meaning he was free to depart for Paris at any time from April 28 on.

179 *"more like a funeral procession"* Ibid., 178.

181 *"It's the weather"* Ibid., 182.

181 *"Get up!"* Balchen, 98.

181 *"Now, the intangible"* TSOSL, 184.

182 *"If the* Spirit" Ibid.

182 *"A group of about six"* Cassagneres, *The Untold Story of the* Spirit of St. Louis, 68.

183 *"the most breathless thing"* Vescey and Dade, 153.

183 *"There was no cheer"* Ibid. The number of actual eyewitnesses to Lindbergh's takeoff varies widely. See the article by Allen Richter in the *NYT*, May 19, 2002.

15. We Two
A useful hour-by-hour overview of Lindbergh's flight from takeoff to touch-down can be found in Cassagneres, *The Untold Story of the* Spirit of St. Louis, 70–82.

184 *"Now it is not"* "Lindbergh's Flight," *Time*, April 13, 1931. A recording of the German opera is available at the Vincent Voice Library (call no. DB2896).
186 *"a hopeless hunt"* TSOSL, 270.
186 *"I stood nearby"* Ibid., 270–271.
186 *"curtain off in her mind"* Ibid., 231.
187 *"The sleet began"* CAL, "Lindbergh's Own Story." This is a compilation of the flier's syndicated *NYT* articles ghostwritten by reporters Carlisle MacDonald and Edwin L. James after his arrival in Paris.
187 *Captain Lindbergh, we're with you NYT*, May 21, 1927.
187 *"With these instruments"* Chicago Tribune, September 30, 1928.
188 *"Every cell"* TSOSL, 354.
189 *"I think half of America"* Elinor Smith Sullivan interview, "Heaven and Earth."
189 *"Its successful flight"* NYT, May 21, 1927.
189 *"If Lindbergh is successful"* Ibid.
189 *"He is known"* Ibid.
190 *"I feel very sorry"* Montague, 76.
190 *"But then I figured"* "Lindbergh's Own Story."
190 *"big ebony Harvey"* Wales, "Formidable!"
191 *"His calm courage"* NYT, May 21, 1927.
191 *"considered doubtful"* Quoted in Mosley, 104.
191 *"It was a lovely"* Shirer, 332.
191 *"It will be"* LPP, May 21, 1927.
192 *"Paris, which carries"* La Liberté, May 21, 1927.
192 *"There was no moon"* "We," 218.
193 *"Numerous shorelines"* Ibid., 219–220.
193 *"suddenly in the tail"* AOV, 12.
193 *"used to take"* WP, June 11, 1927.
193 *"There was this doctor"* Vescey and Dade, 152.
195 *"Here are human beings"* TSOSL, 463.
195 *"In the subway"* Brooklyn Eagle, May 22, 1927.
196 *"moved the plane"* Stewart and Laitin, "Lucky to Be Lindy."
196 *"Corn beef hash"* Brooklyn Eagle, May 22, 1927.
196 *"Is this about Lindbergh?"* Detroit Free Press, May 22, 1927.

196 *"rise to your feet"* *NYT*, May 21, 1927.
196 *"Lindbergh Flies Alone"* *New York Sun*, May 21, 1927.
197 *"From now on"* *TSOSL*, 485.
197 *"Sometime in the afternoon"* Hawkins, 135.
198 *"That fellow"* *"We saw him land!"* *Smithsonian*, May 2002.
198 *"As we waited"* Ibid.
198 *"The* Spirit of St. Louis *is a wonderful plane"* *TSOSL*, 486.
199 *"Suddenly,"* recalled Deutsch Armand Deutsch interview, "Heaven and Earth."
200 *"with the night so clear"* *TSOSL*, 486.
200 *"One second I was"* "We saw him land!"
200 *"was one of jubilation and disbelief"* Deutsch interview.
200 *"yelling and out of breath"* Ahrendt, "Paris 1926–1928."
201 *"Mr. Bruhn called"* Diary of Margo Behan, private collection.
201 *"I'm probably the only living person"* "Interview with Flora Elizabeth Reynolds," University History Series, Regional Oral History Office, Bancroft Library, University of California at Berkeley.
201 *"Before Lindbergh, I had no idea"* Muheim, "My Life with the Lone Eagle."
202 *"People became restless"* *Brooklyn Eagle*, May 22, 1927.
202 *"A young Minnesotan"* Fitzgerald, "Echoes of the Jazz Age."
203 *"a celebration"* Byrd, *Skyward*, 241.
203 *"I just want"* Ibid.
204 *"two characters such as"* *NYT*, May 22, 1927.
204 *"Due to the crowning blow"* Ibid.
204 *"Yes, it's off"* Ibid.

16. "Vive l'Amérique!"
Two newsreels of interest, "Lindbergh Arrives in Paris" (Pathé News) and "Lindbergh's Flight and Return" (Fox News/Kinograms), are accessible through the Internet Archive at http://www.archive.org/.

205 *"You were strong"* Weiss, *La Bataille de l'Atlantique*, 65–66.
205 *"I am Lindbergh."* LPP, May 22, 1927. Before leaving New York, Lindbergh had sold the exclusive rights to his story to the *New York Times*, but exclusivity—and ethics—were ignored as highly competitive news agencies scrambled to cover his arrival in Paris. For some interesting first-person insights into the workings of the press during the flier's week in France, see Berger, 291–305; Hawkins, 133–138; Shirer, 323–344; Root, 28–37; and Wales, "Formidable!" The most memorable question put to Lindbergh came from Hank Wales, a reporter for the Paris edition of the *Chicago Tribune*. "Say, Lindy," he asked during the hero's first formal news conference, "did you have a crapper on that plane?"
205 *"I am Charles Lindbergh!"* *NYT*, May 26, 1927.
205 *"Good. Help me out of my box!"* "New York–Paris," *Flight*, May 26, 1927.

205   *"Well, here we are"*   *Brooklyn Eagle*, May 22, 1927.

205   *"Are there any mechanics here?"*   *TSOSL*, 495. Lindbergh addressed other falsehoods about his first moments in France: "When I landed at Paris, I did not announce my name, or request a cigarette or a glass of milk, or say 'Well, I made it,' or inquire as to whether I had landed at Paris. . . . After being swept away by the crowd, many of the reporters on the aerodrome sent back to their organizations partly imaginary accounts of my landing. There was considerable difference as to what took place and what my words were likely to be." Ibid., 548.

206   *"conveyed no emotion whatsoever"*   Coppens, "La veridique histoire de arrive de Charles Lindbergh au Bourget."

207   *"A young man, almost a child"*   *Excelsior*, May 22, 1927.

207   *"The admirable and splendid effort"*   *Comoedia*, quoted in *LPP*, May 22, 1927.

207   *"this daring human bird"*   *LM*, May 22, 1927.

207   *"There is glory"*   *Victoire*, quoted in *LPP*, May 22, 1927.

207   *"In Lindbergh we salute A MAN"*   *L'Humanité*, May 22, 1927.

208   *"we do not wish to see"*   *L'Ouevre*, May 22, 1927.

208   *"The victory of Lindbergh is"*   Francueil, "Un Heros Légendaire Charles Lindbergh."

209   *"tickled the fancy"*   *WP*, May 23, 1927.

209   *"enthusiastic admiration"*   *The Flight of Captain CAL from New York to Paris*, 18.

209   *"the champion stenographer"*   *NYT*, June 24, 1927.

209   *"is a cockleshell"*   *New York World*, May 23, 1927.

210   *"grateful to the French people"*   *WP*, May 23, 1927.

210   *"We'd have preferred"*   Flanner, 23.

210   *"What a shame"*   Weiss, *La Bataille de l'Atlantique*, 37.

210   *"Cable him to stay"*   *Paris-Soir*, quoted in Mosely, 402.

210   *"A great shout erupted!"*   *LPJ*, May 23, 1927.

211   *"I wanted to make"*   Beamish, 50–51.

211   *"Let them be my lucky charm!"*   *LPJ*, May 23, 1927.

211   *"pleased the sentimental crowd"*   Ibid.

211   *"Who can say"*   Beamish, 55–56.

212   *"This feat of yours"*   Ibid., 56.

212   *"We followed Lindbergh"*   Root, 36.

212   *"grabbed him and still haven't"*   *L'Humanité*, May 24, 1927.

213   *"From the moment I woke"*   *AOV*, 314.

213   *"All the signs"*   *NYT*, May 24, 1927.

213   *"How sad it would have been"*   Pierre Weiss, "Lindbergh," *L'Aerophile*, June 1–15, 1927, quoted in Wohl, *The Spectacle of Flight*, 26.

213   *"Have you seen him?"*   *L'Humanité*, May 24, 1927.

214   *"Well, Mr. Orteig"*   *NYT*, June 11, 1927.

214   *"I knew Coli particularly well"*   *LPP*, May 22, 1927.

214   *"I feel a lot lighter"*   *NYT*, May 23, 1927.

216 *He circled the Eiffel Tower*   TD, 6–8.

217 *"a marvelous young chap"*   WP, June 1, 1927. London journalists joked about Lindbergh's "endurance record" as he was shuttled from ceremony to ceremony, but they, too, took time to honor him. The directors of the *Daily Mail* presented him with a gold cup while the Association of American Correspondents offered their dinner guest a "special course": five sandwiches and a canteen of water. For a fuller account of Lindbergh's reception in Belgium and England, see *"We,"* 247–264, and "London's Welcome to Lindbergh," *Flight*, June 2, 1927.

217 *"Now tell me, Captain Lindbergh"*   Mosely, 116.

217 *"found that it didn't"*   Gill, 166.

17. "Lindbergh Is Our Elijah"

218 *"The Nation is glad"*   WP, June 12, 1927.

218 *"the greatest feat of a solitary man"*   New York World, May 21, 1927.

219 *"If you will sit down"*   Green, "What Lindbergh Found in His Mail Bag."

219 *"Lindbergh had better get"*   Davis, 219.

219 *"commercialize his stunt"*   Ibid., 220.

219 *"You are in for it now"*   Bruno and Dutton, "Lindbergh, the Famous Unknown."

220 *"The parade that went"*   Sullivan interview.

221 *"We measure heroes"*   NYT, June 14, 1927.

222 *"two thoughts in mind"*   TD, 43–49. The U.S. Treasury determined that the federal tax liability on the Orteig Prize would reduce the $25,000 windfall to $23,766.25.

223 *"I was so filled up"*   Bruno and Dutton, "Lindbergh, the Famous Unknown."

224 *"Colonel Lindbergh is a messenger"*   Berg, 170.

224 *"Fair-haired Apollo"*   Green, "What Lindbergh Found in His Mail Bag."

224 *One canned message read*   "Suggested Telegrams," New Yorker, June 18, 1927.

224 *"The stiff military bearing"*   NYT, June 12, 1927.

225 *The power of radio*   For a transcript of the complete NBC broadcast, see WP, June 12, 1927. An audio copy is available at the LOC.

225 *"Americans had known national figures"*   Kyvig, 83–84.

225 *"The popularity of Lindbergh"*   NYT, June 12, 1927.

225 *"has shown us that"*   Mullett, "The Biggest Thing That Lindbergh Has Done."

226 *musical tributes*   Kowalke, "Music in the Air." For some opportunists in the music industry, Lindbergh's flight was one of the best things ever to happen to them. Vernon Dalhart, a country singer who spent much of the 1920s singing about trains and shipwrecks, used a variety of pseudonyms to record Lindbergh songs for eleven different labels. Songwriter Alma Valentine produced at least ten pieces of sheet music about the aviator.

An audio sampling of Lindbergh-inspired songs is available at the Vincent Voice Library.

226 *"For Lindbergh, oh what a Wonder Boy"* On the 78-rpm Victor recording of "Lindbergh (Eagle of the USA)," studio engineers replicated the sound of the *Spirit of St. Louis's* spinning propeller by having an electric fan blade hit a deck of playing cards—reportedly the first-ever use of a sound effect on a record.

226 *The excesses of Lindy mania* Quoted in Roberts, 47–49.

227 *"Sooner or later he will leave"* *New Yorker*, June 18, 1927.

227 *"tried to convince everyone"* *AOV*, 83.

228 *"Is it true, Colonel"* Keyhoe, *Flying with Lindbergh*, 17.

228 *"They must be afraid we'll escape"* Ibid., 222.

229 *"never averse to cashing in"* Bruno and Dutton, "Lindbergh, the Famous Unknown."

230 *"We" was an instant best seller* Lindbergh heartily disliked the title of his first book. As he explained in 1968: "I never used the term 'We' to refer to the *Spirit of St. Louis* and myself. This was a newspaper concoction or misconception. I used 'We' to refer to the men, including myself, who were members of the *Spirit of St. Louis* organization by which the purchase of the plane and the costs of the flight to Paris were financed." Cassagneres, *The Spirit of Ryan*, 41.

231 *"This is more of your self-sureness"* "Letters," *Time*, August 1, 1927.

231 *"They flew over the forest"* Jean-Brunhes, "L'Enigme Des Avions Transatlantiques Disparus."

18. Two More Across

233 *"Now that three American planes"* *NYT*, July 5, 1927.

233 *"Why don't you tell us"* "Godspeed," *New Yorker*, June 18, 1927.

234 *"He isn't really going!"* Grace Levine and Carisi quotes from Montague, 85–86.

234 *"If you'll take me along"* Chamberlin, 42.

236 *"appeared to have sprung out of the sea"* Ibid., 78.

236 *"The noise of your propeller"* *TD*, 32.

236 *"pointed the Bellanca straight over"* Chamberlin, 79.

236 *"Charlie's is a greater feat"* Ibid., 80.

237 *"Never in my life"* Ibid., 91.

238 *"Lindbergh was lucky"* "Chamberlin & Levine," *Time*, June 20, 1927. Recordings of Chamberlin and Levine being interviewed in Germany are available at the Vincent Voice Library (call nos. DB1717 and DB1718).

239 *"The fact of the matter was"* Chamberlin, 160.

239 *"The anti-Semites in Germany"* *Der Tog*, June 7, 1927.

239 *"'Levine and His Flying Machine'"* Slobin, 199–202. Cantor worked Levine into his Ziegfeld Follies act. Challenged on stage to name all the famous aviators of 1927 besides Lindbergh, Cantor would respond:

"Well—Chamberlin, Levine, Ruth Elder, Levine, Commander Byrd, Levine." "Who else?" "Did I mention Levine?" (Cantor, 189). Several of the songs Levine inspired were borrowed from "Ha'Tikvah" ("The Hope"), a popular standard that today is Israel's official national anthem. Within days of the *Columbia*'s arrival in Germany, Joseph Feldman and his orchestra were performing "Levine": "Rejoice Jews, rejoice all / Because we have a right to brag / The news has just come in from Berlin / A Jewish son has just arrived."

240   *"Are the pennies worth"*   *Der Tog*, June 8, 1927.

240   *"spurned the holiness of the Sabbath"*   Ibid., June 9, 1927.

240   *"I am here as an American"*   *NYT*, Oct. 18, 1927.

240   *"Lindbergh is a fine fellow"*   *NYT*, June 7, 1927. In the aftermath of the *Columbia*'s flight, reporter L. B. Linder took to New York's streets to gather the reactions of ordinary Jews. "On Second Avenue near a theater, several Jewish girls and boys stand looking at a poster of Lindbergh displayed in the window of an ice cream parlor. The girls can't take their eyes off Lindbergh. One of the young girls opines that 'Lindy's' trip is more important than Levine's. Firstly, he was the first to fly across the ocean, and secondly he flew alone. 'That's a hero for you. Young Lindy, boy!' Resentful of the girl's fascination of Lindy, one of the young boys tries to prove that Levine is more of a hero than Lindy . . . given the fact that Levine didn't fly alone, if there had been a mishap, then two men would have been lost instead of one. Another girl breaks in, insisting that it's not such a big thing when two fly together, since one can sleep while the other flies. 'That's right!' pipes up the first girl, with half-closed eyes, and adds in English: 'I would love to sit by Lindbergh's right side and help him stay awake.'" *Der Tog*, June 9, 1927.

241   *"I had determined not to wait"*   Byrd, *Skyward*, 244.

241   *"If you don't get going"*   Glines, 45. "It could be said that the Orteig Prize simply confused matters for Byrd. Had others left untouched the problem of flying from New York to Paris, he would have solved it in his own time—for he thoroughly intended to solve it. By sharpening public interest, the Orteig Prize created problems for Byrd. Having become an expert publicist himself, he knew how vital it was to have a 'first flight' or some such heroic tag for any exploratory effort." Hoyt, 133.

242   *"Above the ocean at night"*   Byrd, *Skyward*, 258.

244   *"Do you think we failed?"*   Hawkins, 142. There are wildly conflicting stories as to what transpired aboard the *America* during its flight, especially in regard to who piloted the plane and when. For a distillation of the various accounts see Rose, 158–161.

244   *"Fifteen years ago only dreamers"*   *NYT*, July 5, 1927. From a technological standpoint, the most critical feature of the three successful American crossings was their fuel-efficient and utterly dependable power plant. (By comparison, the earth inductor compass each plane carried malfunctioned at some point.)

While the Wright Whirlwind pulled Lindbergh, Chamberlin, and Byrd to glory, its inventor, Charles L. Lawrance, was unknown to the general public. "Everybody remembers Paul Revere," Lawrance said philosophically, "but nobody knows the name of his horse" (Ware, "Deus Ex Machina"). The aviation industry appreciated Lawrance's achievement, however, awarding him its highest honor, the Collier Trophy, in 1927.

244   *"Your courage gave me courage"*   WP, June 7, 1927. A controversy arose when Byrd and Noville, both career naval officers, were awarded the Distinguished Flying Cross, and Acosta and Balchen were not. The explanation that the medal was restricted to U.S. military personnel failed to satisfy critics.

245   *"This seems to be"*   NYT, July 19, 1927.

245   *"This third American success"*   Bouché, "Le Voyage Dramatique de l'*America*."

19. The Atlantic No Longer Exists

A comprehensive tabulation of flights attempted across the North Atlantic during the interwar (1919–1939) period can be found in McDonough, 116–124.

246   *"We will go"*   Proofread galleys of "Lindbergh et l'Océan" [1934], Bibesco papers, box 282, folder 11.

247   *"Americans succeeded"*   Le Figaro, June 3, 1927.

248   *"For six months"*   NYT, June 9, 1927.

248   *"We must declare"*   Quoted in Montague, 141. French journalist Jacques Mortane reminded his countrymen that it was not unusual for citizens of any nation to patronize products of foreign design. "No doubt those who want so much to see the first attempt made in a French plane are not proposing to be passengers themselves," he quipped. LPJ, July 10, 1927.

249   *"He had the kind of face"*   NYT, October 18, 1927.

249   *"Then the fun began"*   Ibid.

249   *"stood there helpless"*   Quoted in Roseberry, *The Challenging Skies*, 129.

249   *"I am not going to chase"*   NYT, August 30, 1927.

249   *"It was not Levine's money"*   Ibid., August 31, 1927.

250   *"send a battleship to Europe"*   Ibid., September 21, 1927.

250   *"You came back too late!"*   New York World, October 18, 1927.

251   *"to hop off blindly"*   Allen, *Only Yesterday*, 184–185. For a comprehensive account of 1927's "death flights" see Hamlen, 227–359.

251   *"During this experimental period"*   "Comments on Death Flights," Literary Digest, September 24, 1927.

253   *"French aviation had been"*   LM, October 20, 1927.

254   *"all the personal qualities"*   NYT, April 8, 1928.

254   crossing of the Bremen   French reaction to the flight was captured in the tepid response of François Coli's mother. "The success of the Germans proved that my son was right when he declared that the feat was possible. In 1921 he had already traced out the route they followed. If honor goes

to the Germans for the first westward crossing of the Atlantic on that route, the honor for the first attempt must go to my son and to Captain Nungesser" (*NYT*, April 15, 1928). America's response was much warmer. The *Bremen*'s crew—which consisted of Baron Guenther von Huenefeld, Captain Hermann Koehl, and Major James Fitzmaurice, an Irishman— was greeted by huge crowds in New York. President Coolidge presented them with the Distinguished Flying Cross, the first time non-Americans had received the award.

254   *"I would so much have liked"*   *Le Peuple*, August 10, 1928.

255   *"ill-prepared and badly worked"*   *NYT*, Sept. 22, 1928.

257   *"Would you be willing"*   Reveilhac, 192–193.

257   *"An airman at the bottom"*   *NYT*, August 31, 1927.

258   *"I'm attempting Paris-to-New York"*   Reveilhac, 247.

259   *"We'll start"*   De la Croix, 178.

260   *"the song of the motor"*   *NYT*, September 4, 1930.

260   *"He said he never"*   Vescey and Dade, 224.

261   *"There is something about"*   *NYT*, October 17, 1930.

261   *"I think we are about the last"*   Ibid., November 2, 1930.

262   *"entered into History"*   *Le Figaro*, September 24, 1930.

262   *"big mid-ocean landing fields"*   Beamish, 47.

263   *"These liners will probably be"*   Stearns, "Babies Born Today May See—."

263   *"Scientists and designers"*   Beamish, 212.

263   *"Prior to Lindbergh's flight"*   "Progress Since Lindbergh's Flight," *Aero Digest*, May 1928.

Epilogue. Restless Spirits

264   *"New York to Paris"*   TSOSL, 14.

264   *A few days later, Pan American*   Sikorsky Manufacturing Company became a part of United Aircraft and Transport (later United Technologies Corporation) in 1929 and moved to Stratford, Connecticut. During the 1930s Igor Sikorsky designed Pan American's famous "flying clippers," the first airliners to cross the Pacific and Atlantic oceans. Despite his success with fixed-wing and amphibian aircraft, Sikorsky's greatest contribution to aviation was in the field of rotorcraft. He created the first mass-produced helicopter in 1942; today his company continues to be one of the world's leading helicopter manufacturers. Sikorsky was eighty-three when he died in his sleep at his Connecticut home on October 26, 1972.

264   *"You may, indeed, look back"*   TD, 27–28. The combination of Prohibition and the Depression was a double blow to the Brevoort's fortunes. "Mr. Orteig's lease had called for $25,150 a year up to 1928 and $43,500 thereafter. He surrendered it to the landlord in 1932" (*New York Sun*, October 16, 1935). Orteig's sons continued to operate the Lafayette through its final dinner on March 31, 1949. Both hotels eventually were replaced by apartment buildings.

267   *"Because he didn't fly over the North Pole"*   Glines, 246–247. Of the two
      other members of the *America*'s crew, the phlegmatic George Noville
      accompanied Byrd on several subsequent expeditions, while Bert Acosta
      continued to bounce erratically between bar stool and hangar. Acosta,
      whose colorful exploits included briefly flying for the Yankee Squadron
      in the Spanish Civil War, died of tuberculosis in a Denver asylum on
      September 1, 1954. He was fifty-nine. Noville retired as a lieutenant
      commander and started an aeronautical engineering consulting firm in
      California. He died on January 3, 1963, at age seventy-two.

267   *"the biggest and most successful fraud"*   Montague, 283. The debate over
      Byrd's North Pole claims continues to this day. For contrasting views
      of the controversy and insights into the relationship between Balchen
      and Byrd, see Glines, 252–267, and Rose, 113–143. Byrd's "lost diary" is
      examined in detail in *To the Pole: The Diary and Notebook of Richard E. Byrd,
      1925–1927*, edited by Raimund E. Goerler, the archivist who found it in
      the Byrd papers at Ohio State University.

268   *"taken it on the chin"*   *NYT*, September 13, 1934.

268   *"knew that he was a famous flyer"*   Levine FBI file no. 93-7651.

269   *"But now he's talking politics"*   *NYT*, November 15, 1941.

270   *"I'd like to tell you more"*   Vescey and Dade, 129.

270   *"He could not be completely open"*   Reeve Lindbergh, *Forward from Here*,
      218.

270   *"Io Victis"*   Prince, "Io Victis: Nungesser-Coli."

272   *"What lends credence"*   Hansen, "The Unfinished Flight of the *White
      Bird*."

272   *"The frail plane"*   *WP*, August 13, 1972.

273   *"figure of Lindbergh remains for us"*   *L'Intransigeant*, quoted in *NYT*, June
      7, 1927.

273   *"I am convinced"*   *NYT*, April 15, 1928. See Wohl, *A Passion for Wings*,
      229–240, for a discussion of Guynemer's "ascension" in French mythology.

Bibliography

The following list includes books, articles, reports, pamphlets, and other materials that provided the author with specific references or general background for *The Big Jump*. It includes sources cited in the notes.

Abbot, Patrick. *Airship: The Story of R.34 and the First East-West Crossing of the Atlantic by Air*. New York: Charles Scribner's Sons, 1973.

Abels, Jules. *In the Time of Silent Cal*. New York: G. P. Putnam's Sons, 1969.

Aircraft Yearbook. New York: Aeronautical Chamber of Commerce of America, 1925–1928.

Alcock, Sir John, and Sir Arthur Whitten Brown. *Our Transatlantic Flight*. London: William Kimber, 1969.

Allen, Frederick Lewis. *Only Yesterday: An Informal History of the 1920s*. New York: Harper & Brothers, 1931.

Allen, Peter. *The 91 before Lindbergh*. Shrewsbury, U.K.: Airlife, 1984.

Appel, Joseph H. *The Business Biography of John Wanamaker*. New York: Macmillan, 1930.

Balchen, Bernt. *Come North with Me*. New York: E. P. Dutton, 1958.

Baldwin, Neil. *Henry Ford and the Jews: The Mass Production of Hate*. New York: Public Affairs, 2001.

Beamish, Richard J. *The Story of Lindbergh, the Lone Eagle*. New York: International Press, 1927.

Beauregard, Nettie H. *Lindbergh's Decorations and Trophies*. St. Louis: Missouri Historical Society, 1935.

Bellonte, Maurice. *Le Premier Paris–New York*. Paris: Plon, 1976.

Berg, A. Scott. *Lindbergh*. New York: G. P. Putnam's Sons, 1998.

Berger, Meyer. *The Story of the* New York Times, *1851–1951.* New York: Simon & Schuster, 1951.

Berget, Alphonse. *L'Air.* Paris: Larousse, 1927.

Boorstin, Daniel J. *The Image: A Guide to Pseudo Events in America.* New York: Atheneum, 1987.

Bordeaux, Henry. *Georges Guynemer: Knight of the Air.* 1918. Reprint, New York: Arno Press, 1972.

Bowen, Ezra. *Knights of the Air.* Alexandria, Va.: Time-Life Books, 1980.

Boyne, Walter J. *The Smithsonian Book of Flight.* Washington, D.C.: Smithsonian Books, 1987.

Brinnin, John Malcolm. *The Sway of the Grand Salon: A Social History of the North Atlantic.* New York: Delacorte Press, 1971.

Broer, Lawrence, and John D. Walther, eds. *Dancing Fools and Weary Blues: The Great Escape of the Twenties.* Bowling Green, Ohio: Bowling Green University Press, 1990.

Brown, Sir Arthur Whitten. *Flying the Atlantic in Sixteen Hours.* New York: Frederick A. Stokes, 1920.

Burns, Ric, and James Sanders. *New York: An Illustrated History.* New York: Alfred A. Knopf, 2005.

Byrd, Richard E. *Skyward.* New York: G. P. Putnam's Sons, 1928.

Cain, Anthony Christopher. *The Forgotten Air Force: French Air Doctrine in the 1930s.* Washington, D.C.: Smithsonian Institution Press, 2002.

Caloyanni, Emmanuel. *René Couzinet: Avionneur de Lindbergh à Mermoz.* Paris: Geste, 2001.

Cantor, Eddie, with David Freedman. *My Life Is in Your Hands.* New York: Blue Ribbon, 1932.

Carpenter, Humphrey. *Geniuses Together: American Writers in Paris in the 1920s.* Boston: Houghton Mifflin, 1988.

Carpentier, Georges. *Mon Match avec La Vie.* Paris: Flammarion, 1954.

Cassagneres, Ev. *The Spirit of Ryan.* Blue Ridge Summit, Pa.: TAB Books, 1982.
———. *The Untold Story of the* Spirit of St. Louis. New Brighton, Minn.: Flying Books International, 2002.

Chadeau, Emmanuel. *De Bleriot à Dassault: L'Industrie Aéronautique en France, 1900–1950.* Paris: Fayard, 1987.

Chamberlin, Clarence D. *Record Flights.* New York: Dorrance, 1928.

Christienne, Charles, and Pierre Lissarrague. *A History of French Military Aviation.* Translated by Frances Kianka. Washington, D.C.: Smithsonian Institution Press, 1986.

Corrigan, Douglas. *That's My Story.* New York: E. P. Dutton, 1938.

Cortet, Pierre. *Potez 25.* Outreau, France: Lela Presse, 1998.

Crouch, Tom D., ed. *Charles A. Lindbergh: An American Life.* Washington, D.C.: National Air and Space Museum, 1977.

Dark, Sidney. *Paris.* New York: Macmillan, 1941.

Davis, Kenneth S. *The Hero: Charles A. Lindbergh and the American Dream.* Garden City, N.Y.: Doubleday, 1959.

De la Croix, Robert. *They Flew the Atlantic.* Translated by Robert Fitzgerald. London: Frederick Muller, 1958.

Delear, Frank J. *Igor Sikorsky.* New York: Dodd, Mead, 1969.

Denis, Albin. *L'Historique de l'Escadron de Chasse 1/3 "Navarre" de 1915 à 1999.* Paris: Maillard, 2000.

Dierikx, M. L. J., and Marc Dierikx. *Fokker: A Transatlantic Biography.* Washington, D.C.: Smithsonian Institution Press, 1997.

Douglas, Ann. *Terrible Honesty: Mongrel Manhattan in the 1920s.* New York: Farrar, Straus & Giroux, 1995.

Driggs, Laurence La Tourette. *Heroes of Aviation.* Boston: Little, Brown, 1927.

Dwiggins, Don. *The Barnstormers.* New York: Grosset & Dunlap, 1968.

Faure-Favier, Louise. *Guide de L'Aéroport du Bourget.* Paris: Pierre Lecerf, 1926.

Felix, David. *Protest: Sacco-Vanzetti and the Intellectuals.* Bloomington: Indiana University Press, 1965.

Fielding, Raymond. *The American Newsreel, 1911–1967.* Norman: University of Oklahoma Press, 1972.

Fife, George Buchanan. *Lindbergh: The Lone Eagle.* Cleveland: World Syndicate, 1927.

Flanner, Janet. *Paris Was Yesterday, 1925–1939.* Edited by Irving Drutman. New York: Popular Library, 1968.

Fokker, Anthony H. G., and Bruce Gould. *Flying Dutchman.* New York: Henry Holt, 1931.

Fonck, René. *Ace of Aces.* Edited by Stanley M. Ulanoff. 1920. Reprint, Garden City, N.Y.: Doubleday, 1967.

Franks, Norman L. R., and Frank W. Bailey. *Over the Front: A Complete Record of the Fighter Aces and Units of the United States and French Air Services, 1914–1918.* London: Grub Street, 1992.

———. *The Storks: The Story of France's Elite Fighter* Groupe de Combat 12 (Les Cigognes) *in World War I.* London: Grub Street, 1998.

Funderbunk, Thomas. *The Fighters: The Men and Machines of the First World War.* New York: Grosset & Dunlap, 1965.

Garreau, Charles. *Nungesser et Coli: Premiers Vainqueurs de l'Atlantique.* Paris: Aéropole, 1990.

Gilbert, Felix, and David Clay Large. *The End of the European Era: 1890 to the Present.* 5th ed. New York: W. W. Norton, 2002.

Gill, Brendan. *Lindbergh Alone.* New York: Harcourt Brace Jovanovich, 1977.

Glines, Carrol V. *Bernt Balchen: Polar Aviator.* Washington, D.C.: Smithsonian Institution Press, 2000.

Goerler, Raimund E., ed. *To the Pole: The Diary and Notebook of Richard E. Byrd, 1925–1927.* Columbus: Ohio State University Press, 1998.

Goldstein, Laurence. *The Flying Machine and Modern Literature.* Bloomington: Indiana University Press, 1986.

Guggenheim, Harry F. *The Seven Skies.* New York: G. P. Putnam's Sons, 1928.

Gunston, Bill. *World Encyclopedia of Aero Engines.* 5th ed. Stroud, U.K.: Sutton, 2006.

———. *World Encyclopedia of Aircraft Manufacturers.* 2nd ed. Stroud, U.K.: Sutton, 2005.

Guttman, Jon. *Spad VII Aces of World War I.* Oxford, U.K.: Osprey, 2001.

———. *SPA124 Lafayette Escadrille: American Volunteer Airmen in World War I.* Oxford, U.K.: Osprey, 2004.

Haines, Lynn and Dora B. *The Lindberghs.* New York: Vanguard, 1931.

Hall, Nova. *Spirit and Creator: The Mysterious Man behind Lindbergh's Flight to Paris.* Sheffield, Mass.: Safe Goods, 2003.

Hartney, Harold E. *Up and At 'Em.* Edited by Stanley M. Ulanoff. 1940. Reprint, Garden City, N.Y.: Doubleday, 1971.

Hawker, H. G., and K. Mackenzie Grieve. *Our Atlantic Attempt.* London: Methuen, 1919.

Hawker, Muriel. *H. G. Hawker, Airman: His Life and Work.* London: Hutchinson, 1922.

Hawkins, Eric, and Robert N. Sturdevant. *Hawkins of the Paris Herald.* New York: Simon & Schuster, 1963.

Hemingway, Ernest. *A Moveable Feast.* 1964. Reprint, London: Vintage, 2000.

Hertog, Susan. *Anne Morrow Lindbergh: Her Life.* New York: Doubleday, 1999.

Hirschauer, L., and C. Dollfus, eds. *L'Année Aéronautique.* Paris: Dunod, 1925–1928.

Hoare, Robert J. *Wings Over the Atlantic.* Boston: Charles T. Branford, 1957.

Hoffman, Paul. *Wings of Madness: Alberto Santos-Dumont and the Invention of Flight.* New York: Hyperion, 2003.

Horne, Alistair. *Seven Ages of Paris.* New York: Alfred A. Knopf, 2002.

Hoyt, E. P. *The Last Explorer: The Adventures of Admiral Byrd.* New York: John Day, 1968.

Hudson, Kenneth, and Julian Pettifer. *Diamonds in the Sky: A Social History of Air Travel.* London: Bodley Head/BBC, 1979.

Hughes, Judith M. *To the Maginot Line: The Politics of French Military Preparation in the 1920s.* Cambridge, Mass.: Harvard University Press, 1971.

Huttig, Jack. *1927: Summer of Eagles.* Chicago: Nelson-Hall, 1980.

Jablonski, Edward. *Atlantic Fever.* New York: Macmillan, 1972.

Jackson, Kenneth T., ed. *The Encyclopedia of New York City.* New Haven, Conn.: Yale University Press, 1995.

James, Rian. *Dining in New York.* New York: John Day, 1930.

Jones, Colin. *Paris: The Biography of a City.* New York: Viking, 2005.

Jullian, Marcel. *Le Chevalier du Ciel: Charles Nungesser.* Paris: Amiot-Dumont, 1953.

Kaplan, Justin. *Mr. Clemens and Mark Twain.* New York: Simon & Schuster, 1966.

Kerr, John. *Land, Sea and Air: Reminiscences of Mark Kerr.* New York: Longmans, Green, 1927.

Keyhoe, Donald E. *Flying with Lindbergh.* New York: G. P. Putnam's Sons, 1928.

Kyvig, David E. *Daily Life in the United States, 1920–1940.* Chicago: Ivan R. Dee, 2004.

Lalanne, Alain J-B. *Du Béarn à New York: Raymond Orteig (1870–1939), Histoire d'un mécène de l'aviation.* Pau, France: Marrimpouey, 2004.

Lardner, John. "The Lindbergh Legends." In *The Aspirin Age:1919–1941.* Edited by Isabel Leighton. New York: Simon & Schuster, 1949.

Larson, Bruce L. *Lindbergh of Minnesota: A Political Biography.* New York: Harcourt Brace Jovanovich, 1973.

Leinwand, Gerald. *1927: The High Tide of the Twenties.* New York: Four Walls Eight Windows, 2001.

Lerner, Michael A. *Dry Manhattan: Prohibition in New York City.* Cambridge, Mass.: Harvard University Press, 2007.

Les Grands Dossiers de L'Illustration. *L'Épopée de l'Aviation: Histoire d'un Siècle 1843–1944.* Paris: Le Livre de Paris, 1987.

Lewis, W. David. *Eddie Rickenbacker: An American Hero in the Twentieth Century.* Baltimore: Johns Hopkins University Press, 2005.

Lindbergh, Anne Morrow. *Bring Me a Unicorn: Diaries and Letters, 1922–1928.* New York: Harcourt Brace Jovanovich, 1971.

Lindbergh, Charles A. *Autobiography of Values.* New York: Harcourt Brace Jovanovich, 1992.

———. *Boyhood on the Upper Mississippi.* St. Paul: Minnesota Historical Society, 1972.

———. *Of Flight and Life.* New York: Charles Scribner's Sons, 1948.

———. *The Spirit of St. Louis.* 1953. Reprint, St. Paul: Minnesota Historical Society Press, 1993.

———. *"We."* New York: G. P. Putnam's Sons, 1927.

Lindbergh, Reeve. *Under a Wing: A Memoir.* New York: Simon & Schuster, 1998.

———. *Forward from Here.* New York: Simon & Schuster, 2008.

Lodge, John C., with M. M. Quaife. *I Remember Detroit.* Detroit: Wayne State University Press, 1949.

Longstreet, Stephen. *The Canvas Falcons.* New York: World, 1970.

Lotti, Armand. *L'Oiseau Canari: Première française sur l'Atlantique Nord.* Paris: Calmann-Lévy, 1968.

Lovell, Mary S. *The Sound of Wings: The Life of Amelia Earhart.* New York: St. Martin's Press, 1989.

Macmillan, Margaret. *Paris 1919: Six Months That Changed the World.* New York: Random House, 2002.

Mason, Herbert Molloy Jr. *High Flew the Falcons: The French Aces of World War I.* Philadelphia: J. B. Lippincott, 1965.

Maxtone-Graham, John. *The Only Way to Cross.* New York: Macmillan, 1972.

McDonough, Kenneth. *Atlantic Wings: The Conquest of the North Atlantic 1919–1939.* Hertfordshire, U.K.: Model Aeronautical Press, 1966.

McFarland, Gerald W. *Inside Greenwich Village: A New York City Neighborhood, 1898–1918.* Amherst: University of Massachusetts Press, 2001.

Mee, Charles L. Jr. *The End of Order: Versailles 1919.* New York: E. P. Dutton, 1980.

Micelli, Corrine, and Bernard Palmieri. *René Fonck: L'As des As, l'Homme.* Paris: Économica, 2007.

Miller, John J., and Mark Molesky. *Our Oldest Enemy: A History of America's Disastrous Relationship with France*. New York: Doubleday, 2004.

Miller, Nathan. *New World Coming: The 1920s and the Making of Modern America*. New York: Scribner, 2003.

Montague, Richard. *Oceans, Poles and Airmen*. New York: Random House, 1971.

Mortane, Jacques. *La Chevauchée des Mers: Bleriot, Garros, Lindbergh*. Paris: Baudiniere, 1927.

———. *Nungesser: Les Grandes Heures de Sa Vie*. Paris: Bernardin-Bechet, 1927.

Mosely, Leonard. *Lindbergh: A Biography*. Garden City, N.Y.: Doubleday, 1976.

Mott, T. Bentley. *Myron T. Herrick, Friend of France*. Garden City, N.Y.: Doubleday, 1929.

Nevin, David. *The Pathfinders*. Alexandria, Va.: Time-Life Books, 1980.

Nielson, Dale, ed. *Saga of the Air Mail Pioneers*. Washington, D.C.: Air Mail Pioneers, 1962.

O'Callaghan, Timothy J. *The Aviation Legacy of Henry & Edsel Ford*. Ann Arbor, Mich.: Proctor, 2000.

O'Neil, Paul. *Barnstormers and Speed Kings*. Alexandria, Va.: Time-Life Books, 1980.

Parmentier, Florian. *Le Roman de Nungesser*. Paris: Paul Dupont, 1946.

Patterson, Jerry E. *Fifth Avenue: The Best Address*. New York: Rizzoli, 1998.

Paxton, Robert O. *Vichy France: Old Guard and New Order 1940–1944*. New York: Columbia University Press, 1982.

Peden, Charles. *Newsreel Man*. Garden City, N.Y.: Doubleday, 1932.

Perrin, Claude. *Rene Fonck, 1894–1953: As Des As et Visionnaire*. Paris: Officine, 2002.

Pitois, Étienne Pitois. "Notre Propagande Aéronautique Est-elle Suffisante?" in *Annuaire de l'Aéronautique 1926*. Paris: Roufeé, 1926.

Ponce de Leon, Charles L. "The Man Nobody Knows: Charles A. Lindbergh and the Culture of Celebrity," in Dominick A. Pisano, ed., *The Airplane in American Culture*. Ann Arbor: University of Michigan Press, 2003.

Prudhomme, Arnaud. *Pierre Levasseur et Ses Avions*. Paris: TMA, 2002.

Putnam, George Palmer. *Wide Margins: A Publisher's Autobiography*. New York: Harcourt, Brace, 1942.

Report of the Daniel Guggenheim Fund for the Promotion of Aeronautics 1926 and 1927. New York: Daniel Guggenheim Fund, 1928.

Reveilhac, Jean. *Dieudonné Costés: La vie glorieuse et troublée du géant de l'air*. Paris: France-Empire, 1983.

Reynolds, Bruce. *Paris with the Lid Lifted*. New York: George Sully, 1927.

Reynolds, Michael. *Hemingway: The Paris Years*. New York: W. W. Norton, 1999.

Reynolds, Quentin. *They Fought for the Sky*. New York: Holt, Rinehart & Winston, 1957.

Roberts, Randy, and David Welky, eds. *Charles A. Lindbergh: The Power and Peril of Celebrity 1927–1941*. Maplecrest, N.Y.: Brandywine Press, 2003.

Robie, Bill. *For the Greatest Achievement: A History of the Aero Club of America and the National Aeronautic Association*. Washington, D.C.: Smithsonian Institution Press, 1993.

Roger, Philippe. *The American Enemy: The History of French Anti-Americanism.* Chicago: University of Chicago Press, 2005.

Root, Waverly. *The Paris Edition: The Autobiography of Waverly Root, 1927–1934.* Edited by Samuel Abt. San Francisco: North Point Press, 1987.

Rose, Lisle A. *Explorer: The Life of Richard E. Byrd.* Columbia: University of Missouri Press, 2008.

Roseberry, C. R. *The Challenging Skies: The Colorful Story of Aviation's Most Exciting Years, 1919–1939.* Garden City, N.Y.: Doubleday, 1966.

———. *Glenn Curtis: Pioneer of Flight.* Garden City, N.Y.: Doubleday, 1972.

Rosenberg, Barry, and Catherine Macaulay. *Mavericks of the Sky: The First Daring Pilots of the U. S. Air Mail.* New York: William Morrow, 2006.

Ross, Walter S. *The Last Hero: Charles A. Lindbergh.* New York: Harper & Row, 1964.

Rostand, Edmond. *Le Cantique de l'Aile.* Paris: Charpentier, 1922.

Rowe, Percy. *The Great Atlantic Air Race.* London: Angus & Robertson, 1977.

Saint-Exupéry, Antoine de. *Le Petit Prince.* 1943. Reprint, Paris: Poche, 1994.

Scheppler, Robert H. *Pacific Air Race.* Washington, D.C.: Smithsonian Institution Press, 1988.

Shirer, William L. *20th Century Journey: A Memoir of a Life and the Times.* Vol. 1, *The Start: 1904–1930.* New York: Simon & Schuster, 1976.

Sloan, John. *New York Etchings, 1905–1949.* New York: Dover, 1978.

Slobin, Mark. *Tenement Songs: The Popular Music of the Jewish Immigrants.* Urbana: University of Illinois Press, 1982.

Smith, Elinor. *Aviatrix.* New York: Harcourt Brace Jovanovich, 1981.

Smith, Herschel. *A History of Aircraft Piston Engines.* Manhattan, Kan.: Sunflower University Press, 1993.

Smith, Richard K. *First Across!: The U.S. Navy's Transatlantic Flight of 1919.* Annapolis, Md.: Naval Institute Press, 1986.

Solberg, Carl. *Conquest of the Skies: A History of Commercial Aviation in America.* Boston: Little, Brown, 1979.

Spenser, Jay P. *Bellanca C. F.: The Emergence of the Cabin Monoplane in the United States.* Washington, D.C.: Smithsonian Institution Press, 1982.

Steirman, Hy, and Glenn D. Kittler. *Triumph: The Incredible Saga of the First Transatlantic Flight.* New York: Harper & Brothers, 1961.

Stoff, Joshua. *Charles A. Lindbergh: A Photographic Album.* New York: Dover, 1995.

Stoff, Joshua, and William Camp. *Roosevelt Field: World's Premier Airport.* Terre Haute, Ind.: SunShine House, 1992.

Stokes, Horace Winston. *Mirrors of the Year: A National Revue of the Outstanding Figures, Trends and Events of 1927–28.* New York: Frederick A. Stokes, 1928.

Stout, William B. *So Away I Went.* New York: Bobbs Merrill, 1951.

Sufrin, Mark, and Richard Smith. *The Brave Men.* New York: Platt & Munk, 1967.

Sullivan, Mark. *Our Times: The United States 1900–1925.* Vol. VI, *The Twenties.* New York: Charles Scribner's Sons, 1935.

Tardieu, André. *France and America.* New York: Houghton Mifflin, 1927.

Taylor, Michael J. H., ed. *Jane's Encyclopedia of Aviation*. New York: Portland House, 1989.

Testimonial Dinner Given to Mr. Raymond Orteig by His Friends. New York: Privately published, 1928.

Thomas, Lowell. *European Skyways: The Story of a Tour of Europe by Airplane*. Boston: Houghton Mifflin, 1927.

———. *The First World Flight*. Boston: Houghton Mifflin, 1925.

Thomas, Lowell, and Lowell Thomas Jr. *Famous First Flights That Changed History*. 1968. Reprint, Guilford, Conn.: Lyons Press, 2004.

Thompson, J. Lee. *Politicians, the Press, and Propaganda: Lord Northcliffe and the Great War, 1914–1919*. Kent, Ohio: Kent State University Press, 2000.

Toland, John. *Ships in the Sky: The Story of the Great Dirigibles*. New York: Henry Holt, 1957.

Vale, Charles, ed. *The Spirit of St. Louis: One Hundred Poems*. New York: George H. Doran, 1927.

Van Every, Dale, and Morris De Haven Tracy. *Charles Lindbergh: His Life*. New York: D. Appleton, 1927.

Vescey, George, and George C. Dade. *Getting off the Ground: The Pioneers of Aviation Speak for Themselves*. New York: E. P. Dutton, 1979.

Vigilant [Claud W. Sykes]. *French Warbirds*. London: J. Hamilton, 1937.

Villard, H. S. *Contact: The Story of the Early Birds*. New York: Thomas Y. Crowell, 1968.

Wagner, William. *Ryan, the Aviator: Being the Adventures and Ventures of Pioneer Airman and Businessman, T. Claude Ryan*. New York: McGraw-Hill, 1971.

Walker, Stanley. *The Night Club Era*. New York: Frederick A. Stokes, 1933.

Wallace, Graham. *The Flight of Alcock and Brown 14–15 June 1919*. London: Putnam, 1955.

Waller, Douglas C. *A Question of Loyalty: Billy Mitchell and the Court-Martial That Gripped a Nation*. New York: Harper Collins, 2004.

Walsh, George. *Gentleman Jimmy Walker: Mayor of the Jazz Age*. New York: Praeger, 1974.

Watkins, Paul. *In the Blue Light of African Dreams*. New York: Avon, 1992.

Weber, Ronald. *News of Paris: American Journalists in the City of Light between the Wars*. Chicago: Ivan R. Dee, 2006.

Wecter, Dixon. *The Hero in America: A Chronicle of Hero-Worship*. New York: Charles Scribner's Sons, 1941.

Weiss, Pierre. *La Bataille de l'Atlantique*. Paris: Eugène Figuière, 1928.

West, James E. *The Lone Scout of the Sky*. Philadelphia: Boy Scouts of America, 1928.

Wetzsteon, Ross. *Republic of Dreams: Greenwich Village—the American Bohemia, 1910–1960*. New York: Simon & Schuster, 2002.

Wilbur, Ted. *The First Flight across the Atlantic*. Washington, D.C.: Smithsonian Institution, 1969.

Wilkinson, Paul H. *Aircraft Engines of the World*. New York: Paul H. Wilkinson, 1941.

Wilson, Edmund. *The American Earthquake: A Documentary of the Twenties and Thirties*. New York: Farrar, Straus & Giroux, 1958.

Wiser, William. *The Crazy Years: Paris in the Twenties*. New York: Atheneum, 1983.

Wohl, Robert. *A Passion for Wings: Aviation and the Western Imagination, 1908–1918*. New Haven, Conn.: Yale University Press, 1994.

———. *The Spectacle of Flight: Aviation and the Western Imagination, 1920–1950*. New Haven, Conn.: Yale University Press, 2005.

Wykes, Alan. *Air Atlantic*. New York: David White, 1969.

Zulker, William Allen. *John Wanamaker, King of Merchants*. Wayne, Pa.: Eaglecrest Press, 1993.

Periodicals and Web Articles

Ahrendt, Karl. "Paris 1926–1928." http://karlahrendt.com/paris_1926.htm

"The Air Horse." *Time*, February 13, 1928.

"America from the French View." *Literary Digest*, June 4, 1927.

"An American Epic." *Time*, September 14, 1953.

"Aviation's Future as Seen by Experts." *Literary Digest*, June 25, 1927.

"Believe It or Not." *Time*, March 26, 1928.

Bell, Monta. "Movies and Talkies." *North American Review*, October 1928.

Bennett, Floyd. "Our Flight over the North Pole." *Aero Digest*, September 1926.

Benoit-Levy, Georges. "Une Exposition et un Congres Urbains a New-York." *L'Illustration*, October 10, 1925.

Berliner, Don. "The Big Race of 1910." *Air & Space/Smithsonian*, January 2010.

Bouché, Henri. "L'Exploit de Costes et de Bellonte." *L'Illustration*, September 13, 1930.

———. "Les Grands Avions et la Traversée de l'Atlantique." *L'Illustration*, December 24, 1927.

———. "Où en Est l'Aviation?" *L'Illustration*, December 11, 1926.

———. "Vingt-quatre Records du Monde Deviennent Français." *L'Illustration*, November 28, 1925.

———. "Le Voyage Dramatique de l'*America*." *L'Illustration*, July 9, 1927.

Boyer, Jacques. "Les aviateurs aux hautes altitudes et les expériences physiologiques de l'Institut aérotechnique." *La Nature*, no. 2422 (September 4, 1920).

Boyne, Walter J. "The Rocket Men." *Air Force Magazine*, September 2004.

Brock, B. I. "When Hotels Mirrored New York's Life." *New York Times Magazine*, March 6, 1932.

Brown, Dave. "Young Man with a Plane." *St. Louis Globe-Democrat Sunday Magazine*, May 21, 1967.

Brown, K. V. "Flight That Tied the World Together." *Popular Mechanics*, May 1967.

Bruno, Harry A., and William S. Dutton. "Lindbergh, the Famous Unknown." *Saturday Evening Post*, October 21, 1933.

Byrd, Richard E. "The First Flight to the North Pole." *National Geographic*, September 1926.

———. "Our Transatlantic Flight." *National Geographic*, September 1927.

———. "Why We May Wait 20 Years for Ocean Air Lines." *Popular Science*, August 1927.

Caldwell, Cy. "Atlantic Fever." *Aero Digest*, May 1927.

Carson, Gerald. "Supreme City: New York in the 1920s." *American Heritage*, November 1988.

"Cartwheel." *Time*, October 4, 1926.

Cather, Willa. "Coming, Eden Bower!" *Smart Set*, August 1920.

"Chamberlin & Levine." *Time*, June 20, 1927.

"Chamberlin Visits London." *Flight*, July 14, 1927.

"Chance Writes the Lindbergh Saga." *Literary Digest*, June 18, 1927.

"Comments on Death Flights." *Literary Digest*, September 24, 1927.

Constantin, L. "Les accidents d'aviation au cours des grands raids et le moyen de les eviter." *La Nature*, no. 2764 (July 1, 1927).

Coppens, Willy. "La veridique histoire de arrive de Charles Lindbergh au Bourget." *Icare*, no. 81 (Summer 1977).

Courtois, Philippe. "Les Lignes Farman." *Icare*, no. 82 (Autumn 1977).

Currie, Barton W. "Galahad." *Ladies' Home Journal*, August 1927.

"The de Monge Type 7.5 Monoplane." *Aero Digest*, June 1926.

"Dictionnaire des Pilotes." *Icare*, no. 82 (Autumn 1977).

Dinwiddie, William. "Let's Drop In on England." *Century*, April 1919.

Dowd, George Lee Jr. "The First Plane to Germany." *Popular Science*, August 1927.

"Emigré." *New Yorker*, August 28, 1926.

Enslow, Randy. "Barnstorming with Lindy." *Popular Science*, October 1929.

Erskine, John. "The Example of Lindbergh." *Independent*, June 25, 1927.

———. "Flight: Some Thoughts on the Solitary Journey of a Certain Young Aviator." *Century*, September 1927.

"Fadeout." *Time*, June 27, 1927.

"First Nonstop Transatlantic Flight." www.crocnaraw.co.uk/alcock.html

Fisher, H. H. "France and America." *Independent*, July 16, 1927.

Fitzgerald, F. Scott. "Echoes of the Jazz Age." *Scribner's*, November 1931.

"Flagpole Rooster." *Time*, June 20, 1927.

Flammer, Philip M. "The Rediscovery of René Fonck." *Air University Review* 19, no. 3 (March–April 1968).

Flanner, Janet. "Perfume and Politics." *New Yorker*, May 3, 1930.

"Flight." *Time*, May 30, 1927.

"The Flying World." *Time*, July 18, 1927.

Fonck, René. "Le Danger Aerien Allemand." *Revue des Deux Mondes*, May 1924.

———. "My New York–Paris Flight." *Aero Digest*, June 1926.

Forrest, Leo C. Jr. "Those Willing to Dare." *Naval Aviation News*, March–April 1999.

"Four Men in a Fog." *Time*, July 11, 1927.

"Foxy Father." *Time*, July 21, 1930.

"France Extols Lindbergh's Education." *Literary Digest*, June 25, 1927.

Franck, A. J.-M. "Lindbergh et Ma Vie." *La Nouvelle Revue Française*, no. 176 (May 1928).

Francueil, Claude. "Un Heros Légendaire Charles Lindbergh." *Le Petit Journal Illustré*, June 5, 1927.

Fredette, Raymond H. "The Making of a Hero: What Really Happened Seventy-five Years Ago, After Lindbergh Landed at Le Bourget." *Air Power History*, June 2002.

Gale, Tom. "Mr. Hugh Curran Saw the *Spirit of St. Louis*." www.charleslindbergh .com/mystory/ireland.asp

"Godspeed." *New Yorker*, June 18, 1927.

"Gold and Glory." *Time*, September 12, 1927.

Goldsborough, Brice. "The Earth Inductor Compass." *Aero Digest*, June 1927.

———. "Navigating the Plane." *Annals of the American Academy of Political and Social Science* 131, no. 220 (May 1927).

"The Gossip Shop." *Bookman*, August 1927.

Green, Fitzhugh. "What Lindbergh Found in His Mail Bag." *Popular Science*, October 1927.

Hansen, Gunnar. "The Unfinished Flight of the *White Bird*." *Yankee*, June 1980.

"Harry Hawker, the Britisher Who Took Chances Like a Yank." *Literary Digest*, June 7, 1919.

Hartmann, Gérard. "Les avions de record français (1928–1932)." www .hydroretro.net/etudegh/avionsrecordfrancais192832.pdf

Hellman, Geoffrey T. "The Winged-S." *New Yorker*, August 10, 17, 1940.

Heppenheimer, T. A. "Flying Blind." *American Heritage/Invention & Technology*, Spring 1995.

Hinton, Walter. "The First Trans-Atlantic Flight." *Annals of the American Academy of Political and Social Science* 131, no. 220 (May 1927).

Hollingsworth, Henry. "The Average Man." *Literary Digest*, May 28, 1927.

"Honors for France." *Time*, September 15, 1930.

Horsfall, J. E. "Lindbergh's Start for Paris." *Aero Digest*, June 1927.

"How to Fly." *Time*, May 30, 1927.

"In Paris." *Time*, July 18, 1927.

Jean-Brunhes, Mariel. "L'Enigme des Avions Transatlantiques Disparus." *L'Illustration*, August 13, 1927.

Keyhoe, Donald A. "Dressing Up Aviation." *Aviation*, November 10, 1928.

———. "Lindbergh Tells the Future of Aviation." *Popular Mechanics*, November 1927.

———. "To Paris by Rocket." *This Week*, April 10, 1938.

Klinger, Jerry. "Charles Levine and the First American Jewish Pilot." Jewish Magazine, May 2008. www.jewishmag.com/123mag/jewish-aviators/ jewish-aviators.htm

Knight, Robin. "Lindbergh and the Spirit of Air Travel." *Time*, June 16, 1997.

Kowalke, Kim. "Music in the Air: Lindbergh's Flight Inspired a Myriad of Musical Tributes." www.americancomposersorchestra.org/lindberghmusic.htm

Labadié, Jean. "Fonck Inconnu." *La Science et la Vie*, no. 121 (July 1927).

Lanphier, Thomas G. "Lindbergh's Movie Contract." *Photoplay*, January 1939.

"Le Lieutenant Nungesser." *L'Illustration*, June 22, 1918.

Leighton, Bruce G. "The Limits of Aviation." *Atlantic Monthly*, April 1928.

Létourneau, Émile. "Fonck m'a dit." *Icare*, no. 122 (Autumn 1987).

Lindbergh, Anne Morrow. "Flying Around the North Atlantic." *National Geographic*, September 1934.

Lindbergh, Charles A. "Lindbergh's Own Story." *Current History*, July 1927.

"Lindbergh." *Aviation Quarterly* 3, no. 3 (1977).

"Lindbergh." *Time*, December 26, 1927

"Lindbergh as a Columbus." *Literary Digest*, June 18, 1927.

"Lindbergh, Pilot Extraordinary and Ambassador Plenipotentiary." *St. Nicholas*, July 1927.

"The Lindbergh Saga." *Time*, April 2, 1928.

"Lindbergh, the Symbol." *Outlook*, June 22, 1927.

"Lindbergh Welcomed in Europe." *Aero Digest*, June 1927.

"Lindbergh's Flight." *Time*, April 13, 1931.

"Lindbergh's Leap to Paris and Fame." *Literary Digest*, June 4, 1927.

"Lindy: The Advance Agent of the Air Age." *Literary Digest*, January 7, 1928.

Lissarrague, Pierre. "Il y a cinquante ans . . . l'Atlantique Sud aussi." *Pégase*, October 1977.

"London's Welcome to Lindbergh." *Flight*, June 2, 1927.

"Lunch in America—Breakfast in Europe." *Scientific American*, June 28, 1919.

MacCracken, William P. Jr. "Should Ocean Flying Be Curbed?" *Aero Digest*, October 1927.

Mahoney, B. F. "The Ryan Airlines." *Aero Digest*, August 1926.

Markey, Morris. "Young Man of Affairs." *New Yorker*, September 20, 27, 1930.

McCarthy, Leslie Gibson. "The Spirit of St. Louis." *St. Louis Magazine*, May 2007.

McDermott, Rick. "Lindbergh History April 1926–November 1926." www.charleslindbergh.com/mystory/thompson.asp.

McLaughlin, George F. "The All-Metal Sikorsky." *Aero Digest*, June 1926.

Meyer, Corky. "Lindbergh before Paris." *Flight Journal*, February 2004.

Mogus, Mary Ann. "James DeWitt Hill: Scottdale's Aviation Pioneer." *Westmoreland History*, Winter 2001.

Morrow, Lance. "Lindbergh: The Heroic Curiosity." *Time*, May 23, 1977.

Muheim, Harry Miles. "My Life with the Lone Eagle." *American Heritage*, May–June 1997.

Mullett, Mary B. "The Biggest Thing That Lindbergh Has Done." *American Magazine*, October 1927.

Mumford, Lewis. "The Skyline: A Temple of Beauty Gleams and Patrician Grayness Where Fifth Avenue Meets the Park." *New Yorker*, October 1, 1927.

Nelson, Stewart B. "Airports across the Ocean." *American Heritage/Invention & Technology*, Summer 2001.

Neon. "The Future of Aerial Transport." *Atlantic Monthly*, January 1928.

"The New Craze—Flying the Atlantic." *Flight*, June 23, 1927.

"The New Duration Record." *Flight*, May 5, 1927.

"New York to Berlin." *Time*, June 13, 1927.

"New York–Paris." *Flight*, May 26, 1927.

"New York–Paris Flight a Reality." *Aviation*, May 30, 1927.

"No Tears." *New Yorker*, April 2, 1949.

"Non-stop." *Time*, May 11, 1925.

"On to Paris." *Time*, October 25, 1926.

"Our Winged Ambassador of Good Will." *Herald of Gospel Liberty*, June 8, 1927.

Owen, Russell. "Bellanca at Last Conquers Adversity." *New York Times Magazine*, June 19, 1927.

———. "The Dragon Hunters." *New Yorker*, May 21, 1927.

———. "What's the Matter with Lindbergh?" *American Magazine*, April 1939.

Parfit, Michael. "Flying Where Lindy Flew." *Smithsonian*, October 1987.

"Paris Preliminaries." *Time*, April 25, 1927.

"The Paris–New York Flight." *Flight*, May 12, 1927.

"Passenger Airlines." *Time*, July 4, 1927.

"Passenger Levine." *Time*, October 24, 1927.

Post, Augustus. "Columbus of the Air." *North American Review*, September 1927.

Prince, Charles. "Io Victis: Nungesser-Coli." *Atlantic Monthly*, September 1927.

"Progress Since Lindbergh's Flight." *Aero Digest*, May 1928.

"A Quiet Ace." *New Yorker*, August 21, 1926.

Ramsey, Logan C., and Earle H. Kincaid. "Analysis of Weather Conditions on Recent Transatlantic Flights." *Aero Digest*, October 1927.

"The Realm of Summer Playdays," *Literary Digest*, June 4, 1927.

Régnier, Christian. "Paul Bert and the Birth of Aviation Medicine in France." *Medicographia* 30, no. 4 (2008).

"The Rocket Ship of the Future." *Literary Digest*, June 25, 1927.

Russell, Francis. "Were Sacco and Vanzetti Innocent?" *American Heritage*, June 1962.

"S-35." *Time*, August 23, 1926.

Saladin, Raymond. "Le Différend de l'Atlantique." *La Vie Aérienne* 12, no. 79 (August 15, 1927).

Schloss, Leon. "Requiem for Roosevelt Field 1909–1951." *Pegasus*, May 1952.

Schrock, Rudolph. "The Lone Eagle's Clandestine Nests." *Atlantic Times*, June 2005.

Shoumatoff, Alex. "Russian Blood II: Mopsy, Nika, and Uncle." *New Yorker*, May 3, 1982.

Spark, Nick T. "Secrets of the Spirit: Charles Lindbergh, Donald Hall, and the Plane That Made History." *American Aviation Historical Society Journal* 50, no. 2 (Summer 2005).

"The Spirit of St. Louis." *Flight*, June 9, 1927.

Stearns, Myron M. "Babies Born Today May See—." *Popular Science*, October 1927.

Stewart, James, with Joseph Laitin. "Lucky to Be Lindy." *Collier's*, March 30, 1956.

"Suggested Telegrams." *New Yorker*, June 18, 1927.

Taylor, Ken, and Gary Fisk. "Making the Movie *The Spirit of St. Louis.*" *American Aviation Historical Society Journal* 46, no. 4 (Winter 2001).

"To Europe by Rocket." *Popular Science*, September 1927.

"Tragedy, Rancor." *Time*, July 11, 1927.

Traizet, Jacques. "Premiers Envols Français sur la Route de l'Atlantique Nord." *Icare* no. 157 (Summer 1996).

"The Transatlantic Flight." *Flight*, June 19, 1919.

"The Transatlantic Flight: Hawker and Grieve Retrieved." *Flight*, May 29, 1919.

"Uncle Sam's Second Flying Hop across the Pond," *Literary Digest*, June 25, 1927.

Vaillat, Léandre. "La Première Traversée de l'*Île-de-France.*" *L'Illustration*, August 13, 1927.

Waldemar, Kaempffert. "Going to Europe in 1925." *Ladies' Home Journal*, October 1919.

Wales, Henry. "Formidable!" *Atlantic Monthly*, June 1937.

Ward, John W. "The Meaning of Lindbergh's Flight." *American Quarterly* 10 (Spring 1958).

Ware, Foster. "Deus Ex Machina." *New Yorker*, August 13, 1927.

Warren, Lella. "Before the Flight." *Collier's*, July 18, 1931.

Watter, Michael. "Engineering Aspects of Lindbergh's Transatlantic Flight." *Aero Digest*, October 1927.

"We saw him land!" *Smithsonian*, May 2002.

Wheeler, Curtis. "Lindbergh in New York." *Outlook*, June 22, 1927.

Whitman, Alden. "The Price of Fame." *New York Times Magazine*, May 23, 1971.

"Why the World Makes Lindbergh Its Hero." *Literary Digest*, June 25, 1927.

Wiggens, Bill. "Mystery of the *White Bird.*" *Air Classics*, July 1999.

Wilkinson, Stephan. "The Search for *L'Oiseau Blanc.*" *Air & Space/Smithsonian*, February–March 1987.

Wilson, Eugene E. "The Most Unforgettable Character I've Met." *Reader's Digest*, December 1956.

"Winging." *Time*, May 10, 1926.

"The World's Duration Record," *Flight*, August 27, 1925.

"Wright Whirlwind Engines." *Aero Digest*, September 1926.

"Yellow Giant." *Time*, May 9, 1927.

Government Documents

Charles A. Levine. FBI files nos. 93–7651 and 105–108975.

Meunier, Clement-Pascal. "Nungesser et Coli Disparaissent à Bord de *L'Oiseau Blanc*, Mai 1927." Paris: Ministère des Transports, 1983. Translated by The International Group for Historic Aircraft Recovery.

U.S. Department of State. *The Flight of Captain Charles A. Lindbergh from New York to Paris, May 20–21, 1927, as compiled from the official records of the Department of State.* Washington, D.C.: U.S. Government Printing Office, 1927.

Unpublished Manuscripts

Corum, James S. "A Clash of Military Cultures: German and French Approaches to Technology between the World Wars." Paper for the U.S. Air Force Academy Symposium, September 1994.

Gagnon, Paul A. "French Views of Postwar America, 1919–1932." Ph.D. diss., Harvard University, 1960.

Gournay, Isabelle Jeanne. "France Discovers America, 1917–1939: French Writings on American Architecture." Ph.D. diss., Yale University, 1989.

"Interview with Flora Elizabeth Reynolds." University History Series, Regional Oral History Office, Bancroft Library, University of California at Berkeley.

"The Reminiscences of Clarence Chamberlin." Aviation Project, Oral History Research Office, Columbia University, N.Y.

Archives and Collections

Homer Mulhall Berry Papers. Air Force Historical Research Agency, Maxwell Air Force Base, Ala.

Princess Marthe Bibesco Papers. Harry Ransom Humanities Research Center, University of Texas, Austin.

Bibliothèque Nationale de France, Paris.

George B. Corsa Hotel Collection. New-York Historical Society, New York.

L'Aérophile Collection. Science, Technology, and Business Division, Library of Congress, Washington, D.C.

Lindbergh Family Papers, Minnesota Historical Society, St. Paul, Minn.

Charles A. Lindbergh Orteig Prize Collection 1925–1927, National Air and Space Museum Archives, Smithsonian Institution, Washington, D.C.

Musée de l'Air et de l'Espace, Paris.

St. Louis Mercantile Library, University of Missouri, St. Louis, Mo.

Igor I. Sikorsky Historical Archives, Stratford, Conn.

Vincent Voice Library, Michigan State University, East Lansing, Mich.

Orville and Wilbur Wright Papers. Manuscript Division, Library of Congress, Washington, D.C.

Documentaries

"Heaven and Earth" episode of *The Century.* ABC News, 1999.

"Levine and His Flying Machine." Yiddish Radio Project. National Public Radio, 2002.

"Lindbergh." *The American Experience.* PBS/WGBH, 1999.

Index